# Application of Biostatistics in Cancer Research

# Application of Biostatistics in Cancer Research

Guest Editors

**Alan Hutson**
**Han Yu**

MDPI

Basel • Beijing • Wuhan • Barcelona • Belgrade • Novi Sad • Cluj • Manchester

*Guest Editors*

Alan Hutson
Department of Biostatistics
and Bioinformatics
Roswell Park Comprehensive
Cancer Center
Buffalo
USA

Han Yu
Department of Biostatistics
and Bioinformatics
Roswell Park Comprehensive
Cancer Center
Buffalo
USA

*Editorial Office*

MDPI AG
Grosspeteranlage 5
4052 Basel, Switzerland

This is a reprint of the Special Issue, published open access by the journal *Cancers* (ISSN 2072-6694), freely accessible at: https://www.mdpi.com/journal/cancers/special_issues/JKQSP70KE4.

For citation purposes, cite each article independently as indicated on the article page online and as indicated below:

Lastname, A.A.; Lastname, B.B. Article Title. *Journal Name* **Year**, *Volume Number*, Page Range.

**ISBN 978-3-7258-7168-1 (Hbk)**
**ISBN 978-3-7258-7169-8 (PDF)**
**https://doi.org/10.3390/books978-3-7258-7169-8**

# Contents

# About the Editors

**Alan Hutson**

Alan Hutson is the Chair of Biostatistics and Bioinformatics at Roswell Park Comprehensive Cancer Center and Professor of Oncology. He earned degrees in Statistics from SUNY Buffalo and a PhD from the University of Rochester. After roles at the University of Florida and SUNY Buffalo, where he founded the Department of Biostatistics, he joined Roswell Park in 2005, establishing key shared resources in bioinformatics and informatics. A Fellow of the American Statistical Association, he has over 300 publications, two monographs, and expertise in nonparametric methods and clinical trials. He chairs steering committees for NCI initiatives, including the CIP-Net, CAP-IT, and ARTNet.

**Han Yu**

Han Yu is Co-Director of the CCSG Biostatistics and Statistical Genomics Shared Resource at Roswell Park Comprehensive Cancer Center and Assistant Professor of Oncology. He earned an MD from China Medical University (2010) and a PhD in Biostatistics from the University at Buffalo (2018). Since 2018, he has supported Phase I/II trials, data safety monitoring, and multi-omics research using probabilistic graphical models, network integration, and machine learning. His predictive models excelled in the NCI CPTAC DREAM proteogenomics challenge, advancing precision oncology through biological network and computational approaches.

# Preface

The Reprint, guest-edited by Alan Hutson and Han Yu, curates key articles from the Special Issue "Application of Biostatistics in Cancer Research" in *Cancers*. It highlights innovative biostatistical and computational methods addressing oncology challenges: robust trial design, reliable inference, AI/ML-driven diagnostics, dynamic prognosis, and targeted epidemiology. This collection bridges biostatistics, data science, and precision oncology to advance evidence-based cancer research and patient care. It is addressed to biostatisticians, oncologists, trialists, and computational researchers.

**Alan Hutson and Han Yu**
*Guest Editors*

cancers

MDPI

*Article*

# Robustness Assessment of Oncology Dose-Finding Trials Using the Modified Fragility Index

**Amy X. Shi [1], Heng Zhou [2], Lei Nie [3], Lifeng Lin [4], Hongjian Li [5] and Haitao Chu [6,7,*]**

1 Cardiovascular, Renal and Metabolism (CVRM), Biopharmaceuticals R&D, AstraZeneca, Durham, NC 27703, USA
2 Biostatistics and Research Decision Sciences, Merck & Co. Inc., Rahway, NJ 07065, USA; heng.zhou@merck.com
3 Division of Biometrics IV, OB/OTS/CDER/FDA, Silver Spring, MD 20993, USA; lei.nie@fda.hhs.gov
4 Department of Epidemiology and Biostatistics, Mel and Enid Zuckerman College of Public Health, The University of Arizona, Tucson, AZ 85721, USA; lifenglin@arizona.edu
5 Cardiovascular, Renal and Metabolism (CVRM), Biopharmaceuticals R&D, AstraZeneca, Gaithersburg, MD 20878, USA; hongjian.li@astrazeneca.com
6 Statistical Research and Data Science Center, Pfizer Inc., New York, NY 10001, USA
7 Division of Biostatistics and Health Data Science, The University of Minnesota Twin Cities, Minneapolis, MN 55455, USA
* Correspondence: chux0051@umn.edu

**Simple Summary:** In this article, the authors introduce a new metric called the modified Fragility Index (mFI) to assess the accuracy of determining the maximum tolerated dose (MTD) in early oncology clinical trials. The mFI measures how sensitive the MTD decision is to the inclusion of a few more participants in the trial. The authors analyzed three published cancer trials and found that two trials were robust to adding more participants, indicating that the MTD estimate remained stable. However, in the other trial, the MTD estimate was more fragile and could have changed with just one or two more participants. The mFI metric helps researchers make more reliable decisions about the appropriate MTD. By considering the potential impact of additional participants, researchers can improve accuracy and confidence in dose determination, leading to better treatment outcomes for patients.

**Abstract:** Objectives: The sample sizes of phase I trials are typically small; some designs may lead to inaccurate estimation of the maximum tolerated dose (MTD). The objective of this study was to propose a metric assessing whether the MTD decision is sensitive to enrolling a few additional subjects in a phase I dose-finding trial. Methods: Numerous model-based and model-assisted designs have been proposed to improve the efficiency and accuracy of finding the MTD. The Fragility Index (FI) is a widely used metric quantifying the statistical robustness of randomized controlled trials by estimating the number of events needed to change a statistically significant result to non-significant (or vice versa). We propose a modified Fragility Index (mFI), defined as the minimum number of additional participants required to potentially change the estimated MTD, to supplement existing designs identifying fragile phase I trial results. Findings: Three oncology trials were used to illustrate how to evaluate the fragility of phase I trials using mFI. The results showed that two of the trials were not sensitive to additional subjects' participation while the third trial was quite fragile to one or two additional subjects. Conclusions: The mFI can be a useful metric assessing the fragility of phase I trials and facilitating robust identification of MTD.

**Keywords:** oncology trial; fragility Index; maximum tolerated dose; trial design; dose finding; sensitivity analysis; early stopping

## 1. Introduction

The concept of fragility index (FI) dates back to the 1990s [1,2] as an additional robustness appraisal of "statistical significance" for assessing a difference between two proportions. The FI is defined as the minimum number of participants in a randomized clinical trial that is required to change a statistically significant result to non-significant (or vice versa). Walsh et al. used FI to assess the robustness of statistical significance of 399 randomized trials with binary outcomes in 2014 [3], and found that in 53% of trials, the FI was less than the number of patients lost to follow-up, suggesting that the trials were frequently fragile. The FI complements the hypothesis testing (e.g., $p$-value) and helps to identify less robust (or fragile) trial results. Methods for calculating the FI have been further developed for randomized clinical trials with continuous and survival outcomes [4,5], meta-analyses, and network meta-analyses [6–8]. The FI has been increasingly applied to many medical fields, including oncology, surgery, obstetrics, and gynecology, during the past decade [9–12].

In phase I oncology clinical trials, one of the primary goals is to identify the maximum tolerated dose (MTD), which will be used to guide the recommended dose for later phases. However, there may be concerns about the robustness of the chosen MTD, usually determined based on the data from a small number of participants. Researchers and drug developers are often interested in whether the MTD would change if a few additional patients were added to the dose-finding process. If the MTD decision would not be altered in either direction (i.e., downgrading or upgrading) after adding multiple new subjects, we would have more confidence in the dose level chosen as the MTD. Conversely, if the chosen MTD level would be changed right away after including one additional subject, it would raise substantial concerns about whether the selected MTD was reliable. Thus, we propose a modified Fragility Index (mFI), defined as the minimum number of additional participants that is required to potentially change the estimated MTD, to assess robustness and identify fragile phase I trial results.

We begin with an overview on early phase trials and various dose-finding designs in Section 2. Then we cover the definition of mFI and explain how to estimate mFI in Section 3. Three real oncology trials are used to illustrate how to utilize mFI as a convenient and valuable tool for assessing the robustness and validity of the MTD determination in Section 4. Lastly, we examine the relationship between mFI and early stopping, and discuss the limitations of mFI and potential future research topics.

## 2. Materials and Methods

### 2.1. Dose Finding Designs

A phase I trial is often the first time a new drug is applied in human beings. One of the primary goals is to examine the highest possible dose level subject to the dose-limiting toxicity (DLT) constraints and identify the MTD for later phases. Assuming monotonicity, the target DLT probability is often set at a value between 20% and 40%.

The traditional approaches to selecting the MTD include the "3+3" design [13] and various up-and-down designs [14]. The "3 +3" design is the most used for phase I dose escalation. The implementation is easy and does not require a computer program. The sample size required is often smaller than for the model-based designs. However, it is generally inferior in identifying the MTD [15].

Many novel model-based and model-assisted designs have been proposed to improve the efficiency and accuracy of phase I trials to find the MTD. Model-based approaches include the continual reassessment method (CRM) [16], escalation with overdose controls (EWOC) [17], the Bayesian logistic regression model (BLRM), and the time-to-event CRM (TITE-CRM) [18]. Model-assisted designs [19] include the modified toxicity probability interval (mTPI) [15,20], keyboard design [21], and Bayesian optimal interval (BOIN) [22]. Researchers have compared the differences and summarized relative pros and cons for some designs [23]. Appendix A presents an overview of commonly used designs in more detail.

### 2.2. Fragility Index

The FI was developed by Walsh et al. [3] for two-arm randomized controlled trials with binary outcomes that report the numbers of events and non-events in a $2 \times 2$ frequency table. The aim was to examine whether the statistically significant result of a two-arm trial would be altered with a small change in the number of events. Walsh et al. [3] proposed calculating the FI by changing the event status of a subject in a group with fewer events, re-computing the $p$-value based on the Fisher exact test, and repeating this process until a non-significant $p$-value was reached.

For oncology dose-finding studies, because regulators are often interested in whether the MTD would change if a few additional patients were added to the dose-finding process, we propose a modified Fragility Index (mFI), defined as the minimum number of additional participants required to potentially change the estimated MTD, to assess the robustness and identify fragile trial results. The MTD can be altered in either direction: downgrading to a lower dose level or upgrading to a higher dose level. The aim is to investigate if the MTD decision is sensitive to enrolling a few additional subjects in a phase I dose-finding trial.

Suppose that after a dose-finding trial, we collect the following data: $\boldsymbol{d} = (d_1, d_2, \ldots d_J)$ representing the dosage, $\boldsymbol{n} = (n_1, n_2, \ldots n_J)$ the total number of subjects assigned to each dose level, and $\boldsymbol{y} = (y_1, y_2, \ldots y_J)$ the observed DLT for each dose level. If $t$ more subjects are included for further investigation, the possible number of DLTs could be any value in the list $\{0,\ 1,\ 2,\ \ldots,\ t\}$. We could iterate through the list to see whether the originally chosen MTD in the trial would be overturned. As long as one value in the list $\{0,\ 1,\ 2,\ \ldots,\ t\}$ changes the MTD decision, the mFI is set to be $t$ and we stop the process. If none of the values in the list $\{0,\ 1,\ 2,\ \ldots,\ t\}$ changes the MTD decision, we include one more subject and repeat the same process for the $t+1$ subjects. If any DLT value in the list $\{0,\ 1,\ 2,\ \ldots,\ t+1\}$ changes the MTD decision, we stop the process and conclude that $mFI = t + 1$. To be consistent, it is recommended to use the same dose-finding design as employed in the original trial. However, other dose-finding designs and models can be implemented as supplementary assessments. Figure 1 illustrates the process of obtaining the mFI for a dose-finding trial. The procedure is summarized as follows:

1. Collect data from a completed dose-finding trial, $\boldsymbol{d} = (d_1, d_2, \ldots d_J)$, $\boldsymbol{n} = (n_1, n_2, \ldots n_J)$, $\boldsymbol{y} = (y_1, y_2, \ldots y_J)$. At the dose level of the MTD ($d_{\text{MTD}}$), the number of subjects is $n_{MTD}$ and the number of DLTs is $y_{MTD}$.
2. Start with $t = 1$, i.e., add one additional subject at MTD so that the total number of subjects at the MTD is $n_{MTD} + 1$. Let the DLT outcome at the MTD for this new subject be either 0 or 1, hence the total number of DLTs is either $y_{MTD}$ or $y_{MTD} + 1$. Use the same statistical method as used in the original study for both numbers of DLTs to see whether the resulting new MTD is different from the original MTD. If it is different, set mFI = 1; otherwise, go to the next step.
3. Let $t = t + 1$. The number of subjects at the MTD is $n_{MTD} + t$ and let the number of DLTs at the MTD take any value between 0 and $t$: $y_{MTD}, y_{MTD} + 1, \ldots, y_{MTD} + t$. Use the same statistical method as used in the original study for all DLT outcomes to assess whether the resulting MTD is different. If it is different, set mFI = $t$; otherwise, go to the next step.
4. Repeat step 3 unless MTD has been changed and mFI has been set to a value, or if it reaches a prespecified large value.
5. Once the mFI value is determined, we can calculate the probability of observing the number of DLTs or a more extreme case that would change the MTD decision based on the estimated toxicity probability at the original MTD level, to assess its likelihood. For example, if $t$ patients are added at the original MTD level and if $m$ or fewer DLTs are observed among those new patients, it will change the MTD; the probability of this happening is:

$$Pr(X \leq m) = \sum_{i=0}^{m} Pr(X = i) = \sum_{i=0}^{m} \binom{n_{MTD} + t}{m} p_{MTD}{}^{m} (1 - p_{MTD})^{n_{MTD} + t - m}$$

where $X \sim Bin(p_{MTD}, n_{MTD} + t)$ and $p_{MTD}$ can be estimated using the observed DLT rate at the MTD level.

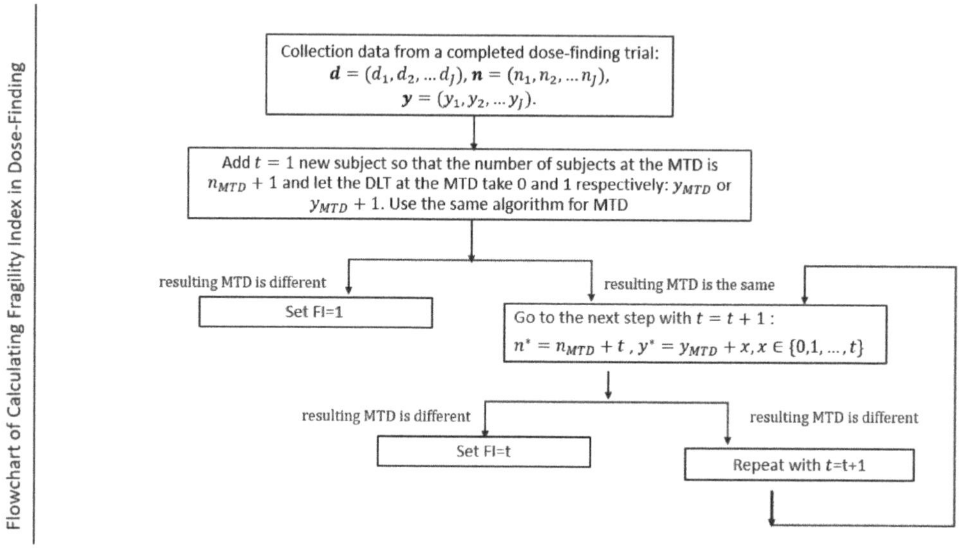


**Figure 1.** Flowchart of Calculating the modified Fragility Index in a Dose-Finding Trial.

We have developed a publicly available R package to provide a convenient way to implement the mFI calculation.

## 3. Results: Three Case Studies

### *3.1. Phase I Dose-Escalation Trial of AUY922*

A first-in-human phase I trial was conducted in patients with advanced solid tumors to determine the MTD of AUY922 inhibitor [24]. An adaptive Bayesian logistic regression model (BLRM) with overdose control was used to assess the relation between dose and DLT probability. The dose started at 2 mg/m$^2$ and upgraded to 4, 8, and 16 mg/m$^2$ with no DLTs. At the next higher dose level of 22 mg/m$^2$, one DLT was observed among 11 patients. No DLT was seen at 28 mg/m$^2$, so the dose was upgraded to 40 mg/m$^2$, at which two of the first seven patients experienced DLTs. The BLRM design supported continued dosing at 40 mg/m$^2$ on the basis of the assessment that the probability of a true DLT probability above 33% was less than 0.25. Therefore, nine additional patients were then dosed and no DLT was observed among these patients. The dose was further extended to 54 and 70 mg/m$^2$, where 2 out of 18 at 54 mg/m$^2$ and 3 out of 24 at 70 mg/m$^2$ had DLT. The final recommended phase II dose (RP2D) was declared at 70 mg/m$^2$. Table 1 displays the dose-finding data of the dose levels, total numbers of subjects treated, numbers of DLTs, and DLT rates for all dose levels.

**Table 1.** Summary of the Data in the Phase I AUY922 Dose-Escalation Trial.

| | Dose Level Index | | | | | | | | |
|---|---|---|---|---|---|---|---|---|---|
| | **1** | **2** | **3** | **4** | **5** | **6** | **7** | **8** | **9** |
| **Dose level (mg/m$^2$)** | 2 | 4 | 8 | 16 | 22 | 28 | 40 | 54 | 70 |
| **Total # subjects treated** | 3 | 3 | 4 | 6 | 11 | 8 | 16 | 18 | 24 |
| **# DLT** | 0 | 0 | 0 | 0 | 1 | 0 | 2 | 2 | 3 |
| **DLT rate (%)** | 0 | 0 | 0 | 0 | 9.1 | 0 | 12.5 | 11.1 | 12.5 |

The mFI was found to be 10, based on both the BLRM and BOIN designs: the MTD did not change until 10 extra subjects were added to the trial at the MTD level of 70 mg/m$^2$ and all those 10 subjects experienced DLT. If we tried fewer subjects, the MTD would not be changed no matter how many subjects experienced DLT. This large mFI value suggests that the result for MTD in this trial was quite robust. One can estimate the probability of having a possible number of DLTs, based on the estimated toxicity probability at the MTD dose level, if 10 more subjects were to be recruited onto the trial. Using a binomial distribution, the chance of having 10 DLTs out of 10 additional subjects is very low, $0.125^{10} < 10^{-8}$, so it is very unlikely that the MTD result would be altered.

The mFI value was the same with the keyboard design, because both BOIN and keyboard are model-assisted designs and use the same isotonic algorithm to compute the MTD. Other dose-finding designs, such as mTPI, gave the same mFI value of 10, whereas the mFI value was 12 when using the CRM algorithm and the mFI value was 8 when using the EWOC algorithm (Table 2).

**Table 2.** The mFI Results of Robustness Assessment for All Three Trials.

| Trials | Dose-Finding Designs | | | | | |
|---|---|---|---|---|---|---|
| | **CRM** | **EWOC** | **BLRM** | **mTPI** | **Keyboard** | **BOIN** |
| 1. AUY922 Dose Escalation | 12 | 8 | 10 | 10 | 10 | 10 |
| 2. Pan-AKT Inhibitor MK-2206 | 10 | 5 | 9 | 18 | 11 | 11 |
| 3. SPRINT Trial | 2 | 2 | 2 | 1 | 1 | 1 |

### 3.2. *Phase I Trial of Pan-AKT Inhibitor MK-2206*

This was a dose-escalation study of continuous oral treatment with the pan-AKT inhibitor MK-2206 in patients with advanced tumors [25]. The drug was administered every other day in 28-day cycles to investigate the safety and MTD. In total, 33 patients were dosed at 30, 60, 75, or 90 mg. The dose finding used a two-stage design. In Stage 1, dose escalation proceeded through dose levels of 30 mg (three subjects), 60 mg (three subjects), and 90 mg (seven subjects). There were 4 out of 7 patients who experienced DLTs at 90 mg. In Stage 2, a new dose of 75 mg was introduced for three patients, whereupon all three developed DLTs. An additional three patients were then enrolled at the lower dose level of 60 mg to check the safety parameters of this dose, and no DLTs were found. Stage 2 included 14 more patients in the expansion phase and observed one DLT. The MTD was established at 60 mg with the mTPI design. The dose-finding data for dose levels, total numbers of subjects treated, numbers of DLTs, and DLT rates are displayed in Table 3.

**Table 3.** Summary of the Data in the Phase I Pan-AKT Inhibitor MK-2206 Trial.

| | Dose Level Index | | | |
|---|---|---|---|---|
| | **1** | **2** | **3** | **4** |
| **Dose level (mg)** | 30 | 60 | 75 | 90 |
| **Total # subjects treated** | 3 | 20 | 3 | 7 |
| **# DLT** | 0 | 1 | 3 | 4 |
| **DLT rate (%)** | 0 | 5.0 | 100 | 57.1 |

As shown in Table 3, the 100% observed DLT rate at the dose level of 75 mg makes it impossible to upgrade from 60 mg to 75 mg. When additional subjects are enrolled, the only possible outcome of changing the MTD is to downgrade. The mFI is 18 according to the mTPI design algorithm. The high mFI value is caused by the 100% DLT rate at the next dose level. The MTD level does not change until 18 extra subjects are added in the trial at the MTD level of 60 mg/m$^2$ and all those subjects experience at least one DLT, the probability of which is extremely low. This suggests that the result for MTD is robust.

As summarized in Table 2, if the keyboard or BOIN design is employed, the mFI is 11, which is still large. Other dose-finding designs give similar mFI values around 10: mFI is 10 with CRM and mFI is 9 with BLRM. However, the mFI is only 5 when using the EWOC algorithm, which may be due to EWOC's over-conservative safety control rule.

### 3.3. *The SPRINT Phase I Trial*

SPRINT was an open-label, single arm, multi-center trial of the MEK 1 inhibitor, selumetinib, in children [26]. The phase I portion of the SPRINT trial evaluated three doses of selumetinib, 20 mg/m$^2$, 25 mg/m$^2$, and 30 mg/m$^2$ in pediatric patients, to identify a suitable dose to be used for the next phase based on all available safety, tolerability, pharmacokinetic, and efficacy data. The objective response rate was similar across 20 to 30 mg/m$^2$ doses: 66.7% (8/12) at 20 mg/m$^2$, 83.3% (5/6) at 25 mg/m$^2$, 50.0% (3/6) at 30 mg/ m$^2$ respectively. The best rate was observed at 25 mg/m$^2$. The tolerability was similar between 20 and 25 mg/m$^2$ doses based on the DLT rates: 2 DLTs out of 12 subjects at 20 mg/m$^2$, 1 DLT out of 6 subjects at 25 mg/m$^2$, and 2 DLTs out of 6 subjects at 30 mg/m$^2$, as shown in Table 4. The dose of 25 mg/m$^2$ was identified as the MTD and the recommended dose for phase II. We used only the tolerability data listed in Table 4 to assess the robustness of the MTD result.

**Table 4.** Summary of the Data in the Phase I SPRINT Trial.

| | Dose Level Index | | |
|---|---|---|---|
| | **1** | **2** | **3** |
| **Dose level (mg/m$^2$)** | 20 | 25 | 30 |
| **Total # subjects treated** | 12 | 6 | 6 |
| **# DLT** | 2 | 1 | 2 |
| **DLT rate (%)** | 16.7 | 16.7 | 33 |

The mFI was found to be 1 with the BOIN algorithm. When one patient was added with no DLT for this new patient, it led to an upgrade to a higher dose level; and the probability of this happening is 0.833, using the observed DLT rate of 16.7%. On the other hand, we investigated downgrading: first, if only one patient is added and that patient develops DLT, the MTD remains the same; then, if two patients are tested additionally and both two patients develop DLT, it results in downgrading to a lower dose level. The probability of these two patients experiencing DLT is 0.028. The mFI would be the 1, since this is the smallest number of subjects needed to alter the MTD. The small mFI indicates the trial's MTD conclusion is not robust if we consider only tolerability data. Other dose-finding designs, such as CRM, EWOC, BLRM, and mTPI, give similar mFI values of either 1 or 2 (Table 2).

### 3.4. *mFI Results Summary*

The mFI results are summarized in Table 2 for all three trials using various dose-finding designs, CRM, EWOC, BLRM, mTPI, keyboard, and BOIN. To be consistent with the original dose-finding process, it is recommended to use the same dose-finding design as employed in the trial for calculating mFI. Other dose-finding models can be implemented as supplementary assessments. There are some variations in the mFI results, as demonstrated by the three trials, but there should be a general pattern or signal in terms of robustness assessment.

The results showed that the first two trials were not sensitive to additional participants, while the third trial is quite fragile to one or two additional subjects being added.

## 4. Discussion and Conclusions

We propose a modified Fragility Index (mFI) to assess the robustness of the MTD determination in early-phase dose-finding trials. The extension of FI in dose-finding trials allows researchers and drug developers to assess whether any additional patients and how many patients should be recruited to achieve a robust MTD decision. Three oncology trials were used to show how to calculate the mFI and assess trial robustness.

In practice, different trials may employ different designs. To be consistent, it is recommended to use the same dose-finding design as employed in the trial for the estimation of mFI. However, other dose-finding designs and models can be implemented as supplementary assessments. Because phase I trials commonly involve a small number of subjects, an mFI value greater than 3 or 5 may intuitively be considered as an indication of robust MTD decision. However, to establish a useful guideline, one would need to systematically evaluate all existing phase I oncology trials and empirically estimate the distribution of mFI. Furthermore, the mFI evaluation may depend on the design used to estimate the MTD. The relative performance of different designs on robust assessment using mFI awaits further research.

Phase I trials can implement rules to stop early if the clinical objectives have been achieved with good confidence. Various stopping rules have been suggested in the literature. O'Quigley et al. [16] proposed a stopping rule based on a confidence interval for CRM and other model-based methods, and Shen and O'Quigley gave a theoretical justification [27]. However, there are some limitations to this approach: (1) the precision level may often require more patients than would be available in an early dose-finding trial and hence, the trial would not halt early in practice; (2) it is questionable whether obtaining a pre-fixed level of precision for the probability of toxicity at the MTD should be a major goal of a trial [28]. On the other hand, O'Quigley and Reiner (1998) [29] estimated the probability that a current recommended dose level will turn out to be the final MTD and the likelihood that all remaining patients will be treated at the current dose level. The trial would be terminated early if the MTD could be predicted with high probability. To implement this stopping rule, one can keep track of the number of times each dose is considered and stop when the dose for an upcoming patient is the same as the dose that was recommended for the previous k (a pre-decided integer) patients in a row. This approach often works out well in practice [28].

Implementing early stopping during a dose-finding trial may first seem quite different from assessing the robustness of a trial using FI, because one is used during a dose-finding trial and the other is considered afterwards. However, they are very much related, because mFI can also be applied in real time during a trial. If a trial has already included a certain number of patients, then what would happen if a few more patients were to be included? Would adding more patients change the current recommended dose? Or would the current recommended dose stay the same, and what probability is associated with that? Therefore, we may want to compare these two approaches via simulations and in practice. As we try to achieve Project Optimus, selecting an optimal biological dose is no longer based just on toxicity, but also other factors, such as efficacy and pharmacokinetic results. Our proposed mFI index can be extended naturally to consider other determining factors beyond safety by incorporating those factors in the decision rule, as shown in the third example.

A related fragility measure is the Robustness Index (RI) proposed by Heston in 2023 [30], which examines how different sample sizes affect statistical significance. When a hypothesis test yields a non-significant result, the original sample size is multiplied by a series of numbers until a significant result is achieved. Conversely, when a test is significant, the original sample size is divided by a series of numbers until the result is no longer significant. The multiplicand or divisor is the RI. However, it is uncertain how the RI can be utilized in a dose-finding trial to determine when the MTD result will change.

The strength of this study is that, to the best of our knowledge, there are scant, if any, existing methods dedicated specifically to evaluating the robustness of results from dose-finding studies. By extending the concept of the FI, this work offers an intuitive way to quantify how the significance of the dose-finding conclusion could change after including additional potential samples. Nevertheless, this study has some limitations. Although our proposed mFI shares the same spirit as the original FI developed by Walsh et al., as both aim at altering the result's significance, they differ in terms of how they achieve the significance change. Specifically, the original FI was intended for general hypothesis testing in relation to treatment effects with binary outcomes in clinical trials, and it modifies the status of binary outcomes (event or no event), with the size of samples in each group remaining fixed. In contrast, in our proposed mFI, like several other extensions of FI for continuous outcomes and survival outcomes [31], the sample sizes in treatment groups or the study are modified. As such, one may argue that the mFI is not a type of FI measure, and we may consider this as an FI-like measure. In addition, our proposed mFI does not account for the likelihood of DLT outcomes among the assumed additional samples for the mFI calculation. It is possible that the DLT outcomes of some samples may not be clinically practical. Baer et al. proposed generalizing the fragility index to a family of fragility indices called incidence fragility indices, permitting only outcome modifications that are sufficiently likely and providing an exact algorithm to calculate the incidence fragility indices [32]. Such a consideration may also be needed when interpreting the mFI results.

**Author Contributions:** Conceptualization, A.X.S. and H.C.; Methodology, A.X.S., H.Z., L.N., L.L., H.L. and H.C.; Software, A.X.S. and H.Z.; Validation, A.X.S., H.Z. and H.C.; Formal analysis, A.X.S.; Data curation, A.X.S. and L.N.; Writing—original draft preparation, A.X.S.; writing—review and editing, A.X.S., H.Z., L.N., L.L., H.L. and H.C.; Visualization, A.X.S.; Supervision, H.C.; Project administration, H.C. All authors have read and agreed to the published version of the manuscript.

**Funding:** This research received no external funding.

**Institutional Review Board Statement:** Not applicable.

**Informed Consent Statement:** Not applicable.

**Data Availability Statement:** The summary level data that support the findings of this study are included in the paper.

**Disclaimer:** This article reflects the views of the authors and should not be construed to represent FDA's views or policies.

**Conflicts of Interest:** The authors declare no conflicts of interest. A.X.S., H.L., H.Z., and H.C. are employed by AstraZeneca, Merck, and Pfizer, and own stocks in those companies. However, all of the contents in this article are strictly educational, instructive, and methodological.

## Appendix A. Overview of Commonly Used Dose Finding Designs

Here, we provide a brief overview of commonly used trial designs. Suppose there are in total J dose levels, $\boldsymbol{d} = (d_1, d_2, \ldots d_J)$, in a phase I dose-finding trial. For dose j (j = 1, 2, . . ., J), the number of patients with a DLT ($y_j$) in a cohort of size $n_j$ is assumed to be binomially distributed $y_j \sim Bin(p_j,\ n_j)$ with the DLT probabilities ($p_j$).

### *A.1. The Continual Reassessment Method (CRM)*

In the CRM design, a parametric model for the dose–toxicity curve is assumed as $p_j = a_j^{\exp(\alpha)}$, where $p_j$ is the true DLT probability at dose level $j$, $\alpha$ is an unknown parameter, and $a_j$ is the initial guess of the DLT probability at dose level $j$ with the constraint of $0 < a_1 < a_2 < \ldots < a_J < 1$. The CRM updates the dose–toxicity curve with the accumulating DLT data across all dose levels and assigns new patients to the optimal dose level, which is defined as the one with the estimated DLT probability being the closest to the target DLT probability, $\phi$. In addition, a safety stopping rule is implemented so that the process is stopped if the DLT probability at the lowest dose ($p_1$) is greater than the target above a pre-specified threshold (for example, 0.95), i.e., $\Pr(p_1 > \phi | D) > 0.95$, where D denotes the trial data.

*A.2. The Escalation with Overdose Control (EWOC)*

As a modification of the CRM, the EWOC employs a two-parameter logistic regression model for extra flexibility in modeling the dose–toxicity curve as $\text{logit}(p_j) = \beta_0 + \beta_1 d_j$, where $(\beta_0, \beta_1)$ are the unknown intercept and slope parameters, and $d_j$ is the dosage of dose level $j$. Thus, the DLT probability of the first dose $d_1$ is $p_1 = \frac{\exp(\beta_0+\beta_1 d_1)}{1+\exp(\beta_0+\beta_1 d_1)}$, and the MTD is $\lambda = \frac{1}{\beta_1}[\log(\phi) - \log(1-\phi) - \beta_0]$. The EWOC treats the first group of patients at the lowest dose and updates the dose–toxicity curve with the accumulating DLT data. The next group of patients are assigned to the optimal dose, which is defined as the one whose mean estimate of the DLT probability is the closest to the target DLT probability $\phi$. The same safety stopping rule is used, i.e., $\Pr(p_1 > \phi|D) > 0.95$.

*A.3. The Bayesian Logistic Regression Model (BLRM)*

This is a two-parameter logistic model, $\text{logit}(p_j) = \log(\alpha) + \beta\log(\frac{d_j}{d^*})$, where $(\alpha, \beta)$ are the two unknown parameters and $d^*$ is the reference dose. Following the paper by Neuenschwander et al. [33], a flat bivariate normal distribution is often used as the prior for $(\log(\alpha), \log(\beta))$. The BLRM requires a predefined probability interval $(\delta_1, \delta_2)$ as the range of acceptable DLT probabilities. For example, $(\delta_1, \delta_2) = (\phi - 0.05, \phi + 0.05)$. The BLRM imposes an overdose control rule, as follows: a dose is considered overdosing if the observed data indicate that the DLT probability at a dose level greater than the upper bound is higher than 0.25, i.e., $\Pr(p_j > \delta_2|D) > 0.25$. The same safety stopping rule as the previous two designs is often used in the BLRM.

*A.4. The Modified Toxicity Probability Interval (mTPI) Design*

The mTPI design uses a beta-binomial model at each dose level: $y_j|n_j, p_j \sim Bin(n_j, p_j)$ and $p_j \sim Beta(1,1)$. Thus, the posterior distribution of the DLT probability at dose j is a beta distribution, i.e., $p_j|n_j, y_j \sim Beta(y_j + 1, n_j - y_j + 1)$. Given a target toxicity probability $\phi$, the mTPI design prespecifies three intervals with two parameters $\delta_1 = \phi - \varepsilon_1, \delta_2 = \phi + \varepsilon_2$, that is, the underdosing interval $(0, \delta_1)$, the acceptable dosing interval $[\delta_1, \delta_2]$, and the overdosing interval $(\delta_2, 1)$, where $0 < \delta_1 < \phi < \delta_2 < 1$. Then, the mTPI design defines a quantity named unit probability mass (UPM), given the posterior distribution of $p_j$ for each of the three intervals as follows:

$$UPM_1 = Pr(p_j < \delta_1|n_j, y_j)/\delta_1,$$

$$UPM_2 = Pr(\delta_1 \leq p_j \leq \delta_2|n_j, y_j)/(\delta_2 - \delta_1),$$

$$UPM_3 = Pr(p_j > \delta_2|n_j, y_j)/(1 - \delta_2).$$

That is, the UPM is the posterior probability that $p_j$ lies in the corresponding interval divided by the length of that interval. The mTPI design determines dose escalation/de-escalation based only on the observed data at the current dose level $j$ as follows:

1. If $UPM_1 = max\{UPM_1, UPM_2, UPM_3\}$, escalate dose to level $j+1$;
2. If $UPM_2 = max\{UPM_1, UPM_2, UPM_3\}$, stay at the current dose level $j$;
3. If $UPM_3 = max\{UPM_1, UPM_2, UPM_3\}$, de-escalate dose to level $j-1$.

Because the three UPMs can be calculated for all outcomes of $n_j$ and $y_j$, dose escalation and de-escalation rules can be determined before the onset of the trial. To avoid treating excessive numbers of participants at extremely toxic dose levels, the mTPI design implements a dose-exclusion rule as follows: if $Pr(p_j > \phi|n_j, y_j) > 0.95$, dose level $j$ and higher doses are excluded in the trial. If the lowest dose is excluded, the trial is stopped for safety.

*A.5. The Keyboard Design*

Yan et al. [21] proposed the keyboard design to improve the performance of the mTPI design, noting that the latter has a high risk of overdosing patients due to the use of the UPM to guide dose escalation. The keyboard design starts by specifying a proper probability interval $I^* = (\delta_1, \delta_2)$ (referred to as the target key) and then forms a series of equal-width keys on both sides of the target key. We denote the resulting intervals/keys as $I_1, \cdots, I_K$. To make the decision for dose transition, given the observed data $(n_j, y_j)$ at the current dose level $j$, the keyboard design defines the "strongest key" as $I_{max} = \text{argmax}\{\Pr(p_j \in I_k); k = 1, \cdots, K\}$, which can be easily obtained using the beta-binomial model as with the mTPI. Statistically, the strongest key represents the interval in which the true toxicity probability is most likely to be located. This intuitive interpretation of the strongest key naturally leads to the following keyboard dose escalation and de-escalation rule:

1. If the strongest key is on the left side of the target key, escalate to the level $j + 1$;
2. If the strongest key is the target key, stay at the current level $j$;
3. If the strongest key is on the right side of the target key, de-escalate to level $j - 1$.

The same dose-exclusion rule as in the mTPI design is also implemented in the keyboard design.

### A.6. The Bayesian Optimal Interval (BOIN) Design

Compared with the mTPI and keyboard designs, which require calculating the posterior distribution of the DLT probabilities, the BOIN design is more straightforward and transparent. Let $\hat{p}_j = \frac{y_j}{n_j}$ denote the observed DLT probability at the current dose level $j$, and $\lambda_e$, $\lambda_d$ denote the predetermined dose escalation and de-escalation boundaries. The BOIN design determines the next dose level as follows:

1. If $\hat{p}_j \leq \lambda_e$, escalate to the level $j + 1$;
2. If $\hat{p}_j \geq \lambda_d$, de-escalate to the level $j - 1$;
3. Otherwise, stay at the current level $j$.

The BOIN design also implements the same dose-exclusion rule as the mTPI and keyboard designs. Due to its straightforward implementation and excellent performance, the BOIN design received a fit-for-purpose designation from FDA as a tool for dose-finding in oncology [34].

## References


1. Feinstein, A.R. The unit fragility index: An additional appraisal of "statistical significance" for a contrast of two proportions. *J. Clin. Epidemiol.* **1990**, *43*, 201–209. [CrossRef] [PubMed]
2. Walter, S. Statistical significance and fragility criteria for assessing a difference of two proportions. *J. Clin. Epidemiol.* **1991**, *44*, 1373–1378. [CrossRef] [PubMed]
3. Walsh, M.; Srinathan, S.K.; McAuley, D.F.; Mrkobrada, M.; Levine, O.; Ribic, C.; Molnar, A.O.; Dattani, N.D.; Burke, A.; Guyatt, G. The statistical significance of randomized controlled trial results is frequently fragile: A case for a Fragility Index. *J. Clin. Epidemiol.* **2014**, *67*, 622–628. [CrossRef] [PubMed]
4. Baer, B.R.; Fremes, S.E.; Gaudino, M.; Charlson, M.; Wells, M.T. On clinical trial fragility due to patients lost to follow up. *BMC Med. Res. Methodol.* **2021**, *21*, 1–11. [CrossRef] [PubMed]
5. Bomze, D.; Asher, N.; Ali, O.H.; Flatz, L.; Azoulay, D.; Markel, G.; Meirson, T. Survival-inferred fragility index of phase 3 clinical trials evaluating immune checkpoint inhibitors. *JAMA Netw. Open* **2020**, *3*, e2017675. [CrossRef]
6. Atal, I.; Porcher, R.; Boutron, I.; Ravaud, P. The statistical significance of meta-analyses is frequently fragile: Definition of a fragility index for meta-analyses. *J. Clin. Epidemiol.* **2019**, *111*, 32–40. [CrossRef]
7. Lin, L. Factors that impact fragility index and their visualizations. *J. Eval. Clin. Pract.* **2021**, *27*, 356–364. [CrossRef]
8. Lin, L.; Chu, H. Assessing and visualizing fragility of clinical results with binary outcomes in R using the fragility package. *PLoS ONE* **2022**, *17*, e0268754. [CrossRef]
9. Lin, L.; Xing, A.; Chu, H.; Murad, M.H.; Xu, C.; Baer, B.R.; Wells, M.T.; Sanchez-Ramos, L. Assessing the robustness of results from clinical trials and meta-analyses with the fragility index. *Am. J. Obstet. Gynecol.* **2023**, *228*, 276–282. [CrossRef]
10. Del Paggio, J.C.; Tannock, I.F. The fragility of phase 3 trials supporting FDA-approved anticancer medicines: A retrospective analysis. *Lancet Oncol.* **2019**, *20*, 1065–1069. [CrossRef]
11. Sanchez-Ramos, L.; Lin, L. Cerclage placement in twin pregnancies with short or dilated cervix does not prevent preterm birth: A fragility index assessment. *Am. J. Obstet. Gynecol.* **2022**, *227*, 338–339. [CrossRef] [PubMed]
12. Tignanelli, C.J.; Napolitano, L.M. The fragility index in randomized clinical trials as a means of optimizing patient care. *JAMA Surg.* **2019**, *154*, 74–79. [CrossRef] [PubMed]

13. Storer, B.E. An evaluation of phase I clinical trial designs in the continuous dose–response setting. *Stat. Med.* **2001**, *20*, 2399–2408. [CrossRef] [PubMed]
14. Gezmu, M.; Flournoy, N. Group up-and-down designs for dose-finding. *J. Stat. Plan. Inference* **2006**, *136*, 1749–1764. [CrossRef]
15. Ji, Y.; Wang, S.-J. Modified toxicity probability interval design: A safer and more reliable method than the 3 + 3 design for practical phase I trials. *J. Clin. Oncol.* **2013**, *31*, 1785. [CrossRef]
16. O'Quigley, J.; Pepe, M.; Fisher, L. Continual reassessment method: A practical design for phase 1 clinical trials in cancer. *Biometrics* **1990**, *46*, 33–48. [CrossRef]
17. Babb, J.; Rogatko, A.; Zacks, S. Cancer phase I clinical trials: Efficient dose escalation with overdose control. *Stat. Med.* **1998**, *17*, 1103–1120. [CrossRef]
18. Cheung, Y.K.; Chappell, R. Sequential designs for phase I clinical trials with late-onset toxicities. *Biometrics* **2000**, *56*, 1177–1182. [CrossRef]
19. Yuan, Y.; Lee, J.J.; Hilsenbeck, S.G. Model-assisted designs for early-phase clinical trials: Simplicity meets superiority. *JCO Precis. Oncol.* **2019**, *3*, 1–12. [CrossRef]
20. Guo, W.; Wang, S.-J.; Yang, S.; Lynn, H.; Ji, Y. A Bayesian interval dose-finding design addressingOckham's razor: mTPI-2. *Contemp. Clin. Trials* **2017**, *58*, 23–33. [CrossRef]
21. Yan, F.; Mandrekar, S.J.; Yuan, Y. Keyboard: A novel Bayesian toxicity probability interval design for phase I clinical trials. *Clin. Cancer Res.* **2017**, *23*, 3994–4003. [CrossRef] [PubMed]
22. Liu, S.; Yuan, Y. Bayesian optimal interval designs for phase I clinical trials. *J. R. Stat. Soc. Ser. C Appl. Stat.* **2015**, *64*, 507–523. [CrossRef]
23. Zhou, H.; Yuan, Y.; Nie, L. Accuracy, safety, and reliability of novel phase I trial designs. *Clin. Cancer Res.* **2018**, *24*, 4357–4364. [CrossRef] [PubMed]
24. Sessa, C.; Shapiro, G.I.; Bhalla, K.N.; Britten, C.; Jacks, K.S.; Mita, M.; Papadimitrakopoulou, V.; Pluard, T.; Samuel, T.A.; Akimov, M. First-in-human phase I dose-escalation study of the HSP90 inhibitor AUY922 in patients with advanced solid tumors. *Clin. Cancer Res.* **2013**, *19*, 3671–3680. [CrossRef]
25. Yap, T.A.; Yan, L.; Patnaik, A.; Fearen, I.; Olmos, D.; Papadopoulos, K.; Baird, R.D.; Delgado, L.; Taylor, A.; Lupinacci, L. First-in-man clinical trial of the oral pan-AKT inhibitor MK-2206 in patients with advanced solid tumors. *J. Clin. Oncol.* **2011**, *29*, 4688–4695. [CrossRef]
26. Food and Drug Administration. *NDA Multi-Disciplinary Review and Evaluation NDA 213756 for Koselugo (Selumetinib)*; Food and Drug Administration: Silver Spring, MD, USA, 2020.
27. Shen, L.Z.; O'quigley, J. Consistency of continual reassessment method under model misspecification. *Biometrika* **1996**, *83*, 395–405. [CrossRef]
28. Devlin, S.M.; Iasonos, A.; O'Quigley, J. Stopping rules for phase I clinical trials with dose expansion cohorts. *Stat. Methods Med. Res.* **2022**, *31*, 334–347. [CrossRef]
29. O'quigley, J.; Reiner, E. A stopping rule for the continual reassessment method. *Biometrika* **1998**, *85*, 741–748. [CrossRef]
30. Heston, T.F. The robustness index: Going beyond statistical significance by quantifying fragility. *Cureus* **2023**, *15*, e44397. [CrossRef]
31. Caldwell, J.-M.E.; Youssefzadeh, K.; Limpisvasti, O. A method for calculating the fragility index of continuous outcomes. *J. Clin. Epidemiol.* **2021**, *136*, 20–25. [CrossRef]
32. Baer, B.R.; Gaudino, M.; Charlson, M.; Fremes, S.E.; Wells, M.T. Fragility indices for only sufficiently likely modifications. *Proc. Natl. Acad. Sci. USA* **2021**, *118*, e2105254118. [CrossRef] [PubMed]
33. Neuenschwander, B.; Branson, M.; Gsponer, T. Critical aspects of the Bayesian approach to phase I cancer trials. *Stat. Med.* **2008**, *27*, 2420–2439. [CrossRef] [PubMed]
34. Food and Drug Administration. Drug Administration. Drug Development Tools: Fit-for-Purpose Initiative. In *Guidance for Industry*; FDA (Food and Drug Administration): Silver Spring, MD, USA, 2021.

*cancers*

MDPI

*Article*

# Deep Learning for Melanoma Detection: A Deep Learning Approach to Differentiating Malignant Melanoma from Benign Melanocytic Nevi

**Magdalini Kreouzi [1], Nikolaos Theodorakis [2,3,4,5], Georgios Feretzakis [5], Evgenia Paxinou [5], Aikaterini Sakagianni [6], Dimitris Kalles [5], Athanasios Anastasiou [7], Vassilios S. Verykios [5,*] and Maria Nikolaou [3]**

1 Department of Internal Medicine & 65+ Clinic, Amalia Fleming General Hospital, 14, 25th Martiou Str., 15127 Melissia, Greece; kreouzi.m@live.unic.ac.cy

2 NT-CardioMetabolics, Clinic for Metabolism and Athletic Performance, 47 Tirteou Str., 17564 Palaio Faliro, Greece; n.theodorakis@flemig-hospital.gr

3 65+ Outpatient Clinic, Amalia Fleming General Hospital, 14, 25th Martiou Str., 15127 Melissia, Greece; m.nikolaou@flemig-hospital.gr

4 School of Medicine, National and Kapodistrian University of Athens, 75 Mikras Asias, 11527 Athens, Greece

5 School of Science and Technology, Hellenic Open University, 18 Aristotelous Str., 26335 Patras, Greece; georgios.feretzakis@ac.eap.gr (G.F.); paxinou.evgenia@ac.eap.gr (E.P.); kalles@eap.gr (D.K.)

6 Intensive Care Unit, Sismanogelio General Hospital, 37 Sismanogleiou Str., 15126 Marousi, Greece; sakagianni@sismanoglio.gr

7 Biomedical Engineering Laboratory, National Technical University of Athens, 15773 Athens, Greece; aanastasiou@biomed.ntua.gr

* Correspondence: verykios@eap.gr

**Simple Summary**

Melanoma is a dangerous type of skin cancer that can grow quickly and spread to other parts of the body, making early detection and diagnosis essential for saving lives. However, it can be difficult to tell the difference between melanoma and harmless skin spots, even for experts. This study explores how advanced computer technologies called convolutional neural networks (CNNs) can help detect melanoma more accurately. These systems analyze skin images and identify patterns that indicate whether a spot is likely to be cancerous. We compared four different types of CNN to find the best balance between accuracy and efficiency. Our findings show that some models are not only highly accurate but also fast and lightweight, making them suitable for use in clinics or even on mobile devices. This research highlights the potential of artificial intelligence to assist doctors and improve early melanoma detection, ultimately saving more lives.

**Abstract**

**Background/Objectives**: Melanoma, an aggressive form of skin cancer, accounts for a significant proportion of skin-cancer-related deaths worldwide. Early and accurate differentiation between melanoma and benign melanocytic nevi is critical for improving survival rates but remains challenging because of diagnostic variability. Convolutional neural networks (CNNs) have shown promise in automating melanoma detection with accuracy comparable to expert dermatologists. This study evaluates and compares the performance of four CNN architectures—DenseNet121, ResNet50V2, NASNetMobile, and MobileNetV2—for the binary classification of dermoscopic images. **Methods**: A dataset of 8825 dermoscopic images from DermNet was standardized and divided into training (80%), validation (10%), and testing (10%) subsets. Image augmentation techniques were applied to enhance model generalizability. The CNN architectures were pre-trained on ImageNet and customized for binary classification. Models were trained using the Adam optimizer and evaluated based on accuracy, area under the receiver operating characteristic curve (AUC-ROC), inference time, and model size. The statistical significance of the differences was assessed using McNemar's test. **Results**: DenseNet121 achieved the highest accuracy (92.30%) and an AUC of 0.951, while ResNet50V2 recorded the highest AUC (0.957). MobileNetV2 combined efficiency with competitive performance, achieving a 92.19% accuracy, the smallest model size (9.89 MB), and the fastest inference time (23.46 ms). NASNetMobile, despite its compact size, had a slower inference time (108.67 ms), and slightly lower accuracy (90.94%). Performance differences among the models were statistically significant ($p < 0.0001$). **Conclusions**: DenseNet121 demonstrated a superior diagnostic performance, while MobileNetV2 provided the most efficient solution for deployment in resource-constrained settings. The CNNs show substantial potential for improving melanoma detection in clinical and mobile applications.

**Keywords:** melanoma detection; convolutional neural networks; artificial intelligence; skin cancer diagnosis; dermoscopic images; deep learning models; medical imaging; early cancer detection

## 1. Introduction

Melanoma, a malignant neoplasm originating from melanocytes, the pigment-producing cells in the epidermis, is an aggressive and life-threatening form of skin cancer. Characterized by its propensity for rapid proliferation and metastatic dissemination, melanoma accounts for the majority of skin-cancer-related mortalities worldwide, despite representing a small fraction of skin cancer diagnoses. The pathogenesis of melanoma involves a complex interplay of genetic mutations, such as alterations in the *BRAF*, *NRAS*, and *CDKN2A* genes, and environmental factors like ultraviolet radiation exposure. Clinically, melanoma may mimic benign melanocytic lesions, including nevi, rendering early detection a significant diagnostic challenge. Delayed or inaccurate diagnoses are associated with poorer prognoses, as the disease rapidly progresses from localized cutaneous lesions to regional lymph node involvement and distant organ metastasis. Consequently, precise differentiation between malignant melanoma and benign melanocytic nevi is critical for timely therapeutic intervention, which can drastically improve survival rates and reduce morbidity [1].

The traditional diagnostic landscape, including visual inspection and dermoscopy, relies heavily on dermatological expertise, leading to considerable inter-observer variability. The advent of artificial intelligence (AI) and deep learning (DL) in medical imaging, however, has heralded a paradigm shift in melanoma diagnosis, enabling automated, reproducible, and highly accurate evaluations. Recent advancements in convolutional neural networks (CNNs) have positioned these architectures at the forefront of melanoma detection research. CNNs excel in analyzing complex patterns and subtle visual features, making them particularly effective for medical imaging tasks, including the classification of skin lesions. Studies underscore the capability of CNNs to achieve diagnostic accuracies comparable to, or even surpassing, those of experienced dermatologists. These models leverage large datasets of dermoscopic images to differentiate melanoma from benign conditions such as melanocytic nevi and other skin abnormalities with remarkable precision [2,3].

Systematic reviews, such as those by Wu et al. (2022) and Magalhães et al. (2024), highlight the growing body of evidence supporting the use of deep learning in skin cancer detection. These studies have identified key factors influencing model performance, including dataset quality, image resolution, and annotation accuracy [4,5]. Additionally, Gautam et al. (2024) demonstrated the potential of CNNs to generalize across diverse lesion types, such as vascular lesions and keratoses, while maintaining robust performance in melanoma detection [6]. One of the significant challenges in melanoma detection is the subtlety of visual differences between malignant and benign lesions, which can often confound traditional diagnostic approaches. Deep learning models, particularly CNNs, have proven adept at capturing these nuanced distinctions. For instance, Winkler et al. (2023) discuss the effectiveness of integrating patient metadata with image features to enhance model predictions. This multimodal approach has been shown to improve diagnostic accuracy, particularly in cases with atypical clinical presentations [7].

Furthermore, the use of transfer learning and pre-trained models, as explored by Naeem et al. (2020) and Dildar et al. (2021), has significantly reduced the computational and data requirements for training CNNs in melanoma detection. These techniques allow for the adaptation of existing high-performance models to specific dermatological tasks, accelerating the deployment of AI solutions in clinical settings [8,9]. Systematic reviews, such as the study by Kassem et al. (2021), provide critical insight into the relative strengths and limitations of various deep learning architectures [10]. These works emphasize the importance of balancing sensitivity and specificity, as over-diagnosis of benign lesions can lead to unnecessary biopsies and patient anxiety.

Despite these advancements, challenges remain. Issues such as dataset bias, class imbalance, and the interpretability of deep learning models have been highlighted by multiple authors, including Efimenko et al. (2020) and Popescu et al. (2022) [11,12]. Addressing these limitations is vital to ensuring the reliable adoption of CNN-based systems in clinical practice. This paper aims to contribute to the growing field of AI-driven dermatology by presenting a novel CNN framework for the differentiation of malignant melanoma from benign melanocytic nevi. By synthesizing insights from the existing literature and leveraging cutting-edge deep learning methodologies, this study seeks to advance the accuracy and accessibility of melanoma detection, ultimately improving patient outcomes and reducing healthcare disparities.

## 2. Materials and Methods

### 2.1. Dataset Preparation

The dataset for this study was obtained from the DermNet repository, a publicly available resource widely used in dermatology research [13]. It contains high-quality images categorized into the following two distinct classes: benign and malignant skin lesions. The dataset comprised 8825 images in total, ensuring a robust foundation for deep learning model training and evaluation [14]. Prior to the analysis, extensive preprocessing was performed to standardize the dataset [15]. Each image underwent careful curation to ensure uniformity in dimensions, format, and quality. All images were resized to a fixed resolution of 224 × 224 pixels, which represents a standard input size for convolutional neural networks (CNNs) and provides a balance between computational efficiency and detail preservation [16].

The organizing of the dataset for the machine learning applications was accomplished using the split-folders library [17]. This tool facilitated the division of the data into the following three essential subsets: training, validation, and testing. A stratified splitting approach was implemented, maintaining an 80-10-10 ratio [18], resulting in 7060 training images, 882 validation images, and 883 testing images. This distribution ensured an even representation of benign and malignant classes across all subsets, preventing any potential class imbalance that could bias model training [19]. The training subset served as the primary data for model fitting, while the validation subset provided crucial feedback during hyperparameter tuning. The testing subset was strictly reserved for the final evaluation, remaining completely isolated from the training process to ensure unbiased assessment of model performance [20].

### 2.2. Image Augmentation

The implementation of image augmentation techniques played a crucial role in enhancing the generalization capability of the CNN models and mitigating the risk of overfitting [21]. This process was executed dynamically during the training phase using TensorFlow's ImageDataGenerator (Google LLC, Mountain View, CA, USA, Version: TensorFlow 2.x) module [22]. The augmentation pipeline began with basic preprocessing, including the rescaling of pixel values to the range [0, 1] for input data normalization [23]. Geometric transformations were then applied, incorporating a rotation range of 30 degrees to account for varying image orientations. Width and height shifts of up to 20% were introduced to simulate different image framing scenarios, while shearing transformations of 20% helped capture varying perspectives [24].

The augmentation process also included zoom variations of 20% to account for different image scales, along with both horizontal and vertical flips to enhance rotational invariance [25]. The fill mode was set to 'nearest' to handle transformed pixel spaces effectively. Additionally, brightness adjustments within a range of [0.8, 1.2] were implemented to simulate varying lighting conditions [26]. These augmentation techniques were exclusively applied to the training dataset, while the validation and testing datasets underwent only basic normalization to maintain evaluation integrity.

### 2.3. Model Architecture

The study implemented a comprehensive comparison of four state-of-the-art CNN architectures, each bringing unique characteristics to the task of skin lesion classification. The DenseNet121 architecture, pre-trained on ImageNet, employs a dense connectivity pattern that promotes feature reuse through direct connections between layers [27,28]. This network, with a model size of 27.86 MB, provides an efficient balance between computational requirements and model complexity. The ResNet50V2, also pre-trained on ImageNet, implements a residual learning framework that facilitates improved gradient flow throughout the network [29]. Despite its larger size of 91.93 MB, this architecture has demonstrated exceptional performance in various computer vision tasks [30].

The NASNetMobile architecture, developed through Neural Architecture Search, was specifically optimized for mobile devices [31]. With a model size of 17.34 MB, it represents a compromise between efficiency and performance. The MobileNetV2 architecture [20] stands out for its lightweight design, employing depth-wise separable convolutions and incorporating inverted residuals and linear bottlenecks. At just 9.89 MB, it offers the most compact solution while maintaining competitive performance [32].

Each of these architectures underwent modification with a custom top layer configuration designed specifically for the binary classification task at hand. This configuration began with a global average pooling layer to reduce spatial dimensions, followed by a batch normalization layer to stabilize training. A dense layer with 512 units and ReLU activation was then implemented, followed by a dropout layer with a rate of 0.5 to prevent overfitting. This was succeeded by another dense layer of 256 units with ReLU activation and a dropout rate of 0.3. The architecture culminated in an output layer with a single unit and sigmoid activation, appropriate for binary classification.

### 2.4. Training Configuration and Optimization

The training process was standardized across all models to ensure fair comparison and reproducible results. The optimization strategy centered on the Adam optimizer (Integrated within TensorFlow by Google LLC, Mountain View, CA, USA, Version: TensorFlow 2.x), selected for its ability to adapt learning rates dynamically and handle sparse gradients effectively. The initial learning rate was set to $1 \times 10^{-4}$, and it was carefully chosen to balance the training speed with the convergence stability. Training proceeded in batches of 32 images, a size that optimized memory utilization while maintaining stable gradient updates. The maximum number of training epochs was set to 50, though early stopping mechanisms were implemented to prevent overtraining.

The loss function employed was binary cross-entropy, which is particularly well-suited for binary classification tasks and provides appropriate gradients for model optimization. To monitor and improve training efficiency, several callback mechanisms were implemented. Early stopping monitored validation loss with a patience of 10 epochs, automatically terminating training when no improvement was observed and restoring the best weights to prevent overfitting. A learning rate reduction scheme was employed that monitored validation loss and reduced the learning rate by a factor of 0.2 when improvement plateaued, with a patience of 5 epochs and a minimum learning rate threshold of 1e-6. Additionally, model checkpointing saved the best-performing model states based on validation accuracy, ensuring that optimal model parameters were preserved.

### 2.5. Model Performance Monitoring and Evaluation

Throughout the training process, comprehensive performance monitoring was implemented to track each model's progress and effectiveness. The primary metrics monitored included accuracy, loss, and area under the receiver operating characteristic curve (AUC-ROC). These metrics were calculated for both the training and validation sets during each epoch, providing immediate feedback on model learning and generalization. The validation metrics served as critical indicators for the learning rate reduction and early stopping mechanisms.

For final model evaluation, a rigorous testing protocol was established using the held-out test dataset. This evaluation included not only accuracy and AUC-ROC measurements but also practical performance metrics such as inference time and model size. Inference time was measured across multiple batches to obtain reliable average values, with standard deviations calculated to assess performance stability. Additionally, McNemar's statistical test was employed to determine the significance of performance differences between model pairs, providing a statistical foundation for model comparison.

### 2.6. Implementation Environment and Technical Infrastructure

The implementation was carried out in a cloud-based environment utilizing Google Colab's GPU runtime (Google LLC, Mountain View, CA, USA), which provided access to NVIDIA's GPU acceleration. This infrastructure choice enabled efficient model training and evaluation while ensuring the reproducibility of the results. The software framework was built on TensorFlow 2.x, leveraging its high-level Keras API for model construction and training. Python 3.10 served as the primary programming language (Python Programming Language Organization: Python Software Foundation, Beaverton, OR, USA), chosen for its robust ecosystem of scientific computing libraries.

The implementation relied on several key supporting libraries, each serving specific functions in the pipeline. NumPy facilitated efficient numerical computations and array manipulations, particularly in data preprocessing and batch handling. Matplotlib was employed for visualization tasks, generating training curves, ROC curves, and performance comparison plots. Scikit-learn provided essential functionality for metrics calculation and statistical analysis, while the split-folders library managed dataset organization and splitting.

### 2.7. Data Management and Storage

To ensure efficient data handling and model persistence, a structured approach to data management was implemented. All preprocessed images were stored in a directory structure that reflected the training, validation, and test splits, facilitating efficient data loading during training. Model checkpoints were saved in the Keras format, preserving both architecture and weights, enabling easy model reloading for further training or deployment. Training logs, including all performance metrics and learning curves, were systematically recorded and stored for subsequent analysis and visualization.

The entire implementation was designed with reproducibility in mind, incorporating fixed random seeds for all stochastic processes. Detailed documentation of the experimental setup, including all hyperparameters and configuration settings, was maintained throughout the study. This comprehensive approach to methodology documentation ensures that the experiments can be reliably reproduced and built upon in future research.

## 3. Results

### 3.1. Model Performance Overview

A comparative analysis of the four deep learning architectures yielded comprehensive insight into their relative strengths and performance characteristics. The investigation encompassed DenseNet121, ResNet50V2, NASNetMobile, and MobileNetV2, each demonstrating distinct performance profiles across multiple evaluation metrics [33]. The evaluation metrics included classification accuracy, area under the curve (AUC), inference time, and model size efficiency, following established evaluation protocols [34].

### 3.2. Receiver Operating Characteristic Analysis

The receiver operating characteristic (ROC) curve analysis, as depicted in Figure 1, revealed notable differences in the discriminative capabilities of the four models [35]. ResNet50V2 achieved the highest AUC score of 0.957, demonstrating a superior ability to distinguish between benign and malignant lesions across various classification thresholds [36]. DenseNet121 followed closely with an AUC of 0.951, while MobileNetV2 and NASNetMobile achieved AUC scores of 0.943 and 0.935, respectively. The ROC curves demonstrate particularly strong performances in the critical low false-positive rate region, with all models showing rapid ascent in true positive rates while maintaining low false positive rates [37].

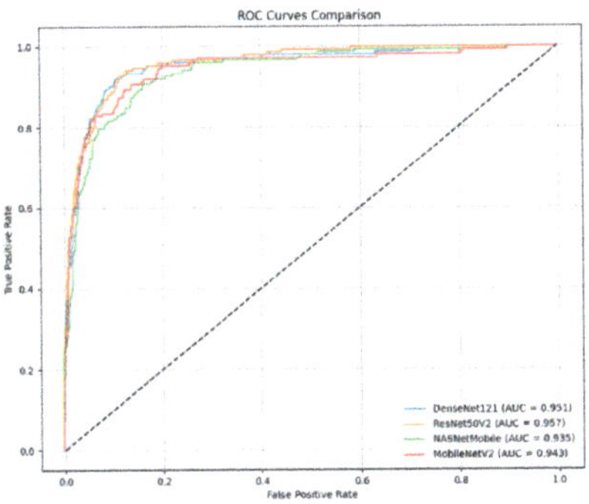


**Figure 1.** ROC curve analysis of the four CNN architectures (ResNet50V2, DenseNet121, MobileNetV2, and NASNetMobile) for melanoma detection, illustrating their discriminative capabilities in differentiating malignant melanoma from benign nevi. ResNet50V2 achieved the highest AUC score (0.957), followed by DenseNet121 (0.951), MobileNetV2 (0.943), and NASNetMobile (0.935). The curves highlight performance differences, particularly in the critical low false-positive rate region, where ResNet50V2 and DenseNet121 excelled.

A detailed examination of the ROC curves reveals that the models' performance differences were most pronounced in the false-positive rate range of 0.1 to 0.3, where ResNet50V2 and DenseNet121 demonstrated marginally better discrimination capabilities. This characteristic is particularly relevant in clinical applications, where minimizing false positives while maintaining high sensitivity is crucial. The convergence of the curves at higher false positive rates suggests comparable performance in high-sensitivity operating points.

### 3.3. *Computational Efficiency and Resource Requirements*

The performance comparison visualization presented in Figure 2 illustrates the stark contrasts in model sizes and inference times among the four architectures [38]. ResNet50V2, while achieving the highest AUC, required substantially more storage space at 91.93 MB, significantly larger than its counterparts [39]. In contrast, MobileNetV2 demonstrated remarkable efficiency with a model size of just 9.89 MB while maintaining competitive classification performance [40]. These findings align with previous studies on model efficiency in medical imaging applications [41].

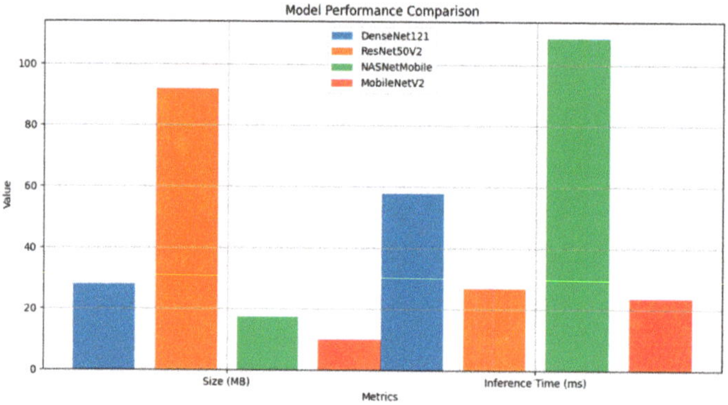


**Figure 2.** Comparison of Model Sizes and Inference Times for CNN Architectures. Comparative visualization of model sizes (in megabytes) and inference times (in milliseconds per image) for the four CNN architectures. MobileNetV2 demonstrated the smallest model size (9.89 MB) and fastest inference time (23.46 ms), showcasing its efficiency for resource-constrained environments. ResNet50V2 achieved strong performance but required more storage space (91.93 MB). NASNetMobile, despite its compact size (17.34 MB), exhibited the longest inference time (108.67 ms).

Inference time analysis revealed equally important distinctions in computational efficiency. MobileNetV2 exhibited the fastest inference time at 23.46 ms per image, closely followed by ResNet50V2 at 26.55 ms. DenseNet121 required moderate computation time at 57.89 m, while NASNetMobile showed the longest inference time at 108.67 ms. These timing differences have significant implications for real-world deployment scenarios, particularly in resource-constrained environments.

### 3.4. *Statistical Significance and Performance Metrics*

McNemar's statistical test revealed significant differences in performance among all model pairs ($p < 0.0001$), confirming that the observed performance variations were not attributable to chance [42]. The strongest statistical differences were observed between NASNetMobile and DenseNet121 (test statistic: 10,076.50), followed by NASNetMobile and MobileNetV2 (test statistic: 5950.10). These results support previous findings on architectural performance differences in medical image classification tasks [43].

### 3.5. Classification Performance Analysis

In terms of raw classification metrics, DenseNet121 achieved the highest accuracy at 92.30%, followed closely by MobileNetV2 at 92.19% and ResNet50V2 at 91.85%. NASNet-Mobile, while showing good overall performance, achieved a slightly lower accuracy of 90.94%. These accuracy figures were complemented by strong precision and recall metrics across all models, with DenseNet121 showing the most balanced performance across all evaluation criteria.

The precision-recall trade-off analysis revealed that all models maintained high precision while achieving good recall rates, with DenseNet121 showing particularly strong performance in balancing these competing metrics. This balance is crucial for clinical applications where both false positives and false negatives carry significant consequences.

### 3.6. Model Stability and Convergence

Model stability and convergence analysis of the training processes demonstrated stable convergence across all architectures, with each model showing consistent improvement in both training and validation metrics throughout the training period. The early stopping mechanisms proved effective in preventing overfitting, with optimal model parameters being successfully captured through the checkpoint system.

## 4. Discussion

### 4.1. CNN in Dermatological Diagnostics

The demonstrated capabilities of convolutional neural networks (CNNs) in melanoma detection highlight their transformative potential in dermatological diagnostics. CNNs excel in recognizing complex patterns in dermoscopic images, often surpassing traditional diagnostic methods. This performance stems from their hierarchical learning structure, where lower layers detect fundamental features such as edges and textures, while deeper layers capture intricate patterns, including asymmetry and irregular pigmentation—hallmarks of malignant melanoma. Studies such as those by Ali et al. (2021) emphasize that CNNs can achieve diagnostic accuracies exceeding 90% when trained on high-quality datasets, challenging even the diagnostic expertise of seasoned dermatologists [44]. Furthermore, advanced augmentation techniques, including zooming, rotation, and flipping, enhance model robustness by exposing it to a broader array of real-world imaging scenarios. This capability is particularly valuable in settings where diagnostic inconsistencies often arise because of inter-observer variability. Multimodal integration, as proposed by Höhn et al. (2021), further extends the utility of CNNs by incorporating clinical metadata alongside image features, enabling nuanced diagnostic interpretations that are indispensable in complex or ambiguous cases [45].

### 4.2. Model Performance

The comparative analysis of the four deep learning architectures provides valuable insights into their potential roles in clinical dermatology applications [46]. DenseNet121's superior overall performance, achieving 92.30% accuracy and an AUC of 0.951, demonstrates the effectiveness of its dense connectivity pattern in capturing intricate features of skin lesions [47]. These findings support previous research on the application of deep learning in dermatological diagnosis [48].

ResNet50V2's achievement of the highest AUC (0.957) indicates its exceptional discriminative ability, particularly in the critical low false-positive rate region. This characteristic is especially valuable in screening applications, where minimizing false alarms while maintaining high sensitivity is paramount. However, the model's substantial size (91.93 MB) presents deployment challenges in resource-constrained environments, necessitating careful consideration of the trade-off between performance and computational requirements.

The remarkable efficiency of MobileNetV2, combining the smallest model size (9.89 MB) with the fastest inference time (23.46 ms) while maintaining competitive accuracy (92.19%), represents a significant advancement in portable diagnostic tools. This architecture's performance characteristics make it particularly suitable for mobile applications and point-of-care devices, where real-time processing and limited computational resources are common constraints.

### 4.3. Computational Efficiency and Resource Utilization

The significant variations in model sizes and inference times among the architectures highlight important considerations for practical deployment [32]. NASNetMobile's unexpectedly long inference time (108.67 ms) despite its relatively compact size (17.34 MB) suggests that architectural complexity does not always translate to better performance [49]. This observation aligns with recent studies on the efficiency-accuracy trade-off in deep learning models [50].

The statistical significance of performance differences among all model pairs, as demonstrated by McNemar's test, confirms that each architecture brings distinct advantages to the task. The strongest statistical differences observed between NASNetMobile and DenseNet121 (test statistic: 10,076.50) suggest fundamental differences in their approach to feature extraction and classification, while the more moderate differences between ResNet50V2 and MobileNetV2 (test statistic: 132.67) indicate closer alignment in their learning strategies.

### 4.4. Limitations

The variation in inference times, particularly NASNetMobile's slower processing speed, suggests opportunities for architecture optimization. Future research could investigate hybrid architectures that combine the efficiency of MobileNetV2 with the feature extraction capabilities of DenseNet121 or ResNet50V2. Additionally, the application of quantization and pruning techniques could further optimize model sizes without significantly compromising performance.

Despite the strong performance across all models, several technical limitations warrant consideration. The current implementation relies on static image input sizes ($224 \times 224$ pixels), which may not be optimal for capturing all relevant diagnostic features in skin lesions of varying sizes [51–53]. Higher-resolution images could preserve critical diagnostic details, particularly for distinguishing subtle features in atypical (or dysplastic) nevi and other challenging cases.

Another limitation lies in the scope of lesion differentiation. While this study focuses on distinguishing benign melanocytic nevi from melanomas, it does not address the more complex challenge of differentiating atypical nevi or non-nevus pigmented neoplasms (e.g., dermatofibromas, lentigines, and seborrheic keratoses) from melanomas. Expanding the dataset to include these lesion types and incorporating a multi-class classification framework will be essential for real-world clinical applicability.

The variation in inference times, particularly NASNetMobile's slower processing speed, underscores the need for further optimization. Investigating hybrid architectures that combine the efficiency of MobileNetV2 with the robust feature extraction capabilities of DenseNet121 or ResNet50V2 could provide a balanced solution. Moreover, quantization and pruning techniques could optimize model sizes and computational efficiency without significantly compromising performance.

Finally, our algorithm does not currently integrate pretest probability into its diagnostic framework. Pretest probability, influenced by factors such as personal and family history of melanoma or prior occurrences, plays a crucial role in clinical decision making. Incorporating patient metadata, such as age, past medical history, family history, clinical history, and lesion location, could improve model performance by addressing the variability in pretest probabilities associated with individual cases.

### 4.5. Clinical Integration and Practical Considerations

The successful deployment of these models in clinical settings requires careful consideration of several factors beyond raw performance metrics [54]. The choice of architecture should be guided by the specific requirements of the deployment environment, available computational resources, and the criticality of real-time response [55]. These considerations align with established guidelines for implementing AI in clinical practice [56].

The high AUC scores across all models suggest their potential value as screening tools, particularly in primary care settings where early detection of suspicious lesions is crucial. However, the implementation of these systems should emphasize their role as assistive tools rather than replacements for clinical expertise. The integration of model uncertainty quantification and explainability mechanisms could enhance their utility in clinical decision support.

### 4.6. Alternative Approaches

Zhang et al. (2023) demonstrated that ViTs, leveraging self-attention mechanisms, outperform traditional CNNs in multi-class classification tasks by capturing global contextual relationships across entire images [57]. Similarly, EfficientNet's compound scaling, as showcased by Tan and Le (2019), allows for increased accuracy while maintaining computational efficiency. Ensemble approaches also provide significant promise for enhancing diagnostic reliability [58]. For instance, Ghosh et al. (2024) demonstrated that a majority voting ensemble of diverse deep learning models effectively reduces the variance and bias, achieving a balanced sensitivity and specificity. Such methods are particularly crucial in minimizing false negatives, which are a critical metric in melanoma detection because of the severe implications of missed diagnoses [59]. Furthermore, the growing interest in hybrid architectures, which integrate traditional handcrafted features with deep learning outputs, underscores the adaptability of CNN systems. Hybrid models can incorporate domain-specific features like lesion texture and color histograms alongside CNN-derived embeddings, resulting in improved accuracy, reaching up to 99% [60].

### 4.7. Future Directions

Several promising avenues for future research emerge from this work. The investigation of ensemble methods combining multiple architectures could leverage the strengths of each model while mitigating their individual limitations. For instance, integrating the robustness of DenseNet121 with the efficiency of MobileNetV2 may enhance both diagnostic performance and deployment feasibility. Ensembles can also improve the generalizability of diagnostic algorithms to diverse lesion types and clinical environments [61–63].

The exploration of few-shot learning techniques offers another promising direction, particularly for addressing rare skin conditions underrepresented in existing datasets. Few-shot learning could enable models to adapt quickly to new classes with minimal labeled data, thereby broadening the scope of automated skin lesion classification and improving diagnostic inclusivity.

Image resolution remains a critical consideration for enhancing diagnostic accuracy. The current study utilized images resized to $224 \times 224$ pixels to optimize computational efficiency, but this resolution may fail to capture finer details essential for differentiating challenging cases, such as atypical nevi or other pigmented lesions. Future research should explore the use of higher-resolution images, such as 1000 × 1000 pixels, which are more reflective of real-world clinical imaging practices. Combining high-resolution inputs with adaptive preprocessing pipelines can optimize image quality and maintain computational feasibility.

Integrating contextual information and patient metadata—such as age, lesion location, clinical history, and family history of melanoma—can significantly enhance diagnostic accuracy. These factors, combined with image-based analysis, would provide more personalized and context-aware predictions, particularly for high-risk individuals with a strong pretest probability of melanoma.

Advanced visualization techniques can also play a pivotal role in improving model interpretability. Developing heatmaps or saliency maps to highlight regions of interest within an image can provide clinicians with valuable insight into the rationale behind model predictions. Such transparency will foster trust in AI-driven diagnostics and support clinical decision making.

Finally, future research should focus on expanding datasets to include a broader range of lesion types, such as atypical nevi and non-nevus pigmented neoplasms (e.g., dermatofibromas, lentigines, and seborrheic keratoses). Including these lesion types would enable the development of more comprehensive multi-class classification frameworks, addressing key gaps in current diagnostic capabilities. By adopting these strategies, advancements in deep learning for melanoma detection can better align with the complexities of real-world clinical practice and provide more robust tools for clinicians.

## 5. Conclusions

This study highlights the transformative potential of convolutional neural networks (CNNs) in melanoma detection, demonstrating their ability to achieve high diagnostic accuracy and efficiency in differentiating malignant melanoma from benign nevi. DenseNet121 emerged as the top-performing architecture, achieving the highest accuracy (92.30%) and an AUC of 0.951, making it suitable for applications requiring precise classification. Meanwhile, MobileNetV2 demonstrated the best balance between accuracy (92.19%) and computational efficiency, with the smallest model size (9.89 MB) and fastest inference time (23.46 ms), offering an ideal solution for resource-constrained environments or mobile diagnostics. These findings underscore the versatility of CNNs in meeting the diverse demands of clinical and point-of-care applications, where both accuracy and efficiency are critical.

Despite these advancements, challenges remain, including the need to address dataset biases, model interpretability, and class imbalances. Future research should explore hybrid and ensemble models to combine the strengths of multiple architectures while leveraging alternative approaches like vision transformers and adaptive preprocessing pipelines to further enhance diagnostic accuracy. The successful integration of AI-driven systems into clinical workflows will require robust validation, clinician-focused training, and mechanisms for explaining model predictions. By addressing these challenges, CNNs can be effectively deployed to complement dermatological expertise, improving early melanoma detection and, ultimately, enhancing patient outcomes.

**Author Contributions:** Conceptualization, M.K.; methodology, G.F., D.K. and V.S.V.; software, A.S.; validation, A.S. and A.A.; formal analysis, G.F., D.K., V.S.V. and A.A.; data curation, N.T.; writing—original draft preparation, M.K., N.T., M.N. and E.P.; writing—review and editing, A.S., G.F., D.K., A.A. and V.S.V.; visualization, A.S.; supervision, M.N. All authors have read and agreed to the published version of the manuscript.

**Funding:** This research received no external funding.

**Institutional Review Board Statement:** Not applicable.

**Informed Consent Statement:** Not applicable.

**Data Availability Statement:** No new data were created in this study. Data sharing is not applicable to this article.

**Conflicts of Interest:** The authors declare no conflicts of interest.

## References


1. Slominski, R.M.; Kim, T.-K.; Janjetovic, Z.; Brożyna, A.A.; Podgorska, E.; Dixon, K.M.; Mason, R.S.; Tuckey, R.C.; Sharma, R.; Crossman, D.K.; et al. Malignant Melanoma: An Overview, New Perspectives, and Vitamin D Signaling. *Cancers* **2024**, *16*, 2262. [CrossRef] [PubMed]
2. Cartocci, A.; Luschi, A.; Tognetti, L.; Cinotti, E.; Farnetani, F.; Lallas, A.; Paoli, J.; Longo, C.; Moscarella, E.; Tiodorovic, D.; et al. Comparative Analysis of AI Models for Atypical Pigmented Facial Lesion Diagnosis. *Bioengineering* **2024**, *11*, 1036. [CrossRef] [PubMed]
3. Ashfaq, M.; Ahmad, A. Skin Cancer Classification with Convolutional Deep Neural Networks and Vision Transformers Using Transfer Learning. In *Advances in Deep Generative Models for Medical Applications*; Springer: Berlin/Heidelberg, Germany, 2023. Available online: https://link.springer.com/chapter/10.1007/978-3-031-46341-9_6 (accessed on 27 November 2024).
4. Wu, Y.; Chen, B.; Zeng, A.; Pan, D.; Wang, R.; Zhao, S. Skin Cancer Classification With Deep Learning: A Systematic Review. *Front. Oncol.* **2022**, *12*, 893972. [CrossRef] [PubMed]
5. Magalhaes, C.; Mendes, J.; Vardasca, R. Systematic Review of Deep Learning Techniques in Skin Cancer Detection. *BioMedInformatics* **2024**, *4*, 2251–2270. [CrossRef]
6. Gautam, S.; Singh, R. Skin Cancer Identification Using Deep Learning. Semantic Scholar. Available online: https://www.semanticscholar.org/paper/Skin-Cancer-Identification-Using-Deep-Learning-Gautam-Singh/bd0306890ef70c6d78782457b99435e2fe4e4c69 (accessed on 1 December 2024).
7. Winkler, J.K.; Blum, A.; Kommoss, K.; Enk, A.; Toberer, F.; Rosenberger, A.; Haenssle, H.A. Assessment of Diagnostic Performance of Dermatologists Cooperating With a Convolutional Neural Network in a Prospective Clinical Study: Human With Machine. *JAMA Dermatol.* **2023**, *159*, 621–627. [CrossRef]
8. Naeem, A.; Farooq, M.S.; Khelifi, A.; Abid, A. Malignant Melanoma Classification Using Deep Learning: Datasets, Performance Measurements, Challenges and Opportunities. *IEEE Access* **2020**, *8*, 110575–110597. [CrossRef]
9. Dildar, M.; Akram, S.; Irfan, M.; Khan, H.U.; Ramzan, M.; Mahmood, A.R.; Alsaiari, S.A.; Saeed, A.H.M.; Alraddadi, M.O.; Mahnashi, M.H. Skin Cancer Detection: A Review Using Deep Learning Techniques. *Int. J. Environ. Res. Public Health* **2021**, *18*, 5479. [CrossRef]
10. Kassem, M.A.; Hosny, K.M.; Damaševičius, R.; Eltoukhy, M.M. Machine Learning and Deep Learning Methods for Skin Lesion Classification and Diagnosis: A Systematic Review. *Diagnostics* **2021**, *11*, 1390. [CrossRef]
11. Efimenko, M.; Ignatev, A.; Koshechkin, K. Review of Medical Image Recognition Technologies to Detect Melanomas Using Neural Networks. *BMC Bioinform.* **2020**, *21* (Suppl. 11), 270. [CrossRef]
12. Popescu, D.; El-Khatib, M.; El-Khatib, H.; Ichim, L. New Trends in Melanoma Detection Using Neural Networks: A Systematic Review. *Sensors* **2022**, *22*, 496. [CrossRef]
13. Ballerini, L.; Fisher, R.B.; Aldridge, B.; Rees, J. A Color and Texture-Based Hierarchical K-NN Approach to the Classification of Non-Melanoma Skin Lesions. *Color Med. Image Anal.* **2013**, *6*, 63–86.
14. Codella, N.C.F.; Gutman, D.; Celebi, M.E.; Helba, B.; Marchetti, M.A.; Dusza, S.W.; Kalloo, A.; Liopyris, K.; Mishra, N.; Kittler, H.; et al. Skin Lesion Analysis Toward Melanoma Detection: A Challenge at the 2017 International Symposium on Biomedical Imaging (ISBI), Hosted by the International Skin Imaging Collaboration (ISIC). In Proceedings of the 2018 IEEE 15th International Symposium on Biomedical Imaging, Washington, DC, USA, 4–7 April 2018; pp. 168–172.
15. Kassani, S.H.; Kassani, P.H. A Comparative Study of Deep Learning Architectures on Melanoma Detection. *Tissue Cell* **2019**, *58*, 76–83. [CrossRef] [PubMed]
16. Krizhevsky, A.; Sutskever, I.; Hinton, G.E. ImageNet Classification with Deep Convolutional Neural Networks. *Adv. Neural Inf. Process. Syst.* **2012**, *25*, 1097–1105. [CrossRef]
17. Jain, A.; Gupta, D.; Tyagi, R. *Deep Learning for Medical Image Analysis*; Academic Press: Cambridge, MA, USA, 2020.
18. Zhang, Z. Improved Adam Optimizer for Deep Neural Networks. In Proceedings of the 2018 IEEE/ACM 26th International Symposium on Quality of Service, Banff, AB, Canada, 4–6 June 2018; pp. 1–2.
19. He, K.; Zhang, X.; Ren, S.; Sun, J. Deep Residual Learning for Image Recognition. In Proceedings of the 2016 IEEE Conference on Computer Vision and Pattern Recognition, Las Vegas, NV, USA, 27–30 June 2016; pp. 770–778.
20. Huang, G.; Liu, Z.; Van Der Maaten, L.; Weinberger, K.Q. Densely Connected Convolutional Networks. In Proceedings of the 2017 IEEE Conference on Computer Vision and Pattern Recognition, Honolulu, HI, USA, 21–26 July 2017; pp. 4700–4708.

21. Shorten, C.; Khoshgoftaar, T.M. A Survey on Image Data Augmentation for Deep Learning. *J. Big Data* **2019**, *6*, 60. [CrossRef]
22. Chollet, F. *Deep Learning with Python*; Manning Publications: Shelter Island, NY, USA, 2017.
23. Howard, A.G.; Zhu, M.; Chen, B.; Kalenichenko, D.; Wang, W.; Weyand, T.; Andreetto, M.; Adam, H. MobileNets: Efficient Convolutional Neural Networks for Mobile Vision Applications. *arXiv* **2017**, arxiv:1704.04861.
24. Russakovsky, O.; Deng, J.; Su, H.; Krause, J.; Satheesh, S.; Ma, S.; Huang, Z.; Karpathy, A.; Khosla, A.; Bernstein, M.; et al. ImageNet Large Scale Visual Recognition Challenge. *Int. J. Comput. Vis.* **2015**, *115*, 211–252. [CrossRef]
25. Zoph, B.; Vasudevan, V.; Shlens, J.; Le, Q.V. Learning Transferable Architectures for Scalable Image Recognition. In Proceedings of the 2018 IEEE/CVF Conference on Computer Vision and Pattern Recognition, Salt Lake City, UT, USA, 18–23 June 2018; pp. 8697–8710.
26. Sandler, M.; Howard, A.; Zhu, M.; Zhmoginov, A.; Chen, L.C. MobileNetV2: Inverted Residuals and Linear Bottlenecks. In Proceedings of the 2018 IEEE/CVF Conference on Computer Vision and Pattern Recognition, Salt Lake City, UT, USA, 18–23 June 2018; pp. 4510–4520.
27. Tan, M.; Le, Q.V. EfficientNet: Rethinking Model Scaling for Convolutional Neural Networks. In Proceedings of the International Conference on Machine Learning, Long Beach, CA, USA, 9–15 June 2019; pp. 6105–6114.
28. Simonyan, K.; Zisserman, A. Very Deep Convolutional Networks for Large-Scale Image Recognition. *arXiv* **2014**, arxiv:1409.1556.
29. He, K.; Zhang, X.; Ren, S.; Sun, J. Identity Mappings in Deep Residual Networks. In Proceedings of the European Conference on Computer Vision, Amsterdam, The Netherlands, 11–14 October 2016; pp. 630–645.
30. Huang, G.; Sun, Y.; Liu, Z.; Sedra, D.; Weinberger, K.Q. Deep Networks with Stochastic Depth. In Proceedings of the European Conference on Computer Vision, Amsterdam, The Netherlands, 11–14 October 2016; pp. 646–661.
31. Zoph, B.; Le, Q.V. Neural Architecture Search With Reinforcement Learning. *arXiv* **2016**, arxiv:1611.01578.
32. Howard, A.; Sandler, M.; Chu, G.; Chen, L.-C.; Chen, B.; Tan, M.; Wang, W.; Zhu, Y.; Pang, R.; Vasudevan, V.; et al. Searching for MobileNetV2. In Proceedings of the 2019 IEEE/CVF International Conference on Computer Vision, Seoul, Republic of Korea, 27 October–2 November 2019; pp. 1314–1324.
33. Esteva, A.; Kuprel, B.; Novoa, R.A.; Ko, J.; Swetter, S.M.; Blau, H.M.; Thrun, S. Dermatologist-Level Classification of Skin Cancer with Deep Neural Networks. *Nature* **2017**, *542*, 115–118. [CrossRef]
34. Yosinski, J.; Clune, J.; Bengio, Y.; Lipson, H. How Transferable Are Features in Deep Neural Networks? *Adv. Neural Inf. Process. Syst.* **2014**, *27*, 3320–3328.
35. Fawcett, T. An Introduction to ROC Analysis. *Pattern Recognit. Lett.* **2006**, *27*, 861–874. [CrossRef]
36. Brinker, T.J.; Hekler, A.; Enk, A.H.; Klode, J.; Hauschild, A.; Berking, C.; Schilling, B.; Haferkamp, S.; Schadendorf, D.; Holland-Letz, T.; et al. Deep Learning Outperformed 136 of 157 Dermatologists in a Head-to-Head Dermoscopic Melanoma Image Classification Task. *Eur. J. Cancer* **2019**, *113*, 47–54. [CrossRef] [PubMed]
37. Powers, D.M.W. Evaluation: From Precision, Recall and F-Measure to ROC, Informedness, Markedness & Correlation. *J. Mach. Learn. Technol.* **2011**, *2*, 37–63.
38. Wang, Z.; Li, H.; Ouyang, W.; Wang, X. Learnable Rich Features for Image Classification. *IEEE Trans. Pattern Anal. Mach. Intell.* **2018**, *40*, 1761–1774.
39. Han, S.; Mao, H.; Dally, W.J. Deep Compression: Compressing Deep Neural Networks with Pruning, Trained Quantization, and Huffman Coding. *arXiv* **2015**, arxiv:1510.00149.
40. Tan, M.; Chen, B.; Pang, R.; Vasudevan, V.; Sandler, M.; Howard, A.; Le, Q.V. MnasNet: Platform-Aware Neural Architecture Search for Mobile. In Proceedings of the 2019 IEEE/CVF Conference on Computer Vision and Pattern Recognition, Long Beach, CA, USA, 15–20 June 2019; pp. 2820–2828.
41. Litjens, G.; Kooi, T.; Bejnordi, B.E.; Adiyoso Setio, A.A.; Ciompi, F.; Ghafoorian, M.; van der Laak, J.A.W.M.; van Ginneken, B.; Sánchez, C.I. A Survey on Deep Learning in Medical Image Analysis. *Med. Image Anal.* **2017**, *42*, 60–88. [CrossRef]
42. Dietterich, T.G. Approximate Statistical Tests for Comparing Supervised Classification Learning Algorithms. *Neural Comput.* **1998**, *10*, 1895–1923. [CrossRef]
43. Ali, S.; Li, J.; Pei, Y.; Khurram, R.; Rehman, K.U.; Rasool, A.B. State-of-the-Art Challenges and Perspectives in Multi-Organ Cancer Diagnosis via Deep Learning-Based Methods. *Cancers* **2021**, *13*, 5546. [CrossRef]
44. Höhn, J.; Hekler, A.; Krieghoff-Henning, E.; Kather, J.N.; Utikal, J.S.; Meier, F.; Gellrich, F.F.; Hauschild, A.; French, L.; Schlager, J.G.; et al. Integrating Patient Data Into Skin Cancer Classification Using Convolutional Neural Networks: Systematic Review. *J. Med. Internet Res.* **2021**, *23*, e20708. [CrossRef]
45. Rajpurkar, P.; Irvin, J.; Zhu, K.; Yang, B.; Mehta, H.; Duan, T.; Ding, D.; Bagul, A.; Langlotz, C.; Shpanskaya, K.; et al. CheXNet: Radiologist-Level Pneumonia Detection on Chest X-Rays with Deep Learning. *arXiv* **2017**, arxiv:1711.05225.
46. Haenssle, H.A.; Fink, C.; Schneiderbauer, R.; Toberer, F.; Buhl, T.; Blum, A.; Kalloo, A.; Hassen, A.B.H.; Thomas, L.; Enk, A.; et al. Man Against Machine: Diagnostic Performance of a Deep Learning Convolutional Neural Network for Dermoscopic Melanoma Recognition in Comparison to 58 Dermatologists. *Ann. Oncol.* **2018**, *29*, 1836–1842. [CrossRef] [PubMed]

47. Phillips, M.; Marsden, H.; Jaffe, W.; Matin, R.N.; Wali, G.N.; Greenhalgh, J.; McGrath, E.; James, R.; Ladoyanni, E.; Bewley, A.; et al. Assessment of Accuracy of an Artificial Intelligence Algorithm to Detect Melanoma in Images of Skin Lesions. *JAMA Netw. Open* **2019**, *2*, e1913436. [CrossRef] [PubMed]
48. Tschandl, P.; Rosendahl, C.; Akay, B.N.; Argenziano, G.; Blum, A.; Braun, R.P.; Cabo, H.; Gourhant, J.-Y.; Kreusch, J.; Lallas, A.; et al. Expert-Level Diagnosis of Nonpigmented Skin Cancer by Combined Convolutional Neural Networks. *JAMA Dermatol.* **2019**, *155*, 58–65. [CrossRef] [PubMed]
49. Cai, H.; Zhu, L.; Han, S. ProxylessNAS: Direct Neural Architecture Search on Target Task and Hardware. In Proceedings of the International Conference on Learning Representations, New Orleans, LA, USA, 6–9 May 2019.
50. Tan, M.; Le, Q.V. EfficientNetV2: Smaller Models and Faster Training. In Proceedings of the International Conference on Machine Learning, Virtual, 18–24 July 2021; pp. 10096–10106.
51. Yao, A.D.; Cheng, D.L.; Pan, I.; Kitamura, F. Deep Learning in Neuroradiology: A Systematic Review of Current Algorithms and Approaches for the New Wave of Imaging Technology. *Radiol. Artif. Intell.* **2020**, *2*, e190026. [CrossRef]
52. Tschandl, P.; Codella, N.; Akay, B.N.; Argenziano, G.; Braun, R.P.; Cabo, H.; Gutman, D.; Halpern, A.; Helba, B.; Hofmann-Wellenhof, R.; et al. Comparison of the Accuracy of Human Readers Versus Machine-Learning Algorithms for Pigmented Skin Lesion Classification: An Open, Web-Based, International, Diagnostic Study. *Lancet Oncol.* **2019**, *20*, 938–947. [CrossRef]
53. Topol, E.J. High-Performance Medicine: The Convergence of Human and Artificial Intelligence. *Nat. Med.* **2019**, *25*, 44–56. [CrossRef]
54. Kelly, C.J.; Karthikesalingam, A.; Suleyman, M.; Corrado, G.; King, D. Key Challenges for Delivering Clinical Impact with Artificial Intelligence. *BMC Med.* **2019**, *17*, 1–9. [CrossRef]
55. Liu, X.; Rivera, S.C.; Moher, D.; Calvert, M.J.; Denniston, A.K.; Ashrafian, H.; Beam, A.L.; Chan, A.W.; Collins, G.S.; Deeks, A.D.J.; et al. Reporting Guidelines for Clinical Trial Reports for Interventions Involving Artificial Intelligence: The CONSORT-AI Extension. *Nat. Med.* **2020**, *26*, 1364–1374. [CrossRef]
56. Vollmer, S.; Mateen, B.A.; Bohner, G.; Király, F.J.; Ghani, R.; Jonsson, P.; Cumbers, S.; Jonas, A.; McAllister, K.S.L.; Myles, P.; et al. Machine Learning and Artificial Intelligence Research for Patient Benefit: 20 Critical Questions on Transparency, Replicability, Ethics, and Effectiveness. *BMJ* **2020**, *368*, l6927. [CrossRef]
57. Zhang, J.; Zhong, F.; He, K.; Ji, M.; Li, S.; Li, C. Recent Advancements and Perspectives in the Diagnosis of Skin Diseases Using Machine Learning and Deep Learning: A Review. *Diagnostics* **2023**, *13*, 3506. [CrossRef]
58. Gautam, R.; Singh, R. EfficientNet: Rethinking Model Scaling for Convolutional Neural Networks. Available online: https://www.researchgate.net/publication/333444574 (accessed on 5 December 2024).
59. Gautam, R.; Singh, R. Melanoma Skin Cancer Detection Using Ensemble of Machine Learning Models Considering Deep Feature Embeddings. Available online: https://www.researchgate.net/publication/381522949 (accessed on 3 December 2024).
60. Roshni Thanka, M.; Edwin, E.B.; Ebenezer, V.; Sagayam, K.M.; Reddy, B.J.; Günerhan, H.; Emadifar, H. A Hybrid Approach for Melanoma Classification Using Ensemble Machine Learning Techniques with Deep Transfer Learning. *Comput. Methods Programs Biomed. Update* **2023**, *3*, 100103. [CrossRef]
61. McKinney, S.M.; Sieniek, M.; Godbole, V.; Godwin, J.; Antropova, N.; Ashrafian, H.; Back, T.; Chesus, M.; Corrado, G.S.; Darzi, A.; et al. International Evaluation of an AI System for Breast Cancer Screening. *Nature* **2020**, *577*, 89–94. [CrossRef] [PubMed]
62. Guo, C.; Pleiss, G.; Sun, Y.; Weinberger, K.Q. On Calibration of Modern Neural Networks. In Proceedings of the International Conference on Machine Learning, Sydney, Australia, 6–11 August 2017; pp. 1321–1330.
63. Rajpurkar, P.; Chen, E.; Banerjee, O.; Topol, E.J. AI in Health and Medicine. *Nat. Med.* **2022**, *28*, 31–38. [CrossRef] [PubMed]

*cancers*

MDPI

*Article*

# Identifying Rural Hotspots for Head and Neck Cancer Using the Bayesian Mapping Approach

**Poornima Ramamurthy [1], John Adeoye [2], Siu-Wai Choi [2], Peter Thomson [1] and Dileep Sharma [1,3,*]**

1 College of Medicine and Dentistry, James Cook University, Smithfield, QLD 4878, Australia; poornima.ramamurthy@jcu.edu.au (P.R.)
2 Oral and Maxillofacial Surgery, Faculty of Dentistry, The University of Hong Kong, Hong Kong, China
3 School of Health Sciences, The University of Newcastle, Ourimbah, NSW 2258, Australia
* Correspondence: dileep.sharma@newcastle.edu.au

**Simple Summary**

Cancers often tend to occur at a higher rate in rural and remote communities due to various reasons. Identifying these cancer hotspots will assist in adequate resourcing of such hotspots. This study was conducted to identify head and neck cancer hotspots in Queensland (QLD), Australia, based on the historical data collected by the cancer register and employing a specialized Bayesian mapping approach. The findings of this study suggested that many rural and remote regions in QLD experience significantly higher head and neck cancer incidence rates and death rates when compared to the QLD state average rates and their surrounding regions. Additionally, a generalized increasing trend of head and neck cancers was noted across the studied period (1982–2018). Although the precise reasons for this increasing trend over time are unclear, a range of factors, such as distance from the tertiary hospitals, lack of awareness of risk factors, behavioral and lifestyle factors, and delayed diagnosis, may be considered to contribute. Our study successfully utilized a robust method to identify head and neck cancer hotspots and will aid in supporting the community and healthcare providers in the region with additional resources to prevent and manage cancer.

**Abstract**

**Background**: The Bayesian mapping approach has not been used to identify head and neck cancer hotspots in Australia previously. This study aims to identify rural communities at risk of head and neck cancer (HNC) for targeted prevention programs. **Methods**: This study included data from 23,853 cases recorded in the Queensland Cancer Register between 1982 and 2018. Outcomes for mapping included incidence, overall mortality, 3-year mortality, and 5-year mortality. Local government areas (LGAs) with a general population aged 15 years and above (according to 2016 census data from the Australian Bureau of Statistics) were utilized for mapping. **Results**: Of the 59 LGAs with higher-than-average risk, 22 predominantly rural and remote LGAs showed statistically significant higher risks of head and neck cancer occurrence. Estimated median standardized mortality ratios (SMRs) ranged from 0.57 to 3.44 and were higher than the state average in 38 LGAs. Four LGAs had the highest mortality—the Shires of Quilpie, Yarrabah, Murweh, and Hinchinbrook. **Conclusions**: Whilst reasons for some LGAs exhibiting higher HNC are unknown, Bayesian mapping highlights these rural and remote regions as worthy of further investigation. In conclusion, the Bayesian disease mapping approach is effective in identifying high-risk communities for HNC. Findings from this study will aid in designing targeted screening and interventions for the prevention and management of head and neck cancer in regional and remote communities through support services such as a cancer navigator.

**Keywords:** rural and remote; cancer; epidemiology; Bayesian mapping

## 1. Introduction

Cancers in the head and neck (HNC) region are known to originate from the mucosal lining of the oral cavity, oropharynx, hypopharynx, larynx, nasopharynx, and sinonasal tract [1]. HNCs are the seventh most common type of cancer in the world, with 660,000 new cases accounting for 5% of total global cancer cases [2,3].

In Australia, 95% of head and neck cancers are squamous cell carcinomas (SCCs) involving the mucosa of the oral cavity, pharynx, and larynx and account for 2–3% of all cancers annually [4,5]. The highest rates of HNC are reported among people living in the Northern Territory with a significant proportion of communities being Aboriginal people and living in rural and remote areas of the state [6]. HNC is known to be a lethal form of cancer as over 50% of diagnosed cases are often diagnosed in the advanced stages of the disease [7]. It is more common in males than females in Australia, and oropharyngeal cancer accounts for nearly 3% of all cancer types [7,8]. Generally, the survival rates are higher due to advancements in treatment approaches and better access in urban areas, but there is a significant reduction in the survival rates of the rural population due to limited access to tertiary care in rural and remote regions [7,9,10]. Additionally, head and neck cancer 10-year observed survival rate for Indigenous Australians (26.5%) is significantly lower than that for non-Indigenous Australians (47.4%), which is a concerning finding [11]. Particularly, Indigenous people living in regional areas are more likely to be diagnosed at an advanced stage of cancer and less likely to receive optimal treatment due to a lack of awareness about the severity of the disease and limited access to healthcare facilities [10,12,13]. This puts the already disadvantaged population at high risk, warranting further screening, education, and awareness programs to facilitate early detection and treatment, thereby improving the overall quality of life.

Bayesian disease mapping is a specialized epidemiological approach used to identify and quantify variations and patterns of diseases among small population areas in a country or state [14,15]. Compared to traditional methods of estimating incidence and mortality ratios in small areas that can provide a value of zero or be susceptible to misinterpretations in areas with small populations, the Bayesian model can provide reliable incidence/mortality estimates by combining observed data (likelihood function) and predicted uncertainty as a measure of one's belief for the estimates before the data are analyzed (prior distribution). This approach has been an effective aid in identifying communities at higher risk of HNC, so that resources and targeted public health screening and healthcare interventions can be optimally planned [14]. Our research team used the Bayesian mapping approach on oral and oropharyngeal carcinomas in Australia recently [16]. However, this approach has not been used to identify HNC hotspots in any of Australia's states with a dataset containing 36 years of cancer data. Hence, this retrospective study was conducted to map and identify HNC hotspots in Queensland, Australia, using the Bayesian mapping approach.

## 2. Material and Methods

### 2.1. Data Collection

Data held by the Queensland Cancer Register (QCR) was accessed for the period 1982–2018 after relevant approvals from the Human Research Ethics Committee at James Cook University (#H8609) and Queensland Health under the Public Health Act 2005. All the data were managed within the Australian Code for the Responsible Conduct of Research.

### 2.2. Data Analysis

Descriptive statistics were performed and presented as tables and text. Head and neck cancer was broadly classified based on its location into cancers involving the external lip, oral cavity, oropharynx, nasopharynx, hypopharynx, larynx, nasal cavity, paranasal sinuses, and salivary glands. This was conducted according to the International Classification of Diseases (ICD-10) codes C00–C14, C30.0, C31, and C32. Outcomes for mapping included the incidence, overall mortality, 3-year mortality, and 5-year mortality of head and neck cancers in Queensland, Australia. Queensland suburbs and localities (SSC) were the spatial units in the original cohort dataset extracted. These SSCs were used to generate higher areal data at the level of the local government areas (LGAs, $n = 78$) from the 2016 Australian census.

To calculate the expected incidence and mortality of head and neck cancer, this study used the LGA population of individuals aged above 15 years based on the 2016 census data recorded by the Australian Bureau of Statistics [1]. The binary adjacency matrix for determining neighborhood dependence and common land boundaries was created using GeoDa (v1.20) with the rook definition. One LGA (Mornington Shire) did not have neighbors during adjacency matrix creation since it comprises islands with no common land boundary. In line with previous adjustments performed for islands in Australia by Duncan et al. [17], the closest neighbor, i.e., Burke Shire, was manually assigned by the team before spatial analysis.

The spatial modeling approach, parameter selection, hyperprior selection, and sensitivity analysis were inspired by our previous analysis of oral cancer data in Hong Kong and Queensland [14,16,18]. In detail, the fully Bayesian method was used to estimate the adjusted incidence and mortality of head and neck cancer, which was implemented using the Gibbs sampling type of Markov Chain Monte Carlo (MCMC) algorithm to sample parameter estimates. Also, a single Markov chain was run for incidence and mortality models. The Besag, York, and Mollie (BYM) method was used to model the incidence and mortality of head and neck cancer. The overall risk effect was assigned vague normal distributions with a mean of 0 and a variance of $10^6$, and conditional autoregressive (CAR) priors were specified to model spatial effects. Noninformative gamma-distributed hyperpriors were also specified in the CAR priors and unstructured effects of the BYM model. The rationale for selecting the BYM method was according to our previous spatial analysis for oral cancer [18], where the model had a lower deviance information criterion and Watanabe–Akaike information criterion compared to the Leroux model.

Overall, 500,000 iterations were conducted with a thinning interval of 20 to ensure independent estimates were sampled. For the incidence and mortality models, the chain had a burn-in of 300,000 iterations to ensure that all nodes converged. The 200,000 iterations that followed were then taken, leading to a sample size of 10,000 estimates. The convergence of the Markov chain was assessed by visualizing the trace, density, and autocorrelation plots and using Geweke's convergence diagnostics.

Median estimates of smoothed incidence and mortality risks were used to draw choropleth maps using the open-source geometry data and shapefiles obtained from the Queensland Government Open Data Portal [19]. LGA boundaries information was also provided by the Queensland Government Department of State Development, Infrastructure, Local Government, and Planning (https://www.statedevelopment.qld.gov.au/__data/assets/pdf_file/0019/42454/local-government-area-boundaries.pdf, accessed on 20 July 2024). Spatial clustering or variation was assessed using the global and local indicator of spatial autocorrelation (LISA)/local Moran's I test, as its sensitivity for quantifying autocorrelation in cancer incidence/mortality estimates have been shown in previous studies [14,16,18,20]. The probability values of these tests were then estimated using Monte

Carlo randomization with 99,999 permutations. When defining spatial clusters or outliers, the lower limit of the 95% credible interval of the smoothed median relative risks was used to determine areas with statistically significant high or low risk for oral cancer incidence and mortality. Statistical and spatial analyses as well as cartography were performed in SPSS v27, R statistical software, WinBUGS, and GeoDa v1.20.

## 3. Results

### 3.1. Patient Cohort

In total, 23,917 patients with head and neck cancers were diagnosed and treated between 1982 and 2018 in Queensland, Australia. Of these, sixty-four patients were excluded from further analysis due to the following reasons: patients aged below 15 years (n = 5), patients with branchial cleft tumors (n = 2), and patients with tumors involving unspecified head and neck sites (n = 57). Consequently, 23,853 patients with HNC were included in the spatial analysis. The age of included patients ranged from 15 to 105 years with a median age (IQR) of 62 (53–71) years. Most patients were between 40 and 64 years old (50.6%), and more males than females (77.5% vs. 22.5%) were noted in the cohort (Table 1). Regarding the site of occurrence, most participants presented with lip cancer (27.3%), oral cavity cancer (25.8%), oropharyngeal cancer (21.5%), and laryngeal cancer (16.9%). As of 1 May 2022, only 40.8% of the patients were alive, and patients' survival times ranged from <1 month to 483 months with a median survival time (IQR) of 81 (27–162) months. Furthermore, 8338 patients (35%) died within five years, while 6714 (28.2%) patients died within three years of their diagnosis. Longitudinal trends of head and neck cancer incidence and mortality rates from 1982 to 2018 are shown in Figures 1 and 2. Head and neck cancer incidence was the highest in 2008, with 29.3 new cases per 100,000, while head and neck cancer mortality was the highest in 2004 (17.3 per 100,000) and 2014 (17.2 per 100,000).

**Table 1.** Patient cohort characteristics.

| Variable | Category | N (%) |
|---|---|---|
| Age | <40 years | 1349 (5.7) |
| | 40–64 years | 12,077 (50.6) |
| | ≥65 years | 10,427 (43.7) |
| Gender | Female | 5362 (22.5) |
| | Male | 18,491 (77.5) |
| Tumor site | Lip | 6512 (27.3) |
| | Oral cavity | 6166 (25.8) |
| | Oropharynx | 5118 (21.5) |
| | Nasopharynx | 334 (1.4) |
| | Hypopharynx | 1261 (5.3) |
| | Larynx | 4024 (16.9) |
| | Nasal cavity and paranasal sinuses | 374 (1.6) |
| | Salivary glands | 64 (0.3) |
| Tumor grade | Well differentiated | 4878 (20.5) |
| | Moderately differentiated | 10,985 (46.1) |
| | Poorly differentiated | 4305 (18.0) |
| | Undifferentiated | 84 (0.4) |
| | Unknown | 3601 (15.1) |
| Status | Alive | 9721 (40.8) |
| | Dead | 14,132 (59.2) |

**Figure 1.** Longitudinal trend of head and neck cancer incidence in Queensland from 1982 to 2018.

**Figure 2.** Longitudinal trend of head and neck cancer mortality in Queensland from 1982 to 2018.

### *3.2. Incidence Risk Mapping*

HNC incidence mapping included 23,853 patients residing in Queensland. The median smoothed standardized incidence ratio (SIR) estimated relative to the population differences in the LGAs ranged from 0.48 in Palm Island Aboriginal Shire to 2.74 in Quilpie Shire (Figure 3A). In comparison to the Queensland average median SIR (1.00), 59 LGAs had a higher risk; however, considering the lower limit of the 95% credible interval (CI), 22 LGAs had significantly higher risks of head and neck cancer occurrence (supplementary data). Twelve LGAs had higher incidence risks exceeding 100% of the Queensland average, while 30 LGAs had incidence risks that were between 1% and 100% higher than the state average. Only Murweh Shire had median smoothed SIR estimates and a 95% CI that was consistently higher than 100% of the Queensland average (2.61 [2.03–3.28]).

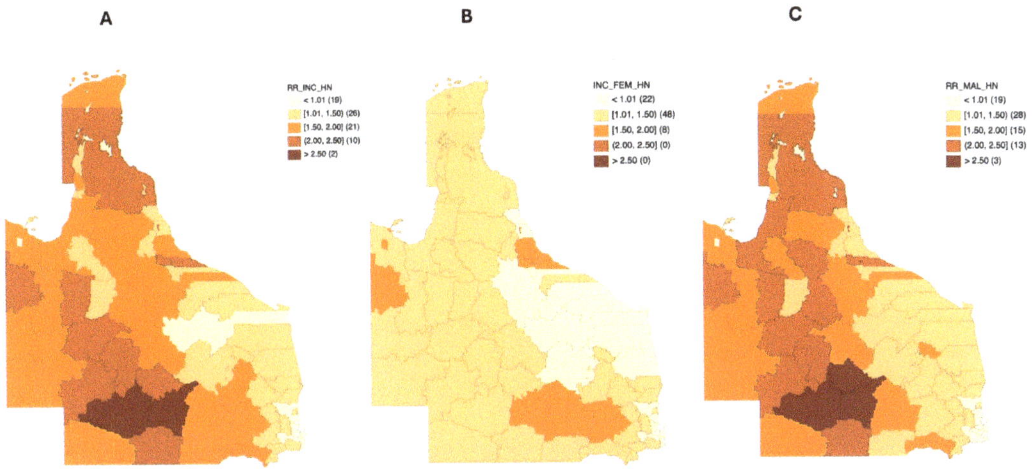


**Figure 3.** Bayesian smoothed median SIR maps for (**A**) head and neck cancer incidence relative risks in all 78 Queensland LGAs, (**B**) head and neck cancer incidence relative risks among females in all 78 Queensland LGAs, and (**C**) head and neck cancer incidence relative risks among males in all 78 Queensland LGAs.

On stratifying head and neck cancer by gender, the median smoothed SIRs for females and males ranged from 0.73 to 1.87 and from 0.54 to 2.80, respectively (Figure 3B,C). For females, 11 LGAs had a significant incidence risk, all of which had median smoothed SIRs between 1% and 100% higher than the average risk (1.16–1.87). The highest incidence risks were observed in Mount Isa City (1.87 [1.38–2.49]). For males, 42 LGAs had significantly higher excess incidence risks than the state average, with a risk distribution similar to that of the total head and neck cancer patients (supplementary data). Twenty-six LGAs had median smoothed SIRs that were between 1% and 100% higher than the state average, while 16 LGAs had a median SIR > 100% of the state average. Likewise, only Murweh Shire had a median smoothed SIR and a 95% CI that was consistently above 100% of the state average (2.69 [2.05–3.49]).

### *3.3. Incidence Risk Mapping by Different Anatomical Sites*

Different patterns in the incidence risk distributions among various LGAs were observed based on the anatomical sites affected by cancer (Figure 4A–F). For lip cancers, median smoothed SIRs ranged from 0.34 to 3.41. Twenty-seven LGAs had a significantly higher incidence risk of lip cancer compared to the Queensland average. Of these LGAs, 13 had excess relative risks between 1% and 100% higher than the state average (1.27–1.77), while 14 had relative incidence risks exceeding 100% of the state average (2.12–3.41). Only Murweh Shire (3.41 [2.33–4.89]) and Maranoa Regional Council (2.88 [2.22–3.71]) had incidence risks that were constantly higher than 100% of the state average according to the lower limit of the 95% credible interval.

Regarding laryngeal cancers, the median smoothed SIR ranged between 0.65 and 2.23 (Figure 4B). Likewise, 33 LGAs had a significantly higher incidence risk for this cancer relative to their total populations and the Queensland average. Only 4 of 33 LGAs had median smoothed SIRs that were above 100% of the state average (2.02–2.23). These LGAs in ascending order of incidence risk distribution were Burdekin Shire, Hinchinbrook Shire, Torres Shire, and Yarrabah Aboriginal Shire. Likewise, 29 LGAs had higher incidence risks ranging between 1% and 100% (1.21–1.95). No LGA had consistent incidence risk estimates exceeding 100% of the state average.

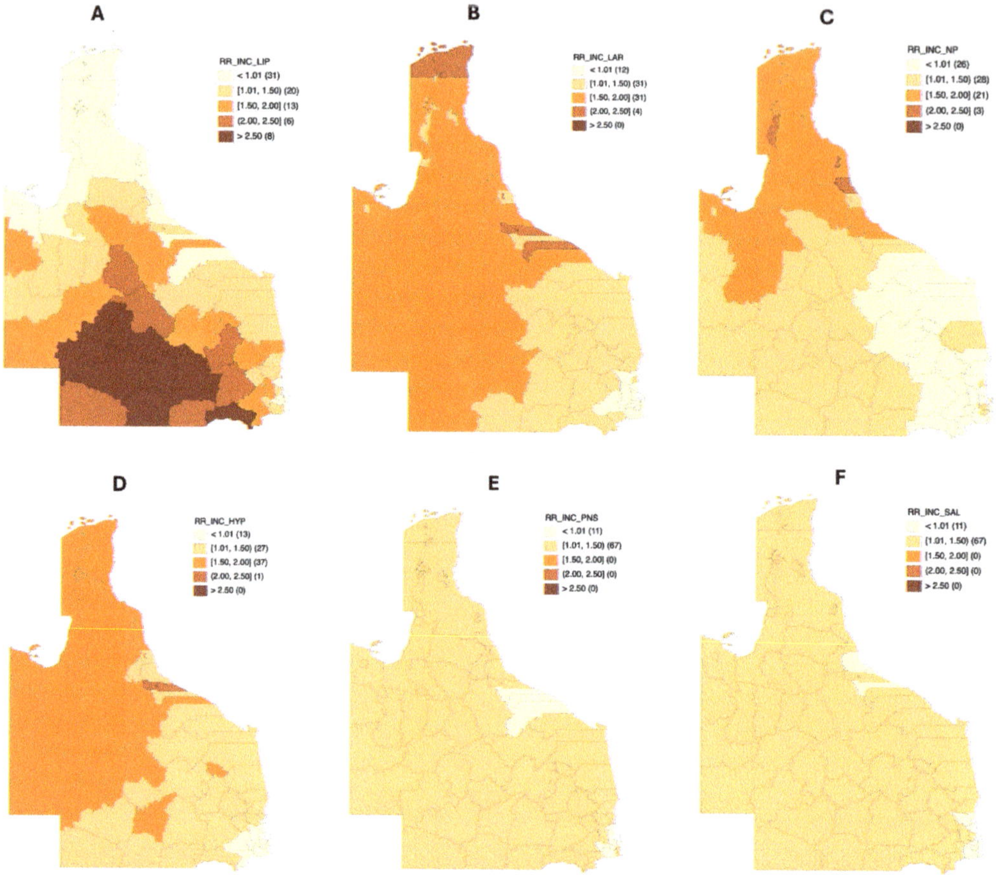


**Figure 4.** Bayesian smoothed median SIR maps for (**A**) lip cancer incidence risks in 78 Queensland LGAs, (**B**) laryngeal cancer incidence risks in 78 Queensland LGAs, (**C**) nasopharyngeal cancer incidence risks in 78 Queensland LGAs, (**D**) hypopharyngeal cancer incidence risks in 78 Queensland LGAs, (**E**) incidence risks for nasal cavity and paranasal sinus malignancies in 78 Queensland LGAs, and (**F**) salivary gland cancer incidence risks in 78 Queensland LGAs.

The distribution of median smoothed estimates for nasopharyngeal cancer incidence in Queensland is shown in Figure 4C. Incidence estimates for this cancer type ranged from 0.62 to 2.50. Only three LGAs (Mareeba Shire, Hinchinbrook Shire, Douglas Shire) had a significantly higher risk of nasopharyngeal cancer incidence above the state average. The median smoothed SIR of these LGAs was from 1.84 to 2.02, and none of them consistently had higher excess relative risks above 100% of the state average (supplementary data).

Incidence risks for hypopharyngeal cancers (Figure 4D) were found to be between 0.69 and 2.04. Nineteen LGAs had significantly higher median smoothed SIR estimates for this cancer type. Seventeen out of 19 LGAs had median incidence estimates between 1% and 100% higher than the state average risk (1.41–1.93), while two LGAs (Hinchinbrook Shire and Northern Peninsula Area Regional Council) had median incidence estimates above 100% higher than the state average risk (2.00–2.04). None of the significant LGAs had credible intervals with the same risk distribution as the median incidence risk estimates.

The median smoothed SIR for nasal cavity and paranasal sinus cancers, as well as salivary gland cancers, was from 0.87 to 1.28 and 0.75 to 1.28, respectively (Figure 4E,F). None of the LGAs had significant incidence risks of these malignancies that were consistently higher than the Queensland average. Thus, these malignancies have low or equivocal risks in the different LGAs of Queensland.

### *3.4. Autocorrelation Analysis for Head and Neck Cancer Incidence*

Global Moran's I (GMI) scatter plots for the incidence risk estimates are shown in Figure 5A–H. The overall incidence risk displayed a significant positive spatial autocorrelation of 0.285 ($p < 0.001$), which was also observed among males (GMI statistic = 0.353; $p < 0.001$). The different cancer types also displayed significant spatial clustering with a GMI statistic that ranged from 0.624 for nasal cavity and paranasal sinus cancers to 0.889 for hypopharyngeal cancers ($p < 0.001$).

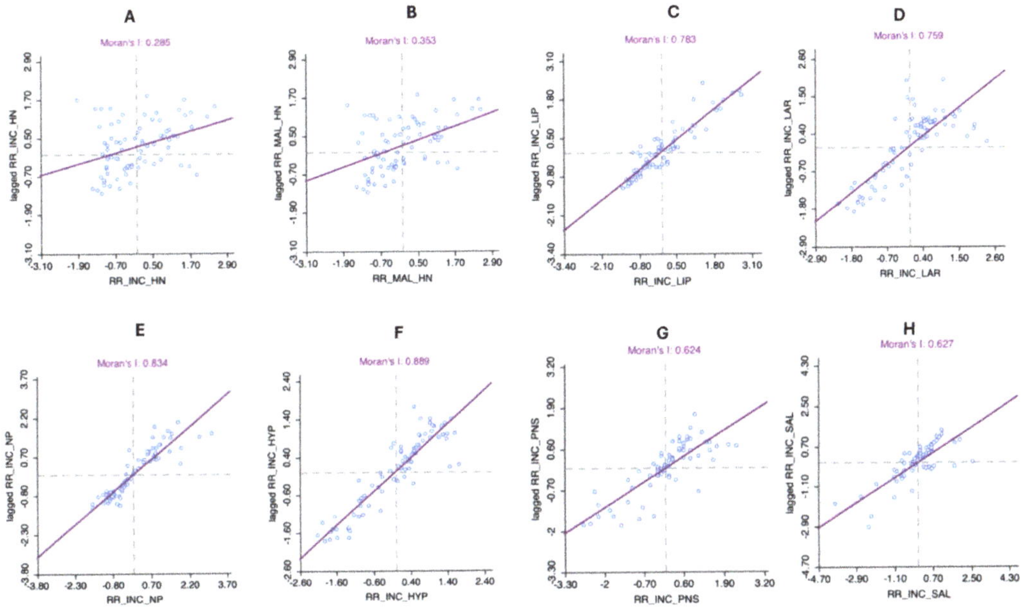


**Figure 5.** Scatter plots for global Moran's I estimation for (**A**) median smoothed SIRs of head and neck cancer in 78 Queensland LGAs, (**B**) median smoothed SIRs of head and neck cancer among males in 78 Queensland LGAs, (**C**) median smoothed SIRs of lip cancer in 78 Queensland LGAs, (**D**) median smoothed SIRs of laryngeal cancer in 78 Queensland LGAs, (**E**) median smoothed SIRs of nasopharyngeal cancer in 78 Queensland LGAs, (**F**) median smoothed SIRs of hypopharyngeal cancer in 78 Queensland LGAs, (**G**) median smoothed SIRs of nasal cavity and paranasal sinus cancers in 78 Queensland LGAs, and (**H**) median smoothed SIRs of salivary gland cancer in 78 Queensland LGAs. Dotted lines in the scatter plots represent the x and y axes of the cartesian plane.

Further analysis to identify spatial clusters and outliers found that higher head and neck cancer incidence risks were clustered around Longreach and Tablelands Regional Councils as well as Mareeba Shire (Figure 6A). In addition to the aforementioned LGAs, Western Downs and Cairns Regional Councils also formed high-risk spatial clusters with their neighbors for head and neck incidence among males (Figure 6B).

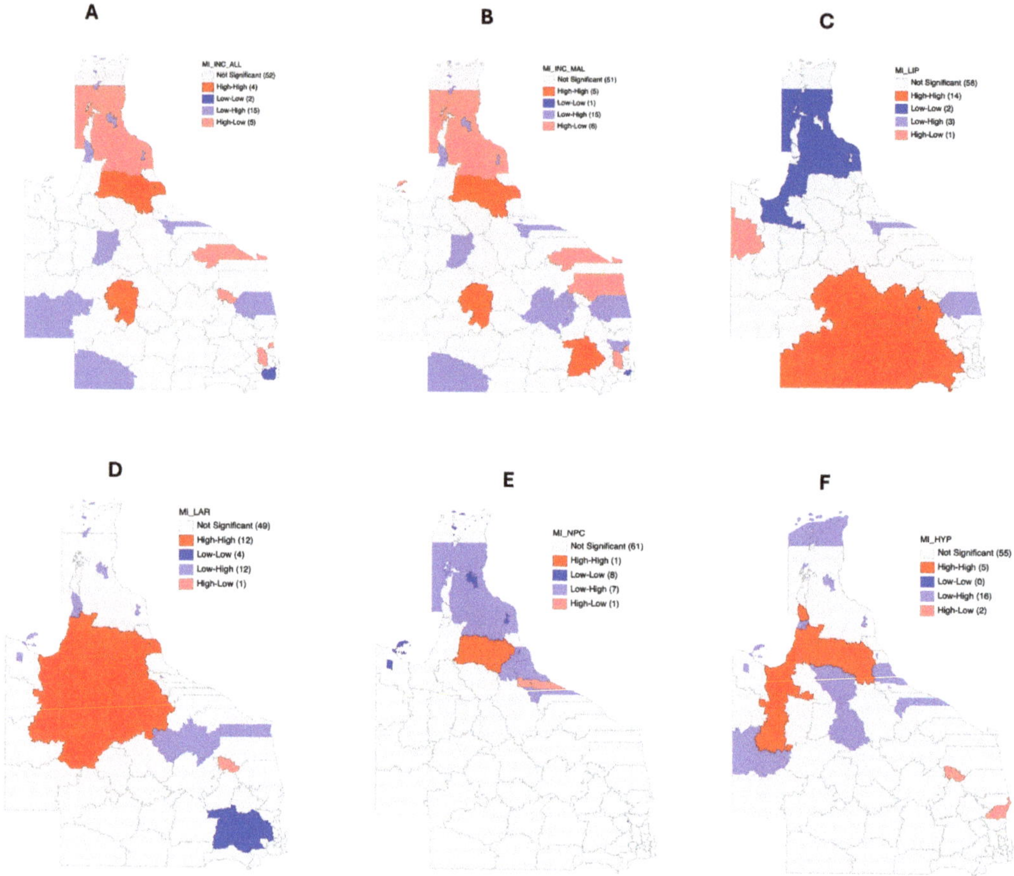


**Figure 6.** Local index of spatial autocorrelation (LISA) maps for (**A**) significant median smoothed SIRs of head and neck cancer in 78 Queensland LGAs, (**B**) significant median SIRs of head and neck cancer among males in 78 Queensland LGAs, (**C**) significant median smoothed SIRs of lip cancer in 78 Queensland LGAs, (**D**) significant median smoothed SIRs of laryngeal cancer in 78 Queensland LGAs, (**E**) significant median smoothed SIRs of nasopharyngeal cancer in 78 LGAs, and (**F**) significant median smoothed SIRs of hypopharyngeal cancer in 78 Queensland LGAs. The terminology "high-high" denotes areas of high incidence located adjacent to another high-incidence area. Similarly, "low-high" denotes areas of high incidence located adjacent to an area with low incidence, and so on.

Fourteen LGAs that formed significant high-risk clusters for lip cancer were identified along with some of their neighbors (Figure 6C). These included Blackall Tambo, Central Highlands, Goondiwindi, Longreach, Maranoa, Toowoomba, and Western Downs Regional Councils, as well as Barcaldine, Banana, Balonne, Murweh, Paroo, Quilpie, and Bulloo Shires. Likewise, 12 significant high-risk LGA clusters were identified for laryngeal cancers, which included Etheridge Shire, Flinders Shire, Mareeba Shire, McKinlay Shire, Richmond Shire, Winton Shire, Carpentaria Shire, Cloncurry Shire, Croydon Shire, Cairns Regional Council, Charters Towers Regional Council, and Tablelands Regional Council, as well as some of their neighbors (Figure 6D).

Mareeba Shire was the only LGA that formed high-risk clusters with some of its neighbors regarding nasopharyngeal cancer incidence (Figure 6E). For hypopharyngeal cancer, five high-high spatial clusters were found which included Mareeba, Douglas, Cloncurry, and Carpentaria Shires, as well as Tablelands Regional Council (Figure 6F). Low-low spatial clusters were only identified for the incidence risks of nasal cavity and paranasal sinus malignancies as well as salivary gland cancers.

### *3.5. Mortality Risk Mapping*

Choropleth maps based on the median smoothed standardized mortality ratio (SMR) of head and neck cancer in Queensland are shown in Figure 7A–C. The median smoothed SMR for head and neck cancer overall mortality was from 0.57 to 3.44. Thirty-eight LGAs had significantly higher-than-state-average (SMR = 1.00) mortality risks. Furthermore, 21/38 LGAs had higher median smoothed SMRs, which were between 1% and 100% over the state average (1.09–1.91), while 17 LGAs had mortality estimates that were above 100% of the state average (2.03–3.44). Of these LGAs with the highest mortality estimates, Quilpie Shire (3.44 [2.07–5.58]), Yarrabah Aboriginal Shire (3.17 [2.05–4.67]), Murweh Shire (3.08 [2.28–4.07]), and Hinchinbrook Shire (2.54 [2.06–3.09]) consistently displayed credible intervals that were also >100% of the state average.

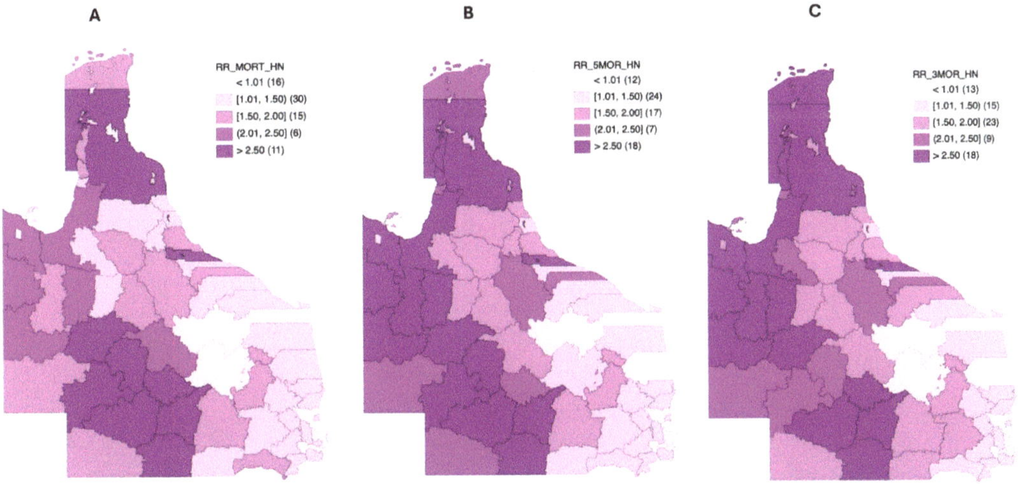


**Figure 7.** Bayesian smoothed median SMR maps for (**A**) head and neck cancer overall mortality risks in all 78 Queensland LGAs, (**B**) head and neck cancer five-year mortality risks in all 78 Queensland LGAs, and (**C**) head and neck cancer three-year mortality risks in all 78 Queensland LGAs.

Regarding the five-year mortality of head and neck cancer in Queensland (Figure 7B), median smoothed SMRs ranged from 0.59 to 5.09 with 41 LGAs having significant mortality risks. Also, 23 of 41 LGAs had median smoothed SMRs that were > 100% higher than the state average (2.12–5.09; supplementary data). Considering the 95% CIs, the highest mortality risks five years after cancer diagnosis were observed in Yarrabah Aboriginal Shire (5.09 [3.23–7.58]), Cook Shire (3.39 [2.37–4.74]), Murweh Shire (3.07 [2.10–4.31]), Mount Isa City (2.77 [2.25–3.38]), and Hinchinbrook Shire (2.69 [2.08–3.44]).

Further stratification based on mortality three years after diagnosis produced median smoothed SMRs that ranged from 0.60 to 5.64. Of the 78 LGAs, 40 had a significantly higher risk of mortality from head and neck cancers 3 years following diagnosis. Also, 23 of the 40 LGAs with significant mortality risks had a risk level that was above 100% of the Queensland average (2.23–5.64). The highest 3-year mortality risks considering the credible intervals and population distribution were observed in seven LGAs. These included Yarrabah Aboriginal Shire (5.64 [3.50–8.63]), Cook Shire (3.44 [2.37–4.90]), Winton Shire (3.40 [2.00–5.76]), Carpentaria Shire (3.21 [2.00–5.08]), Murweh Shire (3.10 [2.07–4.52]), Mount Isa City (2.93 [2.33–3.62]), and Hinchinbrook Shire (2.69 [2.02–3.53]).

### 3.6. Autocorrelation Analysis for Head and Neck Cancer Mortality

The three mortality measures (i.e., overall mortality, 5-year mortality, and 3-year mortality) each showed a significant positive spatial autocorrelation with GMI statistics that ranged from 0.360 to 0.442 ($p < 0.001$; Figure 8A–C).

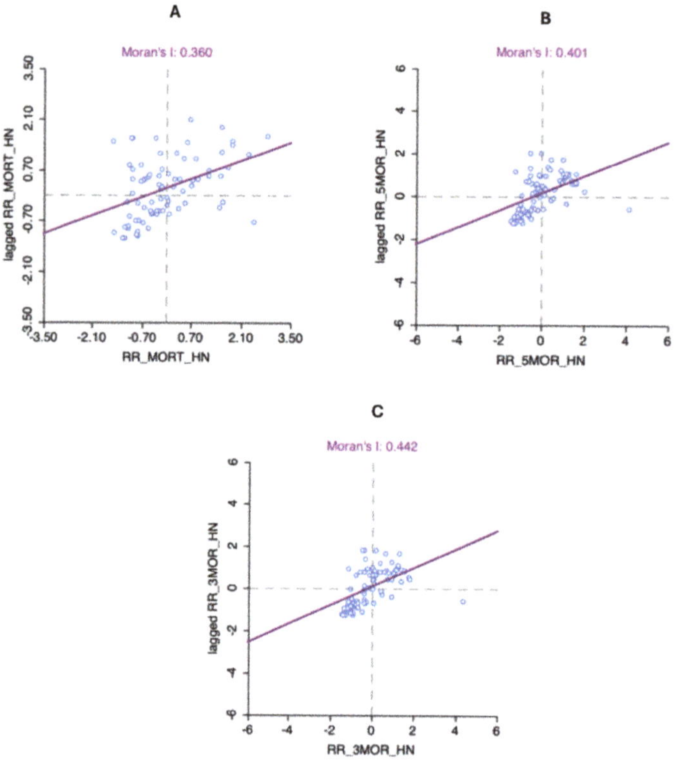


**Figure 8.** Scatter plots for global Moran's I estimation for (**A**) median smoothed overall SMRs of head and neck cancer in 78 Queensland LGAs, (**B**) median smoothed five-year SMRs of head and neck cancer in 78 Queensland LGAs, and (**C**) median smoothed three-year SMRs of head and neck cancer in 78 Queensland LGAs. Dotted lines in scatter plots represent the x and y axes of the cartesian plane.

Further, local index of spatial autocorrelation (LISA) maps for each of the mortality estimates are presented in Figure 9A–C. Three LGAs (Longreach, Western Downs, and Cloncurry Shire) and their neighbors formed high-risk clusters for overall head and neck cancer mortality. For five-year mortality, LISA analysis identified four significant high-risk LGA clusters around Cairns, Longreach, Carpentaria Shire, and Cloncurry Shire (Figure 9B). Furthermore, in addition to these four LGAs, three more LGAs, i.e., Mareeba Shire, Tablelands Regional Council, and Charters Towers Regional Council, formed significant high-risk mortality clusters with their neighbors regarding the three-year mortality of head and neck cancer (Figure 9C).

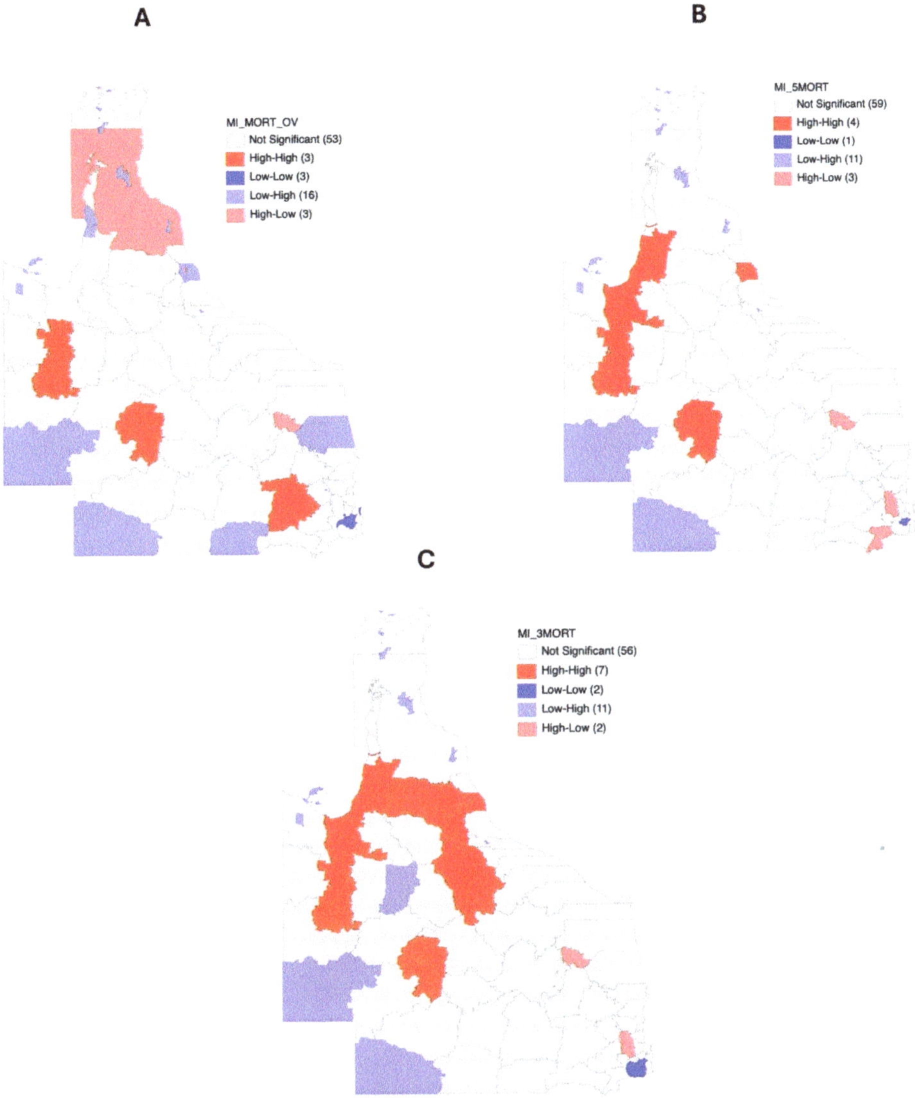


**Figure 9.** Local index of spatial autocorrelation (LISA) maps for (**A**) significant median overall SMRs of head and neck cancer in all 78 Queensland LGAs, (**B**) significant median five-year SMRs of head and neck cancer in all 78 Queensland LGAs, and (**C**) significant median smoothed three-year SMRs of head and neck cancer in all 78 Queensland LGAs.

## 4. Discussion

Cancer is a serious and increasing health issue worldwide, including some forms of HNC expected to increase by up to 70% in case numbers and by 84% in mortality among men by 2050 [21]. In Australia, the state-level cancer registries collate data around individual states and territories, but detailed analyses of this data are minimal. In our current study, which is Australia's largest on HNC, a detailed analysis of the Queensland Cancer Register data from 1982 to 2018 identified 23,853 adult HNC patients and were mapped for incidence and mortality using the Bayesian approach.

The Bayesian statistical approach is a reliable and established methodology used to map disease incidence and mortality risk within well-defined geographic regions employing LGAs or suburbs as units [14,16]. This retrospective study was the first in Australia to map the head and neck cancer hotspots in Queensland state, Australia, using the Bayesian disease mapping approach. Our study showed that at least 22 LGAs had a significantly higher risk of HNC occurrence, with 12 LGAs having incidence risks above 100% of the Queensland average. Most of the LGAs affected are rural or remote communities.

Demographic factors such as gender are known to influence HNC incidence. Previously, the Northern Territory has reported that approximately five times higher in males compared to females [22]. In our study, HNC incidence was strongly influenced by gender, with median smoothed SIRs for females and males ranging from 0.73 to 1.87 and from 0.54 to 2.80, respectively (Figure 3B,C). A recent retrospective study using the Queensland Oncology Repository (QOR), managed by Cancer Alliance Queensland, focused on data from 2013 to 2015 and reported that 77.7% of HNC patients were men, with 45% being over 65 years of age [23]. These findings align with our study, which found that 77.5% were men, and 43.7% were over 65 years of age. Additionally, marital status has been reported to have a protective effect against metastatic HNC, with married people being less likely to present with metastasis and more likely to receive treatment leading to better survival rates [24]. Similar trends of better outcomes for married people were identified in other studies on cancer in general, and specifically on oral cancer [25–27].

Head and neck cancers have previously been reported to have a significant association with treatment-related morbidity and mortality [9]. Our recent study on cancer dataset, focusing on oral cancers (a major subset of HNC), showed that mortality rates have increased in recent years, which can be attributed to factors such as delayed diagnosis and reduced access to services in regional areas of Australia [7]. Additional factors contributing to poorer outcomes after HNC treatment include tumor characteristics and the type and intensity of radiotherapy received, as well as a history of heavy alcohol consumption and limited access due to residence in rural and remote areas [9,23,28,29]. Furthermore, rural residents were reported to travel for treatment and to seek readmission at a different facility from the one that provided the initial treatment [23]. This may be due to the need for frequent travel from rural and remote areas resulting in economic, emotional, and relationship strains [9]. Rurality was also linked to non-treatment for diagnosed HNC in this study, with metropolitan people (9.1%) being less likely to go untreated compared to their rural counterparts (13.7%). This may partly explain the lower overall 2-year survival rates noted in rural cases compared to metropolitan cases (88.7% vs. 75.4%) [23]. Another study involving the Victorian cancer registry explored the role of area-level socio-economic disadvantage on 29 different types of cancers and concluded that 21 types had lower survival rates in more disadvantaged areas [30]. In the case of HNC, inequalities persisted and worsened over the entire period studied (2001–2015), in contrast to many other types of cancers, which showed narrowing disparities [30].

Early detection, prompt referral, and optimal treatment of HNC patients are critical for the commencement of appropriate therapy. In the Australian context, general practitioners (GPs) are invariably the first point of contact for the population and play a pivotal role in fulfilling various functions throughout the cancer care continuum, including facilitating screening and diagnosis, referrals, overseeing the coordination of care delivery, managing the adverse effects of cancer treatment, ensuring survivorship support, and providing palliative care [30–32]. In a recent study exploring the geographic variations in referral practices for patients with suspected HNC in two primary healthcare networks in New South Wales, it was reported that the availability of services was a major factor influencing referral decisions among regional GPs, in contrast to patient symptoms being the key factor for metro GPs [32]. Additionally, less than half of the GPs felt that specialists could examine suspected HNC cases within 2 weeks of referral in regional areas, compared to 70% in metro areas [32]. Similar barriers may be expected in regional QLD, which could, in part, explain higher mortality rates in regional areas as reported in our study.

Holistic management of HNC patients typically involves a multidisciplinary team (MDT) of health professionals delivering clinical care focused on therapeutic and supportive interventions [33]. MDTs are known to significantly improve patient adherence and compliance with therapies by preventing or reducing side effects, thereby contributing to better clinical outcomes [34]. However, access to MDTs for rural and regional communities is often challenging and limited due to ongoing health workforce recruitment and retention issues in most countries, including Australia [35–38]. In this context, the role of cancer or health navigators, particularly in disadvantaged communities, can be a vital link between cancer patients and medical providers in rural and remote communities [39–42]. In some countries, this role is well established and often performed by a nurse, while in others, non-medical professionals provide support to cancer patients [43–45]. In Australia, a critical need for cancer navigators embedded within Aboriginal communities (often residing in rural and remote locations) has been highlighted in multiple studies [46–48]. With the new Australian Cancer Nursing and Navigation Program announced recently, expanding the scope of culturally safe programs is warranted [49]. Particularly, the inclusion of activities around improving cancer awareness within these communities and the implementation of navigator-led preventive programs within the Aboriginal communities can contribute to reducing health inequities.

This is the first study in Australia using the Bayesian approach to identify head and neck cancer hotspots. The dataset utilized in this study was obtained from the QCR, a comprehensive register maintained by Cancer Alliance Queensland. This is the largest population-based cancer registry in Australia and is a unique resource that receives mandatory notifications from all public and private hospitals, nursing homes, and pathology laboratories. Hence, the analyzed data represent the most comprehensive dataset that provides an accurate record of cancer in Queensland since its inception in 1982. In contrast, the interactive Australian Cancer Atlas (v2.0) is accessible online and covers a subset of the data across all cancers reported in Australia, including data from 2010 to 2019 for head and neck cancers' survival rates and diagnosis (https://atlas.cancer.org.au/, accessed on 15 February 2025). However, there are some limitations noted within this retrospective study. The dataset is limited to Queensland state and covers the period from 1 January 1982 to 31 December 2018, making it challenging to generalize trends noted in QLD for the rest of Australia's states and territories. Also, the diagnosis of HNC was based purely on cases with recorded histological evidence of the type and location of cancer. Additionally, the dataset did not record lifestyle behaviors such as smoking and alcohol consumption history among patients diagnosed with any type of cancer. The lack of this data may limit the conclusions drawn in this study since lifestyle factors have a significant effect on the incidence of multiple head and neck cancers across the region studied. Hence, future studies will need to involve a more comprehensive dataset with potential linkage to different datasets held by multiple custodians, such as the Australian Institute of Health and Welfare, state-level cancer registers, and hospital admissions data.

## 5. Conclusions

This paper confirms the effectiveness of identifying at-risk populations for head and neck cancer within Queensland using the Bayesian disease mapping approach. Furthermore, this modeling has also been able to identify the short-term and overall mortality rates of head and neck cancer within QLD so that targeted prevention programs and interventional strategies can be designed and delivered at the community level identified as at-risk or hotspots, predominately in rural and remote regions. The utilization of cancer navigators to deliver holistic cancer care can be expanded to improve cancer awareness in high-risk regions, thereby enhancing the quality of care and access to services in regional communities.

**Supplementary Materials:** The following supporting information can be downloaded at: https://www.mdpi.com/article/10.3390/cancers17050819/s1. LGA level data: Incidence of Head and Neck Cancer (Persons); Incidence of Head and Neck Cancer (Females); Incidence of Head and Neck Cancer (Males); Incidence of Lip cancer; Incidence of Laryngeal cancer; Incidence of Nasopharyngeal cancer; Incidence of Hypopharyngeal cancer; Incidence of Nasal and Paranasal sinus cancer; Incidence of Salivary Gland cancer; Mortality—Head and Neck Cancer (Persons); 3 Year Mortality—Head and Neck Cancer (Persons); 5 Year Mortality—Head and Neck Cancer (Persons).

**Author Contributions:** Conceptualization, P.T., P.R. and D.S.; methodology, J.A., P.R. and S.-W.C.; software, J.A.; validation, J.A. and P.R.; formal analysis, J.A. and P.R.; resources, P.T. and D.S.; data curation, J.A. and P.R.; writing—original draft preparation, P.R., J.A. and D.S.; writing—review and editing, P.T., J.A., P.R. and D.S.; visualization, J.A. and P.R.; supervision, P.T.; project administration, P.T., P.R. and D.S.; funding acquisition, P.T., P.R. and D.S. All authors have read and agreed to the published version of the manuscript.

**Funding:** This research was funded by Tropical Australian Academic Health Centre 2021 Micro-Funding grant number MF0001721. Doctroal candidature of Poornima Ramamurthy (P.R) was supported by Australian Government Research Training Scholarship and Tom and Dorothy Cook Scholarships in Public Health and Tropical Medicine.

**Institutional Review Board Statement:** Ethical approval was obtained from the James Cook University Human Research Ethics Committee (H8609), and further approval for data access from the Queensland Cancer Register was provided by Queensland Health under the PHA 2005.

**Informed Consent Statement:** Patient consent was waived due to the retrospective data analysis approach used in this study.

**Data Availability Statement:** Restrictions apply to the availability of the data. Data were obtained from the Queensland Cancer Register, and forms to request data are available [https://canceralliancegld.health.qld.gov.au/queensland-cancer-register-qcr/ accessed on 15 February 2025] with the permission of Queensland Health under the PHA 2005.

**Conflicts of Interest:** The authors declare no conflicts of interest.

## References

1. Australian Bureau of Statistics. Census DataPacks. Available online: https://www.abs.gov.au/census/find-census-data/datapacks?release=2016&product=GCP&geography=LGA&header=S (accessed on 12 June 2024).
2. Sung, H.; Ferlay, J.; Siegel, R.L.; Laversanne, M.; Soerjomataram, I.; Jemal, A.; Bray, F. Global Cancer Statistics 2020: GLOBOCAN Estimates of Incidence and Mortality Worldwide for 36 Cancers in 185 Countries. *CA Cancer J. Clin.* **2021**, *71*, 209–249. [CrossRef]
3. Johnson, D.E.; Burtness, B.; Leemans, C.R.; Lui, V.W.Y.; Bauman, J.E.; Grandis, J.R. Head and neck squamous cell carcinoma. *Nat. Rev. Dis. Primers* **2020**, *6*, 92. [CrossRef] [PubMed]
4. Koh, J.; Walsh, P.; D'Costa, I.; Bhatti, O. Head and neck squamous cell carcinoma survivorship care. *Aust. J. Gen. Pract.* **2019**, *48*, 846–848. [CrossRef] [PubMed]
5. What Is Head and Neck Cancer? Available online: https://www.headandneckcancer.org.au/head-and-neck-cancer-definition/what-is-oral-cancer/ (accessed on 21 February 2025).
6. Jayaraj, R.; Singh, J.; Baxi, S.; Ramamoorthi, R.; Thomas, M. Trends in incidence of head and neck cancer in the northern territory, Australia, between 2007 and 2010. *Asian Pac. J. Cancer Prev.* **2014**, *15*, 7753–7756. [CrossRef] [PubMed]
7. Sun, A.; Sharma, D.; Choi, S.W.; Ramamurthy, P.; Thomson, P. Oral cancer in Australia: Rising incidence and worsening mortality. *J. Oral Pathol. Med.* **2023**, *52*, 328–334. [CrossRef] [PubMed]
8. Singh, J.; Ramamoorthi, R.; Baxi, S.; Jayaraj, R.; Thomas, M. The risk factors of head and neck cancer and their general patterns in Australia: A descriptive review and update. *J. Environ. Pathol. Toxicol. Oncol.* **2014**, *33*, 45–57. [CrossRef] [PubMed]

9. Pateman, K.A.; Cockburn, N.L.; Batstone, M.D.; Ford, P.J. Quality of life of head and neck cancer patients in urban and regional areas: An Australian perspective. *Aust. J. Rural Health* **2018**, *26*, 157–164. [CrossRef] [PubMed]
10. Condon, J.R.; Zhang, X.; Dempsey, K.; Garling, L.; Guthridge, S. Trends in cancer incidence and survival for Indigenous and non-Indigenous people in the Northern Territory. *Med. J. Aust.* **2016**, *205*, 454–458. [CrossRef] [PubMed]
11. 10-Year Relative Survival—National Cancer Control Indicators. 2022. Available online: https://ncci.canceraustralia.gov.au/outcomes/relative-survival-rate/10-year-relative-survival (accessed on 10 February 2025).
12. National Rural Health Alliance. *Cancer in Rural Australia—Fact Sheet July 2022*; National Rural Health Alliance: Canberra, Australia, 2022; pp. 1–5.
13. Shahid, S.; Teng, T.H.; Bessarab, D.; Aoun, S.; Baxi, S.; Thompson, S.C. Factors contributing to delayed diagnosis of cancer among Aboriginal people in Australia: A qualitative study. *BMJ Open* **2016**, *6*, e010909. [CrossRef] [PubMed]
14. Adeoye, J.; Choi, S.W.; Thomson, P. Bayesian disease mapping and the 'High-Risk' oral cancer population in Hong Kong. *J. Oral Pathol. Med.* **2020**, *49*, 907–913. [CrossRef]
15. MacNab, Y.C. Bayesian disease mapping: Past, present, and future. *Spat. Stat.* **2022**, *50*, 100593. [CrossRef]
16. Ramamurthy, P.; Sharma, D.; Adeoye, J.; Choi, S.W.; Thomson, P. Bayesian Disease Mapping to Identify High-Risk Population for Oral Cancer: A Retrospective Spatiotemporal Analysis. *Int. J. Dent.* **2023**, *2023*, 3243373. [CrossRef] [PubMed]
17. Duncan, E.W.; Cramb, S.M.; Aitken, J.F.; Mengersen, K.L.; Baade, P.D. Development of the Australian Cancer Atlas: Spatial modelling, visualisation, and reporting of estimates. *Int. J. Health Geogr.* **2019**, *18*, 21. [CrossRef]
18. Adeoye, J.A. New World vs Old World: Refining Oral Cancer Screening, Diagnosis, and Prediction. Ph.D. Thesis, The University of Hong Kong, Hong Kong, China, 2023.
19. Queensland Government. Local Government Area Boundaries—Queensland. Available online: https://www.data.qld.gov.au/dataset/local-government-area-boundaries-queensland (accessed on 16 December 2023).
20. Zhang, L.; Wan, X.; Shi, R.; Gong, P.; Si, Y. Comparing spatial patterns of 11 common cancers in Mainland China. *BMC Public Health* **2022**, *22*, 1551. [CrossRef] [PubMed]
21. Bizuayehu, H.M.; Dadi, A.F.; Ahmed, K.Y.; Tegegne, T.K.; Hassen, T.A.; Kibret, G.D.; Ketema, D.B.; Bore, M.G.; Thapa, S.; Odo, D.B.; et al. Burden of 30 cancers among men: Global statistics in 2022 and projections for 2050 using population-based estimates. *Cancer* **2024**, *130*, 3708–3723. [CrossRef] [PubMed]
22. Singh, J.; Jayaraj, R.; Baxi, S.; Ramamoorthi, R.; Thomas, M. Incidence and mortality from mucosal head and neck cancers amongst Australian states and territories: What it means for the northern territory. *Asian Pac. J. Cancer Prev.* **2013**, *14*, 5621–5624. [CrossRef]
23. Foley, J.; Wishart, L.R.; Ward, E.C.; Burns, C.L.; Packer, R.L.; Philpot, S.; Kenny, L.M.; Stevens, M. Exploring the impact of remoteness on people with head and neck cancer: Utilisation of a state-wide dataset. *Aust. J. Rural Health* **2023**, *31*, 726–743. [CrossRef]
24. Inverso, G.; Mahal, B.A.; Aizer, A.A.; Donoff, R.B.; Chau, N.G.; Haddad, R.I. Marital status and head and neck cancer outcomes. *Cancer* **2015**, *121*, 1273–1278. [CrossRef]
25. Dasgupta, P.; Turrell, G.; Aitken, J.F.; Baade, P.D. Partner status and survival after cancer: A competing risks analysis. *Cancer Epidemiol.* **2016**, *41*, 16–23. [CrossRef] [PubMed]
26. Krajc, K.; Mirosevic, S.; Sajovic, J.; Klemenc Ketis, Z.; Spiegel, D.; Drevensek, G.; Drevensek, M. Marital status and survival in cancer patients: A systematic review and meta-analysis. *Cancer Med.* **2023**, *12*, 1685–1708. [CrossRef] [PubMed]
27. Wang, W.; Ramamurthy, P.; Sharma, D.; Choi, S.-W.; Thomson, P. Oral cancer survival and marital status: Observations from an Australian population. *Fac. Dent. J.* **2023**, *14*, 90–96. [CrossRef]
28. Jong, K.E.; Smith, D.P.; Yu, X.Q.; O'Connell, D.L.; Goldstein, D.; Armstrong, B.K. Remoteness of residence and survival from cancer in New South Wales. *Med. J. Aust.* **2004**, *180*, 618–622. [CrossRef]
29. Hegney, D.; Pearce, S.; Rogers-Clark, C.; Martin-McDonald, K.; Buikstra, E. Close, but still too far. The experience of Australian people with cancer commuting from a regional to a capital city for radiotherapy treatment. *Eur. J. Cancer Care* **2005**, *14*, 75–82. [CrossRef]
30. Afshar, N.; English, D.R.; Blakely, T.; Thursfield, V.; Farrugia, H.; Giles, G.G.; Milne, R.L. Differences in cancer survival by area-level socio-economic disadvantage: A population-based study using cancer registry data. *PLoS ONE* **2020**, *15*, e0228551. [CrossRef]
31. Klabunde, C.N.; Ambs, A.; Keating, N.L.; He, Y.; Doucette, W.R.; Tisnado, D.; Clauser, S.; Kahn, K.L. The role of primary care physicians in cancer care. *J. Gen. Intern. Med.* **2009**, *24*, 1029–1036. [CrossRef] [PubMed]
32. Venchiarutti, R.L.; Tracy, M.; Clark, J.A.; Palme, C.E.; Young, J.M. Geographic variation in referral practices for patients with suspected head and neck cancer: A survey of general practitioners using a clinical vignette. *Aust. J. Rural Health* **2022**, *30*, 501–511. [CrossRef]
33. Taberna, M.; Gil Moncayo, F.; Jane-Salas, E.; Antonio, M.; Arribas, L.; Vilajosana, E.; Peralvez Torres, E.; Mesia, R. The Multidisciplinary Team (MDT) Approach and Quality of Care. *Front. Oncol.* **2020**, *10*, 85. [CrossRef] [PubMed]

34. Maslin-Prothero, S. The role of the multidisciplinary team in recruiting to cancer clinical trials. *Eur. J. Cancer Care* **2006**, *15*, 146–154. [CrossRef]
35. Murray, R.B.; Craig, H. A sufficient pipeline of doctors for rural communities is vital for Australia's overall medical workforce. *Med. J. Aust.* **2023**, *219* (Suppl. S3), S5–S7. [CrossRef]
36. Cortie, C.H.; Garne, D.; Parker-Newlyn, L.; Ivers, R.G.; Mullan, J.; Mansfield, K.J.; Bonney, A. The Australian health workforce: Disproportionate shortfalls in small rural towns. *Aust. J. Rural Health* **2024**, *32*, 538–546. [CrossRef] [PubMed]
37. Charlton, M.; Schlichting, J.; Chioreso, C.; Ward, M.; Vikas, P. Challenges of Rural Cancer Care in the United States. *Oncology* **2015**, *29*, 633–640.
38. Levit, L.A.; Byatt, L.; Lyss, A.P.; Paskett, E.D.; Levit, K.; Kirkwood, K.; Schenkel, C.; Schilsky, R.L. Closing the Rural Cancer Care Gap: Three Institutional Approaches. *JCO Oncol. Pract.* **2020**, *16*, 422–430. [CrossRef] [PubMed]
39. Santos Salas, A.; Bassah, N.; Pujadas Botey, A.; Robson, P.; Beranek, J.; Iyiola, I.; Kennedy, M. Interventions to improve access to cancer care in underserved populations in high income countries: A systematic review. *Oncol. Rev.* **2024**, *18*, 1427441. [CrossRef]
40. Balfe, M.; O'Brien, K.; Timmons, A.; Butow, P.; Sullivan, E.O.; Gooberman-Hill, R.; Sharp, L. The unmet supportive care needs of long-term head and neck cancer caregivers in the extended survivorship period. *J. Clin. Nurs.* **2016**, *25*, 1576–1586. [CrossRef] [PubMed]
41. Neadley, K.; Smith, A.; Martin, S.; Boyd, M.; Hocking, C.; Shoubridge, C. Health Navigator intervention to address the unmet social needs of populations living with cancer attending outpatient treatment at a major metropolitan hospital in Australia: Protocol for a mixed-methods feasibility trial. *BMJ Open* **2024**, *14*, e080403. [CrossRef] [PubMed]
42. Stiller, A.; Goodwin, B.C.; Crawford-Williams, F.; March, S.; Ireland, M.; Aitken, J.F.; Dunn, J.; Chambers, S.K. The Supportive Care Needs of Regional and Remote Cancer Caregivers. *Curr. Oncol.* **2021**, *28*, 3041–3057. [CrossRef] [PubMed]
43. Fenton, A.; Downes, N.; Mendiola, A.; Cordova, A.; Lukity, K.; Imani, J. Multidisciplinary Management of Breast Cancer and Role of the Patient Navigator. *Obstet. Gynecol. Clin. N. Am.* **2022**, *49*, 167–179. [CrossRef] [PubMed]
44. Domenico, E.B.L.; Kalinke, L.P. Nurse Navigator of Cancer Patients: Contributions to the discussion on the national stage. *Rev. Bras. Enferm.* **2024**, *77*, e770201. [CrossRef] [PubMed]
45. Emfield Rowett, K.; Christensen, D. Oncology Nurse Navigation: Expansion of the Navigator Role Through Telehealth. *Clin. J. Oncol. Nurs.* **2020**, *24*, 24–31. [CrossRef]
46. Thackrah, R.D.; Papertalk, L.P.; Taylor, K.; Taylor, E.V.; Greville, H.; Pilkington, L.G.; Thompson, S.C. Perspectives of Aboriginal People Affected by Cancer on the Need for an Aboriginal Navigator in Cancer Treatment and Support: A Qualitative Study. *Healthcare* **2022**, *11*, 114. [CrossRef]
47. Bell, L.; Anderson, K.; Girgis, A.; Aoun, S.; Cunningham, J.; Wakefield, C.E.; Shahid, S.; Smith, A.B.; Diaz, A.; Lindsay, D.; et al. "We Have to Be Strong Ourselves": Exploring the Support Needs of Informal Carers of Aboriginal and Torres Strait Islander People with Cancer. *Int. J. Environ. Res. Public Health* **2021**, *18*, 7281. [CrossRef] [PubMed]
48. Valery, P.C.; Bernardes, C.M.; Beesley, V.; Hawkes, A.L.; Baade, P.; Garvey, G. Unmet supportive care needs of Australian Aboriginal and Torres Strait Islanders with cancer: A prospective, longitudinal study. *Support. Care Cancer* **2017**, *25*, 869–877. [CrossRef]
49. Das, M. Australia's new cancer nursing and navigation plan. *Lancet Oncol.* **2024**, *25*, 18. [CrossRef] [PubMed]

*cancers*

MDPI

*Article*

# Improving the Estimation of Prediction Increment Measures in Logistic and Survival Analysis

**Danielle M. Enserro * and Austin Miller**

Department of Biostatistics and Bioinformatics, Roswell Park Comprehensive Cancer Center, Buffalo, NY 14263, USA; austin.miller@roswellpark.org
* Correspondence: danielle.enserro@roswellpark.org

**Simple Summary**

Confidence interval estimation of discrimination improvement measures, including the area under the receiver operating characteristic curve, the net reclassification index, and the integrated discrimination improvement, is an area of ongoing research. The most common confidence interval estimation methods employ normal theory. Literature suggests that degeneration of the normal assumption under the null hypothesis exists, and normal theory confidence intervals estimated may be invalid. Bootstrapped confidence intervals do not rely on normal theory assumptions. We examine the performance of discrimination improvement measures in both the logistic and survival regression context through simulation. Normal theory intervals are only appropriate with a strong effect size of the added parameter, and the percentile bootstrap interval exhibits reasonable coverage while maintaining the shortest width in nearly all simulated scenarios, making this interval the most reliable choice. The intent is that these recommendations improve the accuracy in the estimation and the overall assessment of discrimination improvement.

**Abstract**

**Background/Objectives:** Proper confidence interval estimation of the area under the receiver operating characteristic curve (AUC), the net reclassification index (NRI), and the integrated discrimination improvement (IDI) is an area of ongoing research. The most common confidence interval estimation methods employ asymptotic theory. However, developments demonstrate that degeneration of the normal distribution assumption under the null hypothesis exists for measures such as the change in AUC (ΔAUC) and IDI, and confidence intervals estimated under the normal distribution assumption may be invalid. We aim to study the performance of confidence intervals derived assuming asymptotic theory and those derived with non-parametric bootstrapping methods. **Methods:** We examine the performance of ΔAUC, NRI, and IDI in both the logistic and survival regression context. We explore empirical distributions and compare coverage probabilities of asymptotic confidence intervals with those produced from bootstrapping methods through simulation. **Results:** The primary finding in both the logistic framework and the survival analysis framework is that the percentile CIs performed well regarding coverage, without compromise to their width; this finding was robust in most scenarios. **Conclusions:** Our results suggest that the asymptotic intervals are only appropriate when a strong effect size of the added parameter exists, and that the percentile bootstrap interval exhibits at least a reasonable coverage while maintaining the shortest width in nearly all simulated scenarios, making this interval the most reliable choice. The intent is that these recommendations improve the accuracy in the estimation and the overall assessment of discrimination improvement.

**Keywords:** risk prediction; validation; discrimination; confidence interval estimation; bootstrap

## 1. Introduction

In the pursuit of eradicating cancer, a key area of research is cancer prevention and control. Both observational and treatment trials may assess collected patient risk factors for their associations with cancer survival outcomes, such as objective tumor response, progression-free survival, and overall survival. Cancer risk prediction models can be developed and utilized by health care providers to assess a patient's risk of developing cancer given specific patient characteristics. An example of a model used for breast cancer risk assessment is the National Cancer Institute's Breast Cancer Risk Assessment Tool (BCRAT), which was originally developed by Mitchell Gail and known as the Gail Model [1].

It is important that established risk prediction models are accurate, reliable, and robust for their application in the population at-risk for cancer development or recurrence. The common practice is to develop the risk prediction model on a discovery data set, followed by assessing the model performance through internal or external validation, or some combination [2,3]. The BCRAT model and its performance were later assessed with external validation in a range of diverse populations [4–7]. Common statistical modeling techniques for model development and validation include logistic regression for binary outcomes and Cox proportional hazards (PH) regression for time-to-event outcomes [8].

Risk prediction model validation first requires establishing clinical and statistical significance of the marker of interest [9]. Additionally, model calibration and discrimination should be assessed: calibration quantifies how close the predictions are to the observed outcomes while discrimination quantifies the model's ability to correctly distinguish between events and nonevents [8]. A common area of ongoing research is taking previously developed and validated models and updating them with the addition of new markers to improve both model calibration and discrimination. This paper focuses on the improvement in discrimination by adding a new marker to a standard risk model.

### 1.1. ΔAUC for Evaluating Discrimination Improvement

There are multiple measures for assessing discrimination improvement. The most common metric used in logistic regression is the difference in area under the receiver operating characteristic curve (AUC), where ΔAUC = AUC(expanded model) − AUC(standard model) [10]. The overall C is an extension of the AUC for survival analysis, and ΔC can be calculated as C(expanded model) − C(standard model) [11]. For comparing nested models, a strong added marker should theoretically increase the AUC or the overall C. Pepe et al. demonstrated that if the model is correct under normality, then the significance of the new marker is equivalent to significant improvement in AUC [9]. However, the magnitude of ΔAUC often fails to recognize some promising new markers, the paradox being that a statistically significant marker will fail to produce a large increase in AUC, especially if the standard model's baseline AUC is large [12]. This phenomenon motivated a search for new methods for assessing a predictor's incremental value [13,14].

### 1.2. NRI, NRI > 0, and IDI: Definitions and Controversaries

Pencina et al. proposed new measures for assessing discrimination in logistic regression including a risk-category-based measure known as the net reclassification index (NRI), the continuous NRI (NRI > 0), and the integrated discrimination improvement (IDI) [12,15]. Extensions of these measures were later derived for survival analysis [16]. The NRI attempts to quantify whether a new variable provides clinically relevant improvement in risk prediction, assuming that a valuable marker will tend to increase predicted risks for events and decrease predicted risks for nonevents [12]. Calculation is based on the categorization of model-based predicted probabilities from models being compared into ordinal categories of absolute risk by event status, which are cross-tabulated in a reclassification table. NRI typically assumes either two or three risk categories, but it can also assume many. In the case that risk categories are not clinically assignable, the definition was extended so that model-based predicted probabilities from the standard prediction model and the updated prediction model can be compared directly with NRI > 0 [15]. Finally, IDI accounts for the size of movements up and down in risk categories, jointly quantifying the overall improvement in sensitivity and specificity over all possible cutoffs on the (0, 1) interval [12].

NRI and NRI > 0 have been subject to criticism. Pepe argued that NRI as a single summary measure is less clinically relevant than the event NRI (eNRI) and nonevent NRI (neNRI) as separate components, and Kerr et al. demonstrate scenarios where the sum of eNRI and neNRI mask detriment by the new model within either the events or nonevents [17,18]. NRI's interpretation is commonly mistaken as a proportion, and Pepe argues it is better to interpret eNRI and neNRI separately, since eNRI is the net proportion of events assigned a higher risk and neNRI is the net proportion of nonevents assigned a lower risk [17]. Kerr et al. show that NRI > 0 can be dramatically large in magnitude, even for models with an uninformative added marker, thus alluding that null new markers are predictive and falsely leading investigators to incorrectly assign them roles in risk prediction [18]. Hilden and Gerds argue that the estimation of NRI > 0 and IDI may not be valid with poorly calibrated risk models and that model re-calibration may not correct all issues [19,20]. Leening et al. counter-argue that mean calibration of risk prediction models is automatically achieved by any maximum likelihood estimation (MLE) based algorithm and therefore Hilden and Gerds' example is not applicable [21]. They also reiterate the importance of ensuring properly calibrated models before evaluating the inherent value of an added marker [21]. Additionally, McKeague and Qian show that the empirical distribution of NRI > 0 can be bimodal in nature [22]. With the amount of conflicting literature, investigators should take great care in the estimation and interpretation of NRI, NRI > 0, and IDI, as these measures can be estimated in conjunction with other measures of discrimination improvement such as $\Delta$AUC [17,21].

### *1.3. Challenges in Estimation of Discrimination Improvement Measures*

Proper confidence interval (CI) estimation of these metrics is important to consider. The most common confidence interval estimation methods employ asymptotic theory. However, developments demonstrate that degeneration of the normal distribution assumption under the null hypothesis exists for discrimination improvement metrics, and confidence intervals estimated under the normal distribution assumption may be invalid. Demler et al. demonstrated misuse of the DeLong test comparing AUCs for two nested models, observing that the empirical distribution of $\Delta$AUC was highly right-skewed with the median near zero, suggesting that the distribution of the $\Delta$AUC estimator under the null is dramatically different from the normal distribution assumed by the DeLong test [23]. Additionally, Kerr et al. demonstrated via simulation that the standard error formula of IDI underestimates the standard error, and that the normal theory test testing the null hypothesis of IDI = 0 is not valid due to violation of the normal assumption [24]. We hypothesize that this phenomenon also exists for NRI and NRI > 0. The asymptotic CI formulas rely heavily on the assumption that the distribution of these measures is always normal in nature, which may not be the case, especially for weak added factors. They also rely on proper estimation of standard errors; the developed formulas for the standard errors of NRI and IDI may not be correctly estimating the true variance.

Alternative methods for CI estimation employ bootstrapping techniques and do not assume normality under the null. However, with the potential for large data, deriving CIs from bootstrapping can be computationally intensive, so we must ensure that what we gain from bootstrap CIs is worth the extra time and computer power. In this paper, we examine the performance of ΔAUC, NRI, NRI > 0, and IDI in the binary outcome framework and their extensions in survival analysis. We explore empirical distributions and compare the coverage probabilities for CIs derived from various methods. We consider two event rates, several effect sizes, two sample size options, and two types of censoring for survival analysis. Finally, we make recommendations for CI methods to utilize based on their performance.

## 2. Methods

### 2.1. General Framework: Logistic Regression

We let Y be a binary outcome, where Y = 1 for an event of interest and Y = 0 for a nonevent. We define a column vector X of $p + q$ predictor variables conditional on Y that follows a multivariate normal distribution for nonevents $X \mid Y = 0 \sim N(\mu_0, \Sigma)$ and for events $X \mid Y = 1 \sim N(\mu_1, \Sigma)$. While we assume equal variance for events and non-events, we clarify that this is not a necessary assumption. We assume that Y and X are available for all N patients. We also assume that the $p + q$ predictor variables of X are uncorrelated. We use X to predict Y; a projection based on the full set of $p + q$ predictors compared with a projection based on a reduced set of predictors, $p$, where the reduced model is nested within the full model. In logistic regression, the respective models produce linear coefficient estimates $a' = (a_1, \ldots, a_{p+q})$, based on the full model, and $b' = (b_1, \ldots, b_p)$, based on the reduced model, with risk scores functions of $a'X_{p+q}$ and $b'X_p$. We assume here that higher values of risk scores correspond to a higher probability of the event of interest. We wish to test whether the last $q$ coefficients are equal to 0 and to then determine whether the full model discriminates as well as or better between the two subgroups of Y as compared to the reduced model.

### 2.2. General Framework: Time-to-Event Regression

Logistic regression modeling can be employed in scenarios with full follow-up. While collecting complete follow-up on all participants is ideal, situations without complete follow-up time are more realistic. Survival analysis methods, such as Kaplan–Meier and Cox proportional hazards regressions, have become some of the most used tools in risk prediction modeling [3,8,25]. We assume there is a time-to-event variable T for all individuals, such that $T_i$ represents either when an event has occurred or the time of censoring, where censoring can occur as either loss to follow-up or at the end of the study. All individuals also have an event indicator Y, where Y = 1 for those with the event observed or Y = 0 for those censored. We also have collected data on $p + q$ fixed covariates at baseline in the vector X, made up of $x_1, \ldots, x_{p+q}$. We assume that the censoring is non-informative, meaning that the censoring mechanism is unrelated to the outcome of interest or the covariates, and we also assume right-censoring for the event times. Thus, if the proportionality of hazards assumption is true, we can use the Cox proportional hazards (PH) regression model [26]. The fitted risk model can then be used to estimate the predicted probability of survival within the specified time frame $(0, t)$. Measuring discrimination improvement in survival analysis is complicated by the fact that the event of interest involves a time-to-event component, and the model thus makes predictions about these survival times.

### 2.3. *Measures of Discrimination Improvement*

#### 2.3.1. AUC and Overall C

The area under the receiver operating characteristic (ROC) curve (AUC) is defined as the probability that the risk of event for a randomly selected nonevent is less than the risk of event for a randomly selected event. Given a risk score threshold *t*, sensitivity (or true positive fraction, TPF) is the probability that an event is classified correctly as an event:

$$\text{Sensitivity} = \text{TPF} = \text{P(risk score} > t \mid \text{Y} = 1)$$

Specificity is defined as the probability of correctly classifying a nonevent:

$$\text{Specificity} = \text{P(risk score} < t \mid \text{Y} = 0)$$

Each risk score is compared to *t* for classification of the subject with that risk score to a predicted group, i.e., predicted event vs. predicted nonevent. Subtracting specificity from 1 yields the false positive fraction (FPF):

$$1 - \text{Specificity} = \text{FPF} = \text{P(risk score} > t) \mid \text{Y} = 0)$$

Depending on the choice of threshold *t*, some events and nonevents will be correctly classified while the remainder will be misclassified. Varying *t* yields different pairs of values of TPF and FPF. Plotting these pairs (FPF, TPF) for all possible choices of *t* results in the ROC curve. The AUC is the area under the curve, which ranges from 0.5 (no discriminatory ability) to 1.0 (perfect discrimination).

There is no explicit formula for the AUC, so typically it is estimated by the Mann–Whitney statistic [10]. This is a non-parametric, unbiased estimator, referred to as npAUC and known as the C-statistic [25]., e.g., for the full model discussed with risk scores $a'X_{p+q}$, the formula is

$$\text{C} \equiv \text{npAUC} = \frac{1}{n_0 n_1} \sum\nolimits_{x_i \in Y_0} \sum\nolimits_{x_j \in Y_1} I\left[a' x_i,\ a\prime x_j\right],$$

where $Y_1$ and $Y_0$ are the sets of subjects with and without events, respectively, $n_1$ and $n_0$ are the sizes of the sets, and *I* is given as follows:

$$I\left[a' x_i,\ a\prime x_j\right] = \begin{cases} 1,\ if\ a' x_i < a' x_j \\ 0.5,\ if\ a' x_i = a' x_j \\ 0,\ otherwise \end{cases}$$

DeLong et al. developed an approximate test for testing if two AUCs from different models on the same group of subjects are equal and produced a CI for ΔAUC. The approximate standard error used in both calculations is

$$SE(\Delta AUC) = \left[(1, -1) S (1, -1)\right]^{1/2}$$

where *S* is the estimated variance-covariance matrix of ($npAUC_{p+q}$, $npAUC_p$) [10]. We use the C-statistic as the AUC estimator in this study. To assess improvement in discrimination, we estimate the difference in area under of the receiver operating characteristic curve (AUC) for two models: ΔAUC = AUC(new or updated model) − AUC(standard model) [10].

We now extend the AUC to the survival analysis context. Using the survival regression method described, we denote the predicted survival time for everyone at baseline, $T_1$, $T_2$, ..., $T_n$. We have two categories of subjects at a given time point $T \leq T_{final}$: those who developed the event during the study (Y = 1) and those who were censored (Y = 0).

We denote these actual survival times by $U_1, U_2, \ldots, U_n$. Harrell states that predicted probabilities of survival until any fixed time point (which we denote $V_1, V_2, \ldots, V_n$) can be used in place of the corresponding $T_1, T_2, \ldots, T_n$ if those estimates remain in one-to-one correspondence [25]. M. Pencina et al. show that this point holds true in the most common models in survival analysis, specifically accelerated failure time models and proportional hazards models [11].

Now we consider all pairs of subjects, $(i, j)$, such that $i < j$, to ensure no repetitions. Thus, for a given pair, we have a concordant pair if $U_i < U_j$ and $V_i < V_j$ or $U_i > U_j$ and $V_i > V_j$, and we have a discordant pair if $U_i < U_j$ and $V_i > V_j$ or $U_i > U_j$ and $V_i < V_j$. Since not all pairs will be concordant or discordant due to ties, we can only use the usable pairs of subjects in which at least one had an event in the construction of the C index, resulting in either event vs. event or event vs. nonevent comparisons. The overall C is defined as the proportion of all usable concordant pairs:

$$C = \frac{\pi_c}{\pi_c + \pi_d}$$

where

$$\begin{aligned} \pi_c &= P(U_i < U_j \; and \; V_i < V_j \; or \; U_i > U_j \; and \; V_i > V_j) \\ &= P(U_i < U_j \; and \; V_i < V_j) + P(U_i > U_j \; and \; V_i > V_j) \end{aligned}$$

$$\begin{aligned} \pi_d &= P(U_i < U_j \; and \; V_i > V_j \; or \; U_i > U_j \; and \; V_i < V_j) \\ &= P(U_i < U_j \; and \; V_i > V_j) + P(U_i > U_j \; and \; V_i < V_j) \end{aligned}$$

M. Pencina et al. [11] demonstrate that since *i* and *j* are interchangeable in the definitions of $\pi_c$ and $\pi_d$, and since the V's have a continuous distribution (assuming at least one predictor is continuous), the overall C index reduces to

$$C = \frac{P(U_i < U_j \; and \; V_i < V_j)}{P(U_i < U_j)} = P(V_i < V_j / U_i < U_j).$$

A natural estimate for the overall C is

$$\hat{C} = \frac{1}{Q} \sum_{(i,j) \in O} c_{ij}$$

where O is the set of all usable pairs of subjects $(i, j)$, Q is the total number of usable pairs, and $c_{ij}$ takes on the value of 1 for concordant pairs and 0 otherwise [27]. To assess improvement in discrimination, we estimate the difference in overall Cs for two models: $\Delta C$ = C(expanded model) − C(standard model).

### 2.3.2. NRI, NRI > 0, and NRI(t)

Pencina et al. introduced the net reclassification improvement (NRI) to quantify whether a new variable provides clinically relevant improvement in risk prediction, assuming a valuable new marker will tend to increase predicted risks for events and decrease predicted risks for nonevents [12]. Calculation is based on the categorization of model-based predicted probabilities from the standard risk prediction model and the updated prediction model into clinically meaningful ordinal categories of absolute risk, which are cross-tabulated in a reclassification table. The table tabulates events and nonevents separately. Observations are categorized into the table cells based on assigned risk categories by the standard (old) risk model and the updated (new) risk model. Upward movement is defined as moving into a higher category based on the updated model, while downward movement is defined as moving into a lower category. For those where $Y = 1$, upward movement is preferable while downward movement is problematic. For those where Y = 0, the opposite preferences hold. Thus, the NRI is defined as:

$$NRI = [P(up \mid Y = 1) - P(down \mid Y = 1)] + [P(down \mid Y = 0) - P(up \mid Y = 0)].$$

The quantity in the first bracket is referred to as the event NRI (eNRI), or the net proportion of events assigned a higher risk category. The quantity in the second bracket is referred to as the nonevent NRI (neNRI), or the net proportion of non-events assigned a lower risk category. Each component contains a penalty for any wrong movement in categories. The probabilities can be estimated using sample data obtained from the reclassification table:

$$\hat{P}(\text{up}|Y=1) = \hat{p}_{up,Y=1} = \frac{\#\text{ events moving up}}{\#\text{ events}}$$

$$\hat{P}(\text{down}\,|Y=1) = \hat{p}_{down,Y=1} = \frac{\#\text{ events moving down}}{\#\text{ events}}$$

$$\hat{P}(\text{up}|Y=0) = \hat{p}_{up,Y=0} = \frac{\#\text{ nonevents moving up}}{\#\text{ nonevents}}$$

$$\hat{P}(\text{down}\,|Y=0) = \hat{p}_{down,Y=0} = \frac{\#\text{ nonevents moving down}}{\#\text{ nonevents}}.$$

Thus, NRI can be estimated as

$$\widehat{NRI} = \widehat{eNRI} + \widehat{neNRI}$$

where

$$\widehat{eNRI} = (\hat{p}_{up,Y=1} - \hat{p}_{down,Y=1})$$

$$\widehat{neNRI} = (\hat{p}_{down,Y=0} - \hat{p}_{up,Y=0}$$

The asymptotic standard errors for eNRI and neNRI can be estimated as

$$SE\left(\widehat{eNRI}\right) = \sqrt{\frac{\hat{p}_{up,Y=1} + \hat{p}_{down,Y=1}}{n_1} - \frac{\left(\hat{p}_{up,Y=1} - \hat{p}_{down,Y=1}\right)^2}{n_1}}$$

$$SE\left(\widehat{neNRI}\right) = \sqrt{\frac{\hat{p}_{down,Y=0} + \hat{p}_{up,Y=0}}{n_0} - \frac{\left(\hat{p}_{down,Y=0} - \hat{p}_{up,Y=0}\right)^2}{n_0}}$$

and

$$SE\left(\widehat{NRI}\right) = \sqrt{SE\left(\widehat{eNRI}\right)^2 + SE\left(\widehat{neNRI}\right)^2}$$

where $n_1$ is the number of events and $n_0$ is the number of nonevents [12].

NRI with categories typically assumes either two or three risk categories but can assume up to $k$ risk categories. The choice for risk category cutoffs is of much debate. Pencina et al. recommended that clinically useful category cutoffs should be used, but the choice of category cutoff may not be easy to make [12]. Pencina et al. later recommended that under circumstances that the choice in category cutoff is not obvious, investigators should consider using the event rate as the category cutoff, which yields an NRI measure with relationships with metrics in decision analytics and possesses meaningful interpretations [28].

In the scenario where clinically meaningful categories are not assigned, Pencina et al. extended the definition of NRI so that model-based predicted probabilities from the standard prediction model and the updated prediction model can be compared directly [15]. Instead of tabulating upward and downward movement in categories, increases and decreases in predicted probabilities are tabulated instead. This method of calculating NRI is often referred to as continuous NRI (NRI > 0), which can be defined as follows:

$$\mathrm{NRI} > 0 = [\mathrm{P}(\mathrm{p_{new}} > \mathrm{p_{old}} \mid \mathrm{Y} = 1) - \mathrm{P}(\mathrm{p_{new}} < \mathrm{p_{old}} \mid \mathrm{Y} = 1)]$$

$$- [\mathrm{P}(\mathrm{p_{new}} > \mathrm{p_{old}} \mid \mathrm{Y} = 0) - \mathrm{P}(\mathrm{p_{new}} < \mathrm{p_{old}} \mid \mathrm{Y} = 0)],$$

where $\mathrm{p_{new}}$ are the predicted probabilities from the new updated risk prediction model and $\mathrm{p_{old}}$ are the predicted probabilities from the standard risk prediction model. Similar calculations as those shown above in the definition for NRI with categories can be used for estimating the components of NRI > 0; instead of counting the number of upward and downward movements, the number of observations that satisfy the above risk comparisons are assessed, for both events and nonevents.

The asymptotic standard errors can be estimated as

$$SE\left(e\widehat{NRI > 0}\right) = \sqrt{\frac{\hat{p}_{risk1>risk0,Y=1} + \hat{p}_{risk1<risk0,Y=1}}{n_1} - \frac{\left(\hat{p}_{risk1>risk0,Y=1} - \hat{p}_{risk1<risk0,Y=1}\right)^2}{n_1}}$$

$$SE\left(ne\widehat{NRI > 0}\right) = \sqrt{\frac{\hat{p}_{risk1<risk0,Y=0} + \hat{p}_{risk1>risk0,Y=0}}{n_0} - \frac{\left(\hat{p}_{risk1<risk0,Y=0} - \hat{p}_{risk1>risk0,Y=0}\right)^2}{n_0}}$$

$$SE\left(\widehat{NRI > 0}\right) = \sqrt{SE\left(e\widehat{NRI > 0}\right)^2 + SE\left(ne\widehat{NRI > 0}\right)^2}$$

where each $\hat{p}$ represents the empirical proportions of individuals satisfying their respective criteria and the subscripts *risk1* and *risk0* represent the predicted probability of event in the updated model and the standard model, respectively [15].

NRI was later extended to survival analysis. Chambless et al. express event NRI ($\mathrm{NRI_{Y=1}}$) and nonevent NRI ($\mathrm{NRI_{Y=0}}$) as:

$$NRI_{Y=1} = P(Z_{up}|Y = 1) - P(Z_{down}|Y = 1)$$

$$NRI_{Y=0} = P(Z_{down}|Y = 0) - P(Z_{up}|Y = 0)$$

where overall NRI is estimated as the weighted average of the two quantities:

$$NRI_w = w \cdot NRI_{Y=1} + (1 - w) \cdot NRI_{Y=0},$$

with $w$ between 0 and 1 [16]. A reminder that $Z = X'\beta$, and $Z_{up}$ represents upward movement in risk category or increased risk by the new model while $Z_{down}$ represents downward movement in risk category or decreased risk by the new model. The authors point out that using this notation, the NRI considered by Pencina et al. was $2 \cdot \mathrm{NRI}_{0.5}$, and that the choice of $w$ can be used to reflect relative costs and benefits of improvement in risk prediction [12,16].

Chambless et al. made some modifications to NRI for use in survival analysis, conditioning on time being less than some $t$ [16]:

$$NRI_{Y=1}(t) = P(Z_{up}|Y(t) = 1) - P(Z_{down}|Y(t) = 1),$$

$$NRI_{Y=0}(t) = P(Z_{down}|Y(t) = 0) - P(Z_{up}|Y(t) = 0),$$

$$NRI(t)_w = w \cdot NRI_{Y=1}(t) + (1 - w) \cdot NRI_{Y=0}(t).$$

A count estimator for NRI(t) uses the following proportions for event NRI(t) and nonevent NRI(t):

$$\widehat{NRI}_{Y=1}(t)_{count} = \frac{\sum I(Z_{up}, Y(t) = 1) - \sum I(Z_{down}, Y(t) = 1)}{\sum I(Y(t) = 1)},$$

$$\widehat{NRI}_{Y=0}(t)_{count} = \frac{\sum I(Z_{down}, Y(t) = 0) - \sum I(Z_{up}, Y(t) = 0)}{\sum I(Y(t) = 0)}.$$

We obtain the components of NRI(t) by applying Bayes' theorem:

$$NRI_{Y=1}(t) = \left(\frac{P(Y(t) = 1|Z_{up})\cdot P(Z_{up})}{P(Y(t) = 1)} - \frac{P(Y(t) = 1|Z_{down})\cdot P(Z_{down})}{P(Y(t) = 1)}\right),$$

$$NRI_{Y=0}(t) = \left(\frac{P(Y(t) = 0|Z_{down})\cdot P(Z_{down})}{P(Y(t) = 0)} - \frac{P(Y(t) = 0|Z_{up})\cdot P(Z_{up})}{P(Y(t) = 0)}\right).$$

Assuming $w = 0.5$ and $p = P(Y = 1)$, we obtain

$$NRI = 2\cdot NRI_{0.5}(t) = \frac{(P(Y(t) = 1|Z_{up}) - p)\cdot P(Z_{up}) - (P(Y(t) = 1|Z_{down}) - p)\cdot P(Z_{down})}{p\cdot(1-p)}.$$

Kaplan–Meier estimates are used to estimate $P(Y(t) = 1|Z_{up})$, $P(Y(t) = 1|Z_{down})$, and p = P(Y(t) = 1) to account for censoring, thus giving us our estimate for $NRI_w(t)$ [16]. This expression can be used for both NRI with categories (with upward and downward movement in categories of predicted risks) or for continuous NRI (where predicted risks between new and old models are compared directly), which corresponds nicely to the original derivation of NRI [12,15].

2.3.3. IDI and IDI(t)

Pencina et al. also introduced the integrated discrimination improvement (IDI), which does not require categories, and instead accounts for the size of movements up and down [12]. Using the differences between integrals of sensitivities (IS) and integrals of "one minus specificities" (IP) for models with and without the new variable (i.e., new model vs. standard model), the IDI quantifies jointly the overall improvement in sensitivity and specificity over all possible cutoffs on the (0,1) interval. The IDI is defined as

$$IDI = (IS_{new} - IS_{old}) - (IP_{new} - IP_{old}),$$

where $IS_{new}$ is the integrated sensitivity over all possible cutoffs for the new model (standard plus a new added variable) and $IP_{new}$ is the integrated "one minus specificity" over all possible cutoffs for the new model. $IS_{old}$ and $IP_{old}$ are the same quantities for the standard model. Thus, the IDI is the difference between improvement in average sensitivity and any potential increase in average "one minus specificity".

It has been shown that to estimate IDI using sample data we can use the following equation:

$$\widehat{IDI} = \left(\overline{\hat{p}}_{new,events} - \overline{\hat{p}}_{old,events}\right) - \left(\overline{\hat{p}}_{new,nonevents} - \overline{\hat{p}}_{old,nonevents}\right),$$

where

$$\overline{\hat{p}}_{events} = \frac{\sum_{i \text{ in events}} \hat{p}_i}{\#\, events}$$

is the mean of the model-based predicted probabilities of the event for those who develop the event and

$$\bar{\hat{p}}_{nonevents} = \frac{\sum_{j \text{ in nonevents}} \hat{p}_j}{\# \, nonevents}$$

is the mean of the model-based predicted probabilities of the event for those who do not have the event. These quantities are estimated for both the standard (old) model and the added variable (new) model.

The standard error can be estimated as

$$SE\left(\widehat{IDI}\right) = \sqrt{\left(\widehat{SE}_{events}\right)^2 + \left(\widehat{SE}_{nonevents}\right)^2}$$

where $\widehat{SE}_{events}$ is the standard error of paired differences in new and old model-based predicted probabilities among those with the event and $\widehat{SE}_{nonevents}$ is the corresponding standard error among those without the event [12].

In the extension of IDI for survival analysis, IS(t) is the average sensitivity at time t and IP(t) is the average (1-specificity) at time t. Chambless et al. show that

$$\text{IS}(t) - \text{IP}(t) = R^2(t) = \frac{\text{Var}[S(t|Z)]}{S(t)\cdot[1 - S(t)]}$$

where S(t | Z) is the survival function, S(t) = E[S(t | Z)], and S(t)[1-S(t)] is the variance of the binomial variable 'event have time t' [16]. This ratio is interpreted as the proportion of variance explained by the model and the authors also show that $R^2(t)$ is bounded on the interval [0, 1]. This quantity can be estimated from the fitted survival function, such that

$$\hat{R}^2(t) = \frac{\widehat{\text{Var}}[S(t|Z)]}{\hat{S}(t)\cdot\left[1 - \hat{S}(t)\right]}$$

where $\hat{S}(t)$ is obtained through Kaplan–Meier estimates. By rearranging the definition of IDI presented by M. Pencina et al. such that

$$\text{IDI} = (\text{IS}_{\text{new}} - \text{IP}_{\text{new}}) - (\text{IS}_{\text{old}} - \text{IP}_{\text{old}}),$$

we can see the following holds:

$$\text{IDI(t)} = \text{R}^2\text{(t)}_{\text{new}} - \text{R}^2\text{(t)}_{\text{old}},$$

or the difference in the proportion of variance explained by the new and old models [12,16]. We can estimate IDI(t) by taking the difference between the estimators for $R^2(t)_{new}$ and $R^2(t)_{old}$.

### 2.4. Confidence Interval Estimation

Various methods for confidence interval (CI) estimation exist. The most common estimation methods are intervals derived under normal theory assumptions, or asymptotic CIs [29]. We assume there is a one-sample situation with sample data obtained by random sampling from an unknown distribution $F$, where $F \rightarrow \mathbf{x} = (x_1, x_2, \ldots, x_n)$. Suppose we have a parameter of interest $\theta$ such that $\theta = t(F)$. Let $\hat{\theta} = t(\hat{F})$ be the plug-in estimate of $\theta$ and let $\hat{se}$ be a reasonable estimate of the standard error for $\hat{\theta}$. In most circumstances, as the sample size $n$ increases and grows large, the distribution of $\hat{\theta}$ converges to the normal distribution:

$$Z = \frac{\hat{\theta} - \theta}{\hat{se}} \sim N(0,1)$$

Let $z^{(\alpha)}$ indicate the 100$\alpha$ quantile and $z^{(1-\alpha)}$ indicate the 100(1 − α) quantile of a N(0,1) distribution. The asymptotic CI with coverage probability equal to $1 - 2\alpha$ (where $\alpha$ is equal to the significance level) for a parameter $\theta$ is given by:

$$\left[\hat{\theta} - z^{(1-\alpha)} \cdot \widehat{se},\ \hat{\theta} + z^{(1-\alpha)} \cdot \widehat{se}\right].$$

*SE* represents the standard error and *z* is the critical value from the standard normal distribution [29].

Alternative methods for estimating CIs that do not employ asymptotic theory are CIs estimated with bootstrap techniques. The bootstrap is a data-based simulation method used for statistical inference [29]. The bootstrap distribution of a parameter estimator can be used to calculate a variety of 100(1 − α)% CIs without having to make normal theory assumptions [29]. We explore several types of CIs based on the bootstrap distribution: bootstrap-t, percentile, and bias-corrected percentile (BC), as well as hybrid and bias-corrected and accelerated percentile (BCa) in limited scenarios [29–31].

## 3. Simulation Study Results

For simulations utilizing logistic regression, we defined a vector X of five predictor variables conditional on Y following a multivariate normal distribution such that for nonevents $X \mid Y = 0 \sim N(\mu_0, \Sigma)$ and for events $X \mid Y = 1 \sim N(\mu_1, \Sigma)$, $\mu_0$ = (0.0, 0.0, 0.0, 0.0, 0.0) and $\mu_1$ = (0.7, 0.0, 0.2, 0.5, 0.8) respectfully. Thus, both $x_1$ and $x_5$ are strong predictors of the risk of Y, $x_2$ is a null predictor, $x_3$ is a weak predictor, and $x_4$ is a moderate predictor. We assumed that $x_1$ is the standard predictor and the four other predictor variables to be new candidate markers. Without loss of generality, we assumed that $\boldsymbol{\Sigma}$ is the identity matrix with order $5 \times 5$, which ensures independence among the predictors conditional on event status. We considered event rates of 10% and 50%. We assumed no missing data among N observations and that all N observations were independent. We employed logistic regression to estimate model-based predicted probabilities of the event Y using a function of linear combinations of the predictors described above. We defined the standard model as predicting the risk of event Y from $x_1$ only, resulting in a baseline AUC close to 0.7. We further defined four updated models, each predicting the risk of event Y from $x_1$ plus an additional predictor. For each model, we estimated predicted probabilities of event Y for each observation to estimate the measures of prediction increment quantifying the improvement of the new risk prediction models: ΔAUC, NRI, NRI > 0, and IDI. We considered NRI versions with two and three categories. For 2-category NRI (2catNRI), we chose the event rate as the category cutoff. For 3-category NRI (3catNRI), we used the categories [0.00, 0.05), [0.05, 0.20), and [0.20+) for 10% event rate and [0.00, 0.40), [0.40, 0.60), and [0.60+) for 50% event rate [28].

For the survival analysis, we considered two incidence rates, 10% and 50% (with 90% and 50% expected survival, respectively), over a 10-year follow-up period. We used two different censoring distributions: (1) Type I censoring (time-terminated) and (2) Type II (random censoring; failure-terminated) [8]. We simulated random censoring with the uniform distribution. Failure time assumed a Weibull distribution with shape parameter = 2. The scale parameter varied depending on the target incidence rate and effect size for each model. We defined a vector of five continuous, uncorrelated predictor variables following a multivariate normal distribution, with effect sizes of strong to null. For predictor variables $x_1$, $x_2$, $x_3$, $x_4$, and $x_5$, hazard ratio (HR) values were 2.0, 1.0, 1.2, 1.5, and 2.0, respectively. We assumed $x_1$ to be the established standard predictor, while the four remaining predictors were the candidate variables for model inclusion consideration. We considered the following four comparisons of the standard model (HR = 2.0): (1) standard (HR = 2.0) + null

(HR = 1.0), (2) standard (HR = 2.0) + weak (HR = 1.2), (3) standard (HR = 2.0) + moderate (HR = 1.5), (4) standard (HR = 2.0) + strong (HR = 2.0). We assumed that the event status, failure time (or censoring time), and predictor variables were available for all N observations, as well as independence among observations. After assessing validity of the PH assumption, we employed Cox PH regression to estimate model-based predicted probabilities based on the models described above; for each comparison, we estimated the predicted probability according to the standard model and the predicted probability according to the added variable model. Using these pairs of predicted probabilities, we estimated five measures of prediction increment quantifying the improvement of the new risk prediction models: ΔC, 2catNRI, 3catNRI, NRI > 0, and IDI. We applied the same categories for 2catNRI and 3catNRI that were used in the logistic regression simulations [28].

For both logistic regression and survival analysis, we used n = 100,000 (with 1000 iterations) to construct empirical distributions and samples sizes of n = 2000 and n = 300 to construct bootstrapped 95% CIs with 2000 replications. We repeated the sampling 1000 times to assess coverage probabilities. Since derivations for standard error estimates were not previously provided in the survival analysis extensions, we omitted estimation of CIs assuming asymptotic theory in the survival analysis framework. Data simulation and analyses were completed using SAS software, version 9.4 (Copyright 2002–2012 SAS Institute Inc., Cary, NC, USA). We performed bootstrap analysis with the SAS macro jackboot.sas at http://support.sas.com/kb/24982.html (accessed on 15 October 2016).

Figures 1–4 illustrate the empirical distributions of ΔAUC, IDI, ΔC, and IDI(t) for three of the added-variable regression models. The empirical distributions of 3catNRI, 2catNRI, and NRI > 0 are in Supplemental Figures S1–S11. Each figure illustrates the empirical distribution as the added marker moves closer to the null. The added marker with moderate effect size is omitted, as there is very little change in the shape of distribution until the null added marker. The empirical distributions under the null hypothesis are right-skewed. The histograms for IDI under the logistic framework demonstrate that the standard error appears to be underestimated. To assess where the issues with degeneration began, we also looked at empirical distributions for added markers with effect sizes of 0.1 and 0.05. We observed no change in the shape of the empirical distributions as compared with those for the weak effect size.

Tables 1 and 2 summarize coverage probabilities for considered scenarios in logistic regression. Defining acceptable coverage as 94–96%, acceptable coverage occurs for 26% of asymptotic intervals, 36% for BC intervals, 23% for percentile intervals, and 18% for bootstrap-t intervals. Asymptotic, BC, and bootstrap-t interval methods exhibit low coverage (percentage low: 66%, 57%, and 68%, respectively) whereas the percentile method provides excess coverage (73% high). Likewise, none of the prediction increment measures had at least 50% of scenarios with acceptable coverage: ΔAUC with 47%, 3catNRI and 2catNRI each with 9%, NRI > 0 with 44%, and IDI with 34%. Considering combinations of CI type and prediction measures, the BC method has the best performance for NRI > 0 (69% with acceptable coverage), percentile-based for IDI and ΔAUC (63% and 56%, respectively), and BC for IDI and ΔAUC (56% and 50%, respectively). Coverage was generally too low when adding a null marker, except for percentile CIs, and all CI types for ΔAUC, for which it was high. When adding a moderate or strong marker, most CI methods have appropriate coverage for ΔAUC. There is consistently low coverage by the asymptotic CIs for IDI and 3catNRI, exemplifying the potential underestimation of their standard errors. We also note that the bootstrap-t intervals perform consistently poorly for all versions of NRI, except for 3catNRI with the strongest added marker in the largest sample size. Finally, while the percentile intervals appear to exhibit ≥95% coverage in nearly all scenarios, we do note that this method does not seem to perform well for IDI with a null added marker in the

50% event rate situation; the bootstrap-t interval seems to be the better choice. We also considered hybrid bootstrap intervals and BCa intervals in limited scenarios, and the results are summarized in Supplemental Table S1. We did not observe adequate improvements in coverage with either interval type.

Tables 3 and 4 summarize coverage probabilities of four bootstrapped CI types assuming Type I censoring. Acceptable coverage occurs for 31% of BC intervals, 30% of percentile intervals, 24% of bootstrap-t intervals, and 13% of hybrid intervals. BC, bootstrap-t, and hybrid intervals tend to exhibit low coverage (60%, 63%, and 78% of intervals, respectively) while 68% of percentile intervals tend to have excess coverage. ΔC and IDI have the best chance of acceptable coverage (41%) while both categorical NRIs have the lowest percentages (8% for 3catNRI and 5% for 2catNRI). The BC method has the best performance for NRI > 0 (38% with acceptable coverage) and the percentile method and BC method are best for IDI and ΔC (57% and 50%, respectively, for both measures). In general, coverage is better as the adjusted HR of the added marker increases, with instances of excess or too low of coverage in the weak and null added marker scenarios. Similar results are observed assuming random censoring (Supplemental Tables S2 and S3). The hybrid intervals exhibit some unexpected behavior. The coverage of the hybrid intervals decreases as the adjusted HR of the added marker decreases, with a large increase in coverage under the null. The hybrid interval method adjusts for both bias and skewness, and this interval type has been shown to suffer from low coverage in unexpected situations [29]. In simulation, the expected coverage probability is not achieved under the alternative, and the method appears to over-correct for bias and skewness under the null. For Type I censoring, BC intervals, percentile intervals, and bootstrap-t intervals perform well for ΔC, NRI > 0, and IDI in scenarios with a moderate or strong added marker. For the 50% incidence rate, the hybrid interval also works well for these measures, but there is decreased coverage for the smaller sample size. Overall, issues with acceptable coverage exist for both 3catNRI and 2catNRI. For the null added marker, there are instances of acceptable coverage—most notably hybrid intervals for 3catNRI (assuming large sample size), BC intervals for NRI > 0 (assuming large sample size), and bootstrap-t for IDI (assuming small sample size). For random censoring, there are more noticeable issues with coverage. The BC intervals, percentile intervals, and bootstrap-t intervals still perform well in the moderate to strong added marker scenarios, but there are gaps in good performance. The hybrid interval appears to be a good option for categorical NRI in the null added marker case. Finally, the percentile interval had ≥95% coverage in most scenarios.

Due to the results of the empirical distributions and CI coverage probability analysis, we evaluated bias. Some of the bootstrap methods correct for bias, while others may amplify bias in situations where bias exists and is not properly accounted for. For example, the percentile method performs well for unbiased statistics, but may not perform well when bias is present or for asymmetric sampling distributions. In contrast, the BC method corrects for median bias, not mean bias. Bias of a point estimator $\hat{\theta}$ for a parameter $\theta$ is the difference between the expected value of $\hat{\theta}$ and $\theta$; that is [32]:

$$Bias_{\theta}\hat{\theta} = E_{\theta}\hat{\theta} - \theta$$

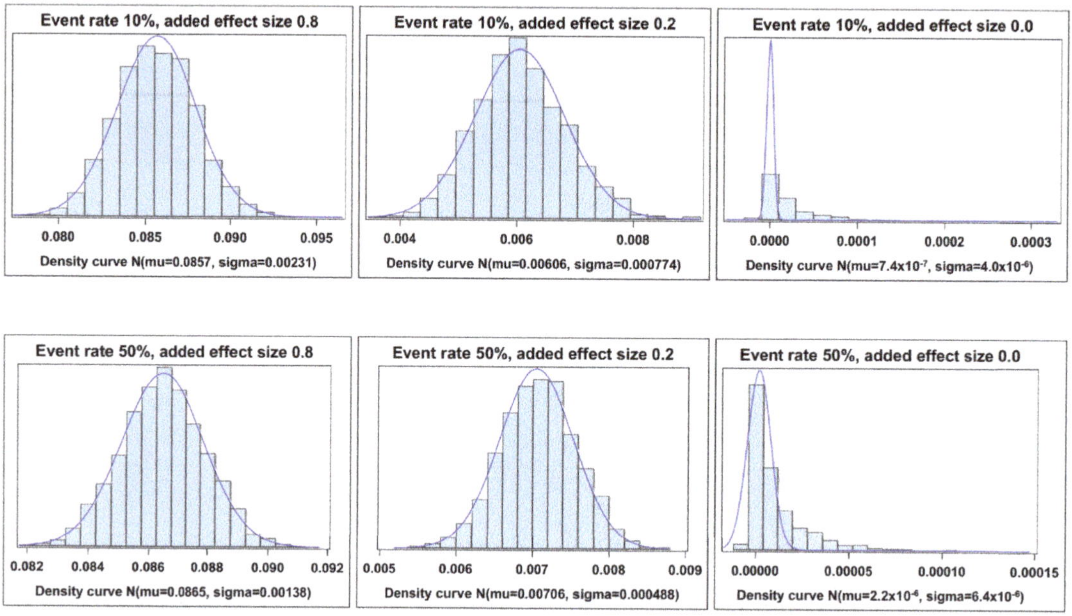


**Figure 1.** Empirical distribution of ΔAUC. Visual representation of the empirical distribution as the added marker effect moves closer to the null.

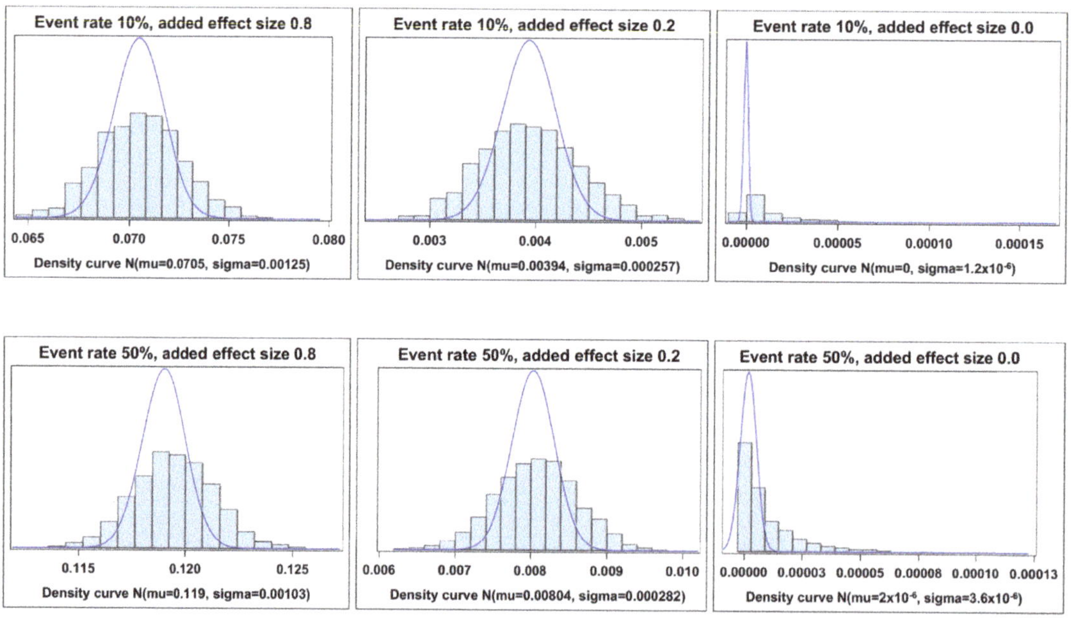


**Figure 2.** Empirical distribution of IDI. Visual representation of the empirical distribution as the added marker effect moves closer to the null.

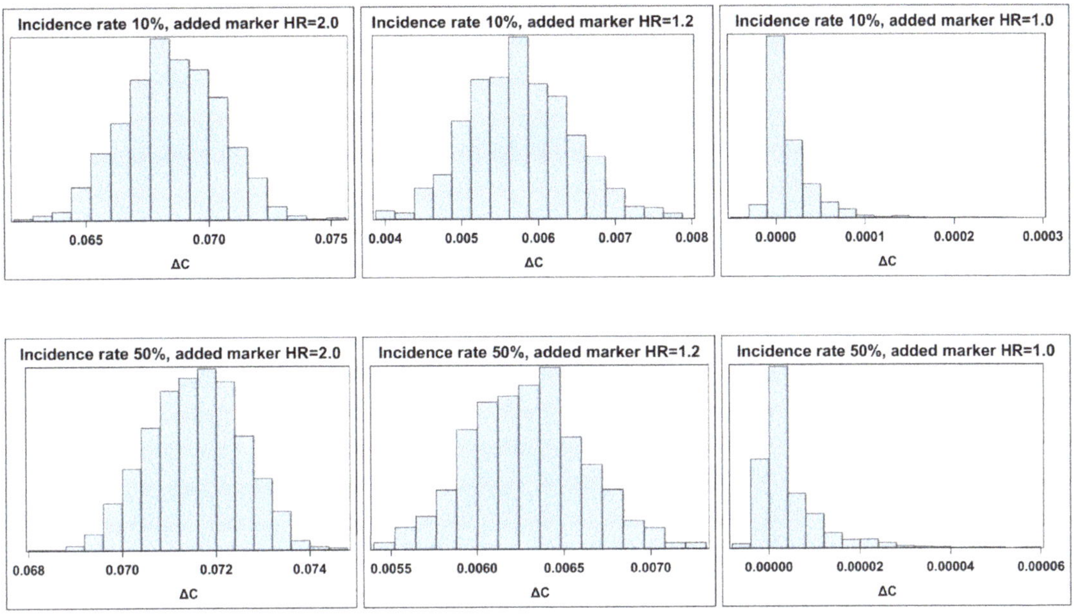


**Figure 3.** Empirical distribution of ΔC assuming Type I censoring. Visual representation of the empirical distribution as the added marker effect moves closer to the null.

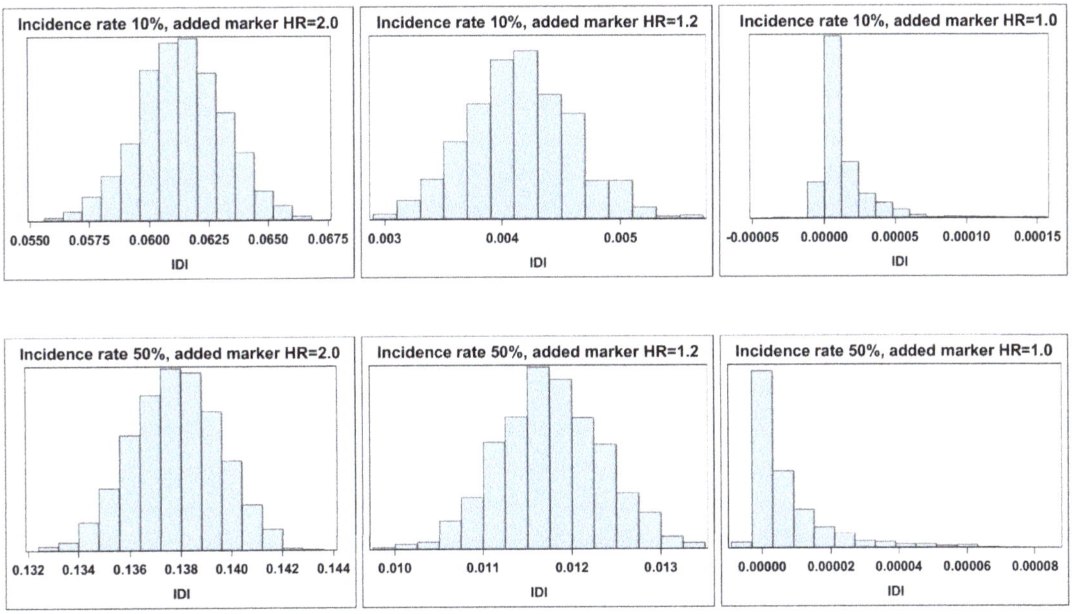


**Figure 4.** Empirical distribution of IDI assuming Type I censoring. Visual representation of the empirical distribution as the added marker effect moves closer to the null.

**Table 1.** Coverage probabilities for 95% confidence intervals with 10% event rate in logistic framework.

| | | | | | | n = 2000 | | | | |
|---|---|---|---|---|---|---|---|---|---|---|
| | | Strong New Marker ($\mu_{Y=1}$ = 0.8) | | | | | Moderate New Marker ($\mu_{Y=1}$ = 0.5) | | | |
| | **ΔAUC** | **3catNRI** | **2catNRI** | **NRI > 0** | **IDI** | **ΔAUC** | **3catNRI** | **2catNRI** | **NRI > 0** | **IDI** |
| **Asymptotic** | 93.7 | 84.4 | 93.4 | 94.4 | 76.1 | 94.3 | 81.2 | 95.1 | 94.5 | 75.2 |
| **Bias Corrected** | 94.6 | 94.5 | 91.0 | 94.6 | 95.5 | 94.8 | 92.8 | 92.4 | 94.7 | 94.2 |
| **Percentile** | 94.7 | 97.0 | 97.5 | 95.5 | 95.4 | 94.7 | 97.4 | 99.1 | 96.2 | 94.0 |
| **Bootstrap-t** | 95.1 | 94.4 | 89.3 | 93.7 | 95.5 | 95.3 | 90.7 | 89.8 | 94.1 | 96.1 |
| | | Weak New Marker ($\mu_{Y=1}$ = 0.2) | | | | | Null New Marker ($\mu_{Y=1}$ = 0.0) | | | |
| | ΔAUC | 3catNRI | 2catNRI | NRI > 0 | IDI | ΔAUC | 3catNRI | 2catNRI | NRI > 0 | IDI |
| **Asymptotic** | 90.6 | 86.4 | 93.5 | 95.4 | 71.0 | 100.0 | 94.6 | 94.1 | 95.8 | 94.0 |
| **Bias Corrected** | 93.3 | 88.0 | 87.6 | 93.8 | 92.7 | 98.4 | 90.5 | 89.7 | 96.0 | 95.5 |
| **Percentile** | 95.5 | 99.5 | 99.4 | 97.7 | 94.8 | 98.9 | 100.0 | 100.0 | 98.4 | 95.9 |
| **Bootstrap-t** | 87.4 | 84.8 | 83.6 | 88.7 | 87.9 | 98.6 | 88.1 | 86.0 | 90.0 | 98.4 |
| | | | | | | n = 300 | | | | |
| | | Strong New Marker ($\mu_{Y=1}$ = 0.8) | | | | | Moderate New Marker ($\mu_{Y=1}$ = 0.5) | | | |
| | ΔAUC | 3catNRI | 2catNRI | NRI > 0 | IDI | ΔAUC | 3catNRI | 2catNRI | NRI > 0 | IDI |
| **Asymptotic** | 92.6 | 80.9 | 93.3 | 94.2 | 76.4 | 88.7 | 78.6 | 92.2 | 93.5 | 71.8 |
| **Bias Corrected** | 94.3 | 91.2 | 91.8 | 95.3 | 95.4 | 92.3 | 87.1 | 87.0 | 92.3 | 92.9 |
| **Percentile** | 94.4 | 97.6 | 99.2 | 97.2 | 94.9 | 95.9 | 99.1 | 99.7 | 98.4 | 94.8 |
| **Bootstrap-t** | 96.0 | 88.8 | 87.5 | 93.6 | 97.3 | 86.4 | 82.8 | 83.0 | 87.3 | 90.5 |
| | | Weak New Marker ($\mu_{Y=1}$ = 0.2) | | | | | Null New Marker ($\mu_{Y=1}$ = 0.0) | | | |
| | ΔAUC | 3catNRI | 2catNRI | NRI > 0 | IDI | ΔAUC | 3catNRI | 2catNRI | NRI > 0 | IDI |
| **Asymptotic** | 88.4 | 79.1 | 91.8 | 96.4 | 75.3 | 99.5 | 89.9 | 93.2 | 93.9 | 96.8 |
| **Bias Corrected** | 91.0 | 83.1 | 85.5 | 89.7 | 85.6 | 98.4 | 88.0 | 87.4 | 94.6 | 94.5 |
| **Percentile** | 97.1 | 99.9 | 100.0 | 97.7 | 97.3 | 98.8 | 100.0 | 100.0 | 98.4 | 95.2 |
| **Bootstrap-t** | 86.1 | 85.0 | 82.8 | 82.2 | 73.3 | 96.9 | 89.7 | 86.7 | 89.0 | 97.8 |

3catNRI categories: [0.00, 0.05), [0.05, 0.20), and [0.20+).

2catNRI categories: [0.00, 0.10) and [0.10+).

**Table 2.** Coverage probabilities for 95% confidence intervals with 50% event rate in logistic framework.

| | | | | | | n = 2000 | | | | |
|---|---|---|---|---|---|---|---|---|---|---|
| | | Strong New Marker ($\mu_{Y=1}$ = 0.8) | | | | | Moderate New Marker ($\mu_{Y=1}$ = 0.5) | | | |
| | **ΔAUC** | **3catNRI** | **2catNRI** | **NRI > 0** | **IDI** | **ΔAUC** | **3catNRI** | **2catNRI** | **NRI > 0** | **IDI** |
| **Asymptotic** | 95.5 | 89.7 | 93.8 | 95.7 | 70.4 | 94.5 | 90.4 | 93.9 | 93.6 | 69.9 |
| **Bias Corrected** | 95.5 | 94.2 | 94.2 | 96.3 | 96.0 | 94.2 | 93.6 | 93.0 | 94.4 | 94.4 |
| **Percentile** | 95.5 | 96.3 | 96.9 | 96.4 | 96.1 | 93.9 | 97.1 | 96.8 | 95.7 | 94.3 |
| **Bootstrap-t** | 95.5 | 93.4 | 93.4 | 94.5 | 96.6 | 94.6 | 91.7 | 91.2 | 94.5 | 95.2 |
| | | Weak New Marker ($\mu_{Y=1}$ = 0.2) | | | | | Null New Marker ($\mu_{Y=1}$ = 0.0) | | | |
| | ΔAUC | 3catNRI | 2catNRI | NRI > 0 | IDI | ΔAUC | 3catNRI | 2catNRI | NRI > 0 | IDI |
| **Asymptotic** | 95.2 | 92.0 | 95.3 | 94.5 | 70.1 | 99.9 | 95.5 | 92.9 | 93.8 | 91.8 |
| **Bias Corrected** | 96.0 | 91.8 | 91.4 | 94.1 | 96.1 | 97.6 | 90.5 | 91.2 | 95.8 | 79.4 |
| **Percentile** | 95.4 | 99.6 | 99.3 | 96.1 | 95.8 | 97.8 | 100.0 | 100.0 | 98.0 | 78.4 |
| **Bootstrap-t** | 95.4 | 88.8 | 88.4 | 94.0 | 96.2 | 97.8 | 88.3 | 89.1 | 90.6 | 96.9 |
| | | | | | | n = 300 | | | | |
| | | Strong New Marker ($\mu_{Y=1}$ = 0.8) | | | | | Moderate New Marker ($\mu_{Y=1}$ = 0.5) | | | |
| | ΔAUC | 3catNRI | 2catNRI | NRI > 0 | IDI | ΔAUC | 3catNRI | 2catNRI | NRI > 0 | IDI |
| **Asymptotic** | 94.4 | 89.8 | 96.1 | 93.8 | 71.7 | 93.1 | 89.8 | 95.0 | 94.3 | 71.4 |
| **Bias Corrected** | 94.9 | 93.5 | 94.0 | 94.0 | 94.3 | 94.9 | 90.6 | 91.5 | 94.9 | 94.5 |
| **Percentile** | 95.0 | 98.4 | 98.7 | 95.9 | 93.8 | 95.2 | 98.2 | 99.1 | 96.5 | 94.8 |
| **Bootstrap-t** | 95.9 | 91.0 | 90.7 | 93.7 | 96.1 | 95.6 | 88.6 | 88.0 | 94.4 | 96.4 |
| | | Weak New Marker ($\mu_{Y=1}$ = 0.2) | | | | | Null New Marker ($\mu_{Y=1}$ = 0.0) | | | |
| | ΔAUC | 3catNRI | 2catNRI | NRI > 0 | IDI | ΔAUC | 3catNRI | 2catNRI | NRI > 0 | IDI |
| **Asymptotic** | 86.6 | 90.0 | 93.3 | 96.3 | 68.4 | 99.9 | 94.8 | 92.2 | 94.1 | 93.6 |
| **Bias Corrected** | 89.9 | 86.8 | 89.8 | 90.8 | 87.0 | 98.2 | 90.2 | 92.1 | 94.3 | 76.9 |
| **Percentile** | 98.8 | 100.0 | 100.0 | 99.1 | 98.1 | 98.4 | 100.0 | 100.0 | 97.3 | 72.1 |
| **Bootstrap-t** | 78.7 | 82.1 | 85.0 | 84.4 | 77.3 | 98.6 | 86.9 | 89.0 | 89.0 | 97.9 |

3catNRI categories: [0.00, 0.40), [0.40, 0.60), and [0.60+).

2catNRI categories: [0.00, 0.50) and [0.50+).

**Table 3.** Coverage probabilities for 95% confidence intervals with 10% incidence rate and type I censoring in survival framework.

| | n = 2000 | | | | | | | | | |
|---|---|---|---|---|---|---|---|---|---|---|
| | **Strong New Marker (Adjusted HR = 2.0)** | | | | | **Moderate New Marker (Adjusted HR = 1.5)** | | | | |
| | **ΔC** | **3catNRI** | **2catNRI** | **NRI > 0** | **IDI** | **ΔC** | **3catNRI** | **2catNRI** | **NRI > 0** | **IDI** |
| **Bias Corrected** | 95.1 | 94.3 | 93.1 | 93.9 | 95.7 | 95.6 | 92.1 | 90.5 | 95.1 | 94.8 |
| **Percentile** | 95.2 | 96.9 | 98.4 | 95.5 | 95.8 | 95.3 | 97.5 | 98.4 | 96.5 | 94.8 |
| **Bootstrap-t** | 95.5 | 93.2 | 92.4 | 93.5 | 96.2 | 96.2 | 90.8 | 90.2 | 94.1 | 96.2 |
| **Hybrid** | 93.6 | 91.8 | 92.5 | 93.3 | 92.8 | 89.9 | 89.6 | 90.5 | 93.7 | 89.1 |
| | **Weak New Marker (Adjusted HR = 1.2)** | | | | | **Null New Marker (Adjusted HR = 1.0)** | | | | |
| | ΔC | 3catNRI | 2catNRI | NRI > 0 | IDI | ΔC | 3catNRI | 2catNRI | NRI > 0 | IDI |
| **Bias Corrected** | 93.2 | 86.0 | 89.2 | 92.5 | 93.2 | 98.3 | 89.1 | 90.1 | 95.0 | 91.2 |
| **Percentile** | 96.9 | 99.6 | 99.9 | 97.6 | 95.2 | 98.8 | 100.0 | 100.0 | 98.2 | 92.0 |
| **Bootstrap-t** | 91.7 | 85.2 | 86.9 | 91.7 | 95.0 | 97.9 | 84.9 | 85.1 | 91.9 | 98.7 |
| **Hybrid** | 75.7 | 86.8 | 90.0 | 91.1 | 76.6 | 100.0 | 94.2 | 90.9 | 90.7 | 100.0 |
| | **n = 300** | | | | | | | | | |
| | **Strong New Marker (Adjusted HR = 2.0)** | | | | | **Moderate New Marker (Adjusted HR = 1.5)** | | | | |
| | ΔC | 3catNRI | 2catNRI | NRI > 0 | IDI | ΔC | 3catNRI | 2catNRI | NRI > 0 | IDI |
| **Bias Corrected** | 94.3 | 90.4 | 91.0 | 92.6 | 94.3 | 87.9 | 85.4 | 90.0 | 91.7 | 91.6 |
| **Percentile** | 94.2 | 97.8 | 99.2 | 97.1 | 94.5 | 95.6 | 99.7 | 99.8 | 98.9 | 96.7 |
| **Bootstrap-t** | 95.3 | 90.9 | 89.1 | 93.1 | 95.2 | 87.3 | 80.5 | 85.5 | 90.0 | 92.1 |
| **Hybrid** | 83.6 | 84.7 | 88.2 | 90.4 | 81.3 | 77.8 | 81.5 | 88.9 | 88.3 | 73.1 |
| | **Weak New Marker (Adjusted HR = 1.2)** | | | | | **Null New Marker (Adjusted HR = 1.0)** | | | | |
| | ΔC | 3catNRI | 2catNRI | NRI > 0 | IDI | ΔC | 3catNRI | 2catNRI | NRI > 0 | IDI |
| **Bias Corrected** | 92.6 | 82.5 | 89.1 | 89.2 | 84.5 | 98.5 | 85.7 | 84.3 | 93.4 | 84.8 |
| **Percentile** | 98.3 | 100.0 | 100.0 | 98.1 | 97.5 | 99.0 | 99.8 | 100.0 | 97.7 | 83.2 |
| **Bootstrap-t** | 82.1 | 73.3 | 79.0 | 87.3 | 82.2 | 96.9 | 78.1 | 77.9 | 90.8 | 95.2 |
| **Hybrid** | 92.4 | 91.0 | 87.9 | 86.5 | 66.3 | 99.7 | 93.3 | 84.1 | 89.6 | 99.7 |

3catNRI categories: [0.00, 0.05), [0.05, 0.20), and [0.20+).
2catNRI categories: [0.00, 0.10) and [0.10+).

**Table 4.** Coverage probabilities for 95% confidence intervals with 50% incidence rate and type I censoring in survival framework.

| | n = 2000 | | | | | | | | | |
|---|---|---|---|---|---|---|---|---|---|---|
| | **Strong New Marker (Adjusted HR = 2.0)** | | | | | **Moderate New Marker (Adjusted HR = 1.5)** | | | | |
| | **ΔC** | **3catNRI** | **2catNRI** | **NRI > 0** | **IDI** | **ΔC** | **3catNRI** | **2catNRI** | **NRI > 0** | **IDI** |
| **Bias Corrected** | 95.6 | 94.1 | 95.2 | 94.5 | 94.5 | 95.0 | 93.4 | 92.9 | 94.5 | 95.7 |
| **Percentile** | 95.9 | 96.0 | 97.0 | 94.9 | 94.6 | 94.6 | 96.9 | 97.3 | 96.5 | 95.3 |
| **Bootstrap-t** | 95.7 | 93.4 | 95.3 | 94.2 | 94.7 | 94.9 | 93.0 | 92.6 | 94.8 | 95.4 |
| **Hybrid** | 95.9 | 93.8 | 95.0 | 94.3 | 94.2 | 94.0 | 93.2 | 92.7 | 94.9 | 95.0 |
| | **Weak New Marker (Adjusted HR = 1.2)** | | | | | **Null New Marker (Adjusted HR = 1.0)** | | | | |
| | ΔC | 3catNRI | 2catNRI | NRI > 0 | IDI | ΔC | 3catNRI | 2catNRI | NRI > 0 | IDI |
| **Bias Corrected** | 94.8 | 91.8 | 92.7 | 93.1 | 94.3 | 99.3 | 92.8 | 86.1 | 96.2 | 97.1 |
| **Percentile** | 94.8 | 98.2 | 99.1 | 94.9 | 94.4 | 99.4 | 100.0 | 100.0 | 98.5 | 97.9 |
| **Bootstrap-t** | 95.7 | 91.7 | 90.5 | 93.4 | 95.3 | 97.9 | 85.8 | 79.4 | 91.9 | 98.6 |
| **Hybrid** | 90.9 | 90.5 | 92.1 | 93.2 | 90.1 | 100.0 | 95.4 | 87.0 | 91.9 | 100.0 |
| | **n = 300** | | | | | | | | | |
| | **Strong New Marker (Adjusted HR = 2.0)** | | | | | **Moderate New Marker (Adjusted HR = 1.5)** | | | | |
| | ΔC | 3catNRI | 2catNRI | NRI > 0 | IDI | ΔC | 3catNRI | 2catNRI | NRI > 0 | IDI |
| **Bias Corrected** | 95.2 | 92.7 | 92.8 | 94.9 | 95.0 | 95.4 | 92.5 | 93.4 | 93.9 | 94.8 |
| **Percentile** | 94.8 | 97.6 | 99.1 | 96.0 | 95.4 | 95.3 | 98.8 | 99.4 | 95.7 | 94.9 |
| **Bootstrap-t** | 95.1 | 92.9 | 91.6 | 94.5 | 95.2 | 95.8 | 92.5 | 91.9 | 93.9 | 96.3 |
| **Hybrid** | 93.3 | 92.0 | 91.8 | 94.1 | 92.6 | 88.3 | 91.3 | 92.3 | 93.6 | 88.5 |
| | **Weak New Marker (Adjusted HR = 1.2)** | | | | | **Null New Marker (Adjusted HR = 1.0)** | | | | |
| | ΔC | 3catNRI | 2catNRI | NRI > 0 | IDI | ΔC | 3catNRI | 2catNRI | NRI > 0 | IDI |
| **Bias Corrected** | 90.4 | 87.0 | 91.4 | 92.8 | 90.4 | 99.4 | 88.7 | 76.2 | 95.0 | 96.9 |
| **Percentile** | 98.0 | 99.8 | 99.9 | 98.9 | 96.8 | 99.5 | 100.0 | 100.0 | 98.6 | 97.6 |
| **Bootstrap-t** | 86.8 | 85.3 | 86.2 | 91.7 | 90.3 | 97.9 | 77.0 | 67.7 | 91.5 | 98.2 |
| **Hybrid** | 80.2 | 89.6 | 89.3 | 91.4 | 73.1 | 99.9 | 93.6 | 74.2 | 91.2 | 100.0 |

3catNRI categories: [0.00, 0.40), [0.40, 0.60), and [0.60+).
2catNRI categories: [0.00, 0.50) and [0.50+).

Thus, positive bias exists when the sample estimate is larger than the population estimate and negative bias exists when the opposite holds. Supplementary Figures S12–S23 show boxplots of bias estimates for all simulated scenarios under both the logistic and survival frameworks. The reference line represents zero bias. In general, the bias distributions are skewed to the right. In the logistic framework, variability in bias increases as the effect size increases for all five measures, with NRI > 0 having the largest variability overall. We also see positive bias with larger magnitudes for all measures in the smaller sample size scenarios. In the survival framework, we observe mean bias of zero for the strongest added markers, with positive bias as the adjusted hazard ratio of the added marker decreases towards the null.

Regarding the CI coverage probabilities, the percentile CIs exhibit coverage of more than 95%, while the other methods yield a coverage too low in more than half of scenarios. Potential issues arise for both coverage extremes. Coverage probabilities below 95% indicate that CIs are too narrow and that Type-I error may be inflated. Coverage probabilities substantially above 95% indicate conservative inference and may be wider than expected. We explored the relationship between the observed coverage probabilities and the widths of the CIs. We constructed boxplots demonstrating the distributions of CI widths. The data for the sample size of 300 are presented in Supplemental Figures S24–S38. Overall, the excess coverage of percentile CIs has not been achieved at the expense of their width. Their width is very similar to the width of the bootstrap BC intervals, yet with better coverage. The asymptotic CIs have the lowest width, but this is also reflected in their low coverage probabilities, further evidence of the potential underestimation of the standard error for some metrics. The bootstrap-t intervals not only demonstrate the most variability in interval width, but they also have consistently poor coverage except with strong added markers in large sample sizes. Additionally, we see an increasing trend in the width of the CIs as the effect size of the added marker increases, with this trend appearing to be most apparent for ΔAUC and IDI. This trend is not present for NRI > 0. It appears that, in general, while the percentile intervals frequently had more than 95% coverage, the widths were shorter when compared with the other CIs we examined. If investigators are looking for a "one size fits all" interval method, the percentile bootstrap interval may be an appropriate choice, as this interval performed the strongest in simulation without exhibiting excess width as compared with the other CI methods. This recommendation requires bootstrapping computations, which can easily be performed in SAS or R. The percentile interval method takes some of the least amount of extra time as compared with the other bootstrap methods. We also observed that the BC method works well for ΔAUC, 3catNRI, jsNRI, NRI > 0, and IDI in situations with a strong added marker and some scenarios with a moderate added marker, depending on event rate and sample size. For CI and standard error estimation from bootstrapping, we recommend that a sufficient number of bootstrap resamples is used; we used B = 2000 for 95% CIs. The number of bootstrap resamples required increases as the desired confidence level increases, which also increases computation time if an interval with more that 95% confidence is desired. However, if the investigator has limited time and wishes to use the asymptotic CI formulas, these formulas would best be used in cases with at least moderate added effect size and with using bootstrap-estimated standard errors, most importantly for IDI and NRI as the asymptotic standard error formulas for these metrics produce CIs with low coverage.

## 4. Conclusions

Discrimination improvement is an important metric to estimate when developing prediction models for assessing cancer risk and establishing new risk factors in oncology research. We summarized several measures used for estimating discrimination improvement: ΔAUC, NRI, NRI > 0, and IDI. We also discussed motivations for their development, definitions, and potential issues with their estimation and use. The motivation for this study was to improve the estimation of these measures, which was studied through simulations targeting confidence interval estimation. The simulation studies performed demonstrate that the assumed normal empirical distributions of these measures break down under the null hypothesis with varying levels of degeneration. This is problematic in estimation of confidence intervals assuming normal theory, which all of these measures assume. Additionally, the asymptotic standard errors for NRI and IDI under the logistic framework appear to be consistently underestimated, decreasing the coverage probability for the asymptotic confidence intervals in nearly all studied scenarios. The primary finding in both the logistic framework and the survival analysis framework is that the percentile CIs performed well regarding coverage, without compromise to their width; this finding was robust in most scenarios. For the simplest recommendation, we suggest the use of the percentile bootstrap interval with enough bootstrap resamples B, with increased B for larger confidence levels of $(1 - \alpha)\%$. The percentile interval method takes the least amount of extra computing time as compared with the other bootstrap methods, and it can be easily estimated with use of SAS, R, or other statistical computing software. However, if investigators wish to apply other bootstrap CI methods, there are other options depending on the desired performance metric, marker strength, incidence rate, and sample size.

There are limitations to this work that should be addressed in future research. While we currently recommend the percentile CIs as the method to use over intervals assuming normal therapy, we acknowledge that further methodological refinements should be considered to possibly enhance the performance of the bootstrapped methods, including a more comprehensive study of bias. We also plan to study the Jackknife technique, acknowledging that it may perform better for small data samples. Additionally, one strength of this work is that we assessed a wide range of possible scenarios to study CI performance in extreme cases. However, we acknowledge that additional simulations should be considered in future work. These should include additional sample size options, other incidence rates, risk models with more predictor variables included, correlated predictors, other censoring distributions, and models accounting for competing risks. We also acknowledge that these recommendations should be tested and validated in real data; at the time writing, we have applied for the use of specific clinical trial data to address this.

**Supplementary Materials:** Supporting information can be downloaded at: https://www.mdpi.com/article/10.3390/cancers17081259/s1.

**Author Contributions:** D.M.E., study design, study analysis, writing, review and editing, final approval; A.M., review and editing, final approval. All authors have read and agreed to the published version of the manuscript.

**Funding:** This research received no external funding.

**Institutional Review Board Statement:** Not applicable.

**Informed Consent Statement:** Not applicable.

**Data Availability Statement:** The original contributions presented in this study are included in the article/Supplementary Material. Further inquiries can be directed to the corresponding author.

**Conflicts of Interest:** The authors declare no conflicts of interest.

## References


1. Gail, M.H.; Brinton, L.A.; Byar, D.P.; Corle, D.K.; Green, S.B.; Schairer, C.; Mulvihill, J.J. Projecting individualized probabilities of developing breast cancer for white females who are being examined annually. *J. Natl. Cancer Inst.* **1989**, *81*, 1879–1886. [CrossRef]
2. D'Agostino, R.B.; Griffith, J.L.; Schmidt, C.H.; Terrin, N. Measures for evaluating model performance. In Proceedings of the Biometrics Section; American Statistical Association: Alexandria, VA, USA, 1997; pp. 253–258.
3. Steyerberg, E.W. *Clinical Prediction Models: A Practical Approach to Development, Validation, and Updating*; Springer Science+Business Media: New York, NY, USA, 2010.
4. Spiegelman, D.; Colditz, G.A.; Hunter, D.; Hertzmark, E. Validation of the Gail et al. model for predicting individual breast cancer risk. *J. Natl. Cancer Inst.* **1994**, *86*, 600–607. [CrossRef]
5. Rockhill, B.; Spiegelman, D.; Byrne, C.; Hunter, D.J.; Colditz, G.A. Validation of the Gail et al. model of breast cancer risk prediction and implications for chemoprevention. *J. Natl. Cancer Inst.* **2001**, *93*, 358–366. [CrossRef]
6. Nickson, C.; Procopio, P.; Velentzis, L.S.; Carr, S.; Devereux, L.; Mann, G.B.; James, P.; Lee, G.; Wellard, C.; Campbell, I. Prospective validation of the NCI Breast Cancer Risk Assessment Tool (Gail Model) on 40,000 Australian women. *Breast Cancer Res. BCR* **2018**, *20*, 155. [CrossRef] [PubMed]
7. Kumar, N.; Singh, V.; Mehta, G. Assessment of common risk factors and validation of the Gail model for breast cancer: A hospital-based study from Western India. *Tzu Chi Med. J.* **2020**, *32*, 362–366. [CrossRef] [PubMed]
8. Harrell, F.E., Jr. *Regression Modeling Strategies: With Applications to Linear Models, Logistic Regression, and Survival Analysis*; Springer: New York, NY, USA, 2001.
9. Pepe, M.S.; Kerr, K.F.; Longton, G.; Wang, Z. Testing for improvement in prediction model performance. *Stat. Med.* **2013**, *32*, 1467–1482. [CrossRef] [PubMed]
10. DeLong, E.R.; DeLong, D.M.; Clarke-Pearson, D.L. Comparing the areas under two or more correlated receiver operating characteristic curves: A nonparametric approach. *Biometrics* **1988**, *44*, 837–845. [CrossRef]
11. Pencina, M.J.; D'Agostino, R.B. Overall C as a measure of discrimination in survival analysis: Model specific population value and confidence interval estimation. *Stat. Med.* **2004**, *23*, 2109–2123. [CrossRef]
12. Pencina, M.J.; D'Agostino, R.B., Sr.; D'Agostino, R.B., Jr.; Vasan, R.S. Evaluating the added predictive ability of a new marker: From area under the ROC curve to reclassification and beyond. *Stat. Med.* **2008**, *27*, 157–212. [CrossRef]
13. Greenland, P.; O'Malley, P.G. When is a new prediction marker useful? A consideration of lipoprotein-associated phospholipase A2 and C-reactive protein for stroke risk. *Arch. Intern. Med.* **2005**, *165*, 2454–2456. [CrossRef]
14. Cook, N.R. Use and misuse of the receiver operating characteristic curve in risk prediction. *Circulation* **2007**, *115*, 928–935. [CrossRef] [PubMed]
15. Pencina, M.J.; D'Agostino, R.B., Sr.; Steyerberg, E.W. Extensions of net reclassification improvement calculations to measure usefulness of new biomarkers. *Stat. Med.* **2011**, *30*, 11–21. [CrossRef]
16. Chambless, L.E.; Cummiskey, C.P.; Cui, G. Several methods to assess improvement in risk prediction models: Extension to survival analysis. *Stat. Med.* **2011**, *30*, 22–38. [CrossRef] [PubMed]
17. Pepe, M.S. Problems with risk reclassification methods for evaluating prediction models. *Am. J. Epidemiol.* **2011**, *173*, 1327–1335. [CrossRef]
18. Kerr, K.F.; Wang, Z.; Janes, H.; McClelland, R.L.; Psaty, B.M.; Pepe, M.S. Net reclassification indices for evaluating risk prediction instruments: A critical review. *Epidemiology* **2014**, *25*, 114–121. [CrossRef]
19. Hilden, J.; Gerds, T.A. A note on the evaluation of novel biomarkers: Do not rely on integrated discrimination improvement and net reclassification index. *Stat. Med.* **2014**, *33*, 3405–3414. [CrossRef]
20. Gerds, T.A.; Hilden, J. Calibration of models is not sufficient to justify NRI. *Stat. Med.* **2014**, *33*, 3419–3420. [CrossRef] [PubMed]
21. Leening, M.J.; Steyerberg, E.W.; Van Calster, B.; D'Agostino, R.B., Sr.; Pencina, M.J. Net reclassification improvement and integrated discrimination improvement require calibrated models: Relevance from a marker and model perspective. *Stat. Med.* **2014**, *33*, 3415–3418. [CrossRef]
22. McKeague, I.W.; Qian, M. An adaptive resampling test for detecting the presence of significant predictors. *J. Am. Stat. Assoc.* **2015**, *110*, 1422–1433. [CrossRef]
23. Demler, O.V.; Pencina, M.J.; D'Agostino, R.B., Sr. Misuse of DeLong test to compare AUCs for nested models. *Stat. Med.* **2012**, *31*, 2577–2587. [CrossRef]
24. Kerr, K.F.; McClelland, R.L.; Brown, E.R.; Lumley, T. Evaluating the incremental value of new biomarkers with integrated discrimination improvement. *Am. J. Epidemiol.* **2011**, *174*, 364–374. [CrossRef] [PubMed]
25. Harrell, F.E., Jr.; Lee, K.L.; Mark, D.B. Multivariable prognostic models: Issues in developing models, evaluating assumptions and adequacy, and measuring and reducing errors. *Stat. Med.* **1996**, *15*, 361–387. [CrossRef]
26. Kalbfleisch, J.D.; Prentice, R.L. *The Statistical Analysis of Failure Time Data*; Wiley: Hoboken, NJ, USA, 1980; pp. 70–118.
27. Nam, B.H.; D'Agostino, R.B. *Goodness-of-Fit Tests and Model Validity*; Birkhauser: Boston, MA, USA, 2002; Chapter 20.

28. Pencina, M.J.; Steyerberg, E.W.; D'Agostino, R.B., Sr. Net reclassification index at event rate: Properties and relationships. *Stat. Med.* **2017**, *36*, 4455–4467. [CrossRef]
29. Efron, B.; Tibshirani, R.J. *An Introduction to the Bootstrap*; Chapman & Hall: New York, NY, USA, 1993.
30. Efron, B. Nonparametric standard errors and confidence intervals (with discussions). *Can. J. Stat.* **1981**, *9*, 139–172. [CrossRef]
31. Hall, P. Theoretical comparison of bootstrap confidence intervals. *Ann. Stat.* **1988**, *16*, 927–953. [CrossRef]
32. Casella, G.; Berger, R.L. *Statistical Inference*; Duxbury: Pacific Grove, CA, USA, 2002.

*cancers*

MDPI

*Article*

# Dynamic Prediction of Rectal Cancer Relapse and Mortality Using a Landmarking-Based Machine Learning Model: A Multicenter Retrospective Study from the Italian Society of Surgical Oncology—Colorectal Cancer Network Collaborative Group

**Rossella Reddavid [1,*], Ugo Elmore [2], Jacopo Moro [1], Paola De Nardi [2], Alberto Biondi [3], Roberto Persiani [3], Leonardo Solaini [4], Donato P. Pafundi [5], Desiree Cianflocca [6], Diego Sasia [6], Marco Milone [7], Giulia Turri [8], Michela Mineccia [9], Francesca Pecchini [10], Gaetano Gallo [11], Daniela Rega [12], Simona Gili [13], Fabio Maiello [14], Andrea Barberis [15], Federico Costanzo [15], Monica Ortenzi [16], Andrea Divizia [17], Caterina Foppa [18,19], Gabriele Anania [20], Antonino Spinelli [18,19], Giuseppe S. Sica [17], Mario Guerrieri [16], Roberto Polastri [14], Francesco Bianco [13], Paolo Delrio [12], Giuseppe Sammarco [21], Micaela Piccoli [10], Alessandro Ferrero [9], Corrado Pedrazzani [8], Michele Manigrasso [7], Felice Borghi [22], Claudio Coco [5], Davide Cavaliere [4], Domenico D'Ugo [3], Riccardo Rosati [2] and Danila Azzolina [23]**

1. Division of Surgical Oncology and Digestive Surgery, Department of Oncology, San Luigi University Hospital, University of Turin, Orbassano, 10043 Turin, Italy; jacopo.moro@unito.it
2. Department of Gastrointestinal Surgery, IRCCS San Raffaele Scientific Institute, School of Medicine, "Vita-Salute" San Raffaele University, 20132 Milan, Italy; elmore.ugo@hsr.it (U.E.); denardi.paola@hsr.it (P.D.N.); rosati.riccardo@hsr.it (R.R.)
3. Fondazione Policlinico Universitario A. Gemelli IRCCS, Università Cattolica del Sacro Cuore, 00168 Roma, Italy; biondi.alberto@gmail.com (A.B.); roberto.persiani@policlinicogemelli.it (R.P.); domenico.dugo@unicatt.it (D.D.)
4. General and Oncologic Surgery, Morgagni-Pierantoni Hospital, Ausl Romagna, 47121 Forlì, Italy; leonardosolaini@gmail.com (L.S.); cavalied@gmail.com (D.C.)
5. Fondazione Policlinico Universitario A. Gemelli IRCCS, UOC Chirurgia Generale 2, 00168 Roma, Italy; donatopaolo.pafundi@policlinicogemelli.it (D.P.P.); claudio.coco@unicatt.it (C.C.)
6. Department of Surgery, S. Croce e Carle Hospital, 12100 Cuneo, Italy; desireecianflocca@live.it (D.C.); diego.sasia@hotmail.it (D.S.)
7. Department of Clinical Medicine and Surgery, Department of Gastroenterology, Endocrinology and Endoscopic Surgery, University of Naples "Federico II", 80138 Naples, Italy; milone.marco.md@gmail.com (M.M.); michele.manigrasso89@gmail.com (M.M.)
8. Division of General and Hepatobiliary Surgery, Department of Surgical Sciences, Dentistry, Gynecology and Pediatrics, University of Verona, 37129 Verona, Italy; giulia.turri89@gmail.com (G.T.); corrado.pedrazzani@gmail.com (C.P.)
9. Department of General and Oncological Surgery, "Umberto I" Mauriziano Hospital, 10128 Turin, Italy; mmineccia@mauriziano.it (M.M.); aferrero@mauriziano.it (A.F.)
10. Unita' Operativa di Chirurgia Generale, D'Urgenza e Nuove Tecnologie, Ospedale Civile S. Agostino-Estense, Azienda Ospedaliero Universitaria di Modena, 41125 Modena, Italy; francescapecc@gmail.com (F.P.); piccoli.micaela@aou.mo.it (M.P.)
11. Department of Surgery, Sapienza University of Rome, 00185 Roma, Italy; gaetanogallo1988@gmail.com
12. Colorectal surgical Oncology, Abdominal Oncology Department, Fondazione Giovanni Pascale IRCCS, 80131 Naples, Italy; daniela.rega@gmail.com (D.R.); p.delrio@istitutotumori.na.it (P.D.)
13. General Surgery Unit, San Leonardo Hospital, ASL-NA3sud, Castellammare di Stabbia, 80053 Naples, Italy; simogili@tin.it (S.G.); bianco.bar@tin.it (F.B.)
14. General Surgery Unit, Department of Surgery, Hospital of Biella, 13875 Biella, Italy; moibaf@gmail.com (F.M.); roberto.polastri@aslbi.piemonte.it (R.P.)
15. Chirurgia Generale ed Epatobiliopancreatica, E.O. Ospedali Galliera, 16128 Genova, Italy; andrea.barberis@galliera.it (A.B.); federico.costanzo@galliera.it (F.C.)
16. Clinica Chirurgica Universita' Politecnica delle Marche, Ospedali Riuniti, 60121 Ancona, Italy; monica.ortenzi@gmail.com (M.O.); guerrieri.m@libero.it (M.G.)
17. Minimally Invasive and Gastrointestinal Surgery Unit, Università e Policlinico Tor Vergata, 00133 Roma, Italy; andreadivizia@gmail.com (A.D.); giuseppe.sica@uniroma2.it (G.S.S.)

[18] Department of Biomedical Sciences, Humanitas University, Via Rita Levi Montalcini 4, Pieve Emanuele, 20072 Milan, Italy; caterina.foppa@hunimed.eu (C.F.); antonino.spinelli@hunimed.eu (A.S.)
[19] IRCCS Humanitas Research Hospital, Via Manzoni 56, Rozzano, 20089 Milan, Italy
[20] Department of Surgical Morphology and Experimental Medicine, AOU Ferrara, 44124 Ferrara, Italy; ang@unife.it
[21] Department of Health Sciences, University of Catanzaro, 88100 Catanzaro, Italy; sammarco@unicz.it
[22] Oncologic Surgery Unit, Candiolo Cancer Institute, FPO-IRCCS, 10060 Turin, Italy; felice.borghi@ircc.it
[23] Department of Environmental and Preventive Sciences, University of Ferrara, Via Fossato di Mortara 64B, 44100 Ferrara, Italy; danila.azzolina@unife.it
* Correspondence: rossella.reddavid@unito.it; Tel.: +39-3479848651

**Simple Summary**

Rectal cancer relapse after curative surgery usually results in poorer survival and quality of life, so early identification of patients at high risk of relapse from rectal tumors is crucial. It is essential to offer risk-based recommendations that address the unique needs of survivors and caregivers while reducing the impact of provider shortages and managing costs for healthcare systems, survivors, and families. This large retrospective study aims to develop a machine learning algorithm using data from the RALAR study for profiling the risk and the onset of rectal cancer relapse after curative resection. Specifically, we proposed a machine learning algorithm that could assist clinicians in predicting patient prognosis by minimizing late relapse diagnosis, consequent delayed treatment, and the inefficient use of economic resources.

**Abstract**

**Background:** Almost 30% of patients with rectal cancer (RC) who submit to comprehensive treatment experience relapse. Surveillance plays a leading role in early detection. The landmark approach provides a more flexible and dynamic framework for survival prediction. **Objective:** This large retrospective study aims to develop a machine learning algorithm to profile the patient prognosis, especially the risk and the onset of RC relapse after curative resection. **Methods:** A cohort of 2450 RC patients were analyzed using landmark analysis. Model A applied a classical cause-specific Cox approach with a landmarking approach, while Model B implemented a landmarking-based RSF (random survival forest) competing risk algorithm. The two models were compared in terms of predictive and interpretative ability. A bootstrapped validation strategy was employed to validate the model's performance and prevent overfitting. The best-performing hyperparameters were selected systematically, ensuring the model's robustness within the landmark approach. The study assessed these factors' importance and interactions using RSF and compared the predictive accuracy to that of the classical Cox model. **Results:** Model B outperformed Model A (mean C-index 0.95 vs. 0.78), capturing complex interactions and providing dynamic, individualized relapse predictions. Clinical factors influencing survival outcomes were identified across time with the landmark approach allowing for more accurate and timely predictions. **Conclusions:** The landmark approach offers an improvement over traditional methods in survival analysis. By accommodating time-dependent variables and the evolving nature of patient data, this approach provides a precise tool for profiling RC survival, thereby supporting more informed and dynamic clinical decision-making.

**Keywords:** rectal cancer; machine learning algorithm; relapse; metastasis; recurrence; landmark analysis; competing events

## 1. Introduction

Rectal cancer (RC) ranks eighth globally, with 729,833 new cases and 343,817 deaths in 2022 [1]. In Italy, in 2024, it is estimated that about 48,706 residents will have experienced colorectal cancer (CRC), with 24,200 cancer-related deaths in 2022 [2]. One-third of new CRC cases are rectal cancer cases.

Patient survival is mainly determined by stage at diagnosis; for stage I, the 5-year survival rate is superior to 90%, decreasing to 70–85% in stage II, 25–80% in stage III, and less than 10% in stage IV [3].

However, almost 30% of patients with locally advanced RC submitted to comprehensive treatment experience relapse (local recurrence and/or distant metastasis) within the first 5 years, with most of them diagnosed before the end of the third year [4]. Due to the high risk of relapse, surveillance plays a crucial role in the early detection and prompt management of RC recurrence.

No consensus has been reached on which type of exams and timing of the testing must be used during surveillance after RC treatment [5].

Typically, postoperative follow-up involves a clinical examination, routine blood tests with tumor markers, and imaging studies. Most global guidelines recommend visiting patients every 3 months for 2 years, every 6 months for 3–5 years, and then once a year [6–8].

Many studies, both randomized controlled trials (RCTs) and observational studies, investigated different types of surveillance to identify the best schedule regarding survival, recurrence detection rate, and the percentage of curative surgery in case of relapse. Three types of surveillance have been proposed and analyzed, including intensive, less intensive, and no follow-up, but no consensus has been found [9].

Furthermore, survival rates are typically static and calculated from the surgery date, without considering the importance of the time elapsed since surgery [10,11]. In this last decade, several authors demonstrated that the risk of death or relapse is related to time after surgery [12,13]. Therefore, the mere evaluation of oncological outcomes at baseline is not enough for long survival in terms of predicting prognosis, resulting in frequent surveillance monitoring and an increased psychological burden on patients. Conditional survival (CS) was recently introduced to provide a personalized prognosis based on the probability of surviving a certain number of years after diagnosis or treatment based on the time the patient has already survived.

However, most survival models fail to account for the time-varying effects of patient disease and procedure-related factors on survival and recurrence risk during follow-up. Landmark analysis addresses this by generating multiple datasets, each capturing the patient population at a specific time. These landmark datasets are then combined into a single "super dataset," which can be analyzed using multivariable regression [14–16].

In this last decade, machine learning (ML) has gained a leading role in the medical field for profiling prognosis in cancer disease. These models can handle complex data interaction and multicollinearity issues by examining structured data derived from images and genetic and electrophysiological records [17]. Several studies reported that the ML technique was successfully employed to predict cancer relapse in different types of tumors, such as colorectal, breast, and gastric [18–20].

Landmarking provides a more realistic and clinically meaningful interpretation of survival outcomes, particularly in oncology, where the influence of prognostic factors may evolve with disease progression and treatment response. However, no efforts are reported in the literature to combine the dynamic landmarking approach with the improved profiling abilities of ML algorithms.

Moreover, the presence of competing risks, such as death from other causes, poses a significant challenge when estimating the probability of relapse and cancer-specific mortality in RC patients. Traditional survival models like Cox regression often struggle to properly account for these competing events, potentially leading to biased risk estimates [21]. In this context, random forest (RF) algorithms for survival analysis, mainly random survival forests (RSF), have emerged as a suitable analysis due to their ability to flexibly handle non-linear relationships, high-dimensional data, and time-dependent variables, all the while accurately incorporating competing risk frameworks. Estimating cumulative incidence functions (CIFs) within a competing risk setting, RF methods provide a more dynamic risk prediction approach, enforcing clinical decision-making for personalized follow-up strategies. Despite these advantages, their application with dynamic landmarking approaches remains scarce [22].

Hence, this large retrospective study aims to develop a landmarking-based RFS competing risk algorithm using data from the RALAR study [23] to profile patient survival and the risk and onset of rectal cancer relapse after curative resection.

## 2. Materials and Methods

The characteristics of this study are reported concisely, as the details have been extensively described in the previous RALAR study [23].

### 2.1. Patient Selection and Dataset

The RALAR database was adopted, and the data were retrospectively collected, including data for patients who submitted to RC resection between January 2000 and December 2016 in 19 Italian colorectal referral centers. All information has been anonymized to prevent patients from being identifiable. Central Ethics Committee approval was obtained by the AOU San Luigi Gonzaga Human Research institutional review board (approval date 23 October 2018, protocol number 15525).

Patients with hereditary malignancies, recurrent rectal cancer, malignant secondary disease dated back less than 5 years, microscopic and macroscopic residual tumors after surgery (R1 and R2), and missing data on life status were not included. After exclusion, 2450 patients were eligible for the study (Figure 1).

All patients were submitted to rectal resection and PME or TME, depending on tumor location, by open or minimally invasive (laparoscopic and robotic) approaches according to the surgeon's preference. Based on the clinical tumor stage, patients underwent neoadjuvant therapy or upfront surgery following updated guidelines.

Adjuvant chemotherapy was administered for selected patients according to pathological tumor stage and patient condition. A multidisciplinary team evaluated every decision.

### 2.2. Statistical Analysis

This study employed a landmarking approach for survival analysis alongside traditional and machine learning-based models. Two methods have been considered for comparison.

(1) Model A: the classical landmark analysis based on the cause-specific Cox model.
(2) Model B: the proposed application of landmarking-based RFS competing risk algorithm.

The primary study outcome is cancer relapse. The proposed Model B treats the relapse as the primary outcome occurring with competing cancer death and death for other causes events.

The goal was to dynamically assess cumulative incidence probabilities over time, accounting for changes in risk factors and patient conditions at predefined time points.

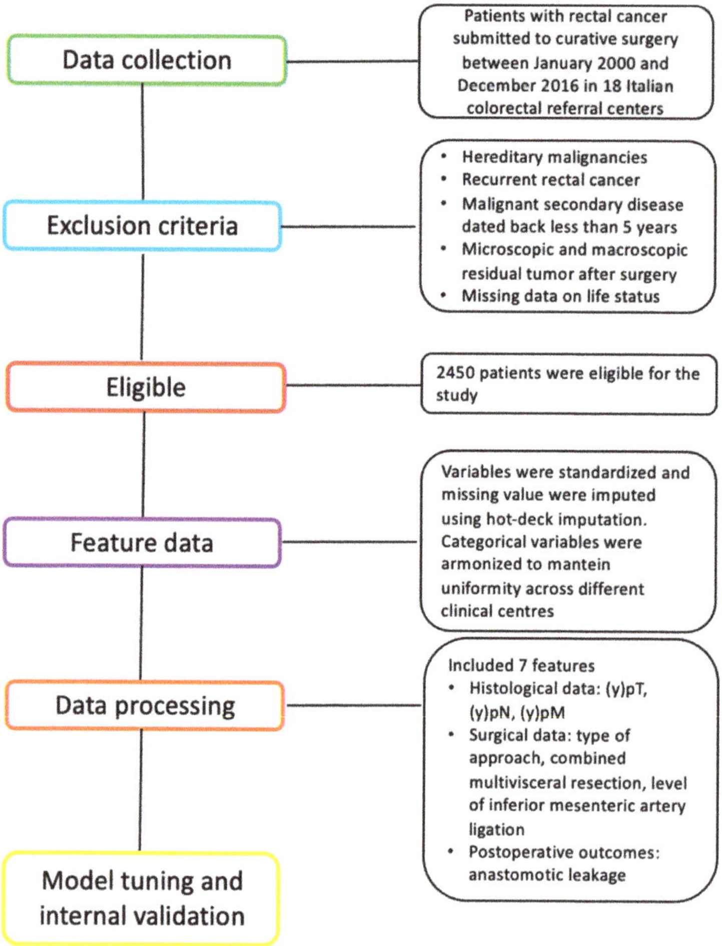


**Figure 1.** Visual diagram of the detailed process for clinical design and data collection.

#### 2.2.1. Data Preparation and Preprocessing

The dataset underwent preprocessing to ensure accuracy and consistency. Given the study's focus on long-term survival, time-to-event variables were computed from the date of surgery to either the occurrence of an event or the last available follow-up.

In landmark analyses, separate datasets are created for each specific time point, including only patients who remain at risk. These datasets are then combined into a single dataset by stacking them together. Landmark time points were selected for one year from the time of surgery up to 15 years.

#### 2.2.2. Data Description

Data have been synthesized as median and interquartile ranges for quantitative variables and absolute and relative frequencies for categorical values. The univariable cause-specific Cox hazard ratio and $p$ values have been reported to describe the effect of patients' characteristics on the hazard of cancer death, death for other causes, and relapse.

### 2.2.3. Landmarking Approach for Time-Varying Risk Estimation

The assumption that hazard ratios remain constant over time is a limitation of traditional survival models. To address this, a landmarking framework was implemented allowing survival estimates to be dynamically updated at multiple time points rather than relying on a single baseline prediction.

In this study, landmark analyses were conducted at one, three, five, and ten years after surgery. This allowed for the assessment of how risk factors influenced survival at different follow-up intervals.

Variables were selected according to clinical judgment. These included age, sex, comorbidities (Charlson score), Body mass index (BMI), American Society of Anesthesiologists (ASA) classification, perioperative treatments (neoadjuvant/adjuvant), smoking status, surgical approach (laparoscopic, open, robotic), inferior mesenteric artery (IMA) ligation level (high tie, low tie), anastomotic dehiscence, combined multivisceral resections (MVR), operative time, blood transfusion, tumor location (high, middle, low), distance from the anal verge, pathological T stage, pathological N stage, pathological TNM stage and tumor grade.

### 2.2.4. Model A: Survival Analysis Using Landmark Cause-Specific Cox Models

Multivariable Cox proportional hazards models were employed to examine the effects of the variables of interest and their interactions with landmark time on cancer mortality, other causes of mortality, and relapse.

Since patients could appear multiple times in the dataset at different landmark time points, a robust [24] sandwich variance estimator was used to account for within-patient correlation due to repeated measures.

### 2.2.5. Model B Machine Learning-Based Competing Risk Survival Analysis: Landmarking with Random Survival Forests

While Cox models assume proportional hazards and linear relationships, these assumptions do not always hold in complex clinical datasets. A landmarking approach was also applied to RSFs to capture non-linear effects and interactions. This machine learning method builds multiple decision trees to estimate survival probabilities without requiring restrictive assumptions about hazard functions.

The schematic diagram (Figure S1, Supplement) illustrates the overall workflow of the machine learning model implemented in this study, combining an RSF algorithm with a landmarking framework to perform dynamic survival prediction in the presence of competing risks.

- √ **Input Layer—Clinical Data and Landmark Time Points**: The model starts with structured clinical data, including baseline and time-varying covariates such as tumor staging, surgical approach, perioperative complications, and comorbidities. For each predefined landmark time point, a subset of patients still at risk is selected to form a "landmark dataset."
- √ **Landmark Dataset Construction**: Separate datasets are generated for each landmark time, capturing the patient profile up to that specific time. These are then stacked together into a "super dataset" while preserving the longitudinal structure of the data. Competing events—cancer-specific death, death from other causes, and relapse—are all considered.
- √ **RSF Model Training**: A random survival forest model is trained using the combined landmark datasets. The RSF, an ensemble of decision trees, learns from the data without assuming proportional hazards or linear relationships. The model captures complex, non-linear associations and interactions among predictors. Before model

fitting, hyperparameter tuning was performed to determine the optimal mtry (number of randomly drawn candidate variables) and node size tuning parameters for a random forest, using out-of-sample error as the evaluation metric. Hyperparameter tuning for RSF was conducted using a grid search strategy. The number of candidate variables considered at each split (mtry) and the minimum node size were tuned by evaluating combinations across predefined ranges: mtry (5 to 15) and node size (5 to 50). The number of trees was fixed at 100 to ensure computational consistency. Model performance for each parameter configuration was assessed using out-of-bag (OOB) error estimates, which serve as internal out-of-sample error measures in ensemble tree models. For each tree, approximately one-third of the samples not included in the bootstrap sample were used to compute the prediction error. The optimal parameter set was defined as the one that minimized the average out-of-bag (OOB) error, measured as the OOB concordance error, across all trees.
Given the longitudinal nature of the landmarking approach, where the same patient may contribute data at multiple time points, cluster-based resampling was employed during bootstrapping. This ensured that repeated measures for a single patient were sampled as a unit, preserving intra-subject correlation and avoiding data leakage between training and validation sets.

√ **Model Outputs—Cumulative Incidence Functions (CIFs)**: For each patient, the RSF produces predicted cumulative incidence functions for each competing event. These CIFs quantify the probability of experiencing relapse or death at future time points, conditional on survival until the landmark. The RSF framework handled competing risks directly by estimating CIF for each event type (cancer-specific death, other-cause death, and relapse), following the methodology proposed by Ishwaran et al. [22]. This non-parametric ensemble method does not rely on Fine–Gray regression but computes CIFs by aggregating over multiple decision trees. Right-censoring was addressed using inverse probability of censoring weighting (IPCW) during tree construction, ensuring unbiased estimation of survival probabilities. Ties in survival times were resolved using standard RSF splitting rules based on ranked survival times.

The feature importance analysis has also been calculated using the minimal depth metric. Minimal depth quantifies the average distance from the root node at which a variable first splits the data across all trees in the forest. Variables that split closer to the root (i.e., with lower minimal depth) are considered more important, as they contribute earlier and more frequently to the prediction process. This method provides a relative ranking of predictors without relying on assumptions of linearity or proportional hazards. While minimal depth captures the algorithmic influence of each variable, it does not reflect effect size or direction and is therefore best interpreted in conjunction with clinical relevance.

Given the presence of multiple competing risks, traditional Kaplan–Meier survival curves were insufficient for accurately estimating event probabilities. Instead, a competing risks framework for RSF was implemented using cumulative incidence functions (CIFs), stratified at each landmark time point. This approach accounted for the fact that a patient who dies from other causes is no longer at risk for cancer-related mortality or relapse.

#### 2.2.6. Validation and Model Performance Assessment

Models A and B were validated through fivefold cross-validation. The performance of each model was assessed using Harrell's concordance index for the Cox models and the RSF models. One hundred bootstrap-based confidence intervals were computed to quantify uncertainty and evaluate the stability of predictions.

#### 2.2.7. Patient Profiling

To visualize the dynamic behavior of cumulative risks predicted by the RSF model (as shown in Section 3.4, two illustrative patient profiles—referred to as "better" and "worse" risk groups—were constructed based on combinations of clinical variables identified as most influential in the model (i.e., those with the lowest minimal depth). These profiles were not derived through data-driven stratification but were manually defined to reflect clinically relevant contrasts in relapse risk.

The better profile represented a low-risk patient characterized by median age (65 years), male sex, medianBMI, minimal comorbidity burden (Charlson score: 0), ASA I–II status, absence of perioperative treatment, non-smoker status, elective laparoscopic approach, high tie ligation of the IMA, no anastomotic dehiscence, no transfusion, no conversion to open surgery, no combined resections, median operative time, mid-to-high tumor localization, early pathologic staging (pT0, pN0, pM0), TNM stage < II, and a median distance from the anal verge.

Conversely, the worse profile simulated a high-risk patient with the same age and sex for comparability. Still, it included high-risk features: maximum BMI, higher comorbidity burden (Charlson score: median), ASA III–IV, urgent surgical setting, open approach, low tie ligation, presence of anastomotic dehiscence, perioperative treatment, smoking, transfusion and conversion during surgery, combined resections, prolonged operative time, low tumor location, advanced pathologic staging (pT4, pN2, pM1), TNM stage > III, and minimal distance from the anal verge.

Cumulative incidence functions (CIFs) for relapse, cancer-related death, and other-cause death were estimated using the trained RSF model at each landmark time point (1, 3, and 5 years). Predictions were generated for the illustrative better and worse patient profiles by applying the model to each profile and computing event-specific CIFs, accounting for right-censoring and competing risks via ensemble averaging and inverse probability of censoring weighting (IPCW).

## 3. Results

### 3.1. Descriptive Statistics

A total of 2405 patients who underwent curative RC resection were included in the analysis. The population's median age was 66.6 years (IQR: 58.2–74.0), with 61.7% being male. The median BMI was 25.3 kg/m$^2$ (IQR: 22.7–27.6), and most patients had a Charlson comorbidity score of 2. Regarding operative risk, 74.4% of patients were classified as ASA I–II, while 25.6% were ASA III–IV. Most procedures were performed laparoscopically (56.5%), with open (35.7%) and robotic (7.8%) approaches used less frequently. Combined MVR were required in 19.7% of cases, and 11.8% experienced anastomotic dehiscence.

Tumor location was predominantly mid- (46.9%) and high-rectal (29.1%), with advanced pathological features present in a substantial proportion of the cohort, including 35.9% with TNM stage >III, 34.6% undergoing combined resections, and 7.8% with peritoneal metastases.

The median follow-up period was 6 years (IQR: 3–8 years). During this time, 187 cancer-related deaths, 474 deaths from other causes, and 202 relapses were observed (Table 1).

Cancer-related mortality was higher in older patients and those with greater comorbidity burdens, such as elevated Charlson and ASA scores. Open surgical approaches and combined MVR were also linked to an increased risk of death from cancer. As expected, advanced disease features (higher TNM stage, positive lymph nodes, and peritoneal metastases) were strongly associated with cancer-specific mortality (Table 1).

**Table 1.** Survival outcomes and clinical characteristics of patients. The table presents cause-specific survival outcomes and clinical characteristics for a cohort of patients, differentiated by outcomes such as death due to cancer, death due to other causes, and relapse. The table includes counts and percentages for each categorical variable, median, and IQR for quantitative variables with cause-specific hazard ratios and *p*-values.

| | | Death for Cancer | | | | Death for Other Causes | | | | Relapse | | | |
|---|---|---|---|---|---|---|---|---|---|---|---|---|---|
| Variables | Overall | No Events | Event | HR | P | No Events | Event | HR | P | No Events | Event | HR | P |
| | N = 2405 | N = 2218 | N = 187 | | | N = 1931 | N = 474 | | | N = 2203 | N = 202 | | |
| **Age (years)** | 66.6 [58.2;74.0] | 66.4 [58.0;73.9] | 69.3 [61.3;75.8] | 1.03 [1.01;1.04] | <0.001 | 64.4 [56.3;70.8] | 74.6 [68.5;79.6] | 1.09 [1.08;1.10] | <0.001 | 66.7 [58.2;74.1] | 66.4 [56.4;73.9] | 1.00 [0.99;1.01] | 0.737 |
| **Gender:** | | | | | 0.171 | | | | 0.001 | | | | 0.096 |
| Female | 921 (38.3%) | 856 (38.6%) | 65 (34.8%) | Ref. | | 768 (39.8%) | 153 (32.3%) | Ref. | | 852 (38.7%) | 69 (34.2%) | Ref. | |
| Male | 1484 (61.7%) | 1362 (61.4%) | 122 (65.2%) | 1.23 [0.91;1.67] | | 1163 (60.2%) | 321 (67.7%) | 1.40 [1.16;1.70] | | 1351 (61.3%) | 133 (65.8%) | 1.28 [0.96;1.71] | |
| **BMI** | 25.3 [22.7;27.6] | 25.4 [22.8;27.7] | 24.9 [22.0;27.2] | 0.96 [0.92;1.00] | 0.081 | 25.3 [22.7;27.6] | 25.4 [22.9;27.5] | 1.01 [0.97;1.04] | 0.726 | 25.2 [22.6;27.5] | 26.1 [24.0;29.0] | 1.06 [1.01;1.11] | 0.012 |
| **Charlson Comorbidity Score** | 2.00 [2.00;3.00] | 2.00 [2.00;3.00] | 2.00 [2.00;3.00] | 1.20 [1.05;1.37] | 0.008 | 2.00 [2.00;3.00] | 3.00 [2.00;3.00] | 1.42 [1.32;1.54] | <0.001 | 2.00 [2.00;3.00] | 2.00 [2.00;3.00] | 1.16 [0.99;1.35] | 0.058 |
| **ASA:** | | | | | 0.011 | | | | <0.001 | | | | 0.42 |
| I–II | 1515 (74.4%) | 1410 (75.0%) | 105 (67.3%) | Ref. | | 1283 (78.1%) | 232 (58.9%) | Ref. | | 1383 (74.5%) | 132 (73.7%) | Ref. | |
| III–IV | 521 (25.6%) | 470 (25.0%) | 51 (32.7%) | 1.54 [1.10;2.15] | | 359 (21.9%) | 162 (41.1%) | 2.19 [1.79;2.68] | | 474 (25.5%) | 47 (26.3%) | 1.15 [0.82;1.60] | |
| **Perioperative treatments:** | | | | | 0.158 | | | | 0.001 | | | | 0.01 |
| No | 287 (19.7%) | 258 (19.4%) | 29 (22.0%) | Ref. | | 227 (18.9%) | 60 (23.3%) | Ref. | | 276 (20.8%) | 11 (8.33%) | Ref. | |
| Yes | 1172 (80.3%) | 1069 (80.6%) | 103 (78.0%) | 0.74 [0.49;1.12] | | 974 (81.1%) | 198 (76.7%) | 0.61 [0.46;0.82] | | 1051 (79.2%) | 121 (91.7%) | 2.20 [1.19;4.09] | |
| **Smoke:** | | | | | 0.886 | | | | 0.425 | | | | 0.903 |
| No | 1156 (75.8%) | 1053 (75.9%) | 103 (74.6%) | Ref. | | 975 (76.1%) | 181 (74.2%) | Ref. | | 1060 (75.7%) | 96 (76.2%) | Ref. | |
| Yes | 370 (24.2%) | 335 (24.1%) | 35 (25.4%) | 1.03 [0.70;1.51] | | 307 (23.9%) | 63 (25.8%) | 1.12 [0.84;1.50] | | 340 (24.3%) | 30 (23.8%) | 0.97 [0.65;1.47] | |
| **Surgical approach:** | | | | | <0.001 | | | | 0.026 | | | | 0.682 |
| Laparoscopic | 1312 (56.5%) | 1242 (58.1%) | 70 (38.5%) | Ref. | | 1078 (57.5%) | 234 (52.6%) | Ref. | | 1208 (56.7%) | 104 (54.7%) | Ref. | |
| Open | 828 (35.7%) | 734 (34.3%) | 94 (51.6%) | 1.93 [1.41;2.63] | | 633 (33.7%) | 195 (43.8%) | 1.02 [0.84;1.24] | | 754 (35.4%) | 74 (38.9%) | 0.95 [0.70;1.29] | |
| Robotic | 181 (7.80%) | 163 (7.62%) | 18 (9.89%) | 1.65 [0.98;2.77] | | 165 (8.80%) | 16 (3.60%) | 0.51 [0.31;0.85] | | 169 (7.93%) | 12 (6.32%) | 0.77 [0.42;1.40] | |
| **Inferior mesenteric artery ligation level:** | | | | | 0.085 | | | | 0.647 | | | | 0.373 |
| High tie | 1752 (85.3%) | 1583 (84.8%) | 169 (90.4%) | Ref. | | 1450 (85.2%) | 302 (85.8%) | Ref. | | 1617 (85.1%) | 135 (88.2%) | Ref. | |
| Low tie | 301 (14.7%) | 283 (15.2%) | 18 (9.63%) | 0.65 [0.40;1.06] | | 251 (14.8%) | 50 (14.2%) | 0.93 [0.69;1.26] | | 283 (14.9%) | 18 (11.8%) | 0.80 [0.49;1.31] | |
| **Anastomotic dehiscence:** | | | | | 0.906 | | | | <0.001 | | | | 0.001 |
| No | 2121 (88.2%) | 1954 (88.1%) | 167 (89.3%) | Ref. | | 1723 (89.2%) | 398 (84.0%) | Ref. | | 1955 (88.7%) | 166 (82.2%) | Ref. | |
| Yes | 284 (11.8%) | 264 (11.9%) | 20 (10.7%) | 0.97 [0.61;1.55] | | 208 (10.8%) | 76 (16.0%) | 1.67 [1.31;2.13] | | 248 (11.3%) | 36 (17.8%) | 1.79 [1.25;2.57] | |
| **Combined multivisceral resections:** | | | | | <0.001 | | | | 0.037 | | | | 0.006 |
| No | 1676 (80.3%) | 1555 (81.7%) | 121 (65.4%) | Ref. | | 1390 (80.8%) | 286 (77.9%) | Ref. | | 1559 (80.8%) | 117 (73.6%) | Ref. | |
| Yes | 412 (19.7%) | 348 (18.3%) | 64 (34.6%) | 2.40 [1.77;3.25] | | 331 (19.2%) | 81 (22.1%) | 1.30 [1.02;1.67] | | 370 (19.2%) | 42 (26.4%) | 1.64 [1.15;2.34] | |
| **Operative time (min):** | 240 [180;300] | 240 [180;300] | 240 [195;300] | 1.00 [1.00;1.00] | 0.809 | 240 [180;300] | 240 [180;300] | 1.00 [1.00;1.00] | 0.033 | 240 [180;300] | 250 [192;312] | 1.00 [1.00;1.00] | 0.029 |
| **Trasfusion:** | | | | | 0.066 | | | | <0.001 | | | | 0.009 |
| No | 1949 (91.6%) | 1805 (91.8%) | 144 (89.4%) | Ref. | | 1575 (92.5%) | 374 (88.0%) | Ref. | | 1782 (91.9%) | 167 (88.8%) | Ref. | |
| Yes | 179 (8.41%) | 162 (8.24%) | 17 (10.6%) | 1.60 [0.97;2.64] | | 128 (7.52%) | 51 (12.0%) | 2.24 [1.67;3.01] | | 158 (8.14%) | 21 (11.2%) | 1.81 [1.15;2.86] | |
| **Conversion:** | | | | | 0.862 | | | | 0.167 | | | | 0.617 |
| No | 1835 (94.2%) | 1707 (94.3%) | 128 (93.4%) | Ref. | | 1452 (94.0%) | 383 (95.0%) | Ref. | | 1684 (94.3%) | 151 (92.6%) | Ref. | |
| Yes | 113 (5.80%) | 104 (5.74%) | 9 (6.57%) | 1.06 [0.54;2.09] | | 93 (6.02%) | 20 (4.96%) | 0.73 [0.47;1.14] | | 101 (5.66%) | 12 (7.36%) | 1.16 [0.64;2.09] | |
| **AV distance:** | 8.00 [6.00;11.0] | 8.80 [6.00;11.0] | 8.00 [6.00;11.0] | 1.00 [0.96;1.04] | 0.987 | 8.00 [6.00;11.0] | 10.0 [6.00;12.0] | 1.05 [1.03;1.08] | <0.001 | 8.00 [6.00;11.0] | 9.00 [6.00;11.0] | 1.03 [0.99;1.07] | 0.161 |
| **Localization:** | | | | | 0.558 | | | | 0.027 | | | | 0.883 |
| High | 682 (29.1%) | 632 (29.2%) | 50 (27.9%) | Ref. | | 532 (28.0%) | 150 (33.6%) | Ref. | | 627 (29.2%) | 55 (27.8%) | Ref. | |
| Middle | 1100 (46.9%) | 1011 (46.7%) | 89 (49.7%) | 1.09 [0.77;1.55] | | 903 (47.5%) | 197 (44.2%) | 0.80 [0.65;0.99] | | 1005 (46.8%) | 95 (48.0%) | 1.05 [0.76;1.47] | |
| Low | 564 (24.0%) | 524 (24.2%) | 40 (22.3%) | 0.89 [0.59;1.35] | | 465 (24.5%) | 99 (22.2%) | 0.72 [0.56;0.93] | | 516 (24.0%) | 48 (24.2%) | 0.97 [0.66;1.43] | Low |

**Table 1.** *Cont.*

| Variables | Overall | Death for Cancer | | | | Death for Other Causes | | | | Relapse | | | |
|---|---|---|---|---|---|---|---|---|---|---|---|---|---|
| | | No Events | Event | HR | P | No Events | Event | HR | P | No Events | Event | HR | P |
| **(y)pT:** | | | | | <0.001 | | | | <0.001 | | | | <0.001 |
| 0 | 223 (9.55%) | 215 (10.0%) | 8 (4.28%) | Ref. | | 187 (9.95%) | 36 (7.89%) | Ref. | | 214 (10.0%) | 9 (4.48%) | Ref. | |
| 1 | 316 (13.5%) | 307 (14.3%) | 9 (4.81%) | 0.74 [0.29;1.93] | | 263 (14.0%) | 53 (11.6%) | 0.88 [0.57;1.34] | | 304 (14.2%) | 12 (5.97%) | 0.84 [0.36;2.01] | |
| 2 | 589 (25.2%) | 565 (26.3%) | 24 (12.8%) | 1.14 [0.51;2.54] | | 481 (25.6%) | 108 (23.7%) | 1.06 [0.73;1.55] | | 553 (25.9%) | 36 (17.9%) | 1.48 [0.71;3.07] | |
| 3 | 1079 (46.2%) | 957 (44.6%) | 122 (65.2%) | 3.73 [1.82;7.63] | | 850 (45.2%) | 229 (50.2%) | 1.62 [1.14;2.31] | | 960 (45.0%) | 119 (59.2%) | 3.27 [1.66;6.44] | |
| 4 | 128 (5.48%) | 104 (4.84%) | 24 (12.8%) | 7.19 [3.23;16.0] | | 98 (5.22%) | 30 (6.58%) | 2.05 [1.26;3.33] | | 103 (4.83%) | 25 (12.4%) | 6.77 [3.16;14.5] | |
| **(y)pM:** | | | | | <0.001 | | | | 0.001 | | | | <0.001 |
| 0 | 2188 (92.2%) | 2060 (94.3%) | 128 (68.4%) | Ref. | | 1755 (92.0%) | 433 (93.3%) | Ref. | | 2030 (93.5%) | 158 (78.6%) | Ref. | |
| 1 | 184 (7.76%) | 125 (5.72%) | 59 (31.6%) | 10.6 [7.77;14.5] | | 153 (8.02%) | 31 (6.68%) | 1.86 [1.29;2.69] | | 141 (6.49%) | 43 (21.4%) | 6.86 [4.87;9.65] | |
| **(y)pN:** | | | | | <0.001 | | | | 0.001 | | | | <0.001 |
| 0 | 1551 (65.4%) | 1489 (68.1%) | 62 (33.2%) | Ref. | | 1243 (65.2%) | 308 (66.0%) | Ref. | | 1452 (66.8%) | 99 (49.5%) | Ref. | |
| 1 | 545 (23.0%) | 473 (21.6%) | 72 (38.5%) | 3.81 [2.72;5.36] | | 439 (23.0%) | 106 (22.7%) | 1.20 [0.96;1.49] | | 489 (22.5%) | 56 (28.0%) | 1.92 [1.38;2.67] | |
| 2 | 277 (11.7%) | 224 (10.2%) | 53 (28.3%) | 7.19 [4.97;10.4] | | 224 (11.8%) | 53 (11.3%) | 1.72 [1.28;2.31] | | 232 (10.7%) | 45 (22.5%) | 4.16 [2.91;5.94] | |
| **Stage (y)pTNM 8th:** | | | | | <0.001 | | | | 0.013 | | | | <0.001 |
| <II | 1541 (64.1%) | 1485 (67.0%) | 56 (29.9%) | Ref. | | 1233 (63.9%) | 308 (65.0%) | Ref. | | 1447 (65.7%) | 94 (46.5%) | Ref. | |
| >III | 864 (35.9%) | 733 (33.0%) | 131 (70.1%) | 5.16 [3.77;7.06] | | 698 (36.1%) | 166 (35.0%) | 1.27 [1.05;1.54] | | 756 (34.3%) | 108 (53.5%) | 2.64 [2.00;3.49] | |

BMI: body mass index; ASA: American Society of Anesthesiologists; min: minutes; AV: anal verge; (y)pT, pathological T stage according to the 8th edition of the TNM classification after neoadjuvant treatment (Y) when administered; (y)pN, pathological N stage according to the 8th edition of the TNM classification after neoadjuvant treatment (Y) when administered; pM, pathological M stage according to the 8th edition of the TNM classification; (y)pTNM, pathological TNM stage according to the 8th edition of the TNM classification after neoadjuvant treatment (Y) when administered; HR: hazard ratio; P: *p*-value.

Older age and a higher Charlson score were significantly associated with increased mortality from other causes. Additional risk factors included higher ASA scores, the occurrence of anastomotic dehiscence, perioperative blood transfusions, and combined MVR. Advanced pathological features, including lymph node involvement and peritoneal metastasis, also contributed to higher mortality from other causes (Table 1).

Relapse was more frequent in patients with higher BMI, those who received perioperative treatments, and those who experienced anastomotic dehiscence. Combined MVR was also associated with a higher relapse rate. As with cancer mortality, advanced pathological staging (positive peritoneal metastases, lymph node involvement, and higher TNM stage) were major predictors of recurrence (Table 1).

### 3.2. Model A

Landmarking Cox's proportional hazards model was applied to evaluate the influence of clinical variables on relapse risk at 1, 3, and 5 years post-surgery, capturing the dynamic nature of prognostic factors over time. The Harrell C index is 0.78 [95% bootstrap CI = 0.75–0.79] for the classical Model A.

The analysis identified combined MVR as consistently associated with an increased risk of relapse across all time points. Similarly, anastomotic dehiscence showed a relevant association with higher relapse risk, particularly in the early postoperative period, although its effect appeared to decrease over time (Table 2). A high tie ligation of the IMA was found to be protective against relapse, with a progressively stronger effect observed at later follow-up times. Distant metastases (pM1) were associated with a higher risk of relapse, significantly closer to the time of surgery, with attenuation of the effect over time.

Regarding pathological staging, lower pT stages (pT0–pT2) were associated with a reduced risk of relapse compared to pT3, with the protective effect being most pronounced in the years after surgery. The distance from the anal verge showed a time-dependent impact with a possible increase in relapse risk over time.

The open surgical approach was associated with a higher risk of relapse compared to laparoscopy, and this effect remained stable throughout the follow-up.

Other factors, such as age, BMI, Charlson score, gender, ASA classification, perioperative treatments, smoking status, conversion to open surgery, and localization of the tumor, did not show notable associations with relapse risk over time in this multivariable setting.

Overall, the landmarking analysis confirmed that relapse risk is dynamic and evolves with time since surgery, with certain risk factors having more pronounced effects at specific follow-up intervals.

### 3.3. Model B

Model B's Harrell C-index performance is notably higher than Model A's (C index = 0.95; 95% CI = 0.82–0.96). The variable importance of clinical predictors across the three competing events (cancer-related mortality, other-cause mortality, and relapse) was evaluated using minimal depth from the random forest models. Variables with lower minimal depth appear closer to the root of the decision trees and are considered more influential for the outcome (Figure 2).

The most important variables for cancer-specific mortality were distant metastases (pM), pathological lymph node involvement (pN), landmarking time, and age. These variables had the lowest minimal depths, highlighting their significant contribution to the model's ability to predict cancer-related death. Pathological features such as TNM stage, distance from the anal verge, and BMI also showed relevance. Conversely, variables like gender, anastomotic leakage, and the level of IMA ligation were less influential in this model (Figure 2).

**Table 2.** Landmark Cox model relapse specific hazard ratios (HRs) and 95% confidence intervals (CIs) for various clinical factors at 1, 3, and 5 years. The Harrell C index is 0.78 [95% bootstrap CI = 0.75–0.79].

| Variables | 1 Year HR (95% CI) | 3 Years HR (95% CI) | 5 Years HR (95% CI) | Global Effect | Interaction with Time |
|---|---|---|---|---|---|
| Age | 1.12 (0.89–1.41) | 0.96 (0.76–1.22) | 0.83 (0.64–1.09) | 0.08 | <0.001 |
| BMI | 1.15 (0.96–1.37) | 1.15 (0.96–1.38) | 1.15 (0.94–1.40) | 0.06 | 0.99 |
| Charlson Comorbidity Score | 1.05 (0.91–1.23) | 0.99 (0.83–1.17) | 0.92 (0.74–1.14) | 0.28 | 0.06 |
| Operative Time | 1.10 (0.88–1.37) | 1.05 (0.81–1.35) | 1.00 (0.74–1.35) | 0.74 | 0.31 |
| Transfusion | 1.60 (0.97–2.64) | 1.33 (0.73–2.41) | 1.11 (0.51–2.43) | 0.06 | 0.2 |
| Conversion | 0.78 (0.42–1.42) | 0.92 (0.50–1.71) | 1.09 (0.53–2.23) | 0.42 | 0.16 |
| AV Distance | 1.68 (0.90–3.14) | 1.33 (0.68–2.58) | 1.05 (0.49–2.26) | 0.07 | 0.04 |
| Landmarking Time | | 0.40 (0.25–0.63) | | 0.02 | |
| Gender—F:M | 0.84 (0.60–1.18) | 0.85 (0.60–1.22) | 0.86 (0.57–1.31) | 0.32 | 0.85 |
| ASA—III-IV:I-II | 0.97 (0.66–1.43) | 0.91 (0.59–1.40) | 0.85 (0.50–1.43) | 0.93 | 0.42 |
| Perioperative Treatments—No:Yes | 0.77 (0.49–1.20) | 0.78 (0.47–1.31) | 0.80 (0.42–1.53) | 0.47 | 0.84 |
| Smoking—Yes:No | 1.07 (0.74–1.55) | 0.99 (0.66–1.49) | 0.91 (0.56–1.49) | 0.81 | 0.28 |
| Surgical Approach—Open: Laparoscopic | 0.59 (0.41–0.85) | 0.58 (0.40–0.85) | 0.57 (0.37–0.89) | 0.03 | 0.48 |
| Surgical Approach—Robotic: Laparoscopic | 0.91 (0.48–1.75) | 1.07 (0.52–2.19) | 1.25 (0.52–3.00) | 0.91 | 0.4 |
| Lower Mesenteric Artery Ligation—Low:High | 0.85 (0.50–1.47) | 0.47 (0.24–0.91) | 0.26 (0.11–0.61) | <0.001 | <0.001 |
| Anastomotic Dehiscence—Yes:No | 1.53 (1.01–2.31) | 1.56 (0.99–2.48) | 1.60 (0.91–2.81) | 0.02 | 0.13 |
| Combined Multivisceral Resections—Yes:No | 1.22 (0.80–1.86) | 1.53 (1.00–2.35) | 1.93 (1.20–3.09) | 0.01 | <0.001 |
| Localization—High:Middle | 0.59 (0.33–1.04) | 0.68 (0.37–1.25) | 0.78 (0.39–1.60) | 0.07 | 0.34 |
| Localization—Low:Middle | 1.33 (0.70–2.52) | 1.15 (0.58–2.27) | 0.99 (0.44–2.20) | 0.1 | 0.26 |
| (y)pT—0:3 | 0.35 (0.16–0.77) | 0.50 (0.23–1.08) | 0.71 (0.31–1.66) | <0.001 | 0.002 |
| (y)pT—1:3 | 0.41 (0.22–0.77) | 0.54 (0.28–1.02) | 0.71 (0.35–1.41) | 0.001 | 0.02 |
| (y)pT—2:3 | 0.55 (0.35–0.86) | 0.58 (0.37–0.93) | 0.62 (0.37–1.06) | 0.01 | 0.28 |
| (y)pT—4:3 | 1.41 (0.82–2.42) | 1.24 (0.67–2.29) | 1.09 (0.51–2.36) | 0.12 | 0.37 |
| (y)pM—1:0 | 4.42 (2.60–7.53) | 3.00 (1.52–5.92) | 2.03 (0.81–5.10) | <0.001 | 0.02 |
| (y)pN—1:0 | 1.40 (0.65–3.02) | 1.46 (0.68–3.13) | 1.53 (0.68–3.47) | 0.28 | 0.99 |
| (y)pN—2:0 | 2.53 (1.13–5.68) | 2.85 (1.24–6.55) | 3.22 (1.24–8.32) | 0.03 | 0.53 |
| (y)pTNM Stage—>III:<II | 0.77 (0.35–1.68) | 0.61 (0.28–1.31) | 0.48 (0.21–1.09) | 0.54 | 0.15 |

CI: 95% confidence intervals; BMI: body mass index; ASA: American Society of Anesthesiologists; min: minutes; AV: anal verge; F: female; M: male; (y)pT, pathological T stage according to the 8th edition of the TNM classification after neoadjuvant treatment (Y) when administered; (y)pN, pathological N stage according to the 8th edition of the TNM classification after neoadjuvant treatment (Y) when administered; pM, pathological M stage according to the 8th edition of the TNM classification; (y)pTNM, pathological TNM stage according to the 8th edition of the TNM classification after neoadjuvant treatment (Y) when administered; HR: hazard ratios. Model B.

In the model for mortality from other causes, age was the dominant predictor, followed by Charlson comorbidity score and operative time, reflecting the relevance of general health status and surgical complexity for non-cancer-related death. Variables related to tumor characteristics (e.g., pT, pN, pM) and perioperative factors (e.g., anastomotic leakage, blood transfusion) contributed less, indicating that patient frailty outweighed tumor burden in predicting other-cause mortality (Figure 2).

Landmarking time, age, and distant metastases (pM) were the most influential variables for relapse prediction. Tumor burden indicators such as pathological tumor stage (pT) and pathological node stage (pN) also played important roles. Notably, combined

MVR, surgical approach, and perioperative complications such as anastomotic leakage had a more modest contribution in this setting (Figure 2).

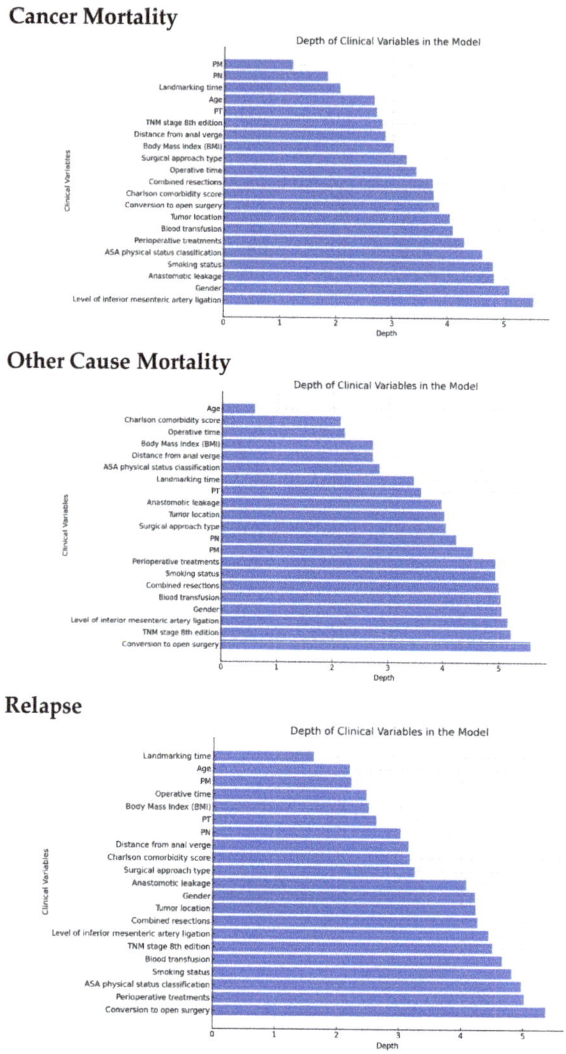


**Figure 2.** Landmark random forest. Minimal depth of clinical variables in decision tree analysis. This figure illustrates the minimal depth at which various clinical variables are used in a decision tree model, which reflects their relative importance in predicting the outcome. Each bar represents the minimal depth where a specific variable first splits the data, with a lower value indicating a higher importance in the model's initial decision-making process. Variables are ranked from top to bottom, starting with those impacting the model as soon as possible (i.e., at the shallowest depth).

### 3.4. Patient Profiling

Figure 3 shows the cumulative incidence functions (CIFs) predicted by the RSF model for cancer-specific mortality, other-cause mortality, and relapse at landmark times of 1, 3, and 5 years. At all time points, predicted cumulative incidence was higher in the worse profile compared to the better profile for each of the three outcomes.

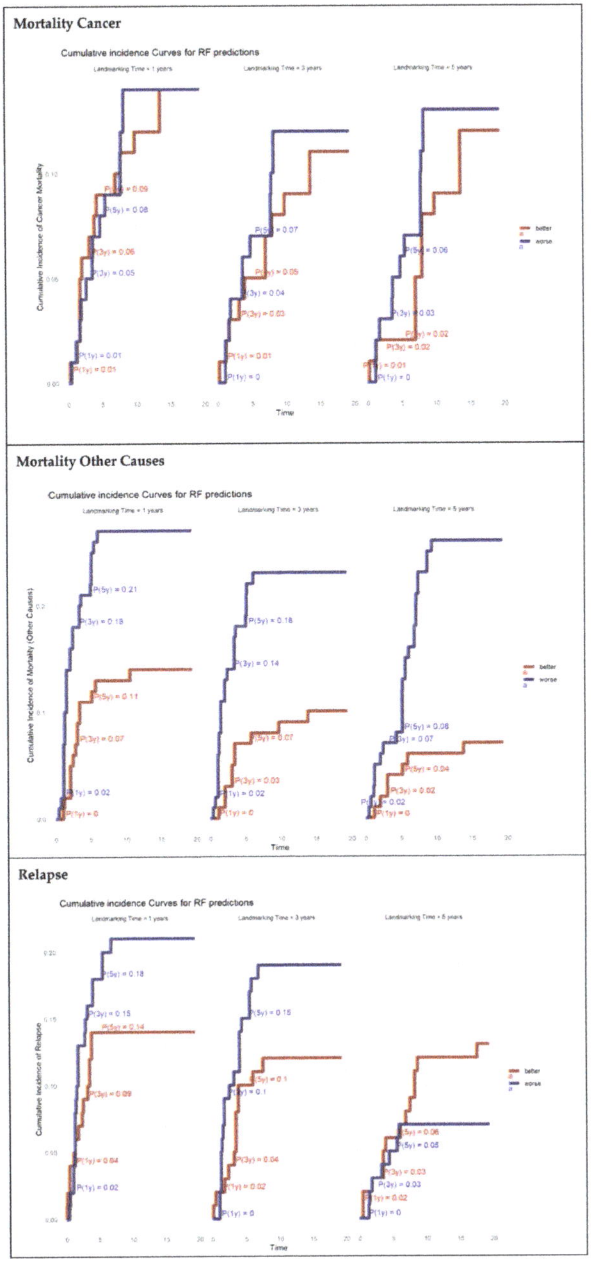


**Figure 3.** Random forest landmark cumulative incidence curves for cancer mortality predictions, mortality for other causes, and relapse. This figure presents the cumulative incidence of cancer mortality predicted by random forest models for landmarking times of 1, 3, and 5 years. Each panel displays curves for two groups classified as "better" (blue) and "worse" (red) based on their risk profiles. The curves illustrate the probability of cancer mortality over time, with annotations showing the probability at specific years, highlighting the differences in outcomes between the groups at these times. The numeric values on the curves represent the cumulative probabilities of mortality, providing insights into the effectiveness of the predictive model over extended periods.

For cancer-specific mortality, the cumulative incidence increased progressively with time and was consistently higher in the worse profile. The difference in predicted risk between the profiles was evident at each landmark and became more pronounced at later time points.

For other-cause mortality, predicted risk also increased over time in both profiles, with a greater rise observed in the worse profile. The curves showed more gradual slopes compared to cancer-specific mortality, with less pronounced differences between profiles.

For a relapse, the predicted cumulative incidence rose rapidly at earlier time points and plateaued more gradually at later landmarks. The worse profile exhibited higher predicted relapse probabilities than the better profile across all landmarks.

### 3.5. Models Comparison

The two modeling approaches demonstrated apparent differences in performance and capabilities. Model A, a traditional cause-specific Cox proportional hazards model with landmarking, achieved a Harrell C-index of 0.78 (95% CI: 0.75–0.79), reflecting moderate discriminative ability. In contrast, Model B, based on a random survival forest (RSF) algorithm within the same landmarking framework, achieved superior predictive performance, with a Harrell C-index of 0.95 (95% CI: 0.82–0.96). While Model A offers high interpretability through hazard ratios, it assumes proportional hazards and linear relationships, which may limit its flexibility in capturing complex interactions. Model B, being non-parametric, efficiently handled non-linear effects and variable interactions without restrictive assumptions. In the Cox model, no formal interaction terms were introduced, as the focus was on estimating time-dependent effects within the landmarking framework. In contrast, the RSF model implicitly captures non-linear effects and complex interactions through recursive partitioning, without requiring pre-specification of interaction terms. While no formal statistical testing of interactions was conducted.

Additionally, Model B explicitly modeled competing risks using cumulative incidence functions, enhancing its applicability in the presence of cancer-related and other-cause mortality. Model B outperformed Model A regarding discrimination, adaptability, and ability to incorporate dynamic, time-varying risk profiles (Table 3).

**Table 3.** Summary comparison of the two predictive models (Model A: Cause-Specific Cox with Landmarking; Model B: Random Survival Forest with Landmarking) used for dynamic relapse and survival prediction in rectal cancer patients. The table outlines key methodological features, assumptions, performance metrics, and interpretability considerations to highlight the strengths and limitations of each approach.

| Feature | Model A (Cause-Specific Cox + Landmarking) | Model B (Random Survival Forest + Landmarking) |
|---|---|---|
| Model Type | Traditional Cox proportional hazards model | Machine learning random survival forest |
| Time-dependency Handling | Handled via landmarking at fixed time points | Handled via landmarking at fixed time points |
| Assumptions | Proportional hazards, linearity | Non-parametric, no proportional hazards assumption |
| Outcome Type | Relapse, with cancer and other-cause death as competing risks | Relapse, with cancer and other-cause death as competing risks |
| Validation Method | fivefold cross-validation, bootstrap CI | fivefold cross-validation, bootstrap CI |
| Performance Metric | Harrell Concordance Index | Harrell Concordance Index |
| Harrell C-Index | 0.78 [95% CI: 0.75–0.79] | 0.95 [95% CI: 0.82–0.96] |
| Interpretability | High (hazard ratios) | Moderate (feature importance via minimal depth) |
| Ability to Capture Non-linear Effects | Limited | High |
| Competing Risks Framework | Handled indirectly through a cause-specific approach | Explicitly modeled with cumulative incidence functions |

A sensitivity analysis using an artificial neural network (ANN) model was performed, demonstrating lower performance compared to the RF algorithm, with a C-index of 0.7 (0.69–0.72); other details are reported in the Supplementary Materials.

## 4. Discussion

The relative survival of patients with RC has improved considerably over the years, especially in more advanced tumor stages. The 5-year survival rate increased for all RC stages combined from 51% to 65% [25]. In the present study, the 5-year overall survival (OS) is 63%, which aligns with literature data. The early detection of relapse at a treatable stage is the main objective of follow-up after curative surgery for RC. Thus, early diagnosis of recurrent RC can increase patient eligibility for many effective treatments, reduce morbidity, and improve overall survival.

Risk assessment of relapse is crucial for early decision-making; several disease-, operative-, and postoperative-related issues should be considered, including the type of approach, combined MVR, level of IMA ligation, locally advanced tumor, lymph-node metastases, distant metastases, and anastomotic leakage.

The open approach resulted in a risk factor for cancer relapse as compared with laparoscopic surgery. Although a very recent RCT from China [26], investigating the non-inferiority of laparoscopic surgery versus the open approach, reported an increased 3-year locoregional recurrence in the open arm compared with the laparoscopic arm (3.7% vs. 2.3%; $p = 0.22$), our results did not align with most of the literature evidence. Specifically, several systematic reviews and meta-analyses [27,28] have shown similar short- and long-term oncological outcomes between the laparoscopic and open approaches. We can justify our findings by suggesting that open surgery was likely administered to more challenging cases, such as those involving locally advanced cancers, tumors invading nearby organs, metastatic disease, and intraoperative adverse events, all of which are widely recognized risk factors for cancer relapse [27].

We were unable to find a study investigating the oncological outcomes of locally advanced RC underwent MVR. However, MVR is usually performed for rectal tumors invading nearby organs (T4b) that are widely recognized as an independent factor for local recurrence [28], corroborating our results.

In the present study, the low tie ligation of IMA is a risk factor for cancer relapse as compared with high ligation. The ligation of the IMA is one of the most relevant procedures during anterior resection for RC to ensure adequate lymphadenectomy and colon mobilization. Compelling evidence suggests that lymph node dissection is mandatory to reduce the risk of local recurrence [29–31]. Some authors argue that low ligation of the IMA does not yield sufficient lymph nodes for oncological safety [32]. In contrast, others contend that routine high tie dissection is unnecessary due to the relatively uncommon occurrence of lymph node metastases at the root of the IMA [33,34]. To date, no consensus has been reached regarding the optimal level of IMA ligation in terms of postoperative complications, quality of life, and oncological outcomes. Our finding adds to the ongoing debate surrounding inferior mesenteric artery ligation.

To our knowledge, a more advanced cancer stage is strictly related to a worse prognosis. Thirty percent of patients with RC stages I–III develop tumor relapse, while up to 65% of patients with stage IV RC experience recurrent disease after curative treatment [27,35].

Finally, a recent meta-analysis, which included 34,487 patients who underwent curative anterior resection for RC, concluded that anastomotic leakage is associated with increased local recurrence and reduced long-term survival [36]. In alignment with the literature data, the present study identified anastomotic leakage after surgery as a leading risk factor for cancer relapse.

To our knowledge, this is the first study to propose an ML algorithm for predicting the risk of relapse, which changes over time after surgery. This is consistent with the new concept of conditional survival. Zheng et al. [12] conducted a retrospective study on 785 patients treated for RC to create CS nomograms that predicted the conditional probability of survival after rectal resection. The author demonstrated that the likelihood of achieving 5-year recurrence-free survival increased from 75.6% immediately after surgery to 93.9% in patients who had already survived for 3 years without recurrence. CS provides a more tailored prognosis over time and helps to calibrate postoperative surveillance strategies. Besides, the CS analysis has already been adopted as a predictor for the risk of relapse in other types of cancer, such as breast [37], hemopoietic [38], liver [39], and esophageal [40].

To date, several professional societies have proposed imaging-based surveillance guidelines for RC. These guidelines are consistent in recommendations for surveillance every 3–6 months for the first 2–3 years after surgery, then every 6 months for a total of 5 years with clinical examination, imaging, and colonoscopy (after 1 year) [6–8]. Despite these differences in the frequency and type of surveillance, there is consensus that overly intensive follow-up does not necessarily yield additional benefits. Additional radiation exposure from surveillance tests could pose risks of developing other types of tumors [41]. Furthermore, it's essential to consider the phenomenon of "scanxiety," a term widely adopted to describe the psychosocial effects of routine surveillance imaging on cancer survivors, which can provoke anxiety and distress in many of them [42].

The findings of this study underscore the value of landmarking as a methodological framework for survival prediction. Landmarking enhances prognostic accuracy and facilitates personalized clinical decision-making by enabling the reassessment of risk factors at multiple time points. Patients do not have a fixed survival probability at the time of surgery; their risk changes as they progress through different stages of follow-up.

Landmarking is particularly useful in oncology, where patients in the early stages have significantly different survival trajectories from those who remain event-free for several years. By updating risk estimates dynamically, clinicians can provide more precise prognostic information and tailor follow-up strategies accordingly. This approach has broader applicability beyond colorectal cancer, extending to other chronic diseases where time-dependent risk assessment is critical.

The integration of landmarking with machine learning-based RSF models provides a flexible and robust framework for survival prediction. By dynamically updating relapses over time and incorporating complex, non-linear interactions among clinical variables, this approach supports more personalized follow-up strategies, enabling the identification of high-risk patients who may benefit from intensified monitoring, while sparing low-risk individuals from unnecessary interventions. Nonetheless, the traditional Cox model remains clinically relevant in scenarios where transparency and interpretability are paramount. For example, when informing guideline development, when communicating prognosis with patients, or in settings with limited computational resources or smaller datasets, the Cox model provides precise hazard ratio estimates that are familiar to clinicians and easier to apply in routine decision-making. In our analysis, the superior performance of the model compared to the widely used ANN model highlights RSF's effectiveness in capturing certain variable relationships within clinical data—relationships that the ANN does not handle as efficiently in this specific context. ANNs are powerful models; they often require larger datasets with complex big data [43,44].

The clinical relevance of our approach lies in its potential to tailor personalized postoperative surveillance. For instance, patients identified as high-risk at a given time point can be prioritized for more intensive imaging and monitoring. In contrast, low-risk patients may be safely followed with less frequent testing, thereby improving resource utilization and patient experience. Beyond improving prognostic accuracy, this model could support more cost-effective follow-up strategies. Current surveillance protocols often apply uniform schedules regardless of individual relapse risk, which can result in unnecessary imaging, laboratory tests, and outpatient visits for low-risk patients while potentially under-monitoring those at higher risk.

By identifying patients with persistently low relapse probabilities, such as those with favorable profiles, follow-up intensity can be safely reduced, thereby lowering healthcare costs and minimizing patient burden from frequent testing and hospital visits. Conversely, intensified surveillance might facilitate earlier detection of recurrence and more timely interventions for high-risk patients, potentially improving outcomes without proportionally increasing costs.

In the context of existing literature, follow-up schemes have been reported to vary widely in cost, ranging from $910 to $26,717 over 5 years, depending on the intensity [9]. A tailored strategy based on our model could optimize resource allocation by concentrating on healthcare efforts where they are most needed. Future prospective studies could simulate the economic impact of risk-adapted surveillance protocols by comparing the cumulative costs and outcomes of standard vs. model-driven follow-up approaches.

This study has many limitations due to its retrospective design and relatively long accrual period. Several issues had important missing data, with a consequently limited number of factors analyzed. Furthermore, many changes concerning perioperative and operative treatment characterized this long accrual interval.

While the RSF model offers the advantage of capturing complex interactions and non-linear effects, its internal measures of variable importance, such as minimal depth, should be interpreted with caution. These rankings are unitless and algorithm-driven, reflecting how early and frequently a variable is used to split nodes across decision trees. Still, they do not provide quantitative estimates of effect size or direct measures of clinical risk. Therefore, the most influential variables for predicting relapse and mortality must be understood in the context of existing clinical evidence and pathophysiology. For example, the prominence of pM and pN status in the model aligns with their well-established prognostic roles in rectal cancer. Ultimately, variable importance metrics are helpful in exploring model behavior, but clinical applicability relies on integrating these results with domain knowledge and individual patient profiles.

Moreover, internal validation through bootstrapping confirms the robustness of the model; external validation with independent datasets should also be important to evaluate its generalizability across diverse ICU settings and patient populations. The modeling framework presented in this study has the potential to support risk-adapted post-operative surveillance in rectal cancer. By integrating time-dependent clinical information and competing risks, the RSF model enables dynamic and individualized prediction of relapse and mortality. This can inform more precise follow-up strategies, such as intensifying imaging schedules for high-risk patients or safely de-escalating surveillance in low-risk cases, ultimately improving clinical decision-making and resource allocation.

To facilitate clinical integration, future work will focus on external validation of the model in independent cohorts from other institutions or population-based registries. Additionally, efforts will be made to translate the model into a user-friendly platform, allowing clinicians to input patient characteristics and receive real-time risk predictions.

## 5. Conclusions

In this era of precision medicine, more tailored surveillance for patients undergoing curative surgery for rectal cancer is needed to obtain early diagnosis of relapses, reduce the cost of ineffective tests, minimize radiation exposure risks, and alleviate negative psychosocial effects. In this study, we analyzed and compared the importance of risk factors for rectal cancer relapse using a machine-learning algorithm. The clinical relevance of our approach lies in its potential to tailor personalized postoperative surveillance.

**Supplementary Materials:** The following supporting information can be downloaded at https://www.mdpi.com/article/10.3390/cancers17081294/s1, Figure S1: Representation of the machine learning model used in this study: a Random Survival Forest (RSF) integrated with a landmarking approach.

**Author Contributions:** Conceptualization, R.R. (Rossella Reddavid) and D.A.; methodology, D.A. and R.R. (Rossella Reddavid); validation, D.A. and R.R. (Rossella Reddavid); formal analysis, D.A.; investigation, U.E., J.M., P.D.N., A.B. (Alberto Biondi), R.P. (Roberto Persiani), L.S., D.P.P., D.C. (Desiree Cianflocca), D.S., M.M. (Marco Milone), G.T., M.M. (Michela Mineccia), F.P. (Francesca Pecchini), G.G., D.R., S.G., F.M., A.B. (Andrea Barberis), F.C., M.O., A.D., C.F., G.A., A.S., M.G., R.P. (Roberto Polastri), F.B. (Francesco Bianco), P.D., G.S., M.P., A.F., C.P., M.M. (Michele Manigrasso), F.B. (Felice Borghi), C.C., D.C. (Davide Cavaliere), D.D., G.S.S., R.R. (Riccardo Rosati), and D.A.; data curation, D.A. and R.R. (Rossella Reddavid); writing—original draft preparation, D.A. and R.R. (Rossella Reddavid); writing—review and editing, R.R. (Rossella Reddavid), U.E., J.M., P.D.N., A.B. (Alberto Biondi), R.P. (Roberto Persiani), L.S., D.P.P., D.C. (Desiree Cianflocca), D.S., M.M. (Marco Milone), G.T., M.M. (Michela Mineccia), F.P. (Francesca Pecchini), G.G., D.R., S.G., F.M., A.B. (Andrea Barberis), F.C., M.O., A.D., C.F., G.A., A.S., M.G., R.P. (Roberto Polastri), F.B. (Francesco Bianco), P.D., G.S., M.P., A.F., C.P., M.M. (Michele Manigrasso), F.B. (Felice Borghi), C.C., D.C. (Davide Cavaliere), D.D., R.R. (Riccardo Rosati) and D.A.; visualization, R.R. (Rossella Reddavid), U.E., J.M., P.D.N., A.B. (Alberto Biondi), R.P. (Roberto Persiani), L.S., D.P.P., D.C. (Desiree Cianflocca), D.S., M.M. (Marco Milone), G.T., M.M. (Michela Mineccia), F.P. (Francesca Pecchini), G.G., D.R., S.G., F.M., A.B. (Andrea Barberis), F.C., M.O., A.D., C.F., G.A., A.S., M.G., R.P. (Roberto Polastri), F.B. (Francesco Bianco), P.D., G.S., M.P., A.F., C.P., M.M. (Michele Manigrasso), F.B. (Felice Borghi), C.C., D.C. (Davide Cavaliere), D.D., R.R. (Riccardo Rosati), D.A.; supervision, R.R. (Rossella Reddavid), U.E., J.M., P.D.N., A.B. (Alberto Biondi), R.P. (Roberto Persiani), L.S., D.P.P., D.C. (Desiree Cianflocca), D.S., M.M. (Marco Milone), G.T., M.M. (Michela Mineccia), F.P. (Francesca Pecchini), G.G., D.R., S.G., F.M., A.B. (Andrea Barberis), F.C., M.O., A.D., C.F., G.A., A.S., M.G., R.P. (Roberto Polastri), F.B. (Francesco Bianco), P.D., G.S., M.P., A.F., C.P., M.M. (Michele Manigrasso), F.B. (Felice Borghi), C.C., D.C. (Davide Cavaliere), D.D., G.S.S., R.R. (Riccardo Rosati) and D.A. All authors have read and agreed to the published version of the manuscript.

**Funding:** This research received no external funding.

**Institutional Review Board Statement:** The study was conducted in accordance with the Declaration of Helsinki and approved by the Central Ethics Committee by the AOU San Luigi Gonzaga human research institutional review board (approval date 23 October 2018, protocol number 15525).

**Informed Consent Statement:** Informed consent was obtained from all subjects involved in the study.

**Data Availability Statement:** The data can be shared up on request.

**Conflicts of Interest:** The authors declare no conflicts of interest.

## Abbreviations

The following abbreviations are used in this manuscript:

| | |
|---|---|
| RC | rectal cancer |
| PME | partial mesorectal excision |
| TME | total mesorectal excision |
| CRT | chemoradio therapy |
| CT | chemotherapy |
| RCT | randomized controlled trial |
| CS | conditional survival |
| AI | artificial intelligence |
| ML | machine learning |
| BMI | body mass index |
| MVR | multivisceral resection |
| CRC | colorectal cancer |
| HR | hazard ratio |
| RF | random forest |

## References


1. Bray, F.; Laversanne, M.; Sung, H.; Ferlay, J.; Siegel, R.L.; Soerjomataram, I.; Jemal, A. Global cancer statistics 2022: GLOBOCAN estimates of incidence and mortality worldwide for 36 cancers in 185 countries. *CA Cancer J. Clin.* **2024**, *74*, 229–263. [CrossRef] [PubMed]
2. I Numeri del Cancro in Italia 2024 P As S I Progressi nelle Aziende Sanitarie per la Salute in Italia. Available online: https://www.cro.sanita.fvg.it/it/news/2024/numeri-cancro-2024.html (accessed on 25 March 2025).
3. Cervantes, A.; Adam, R.; Roselló, S.; Arnold, D.; Normanno, N.; Taïeb, J.; Seligmann, J.; De Baere, T.; Osterlund, P.; Yoshino, T.; et al. Metastatic colorectal cancer: ESMO Clinical Practice Guideline for diagnosis, treatment and follow-up ☆. *Ann. Oncol.* **2023**, *34*, 10–32. [CrossRef] [PubMed]
4. Qiu, J.; Yu, Y.; Wang, Z.; Hong, L.; Shao, L.; Wu, J. Developing Individualized Follow-Up Strategies Based on High-Risk Recurrence Factors and Dynamic Risk Assessment for Locally Advanced Rectal Cancer. *Cancer Med.* **2024**, *13*, e70323. [CrossRef] [PubMed]
5. Kennedy, E.; Zwaal, C.; Asmis, T.; Cho, C.; Galica, J.; Ginty, A.; Govindarajan, A. An Evidence-Based Guideline for Surveillance of Patients after Curative Treatment for Colon and Rectal Cancer. *Curr. Oncol.* **2022**, *29*, 724–740. [CrossRef]
6. Adam, M.; Chang, G.J.; Chen, Y.-J.; Ciombor, K.K.; Cohen, S.A.; Deming, D.; Garrido-Laguna, I.; Grem, J.L.; Buffett Cancer Center Carla Harmath, P.; Randolph Hecht, J.; et al. NCCN Guidelines Version 1.2025 Rectal Cancer Continue NCCN Guidelines Panel Disclosures. 2025. Available online: https://www.nccn.org/professionals/physician_gls/pdf/rectal.pdf (accessed on 25 March 2025).
7. Glynne-Jones, R.; Wyrwicz, L.; Tiret, E.; Brown, G.; Rödel, C.; Cervantes, A.; Arnold, D. Rectal cancer: ESMO Clinical Practice Guidelines for diagnosis, treatment and follow-up. *Ann. Oncol.* **2017**, *28*, iv22–iv40. [CrossRef]
8. Hashiguchi, Y.; Muro, K.; Saito, Y.; Ito, Y.; Ajioka, Y.; Hamaguchi, T.; Hasegawa, K.; Hotta, K.; Ishida, H.; Ishiguro, M.; et al. Japanese Society for Cancer of the Colon and Rectum (JSCCR) guidelines 2019 for the treatment of colorectal cancer. *Int. J. Clin. Oncol.* **2020**, *25*, 1–42. [CrossRef]
9. Lauretta, A.; Montori, G.; Guerrini, G.P. Surveillance strategies following curative resection and non-operative approach of rectal cancer: How and how long? Review of current recommendations. *World J. Gastrointest. Surg.* **2023**, *15*, 177–192. [CrossRef]
10. Silberfein, E.J.; Kattepogu, K.M.; Hu, C.Y.; Skibber, J.M.; Rodriguez-Bigas, M.A.; Feig, B.; Das, P.; Krishnan, S.; Crane, C.; Kopetz, S.; et al. Long-term survival and recurrence outcomes following surgery for distal rectal cancer. *Ann. Surg. Oncol.* **2010**, *17*, 2863–2869. [CrossRef]
11. Fokas, E.; Fietkau, R.; Hartmann, A.; Hohenberger, W.; Grützmann, R.; Ghadimi, M.; Liersch, T.; Ströbel, P.; Grabenbauer, G.G.; Graeven, U.; et al. Neoadjuvant rectal score as individual-level surrogate for disease-free survival in rectal cancer in the CAO/ARO/AIO-04 randomized phase III trial. *Ann. Oncol.* **2018**, *29*, 1521–1527. [CrossRef]
12. Zheng, Z.; Wang, X.; Liu, Z.; Lu, X.; Huang, Y.; Chi, P. Individualized conditional survival nomograms for patients with locally advanced rectal cancer treated with neoadjuvant chemoradiotherapy and radical surgery. *Eur. J. Surg. Oncol.* **2021**, *47*, 3175–3181. [CrossRef]
13. Karagkounis, G.; Liska, D.; Kalady, M.F. Conditional Probability of Survival after Neoadjuvant Chemoradiation and Proctectomy for Rectal Cancer: What Matters and When. In *Diseases of the Colon and Rectum*; Lippincott Williams and Wilkins: Philadelphia, PA, USA, 2019; Volume 62, pp. 33–39.
14. Van Houwelingen, H.C. Dynamic prediction by landmarking in event history analysis. *Scand. J. Stat.* **2007**, *34*, 70–85. [CrossRef]
15. Fontein, D.B.Y.; Klinten Grand, M.; Nortier, J.W.R.; Seynaeve, C.; Meershoek-Klein Kranenbarg, E.; Dirix, L.Y.; van de Velde, C.J.H.; Putter, H. Dynamic prediction in breast cancer: Proving feasibility in clinical practice using the TEAM trial. *Ann. Oncol.* **2015**, *26*, 1254–1262. [CrossRef]
16. Spolverato, G.; Azzolina, D.; Paro, A.; Lorenzoni, G.; Gregori, D.; Poultsides, G.; Fields, R.C.; Weber, S.M.; Votanopoulos, K.; Maithel, S.K.; et al. Dynamic Prediction of Survival after Curative Resection of Gastric Adenocarcinoma: A landmarking-based analysis. *Eur. J. Surg. Oncol.* **2022**, *48*, 1025–1032. [CrossRef] [PubMed]
17. Jiang, F.; Jiang, Y.; Zhi, H.; Dong, Y.; Li, H.; Ma, S.; Wang, Y.; Dong, Q.; Shen, H.; Wang, Y. Artificial intelligence in healthcare: Past, present and future. *Stroke Vasc. Neurol.* **2017**, *2*, 230–243. [CrossRef]
18. Jeon, Y.; Kim, Y.J.; Jeon, J.; Nam, K.H.; Hwang, T.S.; Kim, K.G.; Baek, J.H. Machine learning based prediction of recurrence after curative resection for rectal cancer. *PLoS ONE* **2023**, *18*, e0290141. [CrossRef]
19. Lou, S.J.; Hou, M.F.; Chang, H.T.; Chiu, C.C.; Lee, H.H.; Yeh, S.C.J.; Shi, H.Y. Machine learning algorithms to predict recurrence within 10 years after breast cancer surgery: A prospective cohort study. *Cancers* **2020**, *12*, 3817. [CrossRef]
20. Zhou, C.; Hu, J.; Wang, Y.; Ji, M.H.; Tong, J.; Yang, J.J.; Xia, H. A machine learning-based predictor for the identification of the recurrence of patients with gastric cancer after operation. *Sci. Rep.* **2021**, *11*, 1571. [CrossRef] [PubMed]
21. Berry, S.D.; Ngo, L.; Samelson, E.J.; Kiel, D.P. Competing Risk of Death: An Important Consideration in Studies of Older Adults. *J. Am. Geriatr. Soc.* **2010**, *58*, 783–787. [CrossRef]
22. Ishwaran, H.; Gerds, T.A.; Kogalur, U.B.; Moore, R.D.; Gange, S.J.; Lau, B.M. Random survival forests for competing risks. *Biostatistics* **2014**, *15*, 757–773. [CrossRef]
23. Degiuli, M.; Elmore, U.; De Luca, R.; De Nardi, P.; Tomatis, M.; Biondi, A.; Persiani, R.; Solaini, L.; Rizzo, G.; Soriero, D.; et al. Risk factors for anastomotic leakage after anterior resection for rectal cancer (RALAR study): A nationwide retrospective study of the Italian Society of Surgical Oncology Colorectal Cancer Network Collaborative Group. *Color. Dis.* **2022**, *24*, 264–276. [CrossRef]

24. White, H. A Heteroskedasticity-Consistent Covariance Matrix Estimator and a Direct Test for Heteroskedasticity. *Econom. J. Econom. Soc.* **1980**, *48*, 817. [CrossRef]
25. Brouwer, N.P.M.; Bos, A.C.R.K.; Lemmens, V.E.P.P.; Tanis, P.J.; Hugen, N.; Nagtegaal, I.D.; de Wilt, J.H.W.; Verhoeven, R.H.A. An overview of 25 years of incidence, treatment and outcome of colorectal cancer patients. *Int. J. Cancer* **2018**, *143*, 2758–2766. [CrossRef]
26. Jiang, W.; Xu, J.; Cui, M.; Qiu, H.; Wang, Z.; Kang, L.; Deng, H.; Chen, W.; Zhang, Q.; Du, X.; et al. Laparoscopy-assisted versus open surgery for low rectal cancer (LASRE): 3-year survival outcomes of a multicentre, randomised, controlled, non-inferiority trial. *Lancet Gastroenterol. Hepatol.* **2024**, *10*, 34–43. [CrossRef]
27. Waldenstedt, S.; Bock, D.; Haglind, E.; Sjöberg, B.; Angenete, E. Intraoperative adverse events as a risk factor for local recurrence of rectal cancer after resection surgery. *Color. Dis.* **2022**, *24*, 449–460. [CrossRef]
28. Ozaki, K.; Kawai, K.; Nozawa, H.; Sasaki, K.; Murono, K.; Emoto, S.; Iida, Y.; Ishii, H.; Yokoyama, Y.; Anzai, H.; et al. Therapeutic effects and limitations of chemoradiotherapy in advanced lower rectal cancer focusing on T4b. *Int. J. Color. Dis.* **2021**, *36*, 1525–1534. [CrossRef] [PubMed]
29. Fretwell, V.L.; Ang, C.W.; Tweedle, E.M.; Rooney, P.S. The impact of lymph node yield on Duke's B and C colorectal cancer survival. *Color. Dis.* **2010**, *12*, 995–1000. [CrossRef] [PubMed]
30. Sofia, S.; Degiuli, M.; Anania, G.; Baiocchi, G.L.; Baldari, L.; Baldazzi, G.; Bianco, F.; Borghi, F.; Cavaliere, D.; Coco, C.; et al. Textbook Outcome in Colorectal Surgery for Cancer: An Italian Version. *J. Clin. Med.* **2024**, *13*, 4687. [CrossRef]
31. Degiuli, M.; Arolfo, S.; Evangelista, A.; Lorenzon, L.; Reddavid, R.; Staudacher, C.; De Nardi, P.; Rosati, R.; Elmore, U.; Coco, C.; et al. Number of lymph nodes assessed has no prognostic impact in node-negative rectal cancers after neoadjuvant therapy. Results of the "Italian Society of Surgical Oncology (S.I.C.O.) Colorectal Cancer Network" (SICO-CCN) multicentre collaborative study. *Eur. J. Surg. Oncol.* **2018**, *44*, 1233–1240. [CrossRef]
32. Nakamura, Y.; Yamaura, T.; Kinjo, Y.; Harada, K.; Kawase, M.; Kawabata, Y.; Kanto, S.; Ogo, Y.; Kuroda, N. Level of Inferior Mesenteric Artery Ligation in Sigmoid Colon and Rectal Cancer Surgery: Analysis of Apical Lymph Node Metastasis and Recurrence. *Dig. Surg.* **2023**, *40*, 167–177. [CrossRef]
33. Yoshida, D.; Sugiyama, M.; Nakazono, K.; Oyama, T.; Hasegawa, T.; Kai, S.; Yamamoto, M.; Matsumoto, T.; Kawanaka, H.; Morita, M.; et al. Oncological Impact of the Level of Inferior Mesenteric Artery Ligation in Low Rectal Cancer Surgery. *Anticancer Res.* **2023**, *47*, 3225–3233. [CrossRef]
34. Baik, H.J. To go high, or to go low: The never-ending debate of inferior mesenteric artery ligation. *Ann. Coloproctol.* **2024**, *40*, 1–2. [CrossRef] [PubMed]
35. Van Der Stok, E.P.; Spaander, M.C.W.; Grünhagen, D.J.; Verhoef, C.; Kuipers, E.J. Surveillance after curative treatment for colorectal cancer. *Nat. Rev. Clin. Oncol.* **2017**, *14*, 297–315. [CrossRef] [PubMed]
36. Ma, L.; Pang, X.; Ji, G.; Sun, H.; Fan, Q.; Ma, C.; Koniaris, L.G. The impact of anastomotic leakage on oncology after curative anterior resection for rectal cancer: A systematic review and meta-analysis. *Medicine* **2020**, *99*, E22139. [CrossRef]
37. Zhu, S.; Zheng, Z.; Hu, W.; Lei, C. Conditional Cancer-Specific Survival for Inflammatory Breast Cancer: Analysis of SEER, 2010 to 2016. *Clin. Breast Cancer* **2023**, *23*, 628–639.e2. [CrossRef] [PubMed]
38. Abdallah, N.H.; Smith, A.N.; Geyer, S.; Binder, M.; Greipp, P.T.; Kapoor, P.; Dispenzieri, A.; Gertz, M.A.; Baughn, L.B.; Lacy, M.Q.; et al. Conditional survival in multiple myeloma and impact of prognostic factors over time. *Blood Cancer J.* **2023**, *13*, 78. [CrossRef]
39. Yang, Y.P.; Guo, C.J.; Gu, Z.X.; Hua, J.J.; Zhang, J.X.; Shi, J. Conditional survival probability of distant-metastatic hepatocellular carcinoma: A population-based study. *World J. Gastrointest. Oncol.* **2023**, *15*, 1874–1890. [CrossRef]
40. Xie, S.H.; Santoni, G.; Bottai, M.; Gottlieb-Vedi, E.; Lagergren, P.; Lagergren, J. Prediction of conditional survival in esophageal cancer in a population-based cohort study. *Int. J. Surg.* **2023**, *109*, 1141–1148. [CrossRef] [PubMed]
41. Daly, C.; Urbach, D.R.; Stukel, T.A.; Nathan, P.C.; Deitel, W.; Paszat, L.F.; Wilton, A.S.; Baxter, N.N. Patterns of diagnostic imaging and associated radiation exposure among long-term survivors of young adult cancer: A population-based cohort study. *BMC Cancer* **2015**, *15*, 1–10. [CrossRef]
42. Khatri, R.; Quinn, P.L.; Wells-Di Gregorio, S.; Pawlik, T.M.; Cloyd, J.M. Surveillance-Associated Anxiety After Curative-Intent Cancer Surgery: A Systematic Review. *Ann. Surg. Oncol.* **2024**, *32*, 47–62. [CrossRef]
43. Waqas, M.; Humphries, U.W. A critical review of RNN and LSTM variants in hydrological time series predictions. *MethodsX* **2024**, *13*, 102946. [CrossRef]
44. Pedarzani, E.; Fogangolo, A.; Baldi, I.; Berchialla, P.; Panzini, I.; Khan, M.R.; Valpiani, G.; Spadaro, S.; Gregori, D.; Azzolina, D. Prioritizing Patient Selection in Clinical Trials: A Machine Learning Algorithm for Dynamic Prediction of In-Hospital Mortality for ICU Admitted Patients Using Repeated Measurement Data. *J. Clin. Med.* **2025**, *14*, 612. [CrossRef] [PubMed]

cancers

MDPI

*Article*

# High-Speed Videoendoscopy and Stiffness Mapping for AI-Assisted Glottic Lesion Differentiation

**Magdalena M. Pietrzak [1], Justyna Kałuża-Olszewska [2], Ewa Niebudek-Bogusz [1], Artur Klepaczko [2] and Wioletta Pietruszewska [1,*]**

[1] Department of Otolaryngology, Head and Neck Oncology, Medical University of Lodz, 90-419 Lodz, Poland; magdalena.pietrzak@umed.lodz.pl (M.M.P.); ewa.niebudek-bogusz@umed.lodz.pl (E.N.-B.)

[2] Institute of Electronics, Lodz University of Technology, 90-924 Lodz, Poland; justyna.sujecka@dokt.p.lodz.pl (J.K.-O.); artur.klepaczko@p.lodz.pl (A.K.)

* Correspondence: wioletta.pietruszewska@umed.lodz.pl

**Simple Summary**

Early detection of glottic cancer remains a challenge due to changes in vocal fold biomechanics. This study assessed the Stiffness Asymmetry Index (SAI), derived from high-speed videoendoscopy (HSV), as a quantitative marker of vocal fold stiffness for differentiating benign and malignant glottic lesions. Analysis of 102 participants revealed that SAI (AUC = 0.91, 95% CI: 0.839–0.962) and weighted amplitude asymmetry (AUC = 0.92, 95% CI: 0.85–0.974) effectively distinguished between normal and pathological vocal folds. Machine learning models further improved classification, with an SVM classifier achieving an AUC of 0.93 for organic lesion detection and 0.83 for malignancy differentiation. These findings highlight SAI as a promising non-invasive parameter for early glottic cancer detection, with machine learning enhancing diagnostic accuracy.

**Abstract**

**Objectives**: This study evaluates the potential of high-speed videoendoscopy (HSV) in differentiating between benign and malignant glottic lesions, offering a non-invasive diagnostic tool for clinicians. Moreover, a new parameter derived from high-speed videoendoscopy (HSV) had been proposed and implemented in the analysis for an objective assessment of the vocal fold stiffness. **Methods**: High-speed videoendoscopy (HSV) was conducted on 102 participants, including 21 normophonic individuals, 39 patients with benign vocal fold lesions, and 42 with glottic cancer. Laryngotopographic parameter describing the stiffness of vocal fold (SAI) and kymographic parameters describing amplitude, symmetry, and glottal dynamics were quantified. Statistical differences between groups were assessed using receiver operating characteristic (ROC) analysis and lesion classification was performed using a machine learning model. **Results**: Univariate receiver operating characteristic (ROC) analysis revealed that SAI (AUC = 0.91, 95% CI: 0.839–0.962) and weighted amplitude asymmetry (AUC = 0.92, 95% CI: 0.85–0.974) were highly effective in distinguishing between normophonic and organic lesions ($p < 0.01$). Further multivariate analysis using machine learning models demonstrated improved accuracy, with the SVM classifier achieving an AUC of 0.93 for detecting organic lesions and 0.83 for distinguishing benign from malignant lesions. **Conclusions**: The study demonstrates the potential value of parameter describing the pliability of infiltrated vocal fold (SAI) as a non-invasive tool to support histopathological evaluation in laryngeal lesions, with machine learning models enhancing diagnostic performance.

**Keywords:** glottic cancer; vocal fold stiffness; high-speed videoendoscopy; laryngotopography; Stiffness Asymmetry Index; machine learning; receiver operating characteristic; benign lesions; malignant lesions; kymography; amplitude asymmetry; phase difference of vocal fold oscillations

## 1. Introduction

Dysphonia is usually the first symptom of different disorders of the voice organ including organic lesions as well as functional or inflammatory disorders. The differentiation between possible causes of dysphonia is necessary for adequate treatment modalities. While in benign lesions the main goal is to obtain good quality of voice, the treatment of the malignant lesions is being planned mainly to obtain clear margins. Laryngeal cancer (LC) is one of the most common malignancies in the head and neck region and about 95% is laryngeal squamous cell carcinoma (LSCC) [1]. In the glottis, it usually appears on the mucosal surface of the free margin in the anterior 1/3 of the vocal fold. Early diagnosis of the LSCC is a key point to a complete cure. According to the 5-year survival rate which ranges from 78% in early-stage patients to 34% in advanced cases with metastatic involvement [2]. The histopathological examination remains a gold standard for the diagnosis of organic lesions. However, an effort is made to obtain a highly objective method for the examination before invasive procedures, which could support the diagnosis. Clinical evaluation of the larynx is the first step in the process. An essential point is the white light endoscopy (WLE) which guides treatment planning. However, WLE could be insensitive for early, superficial lesions. Therefore, many studies recommend combining WLE with narrow band imaging (NBI) which asses the vascular patterns [3,4]. European Laryngological Society published a descriptive guideline for vascular changes in lesions of the vocal folds. They pointed out the important value of NBI assessment in the vocal fold lesions. However, authors also stated that NBI examination results must remain as part of other findings e.g., mucosal vibration, vocal fold stiffness [5]. Objective assessment of the vocal fold stiffness had different approaches in time. Firstly it was assessed invasively and, therefore could not be implemented clinically as it caused scaring and required general anesthesia [6]. Then the non-invasive methods were developed based e.g., on the relationship between fundamental frequency (F0) and subglottic pressure (Ps) which allows the clinical use of this parameter [7,8]. According to the endoscopy in larynx, the mucosal wave is commonly assessed and its absence is partly a result of vocal fold stiffness. Commonly laryngovideostroboscopy (LVS) is used for the functional assessment of vocal fold oscillations. This method gives the illusory image of the vocal fold vibrations using the synchronization of strobe light with F0. However, it fails in aperiodic voices or patients who had problems with prolonged phonation, so mostly cases with severe dysphonia. High-speed videoendoscopy (HSV) overcomes some of those problems. This method allows us to obtain the real oscillations of the vocal fold, recording at more than 2000 fps. There are many methods for the objective assessment of HSV among others the laryngotophography (LTG). LTG is a method for the assessment of spatial characteristics. Fourier transformation is used to detect changing in the time brightness of pixels across HSV images [9,10]. In 2022 we proposed implementation of the LTG maps to calculate Stiffness Asymmetry Index (SAI) to provide a quantitative comparison of vibrations between affected and non-affected vocal folds [11].

The goal of the study is to propose the non-invasive approach for differentiation of benign and malignant glottic lesions using a newly proposed parameter describing the vocal fold stiffness (SAI) based on the laryngotopography (LTG) derived from the high-speed videoendoscopy (HSV). Moreover, to implement the new parameter (SAI) in the objective assessment of vocal fold oscillations to support the standard kymographic parameters describing the vocal fold symmetry, amplitude and phase difference with use of machine learning methods.

## 2. Materials and Methods

### 2.1. Study Group

Laryngeal HSV recordings ($n$ = 102) of subjects hospitalized between March 2020 and March 2024 at the Department of Otolaryngology, Head and Neck Oncology, Medical University of Lodz, Poland was taken. The inclusion criteria for the study required that the vocal folds in the recordings were clearly visible during high-speed videoendoscopy (HSV) imaging. Cases where the epiglottis obstructed the anterior commissure, or the arytenoid cartilages obstructed the posterior vocal folds were excluded. The study cohort consisted of 21 normophonic individuals (healthy controls), 39 patients diagnosed with benign vocal fold lesions (such as polyps and cysts), and 42 patients with early malignant lesions (all diagnosed with T1 squamous cell carcinoma of the vocal fold).

According to sex and age in the group of 42 patients with malignant lesions there were 34 males, 8 females, aged from 44 to 91 years, with mean age of 68 years. In the group of 39 patients with benign lesions there were 17 males and 22 females aged from 23 to 77 years, with mean age of 50 years. Normophonic group of 21 patients consists of 7 males and 14 females aged from 22 to 68 years, with a mean age of 43 years.

The final diagnosis of all lesions was confirmed by histopathological examination of tissue specimens obtained from hypertrophic lesions. Patients with bilateral vocal fold lesions or advanced cancer affecting other structures (laryngeal ventricle, vestibular fold, contralateral vocal fold) were excluded from the study.

### 2.2. Equipment and Instrumentation

HSV recordings were carried out using a rigid, oval-shaped endoscope (Xion ϕ10.0, Berlin, Germany) with light input in Storz standard matched to a 4.8 mm fiber optic light cable. The HSV images of the larynx were registered with an Advanced Larynx Imager System (ALIS) manufactured by Diagnova Technologies (Wroclaw, Poland), equipped with an innovative endoscope laser light source (ALIS Lum-MF1) and laryngeal high-speed camera (ALIS Cam HS-1) with a CMOS image sensor with a color filter array (the classic Bayer filter) and a global shutter. Images were recorded 3200 frames per second at 416 × 416 pixels.

### 2.3. Endoscopic Procedure

The high-speed videoendoscopy (HSV) procedure was conducted under controlled conditions, with patients seated in a comfortable position and instructed to maintain stable phonation of the vowel "i" for the duration of the recording at a comfortable level of pitch and volume. The vocal fold movements were captured over a period of a few seconds during sustained phonation. The recordings were carefully reviewed to ensure that no other anatomical structures interfered with the laryngeal views (e.g., epiglottis or arytenoid cartilages obstructing the vocal folds).

### 2.4. Laryngotopographic (LTG) Analysis

Stiffness Asymmetry Index (SAI) was calculated using the laryngotopography (LTG) method. The Fourier Transform was applied on so-called brightness functions defined for every individual pixel within the glottal area. This function is simply a time-series of image pixel brightness values that periodically change due to the vocal folds motion, either obscuring or exposing the glottis lumen. Since the frame rate of the HSV camera used in the study (3200 fps) is much higher than the expected fundamental frequencies range of vocal folds oscillations, the reconstructed brightness functions can be reliably used for signal harmonic analysis. Specifically, Fourier analysis is used to decompose the brightness fluctuations of each pixel over time into frequency components. This enables us to:

#### 2.4.1. Identify Fundamental Frequency (F0) and Harmonic Components

By analyzing pixel intensity variations, we can determine the dominant vibratory frequencies of the vocal folds, distinguishing between normal and pathological oscillations.

#### 2.4.2. Map Spatial Vibratory Patterns

Fourier Transformation is applied across the entire glottic region, creating laryngotopographic maps, which visually represent areas of high and low vibratory activity. These maps are crucial for detecting non-vibratory regions, amplitude asymmetry, and stiffness changes associated with malignancy.

#### 2.4.3. Quantify Oscillatory Behavior in a Standardized Manner

FT-based spectral analysis allows for objective comparison of different glottic regions, reducing observer bias and providing numeric parameters that can be used in machine learning classification.

This method enabled the objective evaluation of the mucosal wave, amplitude asymmetry, and phase difference, with the goal of identifying significant differences between normal and pathological vocal fold movements. The SAI was calculated based on the LTG maps, allowing a quantitative comparison of the vibratory patterns of the affected vocal fold with the non-affected one. Detailed methodology is presented in another publication [12]. In comparison to the published version of the algorithm, for the purpose of the current study we have introduced one major improvement with respect to the lateral separation of the vocal folds. Previously, the user simply indicated the top and the bottom poles of the glottal gap. These two locations determined the symmetry axis of the glottis (see Figure 1a). In the pilot study, this approach ensured accurate division between left and right side. However, there are cases, where the lesion on one side obscures the vocal tissue on the other side, thus disturbing the estimation of the motion dynamics of the unaffected part. Therefore, we modified the procedure of SAI calculation through a more precise delineation of the boundary between the two sides, adapted to the local shape of glottal lesions (Figure 1b).

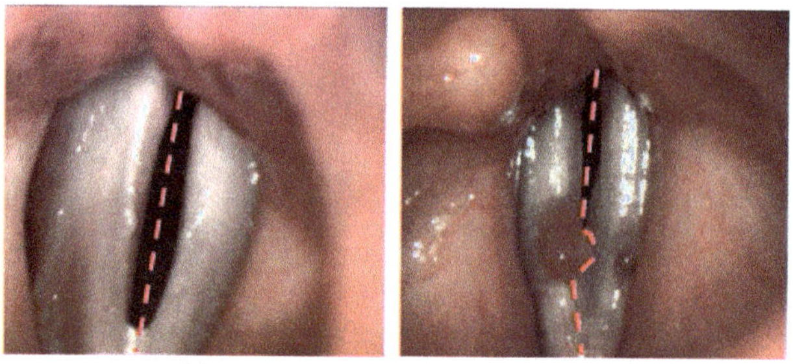

(a) (b)

**Figure 1.** Different approaches for the partitioning of the glottis into left and right side: (**a**) using straight symmetry axis and (**b**) locally adapted boundary to avoid assigning right vocal lesion to the left side.

For the analysis we used short recordings of 625 ms therefore the movement of the endoscope tip is negligible. However, perspective distortion, although a well-recognized issue in endoscopic imaging, remains challenging to fully eliminate. Moreover, studies proved that there is an influence of angle tilt of the endoscope on the parameter values especially those describing the asymmetry [13]. A fundamental approach to mitigating this distortion in laryngoscopy involves ensuring optimal orientation of the endoscope tip, such that the optical axis of the camera is maintained perpendicular to the surface of the vocal folds. Additional strategies include the use of advanced image post-processing techniques to correct distortion effects, as well as the implementation of 3D imaging, which provides depth information and enables more accurate reconstruction of anatomical structures. These techniques are however still in the research and development phase.

Therefore, in this study, video sequences were meticulously acquired with careful attention to optimal endoscope positioning, ensuring reliable quantification of vocal fold dynamics. Furthermore, it is important to highlight that the SAI parameter exhibits inherent robustness to distortions arising from moderately deviated viewing angles. This parameter is calculated as the ratio of the relative vibrating areas of the left and right vocal folds calculated separately. When distortion is minimal, any apparent enlargement on one side effects both the vibrating and total fold areas proportionally, thereby preserving the accuracy of the SAI calculation.

### *2.5. Kymographic Analysis*

The obtained recordings were analyzed with the aid of the Diagnova Technologies software DiagnoScope Specialist ver. 1.3 (Poland) dedicated for ALIS with additional modules. This software provides tools for both short- and long-term kymographic analysis and parameterization. While HSV is the primary imaging modality, our analysis is based on high-speed kymography, which is derived from HSV recordings. For the analysis the software automatically selected a part of the recording 625 ms length. Manual stabilization and centering of the image for each frame was not required, because, in such a short recording time (625 ms), the movement of the endoscope tip is negligible. After this the examiner marked five points on a single representative frame and based on this the vocal folds edges were identified semi-automatically along the whole length of the glottis. In case of any discrepancy the software allows to verify and adjust the automated detection by the examiner. We used the kymography which is a post-processing technique that extracts temporal vibratory information from HSV recordings, enabling quantitative assessment of vocal fold oscillations. In the final step, the software calculated a set of specific parameters to quantify vocal fold dynamics, including amplitude, asymmetry, and phase differences. Those parameters are presented in the Table 1. Their significance were mentioned in the ELS/UEP guidelines as important in the voice assessment [14]. A detailed description of the apparatus and software used is provided in another publication [15]. Detailed explanation with mathematical formulas please see the Supplementary S1.

**Table 1.** Kymographic parameters included in the study and their descriptions. %FL—percent of a vocal fold length.

| | Parameter | Description | | Parameter | Description |
|---|---|---|---|---|---|
| 1 | AmpMaxInd (%FL) | Index of maximum glottal gap amplitude | 20 | OQAvg_3/3 (%) | Open Quotient 1/3 anterior part of the glottis |
| 2 | AmpRMaxInd (%FL) | Index of maximum right vocal fold edge movement amplitude | 21 | AmplAsymAvg (%) | Average amplitude asymmetry |
| 3 | AmpLMaxInd (%FL) | Index of maximum left vocal fold edge movement amplitude | 22 | AmplAsymAvg_1/3 (%) | Average amplitude asymmetry 1/3 posterior part of the glottis |

**Table 1.** *Cont.*

| | Parameter | Description | | Parameter | Description |
|---|---|---|---|---|---|
| 4 | AmpCenter (%FL) | Index of net glottal gap amplitude | 23 | AmplAsymAvg_2/3 (%) | Average amplitude asymmetry 1/3 middle part of the glottis |
| 5 | AmpRCenter (%FL) | Index of net right vocal fold edge movement amplitude | 24 | AmplAsymAvg_3/3 (%) | Average amplitude asymmetry 1/3 anterior part of the glottis |
| 6 | AmpLCenter (%FL) | Index of net left vocal fold edge movement amplitude | 25 | AmplAsymWeighted (%) | Weighted amplitude asymmetry |
| 7 | AmpAvg (%FL) | Average glottal gap amplitude | 26 | PhaseAsymAvg (%) | Average phase asymmetry |
| 8 | AmpAvg_1/3 (%FL) | Glottal gap amplitude 1/3 posterior part of the glottis | 27 | PhaseAsymAvg_1/3 (%) | Average phase asymmetry 1/3 posterior part of the glottis |
| 9 | AmpAvg_2/3 (%FL) | Glottal gap amplitude 1/3 middle part of the glottis | 28 | PhaseAsymAvg_2/3 (%) | Average phase asymmetry 1/3 middle part of the glottis |
| 10 | AmpAvg_3/3 (%FL) | Glottal gap amplitude 1/3 anterior part of the glottis | 29 | PhaseAsymAvg_3/3 (%) | Average phase asymmetry 1/3 anterior part of the glottis |
| 11 | AmpLAvg (%FL) | Average left vocal fold amplitude | 30 | PhaseAsymWeighted (%) | Weighted Average phase asymmetry |
| 12 | AmpRAvg (%FL) | Average right vocal fold amplitude | 31 | Rel2CommonAmplAvg (%) | Average relative to common amplitude ratio |
| 13 | Nonclosing (%FL) | Non-closing part of vocal folds | 32 | PhaseDiffAvg (°) | Average phase difference |
| 14 | Nonopening (%FL) | Non-opening part of vocal folds | 33 | PhaseDiffAvg_1/3 (°) | Average phase difference 1/3 posterior part of the glottis |
| 15 | EffectiveArea (%) | Glottal effective area | 34 | PhaseDiffAvg_2/3 (°) | Average phase difference 1/3 middle part of the glottis |
| 16 | RGGA (%) | Relative Glottal Gap Area | 35 | PhaseDiffAvg_3/3 (°) | Average phase difference 1/3 anterior part of the glottis |
| 17 | OQAvg (%) | Average Open Quotient | 36 | PhaseDiffWeighted (°) | Weighted phase difference |
| 18 | OQAvg_1/3 (%) | Open Quotient 1/3 posterior part of the glottis | 37 | AbsPhaseDiffAvg (°) | Average absolute phase difference |
| 19 | OQAvg_2/3 (%) | Open Quotient 1/3 middle part of the glottis | 38 | AbsPhaseDiffWeighted (°) | Weighted absolute phase difference |

### 2.6. Statistical Analysis

The objective of the statistical analysis was to assess the ability of each parameter to differentiate between benign and malignant patients, as well as distinguish both types of organic lesions from healthy individuals. Before performing group comparisons, we assessed the normality of all 39 kymographic parameters using the Shapiro-Wilk test ($\alpha = 0.05$). Parameters that followed a normal distribution were analyzed using one-way ANOVA. Parameters that did not follow a normal distribution were analyzed using the Kruskal-Wallis test.

To determine which parameters significantly differed between the three patient groups (normophonic, benign, malignant), we applied: one-way ANOVA for normally distributed parameters; Kruskal-Wallis test for non-normally distributed parameters.

For parameters that showed a significant difference in the global ANOVA/Kruskal-Wallis test, we conducted Mann-Whitney U tests for pairwise comparisons: normophonic vs. benign lesions; normophonic vs. malignant lesions; benign vs. malignant lesions. Bonferroni correction was applied to adjust for multiple comparisons.

Six parameters were found to be significantly different across groups: Stiffness Asymmetry Index (SAI); Weighted Amplitude Asymmetry (AmplAsymWeighted); Average Amplitude Asymmetry (AmplAsymAvg); Amplitude Asymmetry (Middle Third) (AmplAsymAvg_2/3); Absolute Phase Difference (AbsPhaseDiffAvg); Weighted Absolute Phase Difference (AbsPhaseDiffWeighted)

For the most significant parameters, Receiver Operating Characteristic (ROC) analysis was conducted to evaluate their classification performance. To compensate for small sample size we had applied ROC analysis with boostrapping. In all simulations, number of bootstrap iterations was set to 1000. Dataset was resampled with replacement so that the size of the resampled data was equal to the original.

The mean metrics were averaged over bootstrap iterations. The 95% confidence bounds were found as 2.5 and 97.5 percentiles of the results obtained through the 1000 repetitions. In this analysis, the ROC curves are interpolated, as the TPR values in different bootstrap run were obtained for different FPRs. The ROC analysis was conducted in two stages: first, to differentiate normophonic patients from those with any organic lesions (benign and malignant), and second, to distinguish between benign and malignant lesions. The Youden Index, sensitivity and specificity with 95% confidence intervals were reported. We have added a definition of the Youden Index, which is used to determine the optimal cut-off threshold for binary classification in our ROC analysis. The Youden Index (J) is calculated as:

$$J = \text{Sensitivity} + \text{Specificity} - 1$$

Youden indexes are calculated for the mean ROC curves, but the threshold cutoff-values can only be given for the full original data. Otherwise, determination of a cutoff value is ambiguous. A higher Youden Index indicates a better balance between sensitivity and specificity, making it a useful metric for selecting the optimal diagnostic threshold for parameters such as SAI and amplitude asymmetry.

### 2.7. Machine Learning Model

To further examine the diagnostic capability of the parameters in the multivariate setting, a machine learning model was developed. The purpose of the study was to build a classifier model for discriminating patients according to the diagnosis (Norm, Benign, and Malignant). With the approach used, there is no need to make assumptions about the type of probability distribution of the data, and the discriminative power of parameters can be evaluated not only individually, but also in their subsets. For the classifier model we chose the Support Vector Machines (SVM) algorithm with the radial basis kernel function [16]. The model was then built using parameters identified as significant using an attributes selection method based on the so-called wrapper approach. The input data was the entire dataset—102 patients described by the 39 parameters listed with the descriptions in the Table 1.

The following analysis steps were performed:

1. Parameter standardization. For each parameter, the mean value and standard deviation were calculated. After subtracting the mean and dividing by the standard deviation, each parameter had mean = 0 and standard deviation = 1. Thus, parameters with a larger range of values had the same effect on the distance metric calculated between data vectors as parameters with a small range.

2. Selection of significant attributes. This step was performed using the sequential floating-forward search (SFFS) algorithm [17]. The exploration of the multidimensional parameter space in search of significant features (providing the best classification of the selected classifier) is done sequentially. First, a single parameter is found that minimizes classification error, and then more features are added or subtracted depending on their impact on the classification accuracy.
3. Training of the final classifier model. The SFFS algorithm terminates when further addition or removal of attributes does not improve classification quality. The final subset is used to develop and test a classifier model of multidimensional data vectors. The following SVM models have been developed:

a. A model for the classification to all 3 classes simultaneously.
b. A binary model to discriminate between Norm and any organic lesion
c. A binary model to discriminate between Malignant and Benign lesions.

In each case, learning and testing of the models was done using 5-fold cross-validation. This means that the dataset was randomly divided into 5 parts. Learning was repeated 5 times, each time a different 4 parts were used to build the model, and testing was performed for the remaining fifth part. This is a major difference from the evaluation of threshold classifiers proposed in statistical analysis, in which the entire data set is used to determine the cutoff value. As common as this is in statistical analysis, the final metrics, such as sensitivity and specificity, are seemingly better than they might actually be if the same cutoff value were used for new patients. Therefore, for binary classifiers in addition to cross-validation, testing was also performed on the entire learning set to enable direct comparison with the results obtained previously.

Moreover, the training and testing of the classifiers described in step 3 were also conducted for the subset of features identified as significant in MCT tests. These experiments allow for the evaluation of the effectiveness of multivariate analysis based on machine learning in comparison to univariate statistical analysis

## 3. Results

### 3.1. Univariate Analysis

The kymographic parameters were compared across three distinct patient groups: normophonic individuals, benign lesion patients, and malignant lesion patients. The statistical comparison revealed six key parameters that differed significantly between all three groups, based on the U Mann-Whitney test ($p < 0.01$). Among these, the Stiffness Asymmetry Index (SAI) emerged as a critical factor, along with two parameters describing phase difference and three parameters quantifying amplitude asymmetry (Table 2). These findings suggest that these parameters provide strong differentiating power when evaluating different types of vocal fold lesions.

The box-and-whisker plot (Figure 2) visually illustrates the distribution of values for these six parameters in the three groups. The median values for these parameters differed significantly between normophonic subjects, benign, and malignant lesion groups. However, no single parameter was able to clearly distinguish between all three groups on its own.

**Table 2.** Parameters which differ simultaneously between the normophonic patients, subjects with benign and malignant lesions (U Mann-Whitney test). Statistic value presents the difference level between investigated groups—the higher is the value of statistic the higher is the measured difference.

| Parameter | Groups | *p*-Value | Statistic |
|---|---|---|---|
| AbsPhaseDiffAvg | Benign vs. Malignant | 0.0096 | 544.5 |
| | Norm vs. Benign | 0.0002 | 169.0 |
| | Norm vs. Malignant | <0.0001 | 132.5 |
| AbsPhaseDiffWeighted | Benign vs. Malignant | 0.0097 | 545.0 |
| | Norm vs. Benign | 0.0004 | 178.5 |
| | Norm vs. Malignant | <0.0001 | 143.0 |
| AmplAsymAvg | Benign vs. Malignant | 0.0001 | 416.0 |
| | Norm vs. Benign | <0.0001 | 124.5 |
| | Norm vs. Malignant | <0.0001 | 62.0 |
| AmplAsymAvg_2/3 | Benign vs. Malignant | 0.0010 | 505.0 |
| | Norm vs. Benign | 0.0001 | 160.0 |
| | Norm vs. Malignant | < 0.0001 | 112.5 |
| AmplAsymWeighted | Benign vs. Malignant | 0.0001 | 412.0 |
| | Norm vs. Benign | <0.0001 | 93.0 |
| | Norm vs. Malignant | <0.0001 | 47.0 |
| SAI | Benign vs. Malignant | <0.0001 | 337.5 |
| | Norm vs. Benign | <0.0001 | 123.5 |
| | Norm vs. Malignant | <0.0001 | 34.0 |

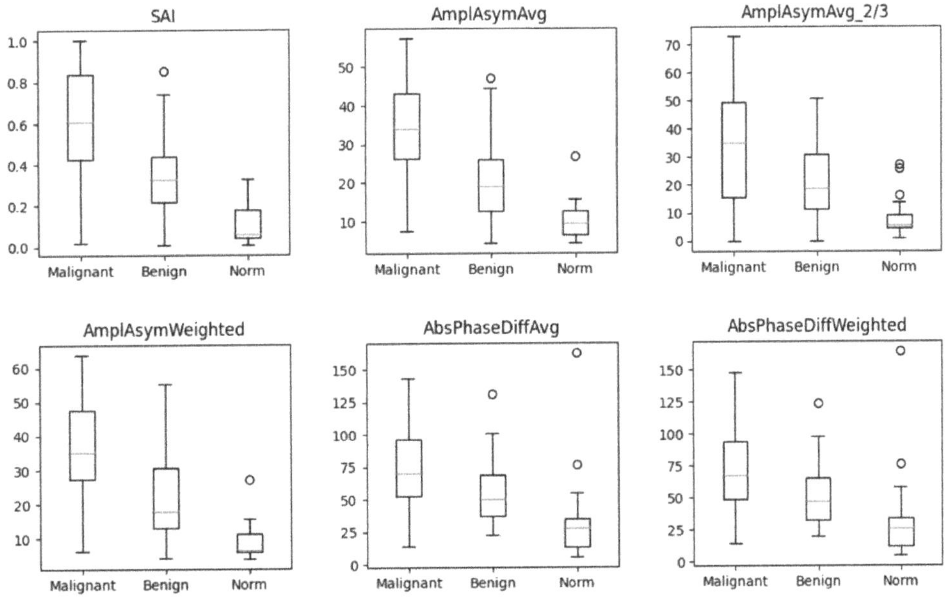


**Figure 2.** Box and whisker plots for six parameters which differ in a significant way simultaneously between normophonic patients, benign and malignant glottic lesion groups. Diagram presents median values of individual vibratory parameters in groups divided by diagnosis, specifically: norm, benign, and malignant. The dots correspond to an elevated value of parameters.

To further assess the discriminatory power of these parameters, ROC curve analysis was conducted. This analysis was performed in two stages: first, to differentiate normophonic individuals from patients with any organic lesion (benign and malignant), and second, to distinguish between benign and malignant lesions.

The best performance in differentiating normophonic subjects from patients with any organic lesion (benign and malignant) was observed for the weighted amplitude asymmetry (AmplAsymWeighted), which yielded an AUC of 0.92 (95% CI: 0.85–0.974) with 83% sensitivity (95% CI: 0.697–0.952) and 92% specificity (95% CI: 0.765–1.0, $p < 0.0001$) indicating excellent discriminative ability. SAI also showed strong performance, with an AUC of 0.91 (95% CI: 0.839–0.962), 83% sensitivity (95% CI: 0.623–0.966) and 90% specificity (95% CI: 0.737–1.0, $p < 0.0001$). Altogether six parameters mentioned above reached AUC values above 0.8, with varying sensitivity and specificity as shown in Figure 3.

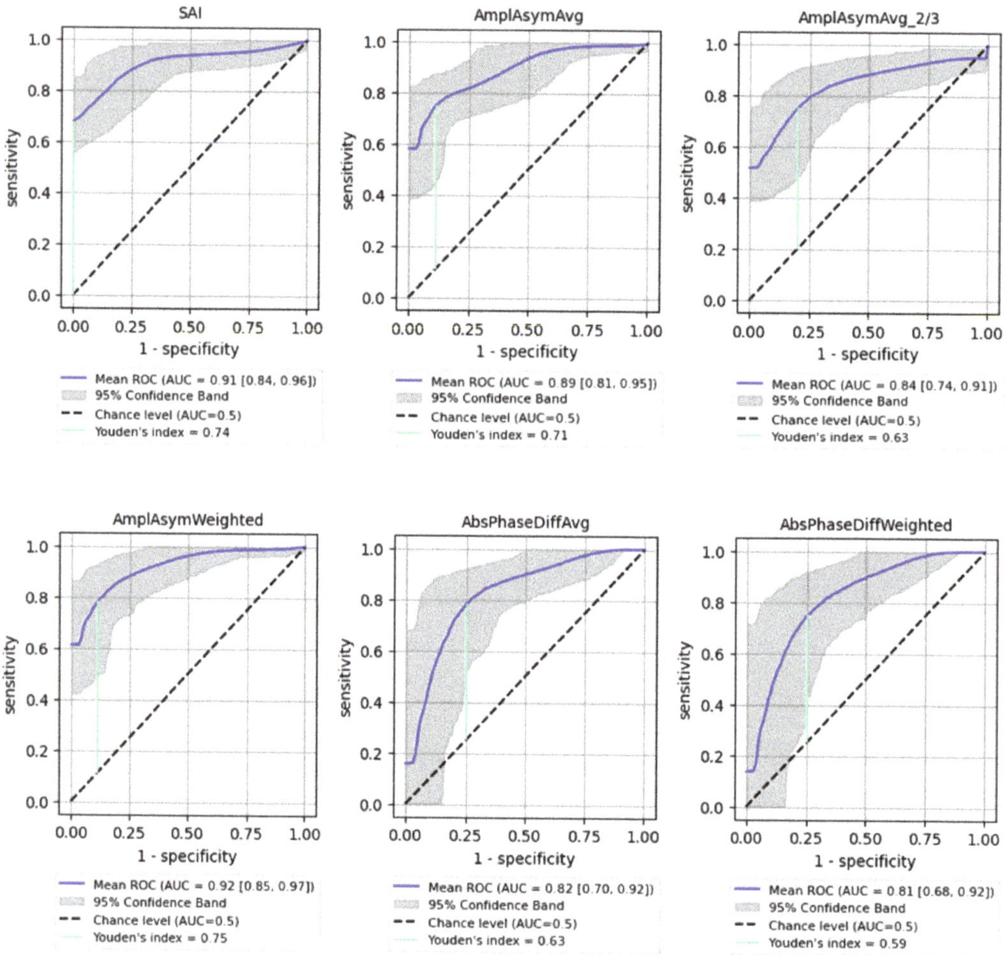


**Figure 3.** ROC curves with bootstrapping for the six best-performing vibratory parameters differentiating normophonic subjects from patients with any organic lesion of the glottis (both benign and malignant) (blue line). *X*- and *y*-axis present sensitivity and 1-specificity of points on the curve. The black line presents an AUC value of 0.5; the aquamarine line presents the value of the Youden index.

The Youden Index was calculated for each parameter, providing a cut-off threshold for detection of organic lesions. The sensitivity and specificity values associated with these cut-off points are summarized in Table 3, indicating high sensitivity and specificity for most parameters, particularly for SAI (0.83 sensitivity, 0.9 specificity). Sensitivity (True Positive Rate): Measures the proportion of actual positive cases correctly identified (i.e., how well the model detects malignant lesions); Specificity (True Negative Rate): Measures the proportion of actual negative cases correctly classified (i.e., how well the model avoids false positives in detecting malignancy).

**Table 3.** Parameters highlighted in the multiple comparison analysis for which ROC analysis with bootstrapping was performed (differentiation of normophonic subjects from patients with any organic lesion of the glottis). The table contains the Youden index values and the corresponding sensitivity and specificity values with 95% confidence intervals. Sensitivity (True Positive Rate): Measures the proportion of actual positive cases correctly identified (i.e., how well the model detects malignant lesions); Specificity (True Negative Rate): Measures the proportion of actual negative cases correctly classified (i.e., how well the model avoids false positives in detecting malignancy).

| | Parameter | Youden's Index (95% CI) | Sensitivity (95% CI) | Specificity (95% CI) |
|---|---|---|---|---|
| 1 | SAI | 0.735 (0.612–0.882) | 0.832 (0.623–0.966) | 0.903 (0.737–1.0) |
| 2 | AmplAsymAvg | 0.715 (0.581–0.833) | 0.777 (0.662–0.903) | 0.938 (0.786–1.0) |
| 3 | AmplAsymAvg_2/3 | 0.633 (0.482–0.788) | 0.764 (0.5–0.911) | 0.869 (0.667–1.0) |
| 4 | AmplAsymWeighted | 0.595 (0.395–0.779) | 0.827 (0.697–0.952) | 0.921 (0.765–1.0) |
| 5 | AbsPhaseDiffAvg | 0.627 (0.435–0.8) | 0.808 (0.587–0.919) | 0.819 (0.636–1.0) |
| 6 | AbsPhaseDiffWeighted | 0.595 (0.395–0.779) | 0.783 (0.625–0.938) | 0.812 (0.571–1.0) |

ROC analysis for distinguishing between benign and malignant lesions showed a generally lower AUC than for detecting the organic lesions. However, SAI remained a significant parameter, achieving an AUC of 0.8 (95% CI: 0.692–0.886) with 73% sensitivity (95% CI: 0.540–0.913) and 81% specificity (95% CI: 0.621–0.955, $p < 0.0001$), while Amplitude Asymmetry parameters (e.g., AmplAsymAvg and AmplAsymWeighted) reached AUC values around 0.75. These values are substantial but lower than those obtained for detecting any organic lesion. Detailed results are shown in Figure 4 and Table 4, illustrating the sensitivity and specificity of each parameter for predicting malignancy.

**Table 4.** Parameters highlighted in the multiple comparison analysis for which ROC analysis was performed (differentiating benign from malignant lesions of the glottis). The table contains the Youden index values, sensitivity and specificity values with 95% confidence intervals.

| | Parameter | Youden's Index (95% CI) | Sensitivity (95% CI) | Specificity (95% CI) |
|---|---|---|---|---|
| 1 | SAI | 0.545 (0.379–0.705) | 0.733 (0.54–0.913) | 0.812 (0.621–0.955) |
| 2 | AmplAsymAvg | 0.538 (0.0.362–0.705) | 0.763 (0.538–0.889) | 0.775 (0.634–0.941) |

**Table 4.** *Cont.*

| | Parameter | Youden's Index (95% CI) | Sensitivity (95% CI) | Specificity (95% CI) |
|---|---|---|---|---|
| 3 | AmplAsymAvg_2/3 | 0.440 (0.259–0.606) | 0.624 (0.375–0.825) | 0.816 (0.629–0.974) |
| 4 | AmplAsymWeighted | 0.503 (0.334–0.667) | 0.725 (0.442–0.895) | 0.778 (0.605–0.976) |
| 5 | AbsPhaseDiffAvg | 0.366 (0.2–0.532) | 0.668 (0.341–0.923) | 0.698 (0.424–0.956) |
| 6 | AbsPhaseDiffWeighted | 0.369 (0.189–0.544) | 0.648 (0.355–0.895) | 0.72 (0.432–0.968) |

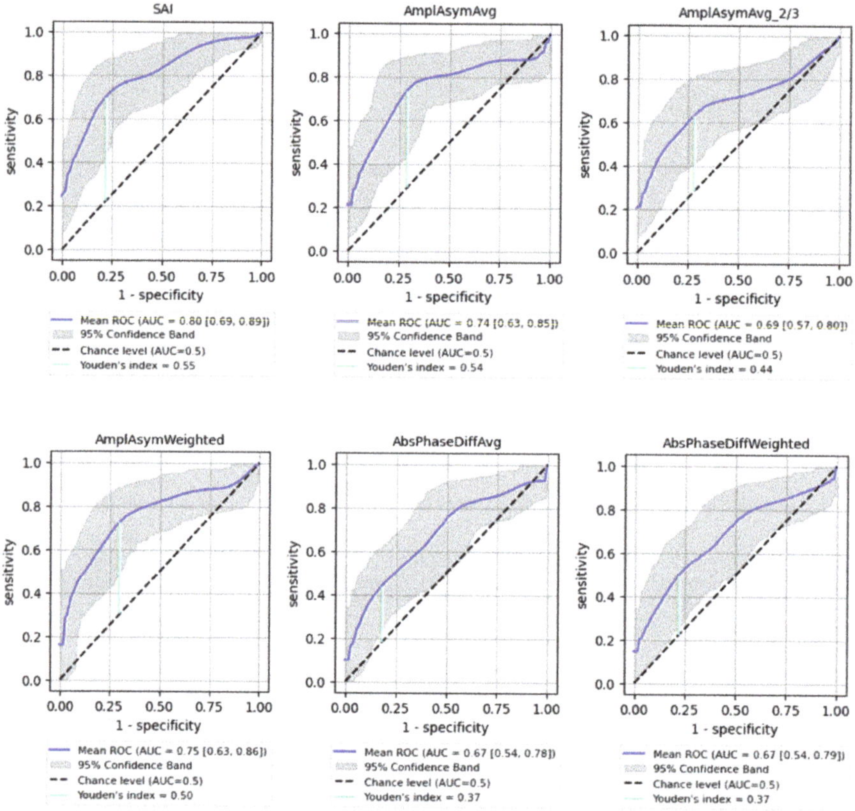


**Figure 4.** ROC curves with bootstrapping for the six best-performing vibratory parameters differentiating benign from malignant lesions of the glottis (blue line). *X*- and *y*-axis present sensitivity and 1-specificity of points on the curve. The black line presents an AUC value of 0.5; the aquamarine line presents the value of the Youden index ending on the curve.

### 3.2. Multidimensional Data Analysis

Given that no single parameter could effectively classify all cases, a machine learning model was employed to improve classification accuracy by considering the interactions between multiple attributes. The analysis used a support vector machine (SVM) classifier, with the sequential floating-forward search (SFFS) algorithm to select the most relevant parameters. The detailed methodology is described in the material and methods section. This approach identified a subset of eight parameters (including SAI, amplitude asymmetry, and phase difference parameters) that significantly improved the classification accuracy.

For the machine learning analysis, the bootstrapping method was applied to the full training dataset, to mimic the workflow applied in the univariate analysis. To follow the established principles of model evaluation in machine learning, it is the cross-validation experiment that should be considered as a more reliable assessment of SVM-associated empirical risk.

### 3.2.1. Classification to 3 Classes

The SFFS-based model showed superior performance compared to the model trained using parameters selected in MCT analysis, correctly classifying 72% of benign lesions, 91% of malignant lesions, and 76% of normophonic subjects. While for MCT it was respectively correctly classified 59% benign lesions, 74% malignant lesions and 67% of normophonic subjects. The results of the SFFS and MCT analyses are presented in the confusion matrices in Figure 5. These findings highlight the effectiveness of integrating multiple attributes within a machine learning framework, which exceeds the predictive performance of individual parameters whose significance was established independently through univariate statistical analysis.

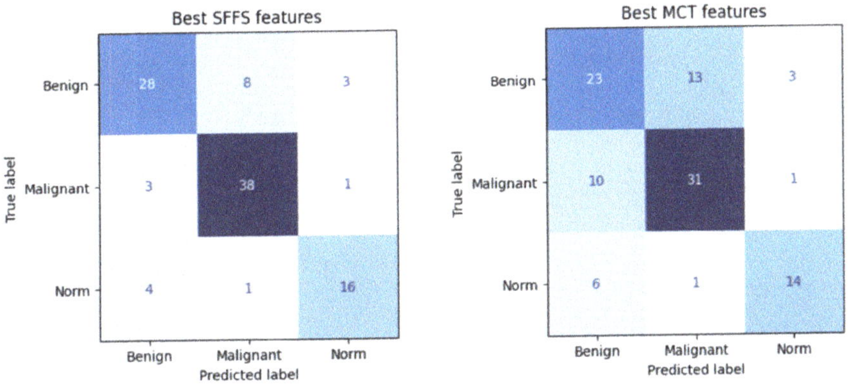


**Figure 5.** Confusion matrix obtained for subsets of significant features determined using the SFFS algorithm and in the MCT univariate analysis. The matrix represents correctly (on the diagonal) and incorrectly (off the diagonal) classified cases. Classifier testing was performed in the 5-fold cross-validation mode.

### 3.2.2. Multidimensional Data Analysis–Classification to 2 Classes: Any Organic Lesion–Norm

The SVM classifier determines the probability of membership in each category for every case being classified. The decision to assign a patient to a specific category is made based on the highest probability. Since the classification outcome, which is the probability of belonging to a selected category, is a continuous value, it is possible to assess the quality of the classification by performing ROC analysis along with the calculation of the standard evaluation metrics, such as balanced accuracy, sensitivity and specificity. In contrast, however, to threshold classifiers built in statistical analysis, the latter two are calculated based on the multidimensional decision hypersurface instead of single cut-off points.

Firstly, a ROC analysis was conducted on the training set to differentiate normophonic subjects from patients with any organic lesion of the glottis, achieving an AUC of 0.99 (95% CI: 0.98–1.0) for the SFFS algorithm and an AUC of 0.97 (95% CI: 0.92–0.99) for the MCT analysis (Figure 6). In case of the SFFS-selected parameters and with lesion class set as a positive label, the model yielded sensitivity of 96% (95% CI: 0.91–1.0), specificity = 99% (95% CI: 0.94–1.0). For MCT-based analysis similar values o sensistivity of 93% (95% CI: 0.84–0.99), specificity = 97% (95% CI: 0.9–1.0)

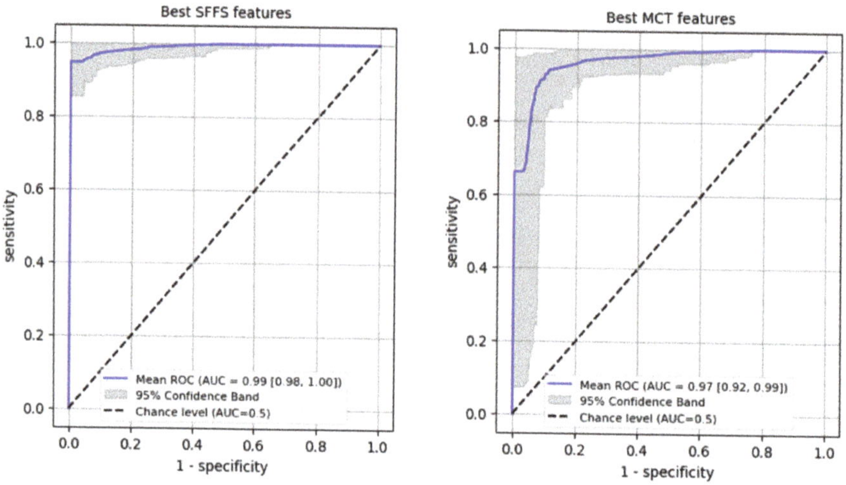


**Figure 6.** ROC curves training set for differentiating normophonic subjects from patients with any organic lesion of the glottis (both benign and malignant).

Subsequently, 5-fold cross-validation testing was conducted to differentiate normophonic subjects from patients with any organic lesion of the glottis, whether benign or malignant. This testing achieved a mean AUC of 0.93 for the SFFS algorithm and a mean AUC of 0.91 for the MCT univariate analysis (Figure 7). The sensitivity metrics remained relatively high, at 97.5% for the SFFS analysis and 93.8% for the MCT analysis. However, specificity decreased to 62% for SFFS and 71% for MCT.

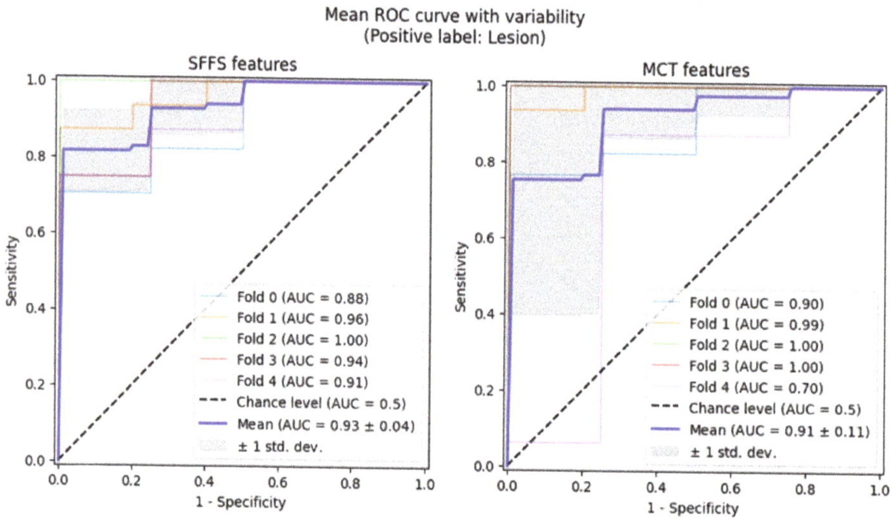


**Figure 7.** ROC curves testing with cross-validation for differentiating normophonic subjects from patients with any organic lesion of the glottis (both benign and malignant).

3.2.3. Multidimensional Data Analysis–Classification to 2 Classes: Malignant Lesion–Benign Lesion

ROC analysis for differentiating benign from malignant lesions of the glottis on the training set was performed reaching AUC 0.97 (95% CI: 0.92–1.0) for SFFS algorithm and AUC 0.92 (95% CI: 0.86–0.97) for MCT univariate analysis (Figure 8). In case of the SFFS-selected parameters and with malignancy class set as a positive label, the model yields sensitivity of 95% (95% CI: 0.85–1.0), specificity = 94% (95% CI: 0.86–1.0). For MCT-selected attributes, sensitivity = 87% (95% CI: 0.74–1.0), specificity = 87% (95% CI: 0.69–1.0).

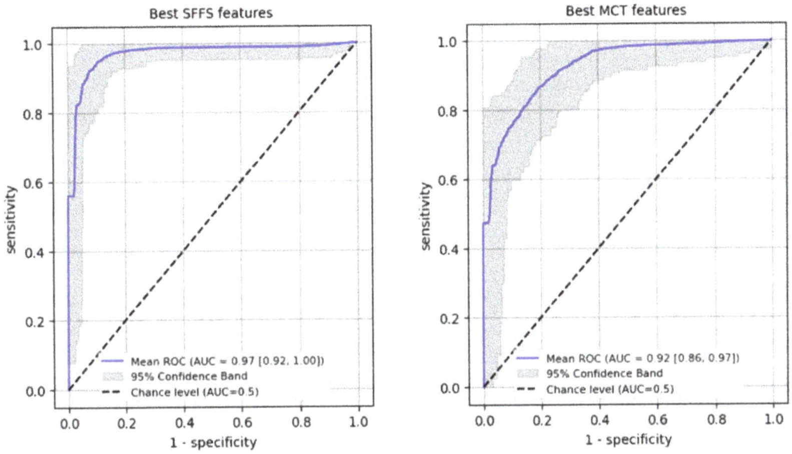


**Figure 8.** ROC curves training set for differentiating benign from malignant lesions of the glottis.

Subsequently, 5-fold cross-validation testing was conducted to differentiate benign from malignant lesions of the glottis. This testing achieved a mean AUC of 0.83 for the SFFS algorithm and a mean AUC of 0.78 for the MCT univariate analysis (Figure 9). Only the specificity for SFFS remains relatively high = 90.6% while the sensitivity = 79.3% for the SFFS and both sensitivity = 66.8%, and specificity = 74.4% for MCT univariate analysis decreased.

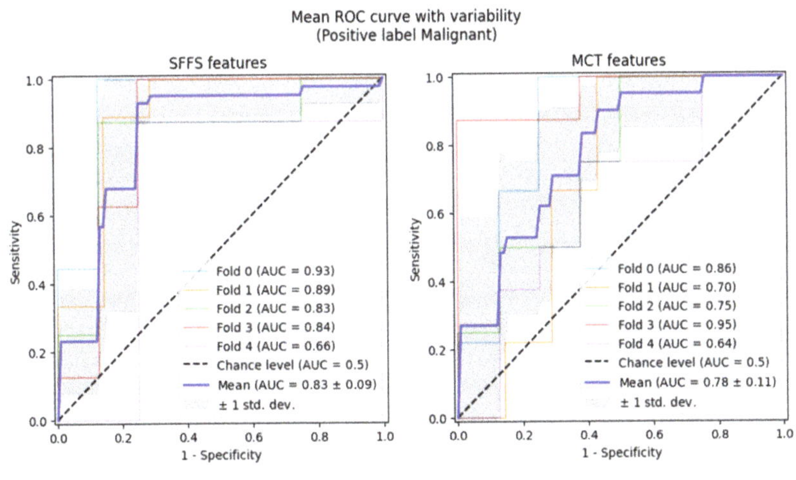


**Figure 9.** ROC curves testing with cross-validation for differentiating benign from malignant lesions of the glottis.

Summarizing, analysis using cross-validation demonstrated that the SVM classifier trained on the SFFS-selected features achieved an AUC of 0.93 in differentiating normophonic subjects from patients with organic lesions and AUC of 0.83 for distinguishing benign from malignant lesions. This underscores the potential of machine learning in enhancing diagnostic accuracy, particularly in the early detection of glottic cancer.

## 4. Discussion

The study shows that Stiffness Asymmetry Index (SAI) is a valuable parameter for detecting organic lesions and predicting malignancy in the vocal folds but it cannot definitively distinguish benign from malignant lesions alone. However, applying the advanced machine learning models, which integrate multiple parameters showed to be promising approach for improving diagnostic accuracy. The findings suggest that SAI, while not sufficient on its own, plays a key role when combined with other dynamic measures of vocal fold function in distinguishing between benign and malignant lesions.

In our study, we assessed vocal fold stiffness as a means of predicting glottic malignancy, using a specially designed Stiffness Asymmetry Index (SAI) derived from the laryngotopographic (LTG) analysis using the High-speed recordings. This index was developed to non-invasively describe the changes in vocal fold structure caused by organic lesions. The results of our study underscore the significant role that vocal fold pliability plays in the diagnosis of glottic lesions, especially when distinguishing between benign and malignant tumors. Growth of the lesion alters the pliability of the vocal fold and it becomes "stiffer" as its ability to vibrate during phonation is reduced. One of the main parts of the vocal fold participating in the vibrations is the membranous portion covering the muscle layer. The wave-like motion of this structure is called mucosal wave and it is only visible during the functional endoscopic examination, such as LVS and HSV. While LVS is commonly used to assess vocal fold vibrations, it fails in cases of aperiodic vibrations, such as those seen in patients with severe dysphonia presented often by patients with glottic cancer. HSV, in contrast, provides a more effective method by recording real-time oscillations thus overcoming the limitations of LVS in such cases [18,19].

Mucosal wave is usually a main part of the subjective assessment of vocal fold vibrations using the HSV along with the glottal closure, symmetry, periodicity and amplitude [20]. These characteristics are commonly assessed subjectively by the clinician as part of glottal function examination, mostly by the LVS. However, a more effective and objective assessment could help clinicians differentiate between the causes of dysphonia [21]. While the benign lesions are usually soft resulting in slight altering of the involved vocal fold's elasticity and pliability, cancerous lesions present different characteristics due to the infiltration of deeper structures. In the case of glottal cancer, studies report the absence of vibratory amplitude in the affected region which could be visualized as a non-vibrating area in LTG. To fill the gap for the objective evaluation of vocal fold pliability which is a crucial aspect in the glottic lesions assessment, we proposed the Stiffness Asymmetry Index (SAI). The parameter describes the stiffness of the affected vocal fold in comparison to non-affected vocal fold based on the LTG maps using the HSV recordings. Due to the high sampling rate, changes in the oscillations are assessed based on the real vocal fold movements allowing the precise evaluation of involved by the lesion areas and their function. Moreover, HSV is successful in the aperiodic vibrations which are often presented in the severe dysphonia caused by the increased mass of vocal folds [22,23].

In our study, the SAI emerged as one of the most promising parameters. It showed excellent performance in detecting any organic lesion and predicting malignancy, both in terms of the area under the ROC curve (AUC) and its sensitivity and specificity (respectively ROC AUC 0.91, 0.8, sensitivity 0.832, 0.733 and specificity 0.903, 0.812). These findings support previous studies that have demonstrated the importance of objective measures in detecting glottic malignancy [12,18]. While benign lesions typically exhibit soft tissue characteristics that result in only slight alterations to vocal fold elasticity, malignant lesions present with more substantial changes due to the infiltration of deeper structures, leading to a reduced mucosal wave and increasing the stiffness of vocal fold. Those changes resulting in the absence of vibratory amplitude in the affected region could be visualized as a non-vibrating area in LTG allows for more accurate discrimination between benign and malignant lesions [18,19].

Besides SAI, the study showed significance of the parameters related to phase difference and amplitude asymmetry of vocal folds which were also significant in our previous study, which focused solely on kymographic parameters for detecting malignancy [24]. These consistent findings highlight the importance of amplitude asymmetry and phase difference in the non-invasive assessment of glottic lesions. In that earlier work, we also evaluated a parameter that specifically measures the amplitude of the vocal fold affected by the lesion. Given the importance of vocal fold pliability and the recommendation by some authors to assess each vocal fold separately, we decided to include this parameter in our analysis [25,26]. This approach indirectly evaluates tissue stiffness by considering the asymmetry between the healthy and affected vocal folds. Average amplitude of affected vocal fold was shown to be a significant predictor of vocal fold malignancy, alongside other kymographic parameters. However, the ROC AUC for this parameter was slightly lower than that obtained for the SAI in this study (0.7 vs. 0.8) [24].

Also in favor of evaluating the two vocal folds separately is the fact that vocal fold stiffness depends on age and gender. It is stated that stiffness of vocal folds is higher in women, and also regardless of gender is associated with aging [8]. By comparing the affected vocal fold to the healthy fold, our approach allows for a more accurate assessment of the lesion's impact on vocal fold function, taking into account these individual differences. Assessment of the tissue stiffness was performed by the LTG to detect periodic and non-periodic vocal fold vibrations in HSV recordings. The method enables quantitative evaluation of the spatial characteristics of the amplitude and phase of phonatory oscillations of the vocal folds due to the Fourier transformation of brightness for each pixel across a sequence of recorded HSV images. Obtained LTG maps present spectral parameters e.g., fundamental frequency and amplitude with assigned pseudocolors for the simple qualitative interpretation. Moreover, LTG visualizes the non-vibrating areas due to the lack of mucosal wave and vibration amplitude which was a base for the creation of the SAI.

Despite the significant differences in the median values of SAI between the groups of patients (norm, benign, malignant) they could not be clearly distinguished based only on this parameter. The median values of SAI were respectively about 0.6 for the malignant lesions, 0.3 for benign lesions, and 0.06 for the normophonic subjects. However, there are cases with very low values of SAI more suitable for the normophonic or benign lesion group that were revealed to be cancerous lesions. Exploring those cases in detail, it appeared they are small superficial lesions, sometimes located in the posterior part of the glottis. Therefore, they were having only a slight influence on the vocal fold oscillations. On the other hand, there were high values of SAI noted for the lesions diagnosed as benign. According to the detailed assessment of the lesions' characteristics, we assumed that it could be a result of hemorrhagic or fibrotic polyps. Those lesions are higher in mass and alter the pliability of the vocal fold more than the jellylike mass of typical polypoid lesions. Moreover, the differences could be caused by the size of the lesions because a big mass could affect the vibrations of healthy vocal fold during the phonatory movements.

Effort is being made to non-invasively classified the glottis lesions before the histopathological examination, which remain the gold standard. The meta-analysis showed that while LVS identifies almost all cases with cancer, only 2/3 of patients with non-invasive lesions are identified as non-cancerous [27]. According to the literature, the best results for the preoperative assessment give the combination of different methods for the endoscopic assessment e.g., functional and with the visualization of the vasculature. Therefore, the authors indicated the need for non-invasive and objective assessment before the surgery [28]. Study performed by Volgger et al. showed that combination of HSV and NBI reach high sensitivity (100%) and specificity (79.4%) in the differentiation between benign/premalignant and malignant lesions [29]. Machine learning techniques, are also being applied to obtain better results, such as the support vector machine (SVM) classifier used in our study, proved to be effective in handling the complex interactions between the parameters characterizing the vocal fold oscillations. The results from the multidimensional data analysis, which integrated multiple parameters including SAI, showed a significant improvement over the univariate analysis. This approach demonstrated better classification accuracy, with the SVM model achieving an AUC of 0.93 for detecting organic lesions (vs. 0.92 for univariate analysis) and 0.83 for distinguishing malignant from benign lesions (vs. 0.79 for univariate analysis). These findings emphasize the potential of machine learning models in clinical applications, where they can enhance diagnostic accuracy by considering the interplay between various parameters. Machine learning methods are now widely implemented in the diagnostic process mainly using the white light and NBI endoscopic images of the larynx to improve the diagnostic process and detect the malignant lesions at the early stage. Zhao et al. investigate different ML models including random forest (RF), support vector machine (SVM), and decision tree (DT), to identify risk factors and predict the malignant lesions using the NBI in a group of 200 patients. The study showed that RF-based model had the best results which were: the accuracy—0.96, precision—0.90, recall 1.00 and F1 index—0.95, and AUC value 0.97. While for the SVM the results were slightly worse than for the RF model: the accuracy—0.91, precision—0.86, recall 0.95 and F1 index—0.90, and AUC value 0.95 but better than in our SVM-based model using the SAI and kymographic parameters based on the HSV [30]. Chinese group evaluate six classical deep learning techniques for the classification of the vocal fold leukoplakia showing the best performance for the GoogLeNet, ResNet, and DenseNe in which the highest overall accuracy of white light image classification is 0.9583, while the highest overall accuracy of NBI image classification is 0.9478 [31]. Other studies proposed also self-made deep-learning algorithms to detect and classify the lesions during the real-time endoscopy obtaining sensitivity for the carcinoma classification between 71% and 78% and for benign vocal cord lesions with a sensitivity between 70% and 82%. That approach could support the clinical decision making during the appointments and it not time consuming like other methods requiring further analysis [32]. The meta-analysis from the 2020 showed that the SVM is the most common algorithm for the detection of voice disorders. [33] However, there are many other well established and self-developed machine learning techniques that give various results for the classification of glottic lesions based on different endoscopic methods.

Besides the use of only one machine learning methods which is SVM in this study, there are several other limitations that should be addressed in future research. First, we included only patients with unilateral lesions, which allowed for direct comparisons between the affected and healthy vocal fold in each patient. While this methodology is robust, it does not fully account for bilateral lesions, which are common in clinical practice.

Besides that, the limitation is the time-consuming nature of the methodology, along with the need for specialized training in the use of HSV and SAI, may limit its widespread adoption in routine clinical settings. Further improvements in the speed and ease of the process, as well as the development of user-friendly software, will be crucial for the implementation of this technique in daily practice [23].

We did not provide the threshold cutoff-values because of the implemented methodology. As we investigated only a group of 102 patients after all exclusions, we had performed a ROC analysis with boostrapping to compensate small sample size. Youden indexes are calculated for the mean ROC curves, but the threshold cutoff-values can only be given for the full original data. Otherwise, determination of a cutoff value is ambiguous.

## 5. Conclusions

In conclusion, Stiffness Asymmetry Index (SAI) is a promising parameter for the non-invasive distinguishing between benign and malignant glottic lesions. Applied to the kymographic analysis using the high-speed videoendoscopy (HSV) By utilizing a support vector machine (SVM) classifier it achieved an AUC of 0.93 for identifying organic lesions and 0.83 for differentiating malignancies from benign lesions, outperforming traditional univariate threshold-based analyses. While no single parameter based on high-speed videoendoscopy (HSV) can definitively predict early glottic cancer, machine learning models which integrate multiple parameters, can further enhance diagnostic performance. The results of this study suggest that SAI, in combination with other kymographic parameters derived from the HSV, could serve as an important adjunct to histopathological evaluation, offering a non-invasive method for early detection and improved clinical decision-making.

**Supplementary Materials:** The following supporting information can be downloaded at: https://www.mdpi.com/article/10.3390/cancers17081376/s1, Supplementary S1—short-term kymographic analysis.

**Author Contributions:** Conceptualization, E.N.-B., W.P., A.K. and J.K.-O.; methodology, E.N.-B., W.P., A.K. and J.K.-O.; software, A.K. and J.K.-O.; validation, E.N.-B. and W.P.; formal analysis, M.M.P., A.K. and J.K.-O.; investigation, M.M.P., E.N.-B. and W.P.; resources, W.P.; data curation, M.M.P., E.N.-B. and W.P.; writing—original draft preparation, M.M.P.; writing—review and editing, E.N.-B., W.P. and A.K.; visualization A.K. and J.K.-O.; supervision, E.N.-B. and W.P.; project administration, M.M.P., E.N.-B. and W.P.; funding acquisition, W.P. All authors have read and agreed to the published version of the manuscript.

**Funding:** This research received no external funding.

**Institutional Review Board Statement:** All procedures performed in studies involving human participants were in accordance with the ethical standards of the institutional and national research committee and with the 1964 Helsinki Declaration and its later amendments or comparable ethical standards. Approval for this study was granted by the Ethical Committee of the Medical University of Lodz (decision no. RNN/96/20/KE 08/04/2020).

**Informed Consent Statement:** Written informed consent was obtained from all individual participants involved in the study.

**Data Availability Statement:** The data presented in this study are available on request from the corresponding author.

**Conflicts of Interest:** The authors declare no conflicts of interest.

## Abbreviations

The following abbreviations are used in this manuscript:

| | |
|---|---|
| SAI | Stiffness Asymmetry Index |
| HSV | High-Speed Videoendoscopy |
| TPR | True Positive Rate |
| FPR | False Positive Rate |
| ROC | Receiver Operating Characteristic |
| AUC | Area Under The Curve |
| SVM | Support Vector Machines |

SFFS Sequential Floating-Forward Search
MCT Multiple Comparisons Test
Abbreviations for parameters with description in Table 1

## References


1. Mody, M.D.; Rocco, J.W.; Yom, S.S.; Haddad, R.I.; Saba, N.F. Head and neck cancer. *Lancet* **2021**, *398*, 2289–2299. [CrossRef]
2. Laryngeal Cancer—Cancer Stat Facts. Available online: https://seer.cancer.gov/statfacts/html/laryn.html (accessed on 23 December 2024).
3. Arthur, C.; Huangfu, H.; Li, M.; Dong, Z.; Asamoah, E.; Shaibu, Z.; Zhang, D.; Ja, L.; Obwoya, R.T.; Zhang, C.; et al. The Effectiveness of White Light Endoscopy Combined With Narrow Band Imaging Technique Using Ni Classification in Detecting Early Laryngeal Carcinoma in 114 Patients: Our Clinical Experience. *J. Voice*, 2023; *Epub ahead of print*. [CrossRef]
4. Piazza, C.; Del Bon, F.; Peretti, G.; Nicolai, P. Narrow band imaging in endoscopic evaluation of the larynx. *Curr. Opin. Otolaryngol. Head Neck Surg.* **2012**, *20*, 472–476. [CrossRef]
5. Arens, C.; Piazza, C.; Andrea, M.; Dikkers, F.G.; Gi, R.E.A.T.P.; Voigt-Zimmermann, S.; Peretti, G. Proposal for a descriptive guideline of vascular changes in lesions of the vocal folds by the committee on endoscopic laryngeal imaging of the European Laryngological Society. *Eur. Arch. Oto-Rhino-Laryngol.* **2016**, *273*, 1207–1214. [CrossRef] [PubMed]
6. Tanaka, S.; Hirano, M. Fiberscopic estimation of vocal fold stiffness in vivo using the sucking method. *Arch. Otolaryngol. Head Neck Surg.* **1990**, *116*, 721–724. [CrossRef] [PubMed]
7. Tseng, W.; Chang, C.; Yang, T.; Hsiao, T. Estimating vocal fold stiffness: Using the relationship between subglottic pressure and fundamental frequency of phonation as an analog. *Clin. Otolaryngol.* **2020**, *45*, 40–46. [CrossRef] [PubMed]
8. Döllinger, M.; Gómez, P.; Patel, R.R.; Alexiou, C.; Bohr, C.; Schützenberger, A. Biomechanical simulation of vocal fold dynamics in adults based on laryngeal high-speed videoendoscopy. *PLoS ONE* **2017**, *12*, e0187486. [CrossRef]
9. Yamauchi, A.; Yokonishi, H.; Imagawa, H.; Sakakibara, K.-I.; Nito, T.; Tayama, N.; Yamasoba, T. Quantification of Vocal Fold Vibration in Various Laryngeal Disorders Using High-Speed Digital Imaging. *J. Voice* **2016**, *30*, 205–214. [CrossRef]
10. Sakakibara, K.I.; Imagawa, H.; Kimura, M.; Yokonishi, H.; Tayama, N. Modal analysis of vocal fold vibrations using laryngotopography. In Proceedings of the 11th Annual Conference of the International Speech Communication Association (INTERSPEECH 2010), Chiba, Japan, 26–30 September 2010; pp. 917–920.
11. Kaluza, J.; Niebudek-Bogusz, E.; Malinowski, J.; Strumillo, P.; Pietruszewska, W. Assessment of Vocal Fold Stiffness by Means of High-Speed Videolaryngoscopy with Laryngotopography in Prediction of Early Glottic Malignancy: Preliminary Report. *Cancers* **2022**, *14*, 4697. [CrossRef]
12. Kałuża, J.; Strumiłło, P.; Niebudek-Bogusz, E.; Pietruszewska, W. Preprocessing of Laryngeal Images from High-Speed Videoendoscopy. In *Information Technology in Biomedicine, Proceedings of the 9th International Conference, ITIB 2022, Kamień Śląski, Poland, 20–22 June 2022*; Springer: Cham, Switzerland, 2022; pp. 132–142.
13. Veltrup, R.; Kniesburges, S.; Semmler, M. Influence of Perspective Distortion in Laryngoscopy. *J. Speech Lang. Hearing Res.* **2023**, *66*, 3276–3289. [CrossRef]
14. Lechien, J.R.; Geneid, A.; Bohlender, J.E.; Cantarella, G.; Avellaneda, J.C.; Desuter, G.; Sjogren, E.V.; Finck, C.; Hans, S.; Hess, M.; et al. Consensus for voice quality assessment in clinical practice: Guidelines of the European Laryngological Society and Union of the European Phoniatricians. *Eur. Arch. Oto-Rhino-Laryngol.* **2023**, *280*, 5459–5473. [CrossRef]
15. Pietruszewska, W.; Just, M.; Morawska, J.; Malinowski, J.; Hoffman, J.; Racino, A.; Barańska, M.; Kowalczyk, M.; Niebudek-Bogusz, E. Comparative analysis of high-speed videolaryngoscopy images and sound data simultaneously acquired from rigid and flexible laryngoscope: A pilot study. *Sci. Rep.* **2021**, *11*, 20480. [CrossRef]
16. Vapnik, V.N. *The Nature of Statistical Learning Theory*; Springer: New York, NY, USA, 2000. [CrossRef]
17. Pudil, P.; Novovičová, J.; Kittler, J. Floating search methods in feature selection. *Pattern Recognit. Lett.* **1994**, *15*, 1119–1125. [CrossRef]
18. Yamauchi, A.; Imagawa, H.; Yokonishi, H.; Sakakibara, K.-I.; Tayama, N. Multivariate Analysis of Vocal Fold Vibrations on Various Voice Disorders Using High-Speed Digital Imaging. *Appl. Sci.* **2021**, *11*, 6284. [CrossRef]
19. Yamauchi, A.; Imagawa, H.; Yokonishi, H.; Sakakibara, K.-I.; Tayama, N. Multivariate Analysis of Vocal Fold Vibrations in Normal Speakers Using High-Speed Digital Imaging. *J. Voice* **2024**, *38*, 10–17. [CrossRef] [PubMed]
20. Tsuji, D.H.; Hachiya, A.; Dajer, M.E.; Ishikawa, C.C.; Takahashi, M.T.; Montagnoli, A.N. Improvement of Vocal Pathologies Diagnosis Using High-Speed Videolaryngoscopy. *Int. Arch. Otorhinolaryngol.* **2014**, *18*, 294–302. [CrossRef]
21. Krausert, C.R.; Olszewski, A.E.; Taylor, L.N.; McMurray, J.S.; Dailey, S.H.; Jiang, J.J. Mucosal wave measurement and visualization techniques. *J. Voice* **2011**, *25*, 395–405. [CrossRef]
22. Powell, M.E.; Deliyski, D.D.; Zeitels, S.M.; Burns, J.A.; Hillman, R.E.; Gerlach, T.T.; Mehta, D.D. Efficacy of Videostroboscopy and High-Speed Videoendoscopy to Obtain Functional Outcomes From Perioperative Ratings in Patients with Vocal Fold Mass Lesions. *J. Voice* **2020**, *34*, 769–782. [CrossRef]

23. Zacharias, S.R.C.; Deliyski, D.D.; Gerlach, T.T. Utility of Laryngeal High-Speed Videoendoscopy in Clinical Voice Assessment. *J. Voice* **2018**, *32*, 216. [CrossRef]
24. Malinowski, J.; Pietruszewska, W.; Kowalczyk, M.; Niebudek-Bogusz, E. Value of high-speed videoendoscopy as an auxiliary tool in differentiation of benign and malignant unilateral vocal lesions. *J. Cancer Res. Clin. Oncol.* **2024**, *150*, 10. [CrossRef]
25. Fehling, M.K.; Grosch, F.; Schuster, M.E.; Schick, B.; Lohscheller, J. Fully automatic segmentation of glottis and vocal folds in endoscopic laryngeal high-speed videos using a deep Convolutional LSTM Network. *PLoS ONE* **2020**, *15*, e0227791. [CrossRef]
26. Gandhi, S.; Bhatta, S.; Ganesuni, D.; Ghanpur, A.D.; Saindani, S.J. High-speed videolaryngoscopy in early glottic carcinoma patients following transoral CO2 LASER cordectomy. *Eur. Arch. Otorhinolaryngol.* **2021**, *278*, 1119–1127. [CrossRef] [PubMed]
27. Mehlum, C.S.; Rosenberg, T.; Groentved, A.M.; Dyrvig, A.-K.; Godballe, C. Can videostroboscopy predict early glottic cancer? A systematic review and meta-analysis. *Laryngoscope* **2016**, *126*, 2079–2084. [CrossRef]
28. Mehlum, C.S.; Kjaergaard, T.; Grøntved, Å.M.; Lyhne, N.M.; Jørkov AP, S.; Homøe, P.; Tvedskov, J.F.; Bork, K.H.; Möller, S.; Jørgensen, G.; et al. Value of pre- and intraoperative diagnostic methods in suspected glottic neoplasia. *Eur. Arch. Otorhinolaryngol.* **2020**, *277*, 207–215. [CrossRef] [PubMed]
29. Volgger, V.; Felicio, A.; Lohscheller, J.; Englhard, A.S.; Al-Muzaini, H.; Betz, C.S.; Schuster, M.E. Evaluation of the combined use of narrow band imaging and high-speed imaging to discriminate laryngeal lesions. *Lasers Surg. Med.* **2017**, *49*, 609–618. [CrossRef]
30. Zhao, W.; Zhi, J.; Zheng, H.; Du, J.; Wei, M.; Lin, P.; Li, L.; Wang, W. Construction of prediction model of early glottic cancer based on machine learning. *Acta Otolaryngol.* **2025**, *145*, 72–80. [CrossRef] [PubMed]
31. You, Z.; Han, B.; Shi, Z.; Zhao, M.; Du, S.; Yan, J.; Liu, H.; Hei, X.; Ren, X.; Yan, Y. Vocal cord leukoplakia classification using deep learning models in white light and narrow band imaging endoscopy images. *Head Neck* **2023**, *45*, 3129–3145. [CrossRef]
32. Wellenstein, D.J.; Woodburn, J.; Marres, H.A.M.; van den Broek, G.B. Detection of laryngeal carcinoma during endoscopy using artificial intelligence. *Head Neck* **2023**, *45*, 2217–2226. [CrossRef]
33. Syed, S.A.; Rashid, M.; Hussain, S. Meta-analysis of voice disorders databases and applied machine learning techniques. *Math. Biosci. Eng.* **2020**, *17*, 7958–7979. [CrossRef]

cancers

MDPI

*Article*

# Benign/Cancer Diagnostics Based on X-Ray Diffraction: Comparison of Data Analytics Approaches

**Alexander Alekseev [1,2], Viacheslav Shcherbakov [1], Oleksii Avdieiev [1], Sergey A. Denisov [1,3], Viacheslav Kubytskyi [1,4], Benjamin Blinchevsky [1], Sasha Murokh [1,5], Ashkan Ajeer [6], Lois Adams [6], Charlene Greenwood [6], Keith Rogers [7,8], Louise J. Jones [7,9], Lev Mourokh [7,10,*] and Pavel Lazarev [1,7]**

1 Matur UK Ltd., 5 New Street Square, London EC4A 3TW, UK; aalexeev@matur.co.uk (A.A.); viacheslav.s@matur.co.uk (V.S.); oavdieiev@matur.co.uk (O.A.); plazarev@matur.co.uk (P.L.)
2 Department of Physics and Technology, Karaganda Buketov University, Karaganda 100028, Kazakhstan
3 Institut de Chimie Physique, UMR8000, CNRS, Université Paris-Saclay, Bât. 349, 91405 Orsay, France
4 Laboratoire de Physique des 2 Infinis Irène Joliot-Curie, UMR9012, CNRS, Université Paris-Saclay, Bât. 209, 91405 Orsay, France
5 Stuyvesant High School, 345 Chambers Street, New York, NY 10282, USA
6 School of Chemical and Physical Sciences, Keele University, Keele ST5 5BG, UK; c.e.greenwood@keele.ac.uk (C.G.)
7 EosDx, Inc., 1455 Adams Drive, Menlo Park, CA 94025, USA
8 Shrivenham Campus, Cranfield University, Swindon SN6 8LA, UK; k.d.rogers@cranfield.ac.uk
9 Barts Cancer Institute, Queen Mary University of London, Charterhouse Square, London EC1M 6BQ, UK; l.j.jones@qmul.ac.uk
10 Physics Department, Queens College, City University of New York, 65-30 Kissena Blvd., Flushing, NY 11367, USA
* Correspondence: lev.murokh@qc.cuny.edu

**Simple Summary**

Breast cancer is the most frequent cancer among women. Currently, histopathological analysis of biopsies is performed for both malignant and benign samples, with no effective triage system to 'fast-track' potential malignant cases. We propose a complementary method of benign/cancer classification based on X-ray scattering. Using and comparing machine learning approaches, we examined over 6000 measurements of benign and cancerous samples from 211 patients, achieving excellent results in distinguishing malignant and benign conditions. This can lead to a significant reduction in the turnaround time for the histopathological analysis and earlier diagnostics of malignancy, with potential impact on the survival rate for breast cancer patients.

**Abstract**

**Background/Objectives:** With the number of detected breast cancer cases growing every year, there is a need to augment histopathological analysis with fast preliminary screening. We examine the feasibility of using X-ray diffraction measurements for this purpose. **Methods:** In this work, we obtained more than 6000 diffraction patterns from 211 patients and examined both standard and custom-developed methods, including Fourier coefficient analysis, for their interpretation. Various preprocessing steps and machine learning classifiers were compared to determine the optimal combination. **Results:** We demonstrated that benign and cancerous clusters are well separated, with specificity and sensitivity exceeding 0.9. For wide-angle scattering, the two-dimensional Fourier method is superior, while for small angles, the conventional analysis based on azimuthal integration of the images provides similar metrics. **Conclusions:** X-ray diffraction of biopsy tissues, supported by machine learning approaches to data analytics, can be an essential tool for pathological services. The method is rapid and inexpensive, providing excellent metrics for benign/cancer classification.

**Keywords:** structural biomarkers; X-ray diffraction; breast cancer diagnostics; machine learning; Fourier transformation

## 1. Introduction

Breast cancer is the most commonly diagnosed cancer among women worldwide. The Lancet Breast Cancer Commission [1] predicts that by 2040, the global incidence of new cases of breast cancer will be more than 3 million per year. In the UK alone, there are 56,800 new cases of breast cancer diagnosed each year, with 11,500 deaths annually [2]. The mortality rate has started to decrease recently [3], which can be attributed to progress in early diagnostics [4,5]. Any delay in cancer detection can be fatal for a patient. All cancers currently require a histopathological examination, but such a procedure also expects the exclusion of benign lesions. Across most services, biopsies with a benign diagnosis are eight times more likely than those with a malignant one. Regardless, all require the same input level, and currently, there is no effective triage system to 'fast-track' potential malignant cases. The diagnostic problem being addressed by this work presents itself as a significant research question, i.e., can new diagnostic methods be developed and introduced into clinical pathways to effectively reduce the interval between clinical presentation and diagnosis?

In an average NHS Trust, there are about 60,000 breast biopsies per year, the majority of which will be benign. This places an enormous burden on Pathology Departments, where only 3% of laboratories are currently fully staffed [6], contributing to significant delays in turnaround time (TAT). Thus, there is a real need to adopt a different approach to tissue diagnostics that can effectively triage samples at an early stage, allowing those with potentially life-threatening conditions to be fast-tracked and, ideally, offering early reassurance to those without significant diseases. This is a component of the diagnostic space that our work is addressing. The problem of minimizing presentation-to-diagnosis time in order to provide improved outcomes is ultimately the issue that the work focuses on. Our solution is a novel diagnostic probe that can deliver significantly enhanced intelligence for clinicians. The work described herein is a step towards this goal.

To address this, we have investigated the feasibility of using the structural biomarkers obtained from X-ray diffraction to rapidly distinguish between cancer and benign breast tissues. Previously, cancer-induced structural changes were examined in two distinct ranges of scattering angles. Small-angle X-ray scattering (SAXS) and wide-angle X-ray scattering (WAXS) are defined to cover the (overlapping) momentum transfer values of $0.1 < q < 5$ nm$^{-1}$ and $3 < q < 45$ nm$^{-1}$, respectively. SAXS probes, for example, modifications to collagen fibril repeat distances [7–10], alterations to the amorphous scattering profile [9–12], and disruption to triglyceride molecular packing [13,14]. For the latter, a diffraction maximum at $q = 1.5$ nm$^{-1}$ is characteristic of healthy tissue, and it has been shown [14] that this peak is absent in benign tissues. In contrast, WAXS addresses modifications to lipid and aqueous components [15–21]. Specifically, it has been shown [13,16] that in cancerous tissues, the intensity of a maximum peak at approximately $q = 14$ nm$^{-1}$ is reduced, while the intensity maximum at approximately $q = 20$ nm$^{-1}$ increases. The first feature is attributed to inter-fatty-acid molecular distances, while the second one is related to the oxygen–oxygen distance in the tetrahedral structure of water. The diminution of the 14 nm$^{-1}$ peak is caused by cancer-altered lipid metabolism, rendering it a potential structural biomarker for cancer.

In the current study, we revisit and extend the measurements of the Breast Cancer Now Biobank (BCNB) [22] samples previously reported in [23] to specifically address the benign/cancer classification and determine the optimal preprocessing and classification methods. We utilize three distinct data representations, one of which is based on the analysis of one-dimensional (1D) momentum transfer profiles obtained after azimuthal integration. This representation was employed in [23]. Another approach was introduced in [24] for XRD-based cancer detection in dogs' claws and implements the Fourier coefficients of this 1D profile. It was demonstrated in [25] for the same dataset of dogs' claws that 2D Fourier analysis of the XRD images, without azimuthal integration, provides better metrics, which is our third data representation method. Various data preprocessing steps are employed, some of which are standard, including principal component analysis (PCA), and some are custom-developed. We use several machine learning classifiers, including Logistic Regression, Random Forest, Support Vector Machine, K-Nearest Neighbor, Naive Bayes Classifier, Light Gradient-Boosting Machine, and XGBoost. The first five classifiers are taken from the scikit-learn library [26,27], while the last two are acquired from [28] and the XGBoost library [29,30], respectively. The code is organized into pipelines, which describe different combinations of preprocessing, processing, and classification steps.

Our analysis shows excellent cancer/benign discrimination, with many pipelines exhibiting a balanced accuracy exceeding 0.9 for patients. In this, the obtained classification metrics are better for the WAXS images. A comparison of the data representation methods demonstrates that the 2D Fourier coefficients have an advantage, whereas, for 1D representation, the conventional approach is preferable to the 1D Fourier transform.

## 2. Materials and Methods

### *2.1. Experimental Design*

#### 2.1.1. Breast Tissue Specimens

To test whether XRD could distinguish between cancer and benign tissue samples, we accessed ex vivo biopsy samples from the Breast Cancer Now Biobank (BCNB). Ethical approval for the project was obtained locally via Keele University (NS-210096) and for the collection and use of specimens via the BCNB (NRES Approval Number 23/EE/0229). These were fresh-frozen (FF) samples, approximately $10 \times 2 \times 2$ mm in size, taken from patients who consented to the BCNB. All cases underwent full histopathological diagnosis on H&E sections and were categorized into invasive cancer or benign lesions. The cancer cohort mainly consisted of invasive ductal carcinoma and invasive lobular carcinoma of different grades. The benign cohort includes various conditions, excluding fibroadenomas and macromastia. The total numbers of patients, samples, and WAXS and SAXS measurements are presented in Table 1. The latter are almost identical, except one more cancerous sample was measured 9 times with SAXS, and one more benign measurement was conducted using WAXS. We obtained two samples from most patients, with a few providing one, three, or four samples. Depending on the size of the sample, it was measured in 4, 5, or 9 points to assess the heterogeneity.

**Table 1.** Numbers of patients, samples, and measurements for WAXS/SAXS.

| | Train | | | Test | | | Total |
|---|---|---|---|---|---|---|---|
| | Benign | Cancer | Total | Benign | Cancer | Total | |
| Patients | 35 | 144 | 179 | 12 | 20 | 32 | 211 |
| Samples | 80 | 283/284 | 363/364 | 25 | 40 | 65 | 428/429 |
| Measurements | 623/622 | 1960/1969 | 2583/2591 | 208 | 256 | 464 | 3047/3055 |

Each tissue specimen was placed into a bespoke aluminum sample holder, 2 mm thick, utilizing a SPEX$^{TM}$ 6 μm thick mylar window film to seal and secure the tissue within a 5 mm aperture.

2.1.2. X-Ray Diffraction (XRD) Measurements

XRD measurements were conducted using a bespoke X-ray diffractometer engineered and built by EosDx, Inc. (Menlo Park, CA, USA), a US-based company developing X-ray scattering for medical diagnostics. The schematic of the device is presented in Figure 1. The radiation produced by the copper-based Incoatec Microfocus Source (Geesthacht, Germany) was collected using two multilayer curved mirror optics, resulting in a low-divergence, monochromatic beam with a wavelength of $\lambda = 0.154$ nm. The two-dimensional detector employed to record the X-ray scatter was a MiniPix SN1442 Si 500 µm detector (ADVACAM, Prague, Czech Republic) with a 256 × 256-pixel array and a 55 × 55 µm pixel size.

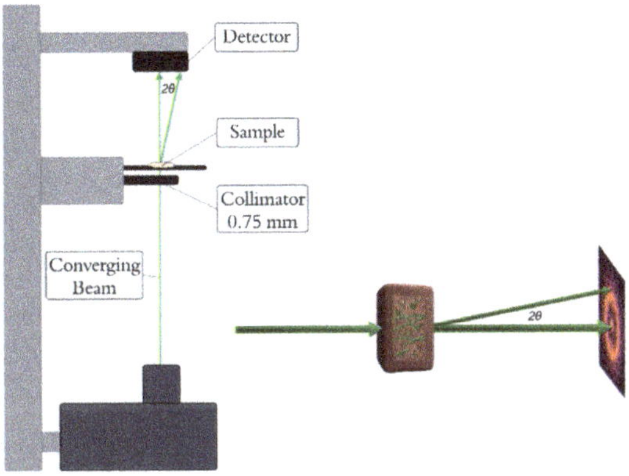


**Figure 1.** Schematic of the diffractometer.

Silver behenate powder (Thermoscientific® 045494.06, Heysham, Lancashire, UK) was scanned (utilizing the bespoke aluminum holders) to allow for accurate sample-to-detector distance calibration. The experimental data were stored as a 256 by 256 matrix of integers representing the photon counts. All the experiments were performed at room temperature (19 °C) under atmospheric pressure. To assess specimen heterogeneity, data were collected from several individual spots on each sample, from 4 to 9, depending on the size of the sample, which resulted in several diffractograms per specimen. The measurements were performed at two specific sample-to-detector distances to examine WAXS (2 cm) and SAXS (16 cm) specifically. Each diffractogram was collected for 1 min for SAXS and 30 s for WAXS, with a count time of 0.1 s. Examples of the XRD images are shown in Figure 2a,b.

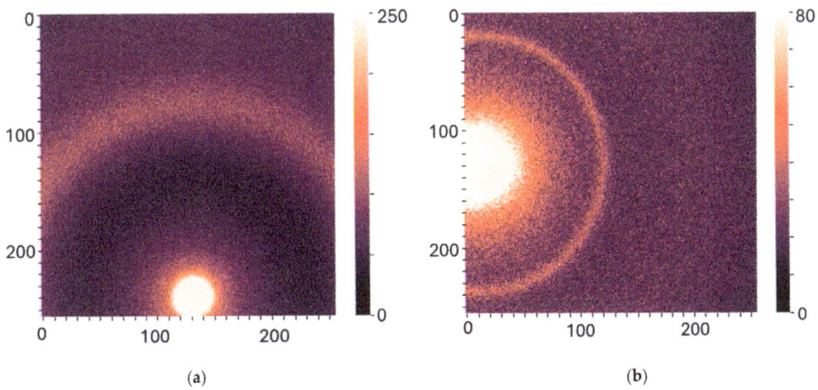


**Figure 2.** X-ray diffraction patterns for (**a**) WAXS and (**b**) SAXS. The labels on both axes are the pixel numbers.

### 2.2. Data Analysis

#### 2.2.1. Image Preprocessing

In total, 3047 WAXS and 3055 SAXS images for 47 benign and 164 cancer patients were collected and examined in this work. The raw XRD data files contained the intensities in the 256 × 256-pixel arrays. In the first preprocessing step, any faulty detector pixels (e.g., dead pixels) were removed.

The maximum difference in sample-to-detector distance, which influences calibration, was within 2.6%. For the 1D models, which include azimuthal integration, automatic calibration was performed using the open-source library PyFAI. For 2D data representation, this error was considered negligible, and no size calibration was performed.

Additional preprocessing steps for the 2D models included normalizing the images outside the primary beam region. Furthermore, to exclude the contributions of random features, the areas outside of the main patterns, which were similar for all images, were nullified. The preprocessed images are presented in Supplemental Materials, Figure S1a,b.

For 1D models, the azimuthal integration was performed using PyFAI to obtain an average radial profile starting from the beam position. It was subsequently represented in terms of the momentum transfer $q = (4\pi \sin\theta)/\lambda$, where $2\theta$ is the scattering angle, tan $2\theta$ is calculated as the ratio of the distances from the pixel to the beam center and from the sample to the detector, and $\lambda$ is the X-ray wavelength. To eliminate artifacts, the full $q$-range was limited to retain $3 \div 20$ nm$^{-1}$ for WAXS and $0.3 \div 3.7$ nm$^{-1}$ for SAXS. The obtained intensities were normalized. The representative curves are shown in Figure 3.

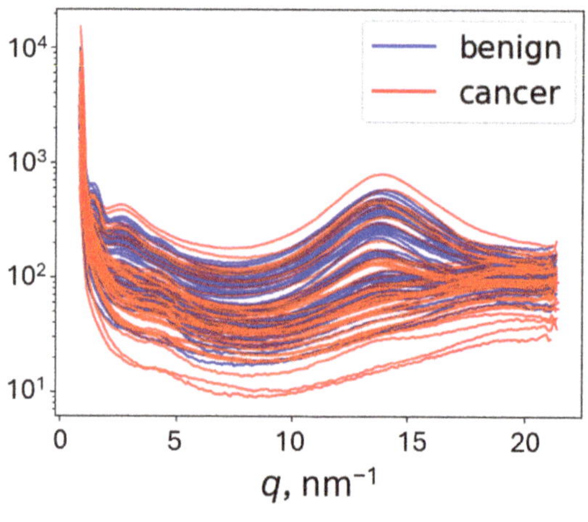


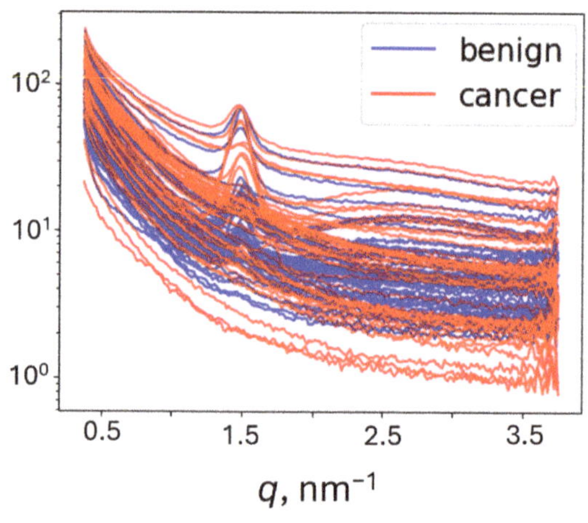


**Figure 3.** The intensity dependencies on the momentum transfer for benign and cancer samples, obtained after azimuthal integration of the XRD patterns measured at a (**a**) sample-to-detector distance of 2 cm (WAXS) and (**b**) sample-to-detector distance of 16 cm (SAXS).

#### 2.2.2. Fourier Coefficient Representation

Both 1D and 2D Fourier transformations were implemented to describe the initial XRD data. The 1D Fourier coefficients were calculated for the azimuthally integrated (*AzI*) curves in Figure 2 using either the Discrete Fourier Transformation implemented in the SciPy and NumPy libraries (*1DF*) or the custom procedure described in [23] (*1DFC*). The slope of the curve was removed for improved Fourier series convergence (*SR*).

The 2D Fourier coefficients (*2DF*) were calculated for the preprocessed XRD data (Figure S1a,b) using the two-dimensional Discrete Fourier Transformation functions provided by the

SciPy and NumPy libraries. This implemented preprocessing enabled analysis of the same area in 2D images, thereby enhancing the influence of cancer on the XRD pattern and reducing the impact of optical alignment. We tested different combinations of Fourier coefficient components: real parts (*Re*), imaginary parts (*Im*), amplitudes (*Am*), and phases (*Ph*).

To eliminate artifacts and accelerate processing, for some pipelines, we employed Low-Pass Fourier Filtration (LPF), which removed high-frequency coefficients. Specifically, for discriminant analysis, 30 coefficients were selected for each curve in the 1D case, and a 20th-order cutoff was implemented in the 2D case to retain only 1257 out of the total 65,536 coefficients.

#### 2.2.3. Measurements-to-Patients Transition

We examined two samples from most patients, with a few providing one, three, or four samples, and each sample was measured multiple times. The model was optimized using all measurements in the training dataset. Then, the class probability of each testing measurement was evaluated using the optimized model, which provided the decision threshold to achieve maximum balanced accuracy. Cancer and benign diagnoses were assigned for each measurement when the probability exceeded or fell below the threshold, respectively. The final diagnosis of a patient was established by averaging all predicted class probabilities for that patient and comparing them with the optimal decision threshold (Figure 4).

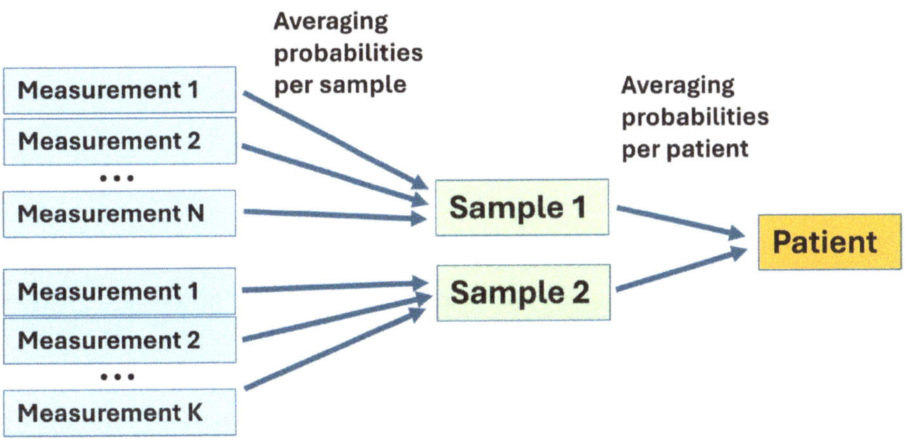


**Figure 4.** The measurements-to-patients transition procedure.

#### 2.2.4. Data Analysis Procedure and Machine Learning Methods

We used Visual Studio (version 1.97.2) and Jupyter Notebook (version 7.2.2) as the primary coding platforms. The majority of preprocessing methods were sourced from the scikit-learn library [27], from which most classifiers were also adopted, except for gradient-boosting algorithms [28–30]. Here, we provide only a brief description of the computation method, as the overall classification algorithm is the same as described in [25], where all details can be found. All preprocessing steps are optional, and they were combined differently in the pipelines. Abbreviations given here in italics will be used in the Results section to describe the pipelines. Optionally, the standardization (*STD*) of Fourier coefficients can be applied before classification. As a dimensionality reduction technique, principal component analysis (PCA) was used with three different numbers of principal components: 3 (*PCA_3*), 50 (*PCA_50*), and 100 (*PCA_100*). Two methods for removing the primary beam were implemented in the code. The beam was removed from the original

for the 1D approach are also reasonably good. The best 1D pipelines based on the 1D Fourier coefficients are ranked 84W–92W, with identical BA_P = 0.91 and AUC_P = 0.9–0.93 for the RF, XGB, KNN, and LGBM classifiers. The conventional 1D analysis is ranked higher, with 43W–48W, yielding BA_P = 0.93 and AUC_P = 0.9–0.93 for the RF, XGB, KNN, SVC, and LGBM classifiers. The LR classifier produces an even higher value, with AUC_P = 0.97. In general, BA_P for 99 out of 574 pipelines exceeds 0.9. For SAXS, the metrics for 2D and conventional 1D are similar, while the best 1D Fourier is ranked 25S, with BA_P = 0.88 and AUC_P = 0.86 for the LR classifier. The results for SAXS are worse than those for WAXS, with only 12 pipelines providing BA_P better than 0.9.

In the analysis of WAXS, the metrics for all classifiers are similar, except for GNB, which showed impressive results only when combined with PCA. It is worth noting that this is the only classifier to perform better with PCA, while all the others showed no improvement. For SAXS, LR and SVC perform better than the others, while KNN performs worse, with metrics sometimes improved by PCA.

To determine the causes of our <1 metrics, we examined the results of the best pipelines for all patients from the testing group. The resulting performances are displayed in Figure 6 for WAXS (a,b) and SAXS (c,d). In this, we also demonstrate the indirect performances of the best WAXS (SAXS) pipelines of all three types on SAXS (WAXS) datasets. They are shown in black, while the best direct ones are in green, blue, and red, depending on the pipeline type.

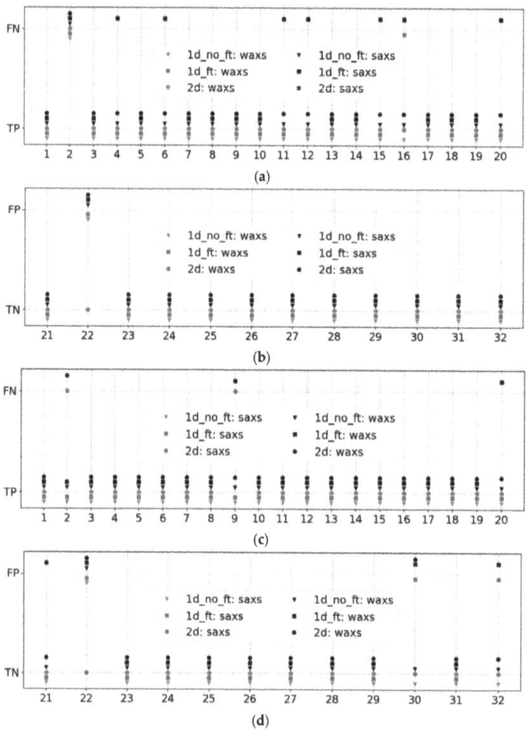


**Figure 6.** Performances of pipelines with best metrics for patients in (**a**) WAXS cancer, (**b**) WAXS benign, (**c**) SAXS cancer, and (**d**) SAXS benign. Cancer patients are numbered from 1 to 20, and benign patients are numbered from 21 to 32. FN, FP, TN, and TP indicate false negative, false positive, true negative, and true positive, respectively.

It is evident from this figure that pipelines with excellent performance on WAXS are not always reliable for the SAXS dataset, and vice versa. A good illustration is Figure 6a, which shows many false-negative results (black squares) for the indirect 1DF pipeline.

This analysis revealed two outstanding patients: Patient 2, with a cancer diagnosis, and Patient 22, with benign conditions. For Patient 2, all pipelines yielded false negatives in WAXS, as did the 2D pipelines in SAXS. For Patient 22, all pipelines, except the direct 2D pipeline, resulted in a false positive. New histopathological analyses were performed for these patients. For Patient 22, a fibroadenoma diagnosis was obtained, which explained the false-positive results, as fibroadenoma patients were not included in the benign training dataset. For Patient 2, the new tissue assessment described the tissue as only 5% invasive ductal carcinoma.

To gain a better understanding of Patient 2, we examined all the measurements of the corresponding samples, along with the class probabilities and optimal decision thresholds, as shown in Figure 7, for the best pipelines of all types.

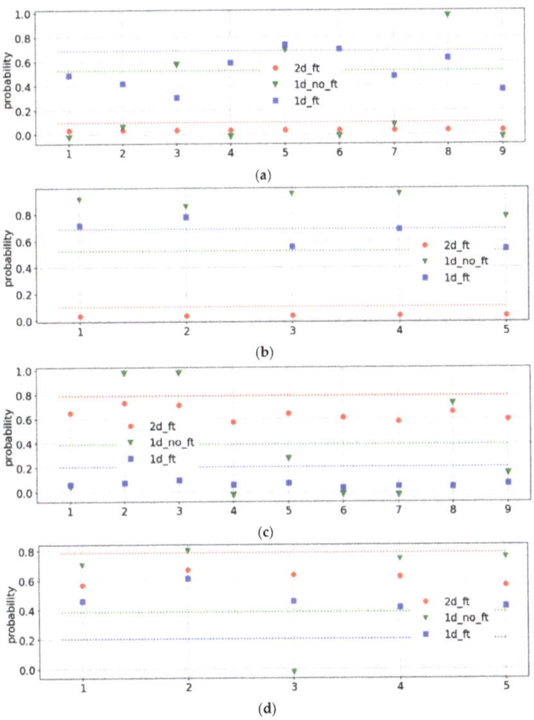


**Figure 7.** Performances of pipelines with best metrics for measurements of Patient 2 for (**a**) WAXS, sample 1, (**b**) WAXS, sample 2, (**c**) SAXS, sample 1, and (**d**) SAXS, sample 2. The horizontal lines are the optimal decision thresholds for the pipelines of the same color.

The two samples belonging to Patient 2 exhibit different behaviors seen in the 1D pipelines, while for the 2D pipelines, they are similar. The first sample, measured at nine points, was closer to the benign response, while the second sample was rather cancerous. However, even in the first sample, the class probabilities for different measurements vary from 0 to 1 in the conventional 1D classification. This agrees with a new tissue assessment reporting that this patient had an initial or even pre-cancerous stage; the tumor microenvironment is not entirely restructured by the cancer cells, and the diffraction patterns strongly depend on the point of measurement. Such non-uniformity of the X-ray scattering is especially seen in the SAXS measurements.

## 4. Discussion

In this study, we measured X-ray diffraction patterns from 211 patients with benign and malignant histological diagnoses. The measurements were performed in two separate ranges of the scattering momentum transfer, varying the sample-to-detector distance of the diffractometer. We compared various data analytics methods with different sets of preprocessing steps and machine learning classifiers (pipelines). We achieved excellent benign/cancer classification, with more than a hundred pipelines having balanced accuracy exceeding 0.9. These results are significantly better than those previously obtained in [23] for part of the dataset. However, it is worth noting that for the present paper, we excluded the "healthy" samples derived from cosmetic procedures and benign samples with confirmed diagnoses of fibroadenoma and macromastia.

We compared three different data representations and demonstrated that the custom-developed approach, based on the 2D Fourier coefficients [25], yields better metrics for wide-angle scattering. For small angles, the results obtained by this approach are similar to those obtained by the conventional method based on azimuthal integration. At the same time, using the Fourier transformation for the examination of the 1D curves [24] does not appear to be beneficial, as the metrics are worse. The standard and custom-developed Fourier transformation procedures produced identical results. Generally, the classification performs better for WAXS measurements than for SAXS.

We also compared various machine learning classifiers and demonstrated that the results are comparable, with minor exceptions. One such exception is the performance of the Logistic Regression. In [25], where X-ray diffraction of dogs' claws was examined, this classifier was worse than any of the others. Here, it provides improved metrics, especially in the SAXS range. A possible explanation is that cancer and benign clusters are well defined, in contrast to dogs' claws, and the straightforward separation using Logistic Regression works well.

We also investigated the reasons why our analysis was non-ideal and identified two outliers in the test dataset, for which almost all pipelines produced either a false negative (for the cancer patient) or a false positive (for the benign patient). A new histopathological tissue assessment revealed that the benign patient had a fibroadenoma, which was an exclusion criterion for the training dataset; therefore, these data do not belong to either of the established clusters. For the data of the second anomalous patient, a similar new tissue assessment showed that this is only 5% invasive ductal carcinoma. A more scrutinized examination of the two samples belonging to this patient revealed the non-uniformity of results between the samples and even within different positions on the same sample. This is expected, as the cancer-induced structural changes have not yet extended to the macroscopic scale in such patients.

The revealed heterogeneity informs us regarding one of the future improvements of our method. In the present work, we employed simple averaging of the results from different measurements and samples, as shown in Figure 4. However, for non-conclusive cases, a more advanced weighted approach could be used. Another improvement can be the inclusion of healthy samples and patients with fibroadenoma and macromastia. In this case, the binary classification would be replaced with a multiclass classification, as several clusters are expected. However, we should emphasize that the present work is only the first step, and further research is necessary with greatly enhanced statistics.

## 5. Conclusions

Our results clearly showed that cancer-induced structural biomarkers can be successfully revealed by X-ray diffraction of human breast tissues. Our prototype measurement system features a variable sample-to-detector distance, enabling it to accommodate a range of momentum transfer values from the SAXS to the WAXS regions. Such measurements probe different independent molecular components of tissues and, therefore, complement each other.

In the present work, we developed and compared various data analytics approaches, which include both conventional 1D data representation based on the azimuthal integration of the diffraction patterns and 1D and 2D Fourier transformations. We obtained excellent performance metrics, especially with 2D Fourier coefficients in the WAXS range. Our measurements and data analysis are fast and inexpensive, making X-ray diffraction a valuable tool for pathological laboratories. Thus, this work makes a significant contribution to the steps required in the development and ultimate deployment of diffraction-based technologies to address the issue of minimizing presentation-to-diagnosis periods. In particular, it identifies optimal data reduction and analysis protocols. The work also provides valuable data and analysis approaches for other research groups studying the exploitation of X-ray scatter signatures for medical diagnostics.

**Supplementary Materials:** The following supporting information can be downloaded at https://www.mdpi.com/article/10.3390/cancers17101662/s1: Table S1: List of abbreviations; Figure S1: The pre-processed images: (a) WAXS and (b) SAXS.

**Author Contributions:** Conceptualization, L.J.J., L.M. and P.L.; methodology, A.A. (Alexander Alekseev), O.A., A.A. (Ashkan Ajeer), C.G., K.R. and P.L.; software, A.A. (Alexander Alekseev), V.S., O.A., S.A.D., V.K., B.B. and S.M.; validation, A.A. (Alexander Alekseev), K.R., L.J.J., L.M. and P.L.; formal analysis, A.A. (Alexander Alekseev) and L.M.; investigation, A.A. (Alexander Alekseev), V.S., O.A., S.A.D., V.K., B.B., S.M., A.A. (Ashkan Ajeer), L.A. and C.G.; resources, C.G., L.J.J. and P.L.; data curation, A.A. (Alexander Alekseev), V.S., O.A., S.A.D., V.K., B.B. and A.A. (Ashkan Ajeer); writing—original draft preparation, A.A. (Alexander Alekseev), L.J.J. and L.M.; writing—review and editing, A.A. (Alexander Alekseev), V.S., V.K., C.G., K.R., L.J.J. and L.M.; visualization, A.A. (Alexander Alekseev), S.M. and L.M.; supervision, C.G., K.R., L.M. and P.L.; project administration, C.G., L.J.J. and P.L. All authors have read and agreed to the published version of the manuscript.

**Funding:** This research received no external funding.

**Institutional Review Board Statement:** Tissue was collected under NRES Approval number 23/EE/0229, approved 21 November 2023, with university ethics approval granted for this research (NS-210096).

**Informed Consent Statement:** Informed consent was obtained from all subjects involved in the study by the Breast Cancer Now Biobank.

**Data Availability Statement:** The files with the XRD patterns for the training and test datasets, as well as the complete tables with sets of metrics obtained from different approaches, are available at https://zenodo.org/records/15129858 (published 3 April 2025). The codes are available upon request.

**Acknowledgments:** The authors wish to acknowledge the role of the Breast Cancer Now Tissue Bank in collecting and making available the samples used in the generation of this publication, and the patients who donated to the Bank. This work acknowledges the support of the National Institute for Health and Care Research Barts Biomedical Research Centre (NIHR203330), a delivery partnership of Barts Health NHS Trust, Queen Mary University of London, St George's University Hospitals NHS Foundation Trust, and St George's University of London.

**Conflicts of Interest:** P.L. is a shareholder of Matur UK, Ltd. and EosDx, Inc. A.Al., V.S., O.A., S.D., V.K., B.B., and S.M. are consultants for Matur UK, Ltd. K.R., L.J., and L.M. are consultants for EosDx,

Inc. The remaining authors declare that the research was conducted in the absence of any commercial or financial relationships that could be construed as a potential conflict of interest.

## References


1. Coles, C.E.; Earl, H.; Anderson, B.O.; Barrios, C.H.; Bienz, M.; Bliss, J.M.; Cameron, D.A.; Cardoso, F.; Cui, W.; Francis, P.A.; et al. The *Lancet* Breast Cancer Commission. *Lancet* **2024**, *403*, 1895–1950. [CrossRef] [PubMed]
2. Available online: https://www.cancerresearchuk.org/health-professional/cancer-statistics/statistics-by-cancer-type/breast-cancer (accessed on 18 March 2025).
3. Siegel, R.L.; Giaquinto, A.N.; Jemal, A. Cancer statistics, 2024. *CA Cancer J. Clin.* **2024**, *74*, 12–49. [CrossRef]
4. Migowski, A. Early detection of breast cancer and the interpretation of results of survival studies. *Cienc. Saude Coletiva* **2015**, *20*, 1309. [CrossRef] [PubMed]
5. Taylor, C.; McGale, P.; Probert, J.; Broggio, J.; Charman, J.; Darby, S.C.; Kerr, A.J.; Whelan, T.; Cutter, D.J.; Mannu, G.; et al. Breast cancer mortality in 500,000 women with early invasive breast cancer diagnosed in England, 1993–2015: Population based observational cohort study. *BMJ* **2023**, *381*, e074684. [CrossRef] [PubMed]
6. Available online: https://www.rcpath.org/discover-pathology/public-affairs/the-pathology-workforce.html (accessed on 18 March 2025).
7. Lewis, R.A.; Rogers, K.D.; Hall, C.J.; Towns-Andrews, E.; Slawson, S.; Evans, A.; Pinder, S.E.; Ellis, I.O.; Boggis, C.R.M.; Hufton, A.P.; et al. Breast cancer diagnosis using scattered X-rays. *J. Synchrotron Rad.* **2000**, *7*, 348–352. [CrossRef]
8. Fernandez, M.; Keyrilainen, J.; Serimaa, R.; Torkkeli, M.; Karjalainen-Lindsberg, M.-L.; Tenhunen, M.; Thomlinson, W.; Urban, V.; Suortti, P. Small-angle x-ray scattering studies of human breast tissue samples. *Phys. Med. Biol.* **2002**, *47*, 577–592. [CrossRef]
9. Sidhu, S.; Siu, K.K.W.; Falzon, G.; Nazaretian, S.; Hart, S.A.; Fox, J.G.; Susil, B.J.; Lewis, R.A. X-ray scattering for classifying tissue types associated with breast disease. *Med. Phys.* **2008**, *35*, 4660–4670. [CrossRef]
10. Conceição, A.L.; Antoniassi, M.; Poletti, M.E. Analysis of breast cancer by small angle X-ray scattering. *Analyst* **2009**, *134*, 1077–1082. [CrossRef]
11. Sidhu, S.; Siu, K.K.W.; Falzon, G.; Hart, S.A.; Fox, J.G.; Lewis, R.A. Mapping structural changes in breast tissue disease using x-ray scattering. *Med. Phys.* **2009**, *36*, 3211–3217. [CrossRef]
12. Conceiçao, A.L.C.; Antoniassi, M.; Geraldelli, W.; Poletti, M.E. Mapping transitions between healthy and pathological lesions in human breast tissues by diffraction enhanced imaging computed tomography (DEI-CT) and small angle x-ray scattering (SAXS). *Radiat. Phys. Chem.* **2014**, *95*, 313–316. [CrossRef]
13. Conceicao, A.L.C.; Meehan, K.; Antoniassi, M.; Piacenti-Silva, M.; Poletti, M.E. The influence of hydration on the architectural rearrangement of normal and neoplastic human breast tissues. *Heliyon* **2019**, *5*, e01219. [CrossRef] [PubMed]
14. Mohd Sobri, S.N.; Abdul Sani, S.F.; Sabtu, S.N.; Looi, L.M.; Chiew, S.F.; Pathmanathan, D.; Chio-Srichan, S.; Bradley, D.A. Structural Studies of Epithelial Mesenchymal Transition Breast Tissues. *Sci. Rep.* **2020**, *10*, 1997. [CrossRef] [PubMed]
15. Kidane, G.; Speller, R.D.; Royle, G.J.; Hanby, A.M. X-ray scatter signatures for normal and neoplastic breast tissues. *Phys. Med. Biol.* **1999**, *44*, 1791. [CrossRef]
16. Poletti, M.E.; Gonçalves, O.D.; Mazzaro, I. X-ray scattering from human breast tissues and breast-equivalent materials. *Phys. Med. Biol.* **2002**, *47*, 47–63. [CrossRef]
17. Oliveira, O.R.; Conceiçao, A.L.C.; Cunha, D.M.; Poletti, M.E.; Pela, C.A. Identification of neoplasias of breast tissues using a powder diffractometer. *J. Radiat. Res.* **2008**, *49*, 527–532. [CrossRef]
18. Conceicao, A.L.C.; Antoniassi, M.; Poletti, M.E. Assessment of the differential linear coherent scattering coefficient of biological samples. *Nucl. Instr. Meth. Phys. Res. A* **2010**, *619*, 67–70. [CrossRef]
19. Griffiths, J.A.; Royle, G.J.; Hanby, A.M.; Horrocks, J.A.; Bohndiek, S.E.; Speller, R.D. Correlation of energy dispersive diffraction signatures and microCT of small breast tissue samples with pathological analysis. *Phys. Med. Biol.* **2007**, *52*, 6151–6164. [CrossRef]
20. Cunha, D.M.; Oliveira, O.R.; Pérez, C.A.; Poletti, M.E. X-ray scattering profiles of some normal and malignant human breast tissues. *X-ray Spectrom.* **2006**, *35*, 370–374. [CrossRef]
21. Conceicao, A.L.C.; Antoniassi, M.; Cunha, D.M.; Ribeiro-Silva, A.; Poletti, M.E. Multivariate analysis of the scattering profiles of healthy and pathological human breast tissues. *Nucl. Instr. Meth. Phys. Res. A* **2011**, *652*, 870–873. [CrossRef]
22. Available online: https://breastcancernow.org/our-research/information-for-researchers/apply-to-our-biobank/ (accessed on 18 March 2025).
23. Denisov, S.; Blinchevsky, B.; Friedman, J.; Gerbelli, B.; Ajeer, A.; Adams, L.; Greenwood, C.; Rogers, K.; Mourokh, L.; Lazarev, P. Vitacrystallography: Structural Biomarkers of Breast Cancer Obtained by X-ray Scattering. *Cancers* **2024**, *16*, 2499. [CrossRef]
24. Alekseev, A.; Yuk, D.; Lazarev, A.; Labelle, D.; Mourokh, L.; Lazarev, P. Canine Cancer Diagnostics by X-ray Diffraction of Claws. *Cancers* **2024**, *16*, 2422. [CrossRef] [PubMed]
25. Alekseev, A.; Avdieiev, O.; Murokh, S.; Yuk, D.; Lazarev, A.; Labelle, D.; Mourokh, L.; Lazarev, P. Fourier Transformation-Based Analysis of X-Ray Diffraction Pattern of Keratin for Cancer Detection. *Crystals* **2025**, *15*, 57. [CrossRef]

26. Pedregosa, F.; Varoquaux, G.; Gramfort, A.; Michel, V.; Thirion, B.; Grisel, O.; Blondel, M.; Prettenhofer, P.; Weiss, R.; Dubourg, V.; et al. Scikit-learn: Machine learning in python. *J. Mach. Learn. Res.* **2011**, *12*, 2825–2830.
27. Available online: https://scikit-learn.org/stable/ (accessed on 18 March 2025).
28. Available online: https://lightgbm.readthedocs.io/en/stable/ (accessed on 18 March 2025).
29. Chen, T.; Guestrin, C. Xgboost: A scalable tree boosting system. In Proceedings of the 22nd ACM SIGKDD International Conference on Knowledge Discovery and Data Mining, San Francisco, CA, USA, 13–17 August 2016; Association for Computing Machinery: New York, NY, USA, 2016; pp. 785–794.
30. Available online: https://xgboost.readthedocs.io/en/stable/ (accessed on 18 March 2025).

*cancers*

MDPI

*Article*

# Optimizing One-Sample Tests for Proportions in Single- and Two-Stage Oncology Trials

**Alan David Hutson**

Roswell Park Comprehensive Cancer Center, Department of Biostatistics and Bioinformatics, Elm and Carlton Streets, Buffalo, NY 14623, USA; alan.hutson@roswellpark.org

**Simple Summary**

Phase II oncology trials often use single-arm designs when randomized trials are too expensive or impractical, such as in rare diseases. These trials typically test whether a treatment's success rate exceeds a specified benchmark. Standard statistical methods, like the exact binomial test or Simon's two-stage design, are commonly used but tend to be conservative, often underestimating the actual probability of incorrectly rejecting a true null hypothesis (Type I error). To address this, a new method is proposed that blends the binomial distribution with simulated normal data to create an unbiased estimate of treatment success. This convolution-based method improves the precision of Type I error control and can lead to more efficient trial designs. It also introduces a new two-stage design that includes an early stopping point for futility, offering flexibility and reduced sample sizes without compromising statistical rigor. Compared to traditional methods, this approach can lower the cost and shorten the duration of trials, making it a promising tool for early-stage oncology research.

**Abstract**

Background/Objectives: Phase II oncology trials often rely on single-arm designs to test $H_0 : \pi = \pi_0$ versus $H_a : \pi > \pi_0$, especially when randomized trials are infeasible due to cost or disease rarity. Traditional approaches, such as the exact binomial test and Simon's two-stage design, tend to be conservative, with actual Type I error rates falling below the nominal $\alpha$ due to the discreteness of the underlying binomial distribution. This study aims to develop a more efficient and flexible method that maintains accurate Type I error control in such settings. Methods: We propose a convolution-based method that combines the binomial distribution with a simulated normal variable to construct an unbiased estimator of $\pi$. This method is designed to precisely control the Type I error rate while enabling more efficient trial designs. We derive its theoretical properties and assess its performance against traditional exact tests in both one-stage and two-stage trial designs. Results: The proposed method results in more efficient designs with reduced sample sizes compared to standard approaches, without compromising the control of Type I error rates. We introduce a new two-stage design incorporating interim futility analysis and compare it with Simon's design. Simulations and real-world examples demonstrate that the proposed approach can significantly lower trial cost and duration. Conclusions: This convolution-based approach offers a flexible and efficient alternative to traditional methods for early-phase oncology trial design. It addresses the conservativeness of existing designs and provides practical benefits in terms of resource use and study timelines.

**Keywords:** perturbation test; exact binomial test; small-sample power; clinical trial

## 1. Introduction

Common designs for phase II oncology trials typically focus on testing the hypothesis $H_0 : \pi = \pi_0$ versus $H_a : \pi > \pi_0$ in a one-arm non-randomized setting. Although randomized trials are generally preferred, considerations such as cost, feasibility, and the rarity of certain cancer types often necessitate the use of single-arm designs. The estimated per-patient cost of conducting an oncology clinical trial was approximately $59,500, as reported by Batelle in 2013 [1]. More recent studies, particularly those involving cellular therapies, report substantially higher costs, in some cases exceeding $500,000 per treatment cycle [2–4]. Consequently, there is a critical need to optimize both phase II and phase III randomized trial designs to shorten trial duration and reduce required sample sizes. These efforts not only address escalating costs but also aim to expedite the availability of effective therapies to cancer patients. The focus of this work is towards optimizing phase II one-arm oncology trials with a binary endpoint in terms of reduced sample size and increased efficiency.

Commonly employed binary endpoints in phase II trials include objective response, complete response, and progression-free, event-free, or overall survival at fixed time points, such as 6 months or 1 year. A key feature of non-randomized, single-arm phase II trials is that, in many cancer indications, the standard-of-care population response rate is sufficiently well-characterized to serve as a comparator. If no promising signal is observed, further development, including progression to a randomized phase II or III trial, is typically not pursued.

In single-stage designs, the hypothesis about a rate or proportion, $H_0 : \pi = \pi_0$ versus $H_a : \pi > \pi_0$, is most often tested using an exact binomial test, where the Type I error rate $\leq \alpha$. In contrast, one-arm two-stage designs commonly employ Simon's two-stage design [5], using either the minimax or optimal design configurations. The minimax design minimizes the total sample size, while the optimal design minimizes the expected sample size under the null hypothesis, where with the constraints are that the Type I error rate $\leq \alpha$ and the Type II error rate $\leq \beta$. Both designs incorporate an interim futility analysis at a predetermined sample size to allow early termination for lack of efficacy. Historically, it is noteworthy that very similar sampling schemes were developed decades earlier in the field of quality control, referred to as double sampling plans [6], with Simon's two-stage design representing a special case of these earlier methods [7].

The issue with both single-stage and two-stage designs is that the exact Type I error rate is often considerably lower than the desired Type I error rate $\alpha$ and the desired power is often larger than the desired power value $1 - \beta$, due to the discreteness of the underlying binomial distribution under both the null and alternative hypotheses for a given design. This phenomenon is illustrated in the so-called saw-tooth plots in Figure 1, which display the exact Type I error across a range of potential null values for $\pi_0$ with sample sizes $n = 10, 20, 30, 40$. As a result, these tests can be conservative in certain scenarios where the exact Type I error rate falls substantially below the target level $\alpha$.

One approach to mitigate this conservatism is to incorporate a continuity correction [8]; however, this does not eliminate the saw-tooth behavior in Type I error control. Similarly, the power function may also exhibit a saw-tooth pattern and can be non-monotonic [9]. For a fixed sample size $n$, there are $n$ discrete values of $\pi_0$ corresponding to $k = 1, 2, \ldots, n$ ($k = 0$ is infeasible), at which the Type I error equals $\alpha$, given by

$$\pi_0 = I_{\alpha}^{-1}(k, n - k + 1), \tag{1}$$

where $I^{-1}$ is the inverse regularized incomplete beta function.

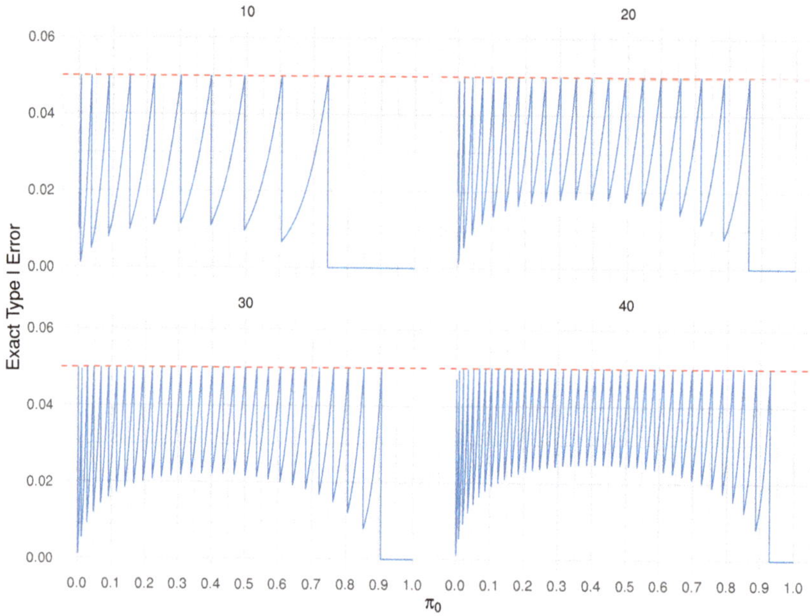


**Figure 1.** Type I error control for exact binomial test as a function of $\pi_0$ values, $n = 10, 20, 30, 40$.

Interestingly, Simon's two-stage design can exhibit the same phenomenon, where the exact Type I error rate is often much lower than the derired Type I error rate $\alpha$. In this case, however, we cannot produce a saw-tooth plot as a function of $\pi_0$ alone, since Simon's two-stage design also depends on the choice of the alternative response rate, denoted $\pi_1 (> \pi_0)$. In Figure 2, we present the exact Type I error rate and power for testing $H_0 : \pi = \pi_0$ versus $H_a : \pi > \pi_0$, with $\pi_0 = 0.1$ and $\pi_1$ varying from 0.19 to 0.8, while fixing $\alpha = 0.05$ and power = 0.80 for the minimax design. As $\pi_1$ increases, the required total sample size decreases, thus reducing the dimensionality of the sample space for design choices. In fact, for this example, there are very few instances where the exact Type I error rate approaches the nominal $\alpha$. For example, when $\pi_1 = 0.35$, the exact Type I error rate is 0.027 with a final stage sample size of $n = 18$. Increasing $\pi_1$ to 0.36 raises the exact Type I error rate to 0.044, with a corresponding final stage sample size of $n = 14$. For smaller values of $n$, the exact Type I error rate can drop as low as 0.015. Similarly, as the sample size decreases with increasing $\pi_1$, the exact power may deviate considerably from the target power.

In this note, we illustrate how a straightforward convolution of a binomial random variable with a simulated normal random variable enables the construction of an unbiased estimator for the rate parameter $\pi$, and facilitates inference for $H_0 : \pi = \pi_0$ versus $H_a : \pi > \pi_0$ with precise Type I error control. This in turn can reduce sample size requirements for both one-stage and two-stage designs.

In Section 2, we define the convolution estimator, derive its density and distribution functions, outline key theoretical properties including its expectation and variance, and present a toy example to demonstrate the $p$-value calculation.

We then provide a detailed comparison of the new convolution-based test with the exact binomial test in terms of Type I error control and power. In Section 3, we introduce a new two-stage design with a futility stopping rule that also achieves precise Type I error control. A direct comparison between the convolution-based two-stage design and Simon's two-stage design is presented.

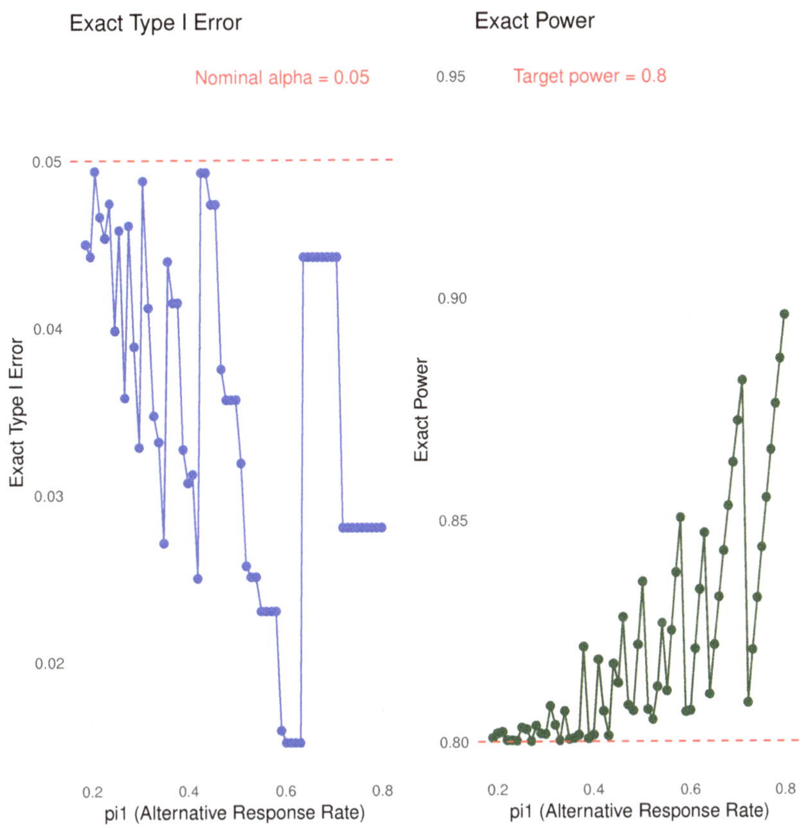


**Figure 2.** Type I error control and power for the mimimax Simon's two-stage design as a function of $\pi_0 = 0.1$ and $\pi_1 = 0.19$ to 0.80.

In Section 4, we provide real-world examples of both one-stage and two-stage designs, demonstrating how the convolution-based approach can reduce the cost and duration of clinical trials based on published design parameters. We conclude with final remarks.

## 2. Convolution Estimator

Our approach for constructing a test of the hypothesis $H_0 : \pi = \pi_0$ versus $H_1 : \pi > \pi_0$, with precise Type I error control, utilizes a convolution-based method, in which synthetic continuous noise is added to discrete binomial data. Specifically, let $Y \sim \text{Binomial}(n, \pi)$ denote the binomial response over $n$ subjects, where $\pi$ is the success probability. Let $X \sim N(0, h)$ be an independent normal random variable with mean 0 and standard deviation $h$. We define the continuous variable $Z = Y + X$ and derive its probability density and cumulative distribution functions.

The probability density function (PDF) of Z, denoted $f_Z(z)$, is obtained by convolving the binomial probability mass function of $Y$ with the normal density of $X$. Since $Y$ is discrete and $X$ is continuous, this results in a finite mixture of normal densities:

$$f_Z(z) = \frac{1}{h\sqrt{2\pi}} \sum_{k=0}^{n} \binom{n}{k} \pi^k (1-\pi)^{n-k} \exp\left(-\frac{(z-k)^2}{2h^2}\right), \quad z \in \mathbb{R}.$$

Each component of the mixture is centered at $k = 0, 1, \ldots, n$, with mixing weights given by the binomial probabilities $\binom{n}{k}\pi^k(1-\pi)^{n-k}$.

Similarly, the cumulative distribution function (CDF) of $Z$, denoted $F_Z(z) = P(Z \leq z)$, is derived by conditioning on the values of $Y$:

$$F_Z(z) = \sum_{k=0}^{n} \binom{n}{k} \pi^k (1-\pi)^{n-k} \Phi\left(\frac{z-k}{h}\right), \quad z \in \mathbb{R}, \tag{2}$$

where $\Phi(u)$ is the standard normal CDF defined as

$$\Phi(u) = \int_{-\infty}^{u} \frac{1}{\sqrt{2\pi}} e^{-t^2/2}\, dt.$$

To understand the properties of the test statistic, we compare the moments of $Y$ and $Z$. The expectation and variance of $Y$ are given by

$$E[Y] = n\pi, \qquad \mathrm{Var}(Y) = n\pi(1-\pi).$$

Since $Y$ and $X$ are independent, the corresponding moments of $Z = Y + X$ follow directly:

$$E[Z] = E[Y+X] = E[Y] + E[X] = n\pi + 0 = n\pi,$$

$$\mathrm{Var}(Z) = \mathrm{Var}(Y+X) = \mathrm{Var}(Y) + \mathrm{Var}(X) = n\pi(1-\pi) + h^2.$$

Thus, the mean of $Z$ remains identical to that of $Y$, while the variance of $Z$ is increased by an additive term $h^2$, capturing the additional variability introduced by the normal perturbation. Throughout this note, we fix the value of $h = 1/100$. Although this results in only a modest increase in the variance of $Z$ we will demonstrate that this small adjustment is sufficient to produce tests with substantially improved power while maintaining the precise Type I error level.

To test $H_0 : \pi = \pi_0$ against $H_1 : \pi > \pi_0$ at significance level $\alpha$, we reject $H_0$ if $Z > c$, where the critical value $c$ is chosen to satisfy

$$1 - \sum_{k=0}^{n} \binom{n}{k} \pi_0^k (1-\pi_0)^{n-k} \Phi\left(\frac{c-k}{h}\right) = \alpha. \tag{3}$$

The solution for $c$ is via numerical methods. Similarly, the $p$-value is given by

$$p = 1 - F_{Z|\pi=\pi_0}(z) = 1 - \sum_{k=0}^{n} \binom{n}{k} \pi_0^k (1-\pi_0)^{n-k} \Phi\left(\frac{z-k}{h}\right), \tag{4}$$

where $z$ is the value of the observed convolution-based test statistic.

Under the alternative hypothesis $H_1 : \pi = \pi_1 > \pi_0$, the corresponding CDF is

$$F_{Z|\pi=\pi_1}(z) = \sum_{k=0}^{n} \binom{n}{k} \pi_1^k (1-\pi_1)^{n-k} \Phi\left(\frac{z-k}{h}\right),$$

and the power of the test at $\pi = \pi_1$ is given by

$$\mathrm{Power}(\pi_1) = 1 - \sum_{k=0}^{n} \binom{n}{k} \pi_1^k (1-\pi_1)^{n-k} \Phi\left(\frac{c-k}{h}\right). \tag{5}$$

### 2.1. Toy Example

We simulated the random variables $Y \sim \text{Binomial}(n = 20, \pi = 0.3)$ and $X \sim \mathcal{N}(0, h^2)$ with $h = \frac{1}{100}$, and computed $Z = X + Y$. For each run, we calculated the convolution-based $p$-value and the exact binomial $p$-value testing $H_0 : \pi = \pi_0$ vs. $H_1 : \pi > \pi_0$.

We see from Table 1 that the convolution-based $p$-values are consistently close to the exact binomial $p$-values, but tend to be slightly smaller due to the smoothing effect introduced by the normal perturbation $X$. The addition of this small normal noise transforms the discrete binomial distribution into a continuous mixture distribution, which leads to slightly different tail probabilities. For runs with larger observed binomial counts $y$, both the convolution and exact tests yield smaller $p$-values, indicating stronger evidence against the null hypothesis $H_0 : \pi = \pi_0$.

**Table 1.** Comparison of mixture-based and exact binomial $p$-values over three simulations.

| Run | $y$ | $x$ | $z = x + y$ | $F_Z(z)$ | Convoution $p$-Value | Exact Binomial $p$-Value |
|---|---|---|---|---|---|---|
| 1 | 4 | 0.007968 | 4.007968 | 0.5832 | 0.4168 | 0.5886 |
| 2 | 11 | 0.014024 | 11.01402 | 0.9999 | 0.0001 | 0.0006 |
| 3 | 3 | 0.008362 | 3.008362 | 0.3701 | 0.6299 | 0.7939 |

### 2.2. Convolution Approach and Exact Binomial Test Comparison

Table 2 presents a Type I error control and power comparison between the convolution-based test and the exact binomial test for a sample size of $n = 10$, across varying null hypotheses $\pi_0 \in \{0.1, 0.2, 0.3, 0.4, 0.5\}$ and corresponding alternatives $\pi_1 \in \{\pi_0, \pi_0 + 0.1, \ldots, \min(\pi_0 + 0.4, 1)\}$. For each $\pi_0$, a critical value $c$ was determined so that the convolution-based test controls the Type I error exactly at level $\alpha = 0.05$, as defined in Equation (3). The corresponding power was computed using Equation (5), noting that power equals the Type I error when $\pi_0 = \pi_1$. In contrast, the exact binomial rejection threshold $k$ was chosen to ensure that the Type I error remained strictly below $\alpha$.

Table 3 reports analogous results for a larger sample size of $n = 20$. As expected, power increases for both methods with larger $n$. Across both settings, the convolution-based test consistently achieves the nominal Type I error and provides greater power than the exact binomial test, particularly when the exact binomial test is overly conservative relative to Type I error control. This improved performance is attributed to the smoothing introduced by the normal perturbation, which results in a more refined and responsive rejection region. These findings underscore the practical utility of the convolution-based test in discrete-data settings, especially when measurement or process noise is present and sample sizes are limited. The only time the classic test and the convolution based test are equivalent are the $n$ values for $\pi_0$ where Equation (1) is satisfied.

**Table 2.** Comparison of power between the mixture-based convolution test and the exact binomial test for sample size $n = 10$, across values of $\pi_0$ and $\pi_1$, $h = 0.01$. The rejection threshold $k$ ensures the binomial test controls Type I error strictly below $\alpha = 0.05$.

| $\pi_0$ | $\pi_1$ | Critical $c$ | Mixture Power | Rejection $k$ | Binomial Power |
|---|---|---|---|---|---|
| 0.1 | 0.1 | 2.9962 | 0.050000 | 4 | 0.012795 |
| 0.1 | 0.2 | 2.9962 | 0.251377 | 4 | 0.120874 |
| 0.1 | 0.3 | 2.9962 | 0.523352 | 4 | 0.350389 |
| 0.1 | 0.4 | 2.9962 | 0.757080 | 4 | 0.617719 |
| 0.1 | 0.5 | 2.9962 | 0.904088 | 4 | 0.828125 |
| 0.2 | 0.2 | 4.0086 | 0.050000 | 5 | 0.032793 |

**Table 2.** *Cont.*

| $\pi_0$ | $\pi_1$ | Critical $c$ | Mixture Power | Rejection $k$ | Binomial Power |
|---|---|---|---|---|---|
| 0.2 | 0.3 | 4.0086 | 0.189362 | 5 | 0.150268 |
| 0.2 | 0.4 | 4.0086 | 0.415895 | 5 | 0.366897 |
| 0.2 | 0.5 | 4.0086 | 0.663109 | 5 | 0.623047 |
| 0.2 | 0.6 | 4.0086 | 0.855538 | 5 | 0.833761 |
| 0.3 | 0.3 | 5.0195 | 0.050000 | 6 | 0.047349 |
| 0.3 | 0.4 | 5.0195 | 0.171407 | 6 | 0.166239 |
| 0.3 | 0.5 | 5.0195 | 0.383292 | 6 | 0.376953 |
| 0.3 | 0.6 | 5.0195 | 0.638272 | 6 | 0.633103 |
| 0.3 | 0.7 | 5.0195 | 0.852383 | 6 | 0.849732 |
| 0.4 | 0.4 | 6.9878 | 0.050000 | 8 | 0.012295 |
| 0.4 | 0.5 | 6.9878 | 0.158735 | 8 | 0.054688 |
| 0.4 | 0.6 | 6.9878 | 0.358174 | 8 | 0.167290 |
| 0.4 | 0.7 | 6.9878 | 0.619691 | 8 | 0.382783 |
| 0.4 | 0.8 | 6.9878 | 0.856551 | 8 | 0.677800 |
| 0.5 | 0.5 | 7.9876 | 0.050000 | 9 | 0.010742 |
| 0.5 | 0.6 | 7.9876 | 0.154390 | 9 | 0.046357 |
| 0.5 | 0.7 | 7.9876 | 0.357879 | 9 | 0.149308 |
| 0.5 | 0.8 | 7.9876 | 0.645587 | 9 | 0.375810 |
| 0.5 | 0.9 | 7.9876 | 0.909147 | 9 | 0.736099 |

**Table 3.** Power comparison between the mixture-based convolution test and the exact binomial test for sample size $n = 20$, across values of $\pi_0$ and $\pi_1$, $h = 0.01$. The rejection threshold $k$ ensures the binomial test controls Type I error strictly below $\alpha = 0.05$.

| $\pi_0$ | $\pi_1$ | Critical $c$ | Mixture Power | Rejection $k$ | Binomial Power |
|---|---|---|---|---|---|
| 0.1 | 0.1 | 4.0143 | 0.050000 | 5 | 0.043174 |
| 0.1 | 0.2 | 4.0143 | 0.386941 | 5 | 0.370352 |
| 0.1 | 0.3 | 4.0143 | 0.772408 | 5 | 0.762492 |
| 0.1 | 0.4 | 4.0143 | 0.951708 | 5 | 0.949048 |
| 0.1 | 0.5 | 4.0143 | 0.994442 | 5 | 0.994091 |
| 0.2 | 0.2 | 7.0045 | 0.050000 | 8 | 0.032143 |
| 0.2 | 0.3 | 7.0045 | 0.281501 | 8 | 0.227728 |
| 0.2 | 0.4 | 7.0045 | 0.638410 | 8 | 0.584107 |
| 0.2 | 0.5 | 7.0045 | 0.892613 | 8 | 0.868412 |
| 0.2 | 0.6 | 7.0045 | 0.983738 | 8 | 0.978971 |
| 0.3 | 0.3 | 9.0186 | 0.050000 | 10 | 0.047962 |
| 0.3 | 0.4 | 9.0186 | 0.249643 | 10 | 0.244663 |
| 0.3 | 0.5 | 9.0186 | 0.593093 | 10 | 0.588099 |
| 0.3 | 0.6 | 9.0186 | 0.874692 | 10 | 0.872479 |
| 0.3 | 0.7 | 9.0186 | 0.983230 | 10 | 0.982855 |
| 0.4 | 0.4 | 11.9910 | 0.050000 | 13 | 0.021029 |
| 0.4 | 0.5 | 11.9910 | 0.229635 | 13 | 0.131588 |
| 0.4 | 0.6 | 11.9910 | 0.562559 | 13 | 0.415893 |
| 0.4 | 0.7 | 11.9910 | 0.865636 | 13 | 0.772272 |
| 0.4 | 0.8 | 11.9910 | 0.985944 | 13 | 0.967857 |
| 0.5 | 0.5 | 13.9918 | 0.050000 | 15 | 0.020695 |
| 0.5 | 0.6 | 13.9918 | 0.224232 | 15 | 0.125599 |
| 0.5 | 0.7 | 13.9918 | 0.568302 | 15 | 0.416371 |
| 0.5 | 0.8 | 13.9918 | 0.890702 | 15 | 0.804208 |
| 0.5 | 0.9 | 13.9918 | 0.995777 | 15 | 0.988747 |

## 3. Two Stage Design

Similar to the one-stage test, we construct a two-stage test of the hypothesis $H_0 : \pi = \pi_0$ versus $H_1 : \pi > \pi_0$, offering precise control of the Type I error rate and allowing for early stopping due to futility. Let the total sample size be $n = n_1 + n_2$. After the first $n_1$ subjects have completed their endpoint assessments, a futility stopping rule is applied.

As in the one-stage design, let $Z_1$ denote the observed value of the convolution-based test statistic after the first $n_1$ subjects, and let $Z_2$ be the corresponding statistic based on an independent second cohort of $n_2$ subjects. Under the null hypothesis $H_0$, define the $p$-values as

$$p_1 = 1 - F_{Z|\pi=\pi_0}(Z_1), \quad p_2 = 1 - F_{Z|\pi=\pi_0}(Z_2),$$

where $p_1$ and $p_2$ follow a uniform $U(0,1)$ distribution by the probability integral transform. The cumulative distribution function $F_{Z|\pi=\pi_0}$ is defined in Equation (4).

Our approach uses a $p$-value threshold at the interim analysis and applies Stouffer's weighted z-score method for the final efficacy analysis [10]. Define the transformed statistics:

$$T_1 = \Phi^{-1}(p_1), \quad \text{based on the first } n_1 \text{ subjects,}$$

$$T_2 = \Phi^{-1}(p_2), \quad \text{based on the second } n_2 \text{ subjects,}$$

where $\Phi^{-1}$ is the quantile function of the standard normal distribution.

The combined test statistic is given by the following:

$$T = \frac{w_1 T_1 + w_2 T_2}{\sqrt{w_1^2 + w_2^2}},$$

where the weights are defined as $w_1 = n_1/n$ and $w_2 = n_2/n$. With this weighting scheme, the statistic $T$ follows a standard normal distribution under $H_0$, i.e., $T \sim \mathcal{N}(0,1)$.

The interim futility rule is to terminate the study early if $p_1 > p_c$, where the threshold $p_c$ may be specified by the user or selected to optimize statistical power or minimize the expected sample size,

$$\text{ESN} = n_1 p_c + n_2(1 - p_c).$$

If the study does not stop early for futility, the final $p$-value is computed as $p = \Phi(T)$, where $\Phi$ denotes the standard normal CDF. The null hypothesis $H_0$ is rejected if $p < \alpha'$, where $\alpha'$ is adjusted to ensure that the overall Type I error rate is controlled at the nominal level $\alpha$.

To determine $\alpha'$, let $a = \Phi^{-1}(p_c)$. The conditional probability of rejecting $H_0$ given that the futility boundary is not crossed is:

$$P(T < c \mid T_1 < a) = \frac{1}{\Phi(a)} \int_{-\infty}^{a} \Phi(\sqrt{2}c - x)\, \phi(x)\, dx,$$

where $\phi$ is the standard normal density function. To ensure the overall Type I error rate is $\alpha$, we solve for $c$ in the equation:

$$p_c \cdot P(T < c \mid T_1 < a) = \alpha,$$

and define the adjusted significance level as $\alpha' = \Phi(c)$, which satisfies $\alpha' > \alpha$. Once $\alpha'$ is determined numerically power can be calculated under $H_1$ via simulation. For a fixed $n$ we can find combinations of $n_1$ and $n_2$ such that the overall $\alpha = 0.05$ and power is greater than or equal to the desired power. Practically speaking one can start at the $n$ determined by the Simon two-stage design and reduce by increments of 1 until the power constraint is no longer satisfied. The search is over values of $n_1$ and $p_c$, with $n_2 = n - n_1$. This will be illustrated in the next section.

### *Convolution Approach and Simon Two-Stage Design Comparison*

There is no straightforward way to directly compare the convolution-based approach with Simon's two-stage design. A key distinguishing feature is that the convolution-based method precisely controls the Type I error rate, whereas Simon's two-stage design may be conservative in some scenarios, as illustrated earlier in Figure 2. In settings where the actual Type I error of Simon's design falls well below the nominal level, the convolution-based method can achieve the same desired power with a smaller sample size, particularly when the difference between $\pi_1$ and $\pi_0$ is substantial.

To illustrate, we consider testing $H_0 : \pi = \pi_0$ versus $H_1 : \pi > \pi_0$ with $\pi_0 = 0.1$ and $\pi_1$ ranging from 0.3 to 0.6 in increments of 0.1. The results of various Simon two-stage designs are presented in Table 4, showing the corresponding total sample size, exact Type I error, power, expected sample size ($EN_0$), and probability of early stopping.

Similarly, Table 5 displays results from the convolution-based two-stage designs across the same values of $\pi_1$. For each design, we considered a range of $p_c$ values from 0.2 to 0.7 in steps of 0.01, and we report the total sample size $n$, stage-wise sample sizes $n_1$ and $n_2$, $p_c$, power, expected sample size (ESN), adjusted $\alpha'$, for testing at the second stage, and the probability of early stopping, which is equal to $1 - p_c$. The designs in Table 5 represent a subset of possible scenarios to provide a concise summary.

The convolution-based approach demonstrates a clear advantage by achieving slightly smaller sample sizes across all settings. Moreover, it is not constrained by the range of early stopping probabilities observed in the Simon designs (approximately 0.549 to 0.810 in our example). Instead, the convolution-based method allows the user to specify any desired $p_c$ (and thus early stopping probability), offering greater flexibility to tailor the design to the specific goals and constraints of a given clinical trial.

**Table 4.** Summary of Simon Two-Stage Designs with one-sided Type I error rate $\alpha = 0.05$, Power = 0.8, $\pi_0 = 0.1$, $h = 0.01$. Designs are shown for various response probabilities $\pi_1$.

| $\pi_1$ | $n$ | $n_1$ | $r_1$ | $r_2$ | Type I Error | Power | $EN_0$ | P (Early Stop) | Method |
|---|---|---|---|---|---|---|---|---|---|
| 0.3 | 25 | 15 | 1 | 5 | 0.033 | 0.802 | 19.5 | 0.549 | Minimax |
| 0.3 | 26 | 12 | 1 | 5 | 0.036 | 0.805 | 16.8 | 0.659 | |
| 0.3 | 27 | 11 | 1 | 5 | 0.040 | 0.806 | 15.8 | 0.697 | |
| 0.3 | 29 | 10 | 1 | 5 | 0.047 | 0.805 | 15.0 | 0.736 | Optimal |
| 0.4 | 13 | 8 | 1 | 3 | 0.031 | 0.802 | 8.9 | 0.813 | Minimax |
| 0.4 | 15 | 4 | 0 | 3 | 0.043 | 0.818 | 7.8 | 0.656 | Optimal |
| 0.5 | 8 | 4 | 0 | 2 | 0.036 | 0.836 | 5.4 | 0.656 | Minimax |
| 0.5 | 9 | 3 | 0 | 2 | 0.041 | 0.828 | 4.6 | 0.729 | Optimal |
| 0.6 | 6 | 3 | 0 | 2 | 0.015 | 0.807 | 3.8 | 0.729 | Minimax |
| 0.6 | 8 | 2 | 0 | 2 | 0.025 | 0.819 | 3.1 | 0.810 | Optimal |

**Table 5.** Summary of Convolution-Based Two-Stage Designs with one-sided Type I error rate $\alpha = 0.05$, Power = 0.8, $\pi_0 = 0.1$, $h = 0.01$. Designs are shown for various response probabilities $\pi_1$.

| $\pi_1$ | $n$ | $n_1$ | $n_2$ | $p_c$ | Power | ESN | $\alpha'$ | P (Early Stop) |
|---|---|---|---|---|---|---|---|---|
| 0.3 | 23 | 16 | 7 | 0.34 | 0.810 | 18.4 | 0.055 | 0.66 |
| 0.3 | 23 | 17 | 6 | 0.32 | 0.807 | 18.9 | 0.056 | 0.68 |
| 0.3 | 23 | 17 | 6 | 0.30 | 0.806 | 18.8 | 0.057 | 0.70 |
| 0.3 | 23 | 15 | 8 | 0.31 | 0.806 | 17.5 | 0.056 | 0.69 |
| 0.3 | 23 | 14 | 9 | 0.37 | 0.806 | 17.3 | 0.054 | 0.63 |
| 0.3 | 23 | 14 | 9 | 0.45 | 0.806 | 18.0 | 0.052 | 0.55 |
| 0.3 | 23 | 14 | 9 | 0.46 | 0.806 | 18.1 | 0.052 | 0.54 |

Table 5. *Cont.*

| $\pi_1$ | $n$ | $n_1$ | $n_2$ | $p_c$ | Power | ESN | $\alpha'$ | P (Early Stop) |
|---|---|---|---|---|---|---|---|---|
| 0.3 | 23 | 16 | 7 | 0.69 | 0.806 | 20.8 | 0.050 | 0.31 |
| 0.3 | 23 | 16 | 7 | 0.36 | 0.805 | 18.5 | 0.054 | 0.64 |
| 0.3 | 23 | 15 | 8 | 0.37 | 0.805 | 18.0 | 0.054 | 0.63 |
| 0.3 | 23 | 13 | 10 | 0.50 | 0.805 | 18.0 | 0.051 | 0.50 |
| 0.3 | 23 | 13 | 10 | 0.53 | 0.805 | 18.3 | 0.051 | 0.47 |
| 0.3 | 23 | 12 | 11 | 0.70 | 0.805 | 19.7 | 0.050 | 0.30 |
| 0.4 | 11 | 8 | 3 | 0.20 | 0.801 | 8.6 | 0.066 | 0.80 |
| 0.4 | 11 | 9 | 2 | 0.21 | 0.801 | 9.4 | 0.064 | 0.79 |
| 0.5 | 7 | 5 | 2 | 0.20 | 0.809 | 5.4 | 0.066 | 0.80 |
| 0.5 | 7 | 5 | 2 | 0.25 | 0.805 | 5.5 | 0.060 | 0.75 |
| 0.5 | 7 | 5 | 2 | 0.30 | 0.801 | 5.6 | 0.057 | 0.70 |
| 0.6 | 5 | 3 | 2 | 0.29 | 0.810 | 3.6 | 0.057 | 0.71 |
| 0.6 | 5 | 3 | 2 | 0.38 | 0.804 | 3.8 | 0.053 | 0.62 |
| 0.6 | 5 | 3 | 2 | 0.40 | 0.801 | 3.8 | 0.053 | 0.60 |
| 0.6 | 5 | 3 | 2 | 0.52 | 0.801 | 4.0 | 0.051 | 0.48 |

## 4. Real World Examples

### 4.1. One-Stage Designs

#### 4.1.1. Example 1

Our first example [11] is from a study of patients with concomitant advanced non-small cell lung cancer (NSCLC) and interstitial lung disease (ILD). This prospective, multicenter, single-arm phase 2 trial investigated the efficacy and safety of albumin-bound paclitaxel (nab-paclitaxel) in combination with carboplatin in patients with both advanced NSCLC and ILD. The primary endpoint was the overall response rate (ORR), testing $H_0 : \pi = \pi_0$ versus $H_1 : \pi > \pi_0$, with $\pi_0 = 0.2$, alternative $\pi_1 = 0.4$, $\alpha = 0.05$, and power = 0.80. Based on an exact binomial test, this required a sample size of $n = 35$. The actual study enrolled $n = 36$ subjects between April 2014 and September 2017, corresponding to an average accrual rate of approximately 1.3 subjects per month.

Using the same design parameters, the convolution-based test would require $n = 32$ subjects to achieve a power of 0.8117, or $n = 31$ for a power of 0.7967, potentially reducing the trial duration by 4 to 5 months with the corresponding cost savings. The $p$-value was $< 0.001$ under both the exact binomial and convolution-based approaches. If a prorated response of 17 out of 31 positive responses were observed, the $p$-value using the convolution-based method would still be $<0.001$.

#### 4.1.2. Example 2

Our next example study[12] enrolled $n = 15$ metastatic prostate cancer patients with AR-V7-expressing circulating tumor cells into a prospective phase II trial. The primary endpoint was PSA response, with hypothesis testing conducted as $H_0 : \pi = \pi_0$ versus $H_1 : \pi > \pi_0$, where $\pi_0 = 0.05$, $\pi_1 = 0.264$, $\alpha = 0.10$, and target power = 0.80. The true Type I error rate for the exact binomial test was 0.0362. A positive outcome in the study was thus defined as $\geq$3 of 15 patients achieving a PSA response.

Using the same design parameters, the convolution-based test would require $n = 11$ subjects to achieve a power of 0.824, or $n = 10$ for a power of 0.793. In the actual trial, 2 out of 15 subjects achieved a PSA response, yielding a $p$-value of 0.14 using the exact binomial test. The convolution-based test yielded a $p$-value of 0.106. Although not statistically significant at the $\alpha = 0.10$ level, this result demonstrates the relative efficiency of the convolution-based approach.

### 4.2. Two-Stage Designs

#### 4.2.1. Example 1

Our next example [13] is based on a study evaluating vinorelbine in advanced non-small cell lung cancer (NSCLC) patients aged 70 years or older. The study employed a multicenter, two-stage phase II design following Simon's optimal method. The primary endpoint was objective response rate (ORR), with hypothesis testing structured as $H_0 : \pi = \pi_0$ versus $H_1 : \pi > \pi_0$, where $\pi_0 = 0.10$, $\pi_1 = 0.25$, $h = 0.01$, $\alpha = 0.05$, and target power = 0.80.

The final sample size under Simon's design was $n = 43$ with an interim futility analysis planned at $n_1 = 18$ subjects. The actual Type I error rate achieved was 0.048. Table 6 presents three example two-stage designs generated using the convolution-based estimator. Notably, if one is willing to delay the interim futility analysis beyond $n_1 = 18$, the total required sample size can be reduced from $n = 43$ to $n = 35$, offering a more efficient design compared to Simon's optimal design alternative. Even maintaining the interim analysis at $n_1 = 18$, the convolution-based approach can still reduce the total sample size to $n = 37$.

**Table 6.** Convolution-based design scenarios for Example 1: Two-stage design.

| $n$ | $n_1$ | $n_2$ | $\pi_c$ | Power | ESN | $\alpha'$ |
|---|---|---|---|---|---|---|
| 35 | 27 | 8 | 0.23 | 0.803 | 28.8 | 0.062 |
| 36 | 24 | 12 | 0.24 | 0.802 | 26.9 | 0.061 |
| 37 | 18 | 19 | 0.56 | 0.801 | 28.6 | 0.051 |

In the observed trial data, 5 of the initial 18 subjects achieved a positive ORR, with a total of 10 ORR responses observed out of 43 by the end of the study. Simon's optimal design specified early stopping for futility if 3 or fewer ORR responses were observed in the first stage, and declared efficacy if 8 or more total responses were observed at the second stage.

For each convolution-based design in Table 6, we retrospectively aligned the observed data to the alternative designs to estimate what would have occurred under those configurations:

- For $n = 35$, $n_1 = 27$: Assuming 7 out of 27 responses, the futility $p$-value was 0.011, below the stopping threshold $\pi_c = 0.23$. The final-stage $p$-value, assuming 8 out of 35 total responses, was 0.0158, significant at the adjusted level $\alpha' = 0.062$.
- For $n = 36$, $n_1 = 24$: Assuming 6 out of 24 responses, the futility $p$-value was 0.002, below $\pi_c = 0.24$. The final-stage $p$-value based on 8 of 36 responses was 0.0162, also significant at $\alpha' = 0.061$.
- For $n = 37$, $n_1 = 18$: Assuming 5 out of 18 responses, the futility $p$-value was 0.015, which is less than $\pi_c = 0.56$. The final $p$-value with 8 of 37 responses was 0.020, significant at $\alpha' = 0.051$.

This example again highlights the potential cost savings and efficiency gains achievable with the convolution-based approach compared to Simon's two-stage design, while maintaining rigorous Type I error control and statistical power.

#### 4.2.2. Example 2

Our next example [14] comes from a publication describing the LuDO-N trial, a phase II, open-label, multicenter, single-arm, two-stage clinical trial in children with high-risk neuroblastoma, utilizing an alternative administration schedule of Lutetium DOTATATE. The primary endpoint is the response rate, assessed by the Revised International Neuroblastoma Response Criteria one month after completion of therapy. Hypothesis testing is structured as $H_0 : \pi = \pi_0$ versus $H_1 : \pi > \pi_0$, where $\pi_0 = 0.2$, $\pi_1 = 0.4$,$h = 0.01$, $\alpha = 0.1$, and the target power is 0.80.

The proposed design follows Simon's Two-Stage Minimax design. Recruitment is expected to be completed within 3–5 years. Based on the specified parameters, the Simon design requires a total sample size of $n = 24$, with a first-stage futility analysis at $n_1 = 14$, yielding a true Type I error rate of 0.0874.

In contrast, an alternative convolution-based design would require a total of $n = 19$ subjects, with $n_1 = 16$ in the first stage, using a futility threshold of $p_c = 0.21$ and a final adjusted significance level of $\alpha' = 0.158$. If the projected recruitment rate is 24 subjects over 5 years (approximately 4.8 subjects per year), the convolution-based design would reduce the total accrual period by roughly one year.

## 5. Conclusions

The convolution-based approach presented in this work offers a flexible and efficient alternative to traditional exact methods for designing and analyzing single-arm phase II oncology trials with binary endpoints. By convolving the binomial distribution with a simulated normal random variable, this method produces an unbiased estimator for the response rate $\pi$ and achieves precise Type I error control. This leads to reduced sample size requirements in both one-stage and two-stage designs, while maintaining desirable operating characteristics.

A significant advantage of the convolution framework is its adaptability. It can be easily modified to incorporate an interim analysis for either futility or combined efficacy and futility, allowing for early decision-making and further optimization of trial resources. Moreover, the convolution-based method provides a smooth and continuous approximation to the binomial tail distribution, making it especially valuable in scenarios where measurement error or process variability exists, and a continuous $p$-value function is preferred.

Overall, this approach enhances the efficiency of early-phase oncology clinical trial design and provides a theoretically sound and practically implementable alternative to exact binomial and Simon's two-stage methods. It holds particular promise for high-cost therapeutic areas, such as oncology and cellular therapies, where efficient trial execution is critical.

**Funding:** This work was supported by the following three NCI grants to Hutson: NRG Oncology Statistical and Data Management Center grant (grant no. U10CA180822); Immuno-Oncology Translational network (IOTN) Moonshot grant (grant no. U24CA232979); Acquired Resistance to Therapy network (ARTNet) grant (grant no.U24CA274159).

**Institutional Review Board Statement:** Not applicable.

**Informed Consent Statement:** Not applicable.

**Data Availability Statement:** The data utilized to illustrate this work is provided in the body of the text in Section 4.

**Acknowledgments:** We wish to thank the reviewers for their thoughtful remarks, which led to an improved version of this manuscript.

**Conflicts of Interest:** The authors declare no conflicts of interest.

## References

1. Prepared by Battelle Technology Partnership Practice. Biopharmaceutical Industry-Sponsored Clinical Trials: Impact on State Economies. Prepared for Pharmaceutical Research and Manufacturers of America (PhRMA). 2015. Available online: http://orclinicalresearch.com/wp-content/uploads/2018/12/battelle-2015-study.pdf (accessed on 8 July 2025).
2. Leighl, N.B.; Nirmalakumar, S.; Ezeife, D.A.; Gyawali, B. An Arm and a Leg: The Rising Cost of Cancer Drugs and Impact on Access. *Am. Soc. Clin. Oncol. Educ. Book. Am. Soc. Clin. Oncol. Annu. Meet.* **2021**, *41*, e1–e12. [CrossRef] [PubMed]
3. Kapinos, K.A.; Hu, E.; Trivedi, J.; Geethakumari, P.R.; Kansagra, A. Cost-Effectiveness Analysis of CAR T-Cell Therapies vs. Antibody Drug Conjugates for Patients with Advanced Multiple Myeloma. *Cancer Control* **2023**, *30*, 1–8. [CrossRef] [PubMed]
4. Hoover, A.; Reimche, P.; Watson, D.; Tanner, L.; Gilchrist, L.; Finch, M.; Messinger, Y.H.; Turcotte, L.M. Healthcare cost and utilization for chimeric antigen receptor (CAR) T-cell therapy in the treatment of pediatric acute lymphoblastic leukemia: A commercial insurance claims database analysis. *Cancer Rep.* **2024**, *Epub ahead of print*. [CrossRef] [PubMed]
5. Simon, R. Optimal two-stage designs for phase II clinical trials. *Control. Clin. Trials* **1989**, *10*, 1–10. [CrossRef] [PubMed]
6. Hamaker, H.C.; van Strik, R. The Efficiency of Double Sampling for Attributes. *J. Am. Stat. Assoc.* **1955**, *50*, 830–849. [CrossRef]
7. Duncan, A.J. *Quality Control and Industrial Statistics*; Irwin: Homewood, IL, USA, 1986.
8. Hutson, A.D. Modifying the Exact Test for a Binomial Proportion and Comparisons with Other Approaches. *J. Appl. Stat.* **2006**, *33*, 679–690. [CrossRef]
9. Chernick, M.R.; Christine, Y.; Liu, C.Y. The Saw-Toothed Behavior of Power Versus Sample Size and Software Solutions: Single Binomial Proportion Using Exact Methods. *Am. Stat.* **2002**, *56*, 149–155. [CrossRef]
10. Whitlock, M.C. Combining probability from independent tests: The weighted Z-method is superior to Fisher's approach. *J. Evol. Biol.* **2005**, *18*, 1368–1373. [CrossRef] [PubMed]
11. Asahina, H.; Oizumi, S.; Takamura, K.; Harada, T.; Harada, M.; Yokouchi, H.; Kanazawa, K.; Fujita, Y.; Kojima, T.; Sugaya, F.; et al. A prospective phase II study of carboplatin and nab-paclitaxel in patients with advanced non-small cell lung cancer and concomitant interstitial lung disease (HOT1302). *Lung Cancer* **2019**, *138*, 65–71. [CrossRef] [PubMed]
12. Boudadi, K.; Suzman, D.L.; Anagnostou, V.; Fu, W.; Luber, B.; Wang, H.; Niknafs, N.; White, J.R.; Silberstein, J.L.; Sullivan, R.; et al. Ipilimumab plus nivolumab and DNA-repair defects in AR-V7-expressing metastatic prostate cancer. *Oncotarget* **2018**, *9*, 28561–28571. [CrossRef] [PubMed]
13. Gridelli, C.; Perrone, F.; Gallo, C.; De Marinis, F.; Ianniello, G.; Cigolari, S.; Cariello, S.; Di Costanzo, F.; D'Aprile, M.; Rossi, A.; et al. Vinorelbine is well tolerated and active in the treatment of elderly patients with advanced non-small cell lung cancer. A two-stage phase II study. *Eur. J. Cancer* **1997**, *33*, 392–397. [CrossRef] [PubMed]
14. Sundquist, F.; Georgantzi, K.; Jarvis, K.B.; Brok, J.; Koskenvuo, M.; Rascon, J.; van Noesel, M.; Grybäck, P.; Nilsson, J.; Braat, A.; et al. A Phase II Trial of a Personalized, Dose-Intense Administration Schedule of 177Lutetium-DOTATATE in Children With Primary Refractory or Relapsed High-Risk Neuroblastoma-LuDO-N. *Front. Pediatr.* **2022**, *10*, 836230. [CrossRef] [PubMed]

*cancers*

MDPI

*Article*

# The Impact of Design Misspecifications on Survival Outcomes in Cancer Clinical Trials

**Fang-Shu Ou *,†, Tyler Zemla † and Jennifer G. Le-Rademacher**

Division of Clinical Trials and Biostatistics, Mayo Clinic, Rochester, MN 55905, USA; zemla.tyler@mayo.edu (T.Z.); le-rademacher.jennifer@mayo.edu (J.G.L.-R.)

* Correspondence: ou.fang-shu@mayo.edu

† These authors contributed equally to this work.

**Simple Summary**

Clinical trial design relies on assumptions that may change over time, potentially affecting the accuracy of results. This study evaluates how deviations in design assumptions impact the statistical power of randomized trials with survival endpoints. Findings show that incorrect assumptions can significantly affect all methods similarly. Thus, it is crucial to base trial designs on the most accurate assumptions and consider potential impacts on statistical power.

**Abstract**

**Background/Objectives**: Results from a well-designed trial provide evidence to support approval of truly effective treatments or discontinuation of ineffective treatments. However, the information available at the time of trial design may be limited which may lead to underpowered trials. This work aims to evaluate the impact of design assumption misspecifications on the statistical power of randomized trials with survival outcomes. **Methods**: The impact of the design assumption misspecifications on statistical power of four different statistical methods was investigated in a simulation study. The methods include the log-rank test, MaxCombo test, the test of difference in survival probability, and test of difference in restricted mean survival time (RMST). The deviations considered include the survival rate in the control arm, the expected treatment effect in terms of magnitude and pattern, accrual rate, and drop-out rate. **Results**: Deviations in the control arm's survival distribution have no impact on the power of the log-rank and MaxCombo tests but it affects the trial duration since trials designed with these tests require the total number of events to be met before the final analysis can be conducted. Misspecified treatment effect has similar effect on the statistical power of all four methods. When the proportional hazards assumption is misspecified, the RMST is more robust with a larger early treatment effect, while the survival probability and the MaxCombo tests are more robust with a larger late treatment effect and crossing hazards. **Conclusions**: Selecting the appropriate statistical tests to design a trial depends on the goal of the trial, the mechanism of action of the experimental treatment, the survival quantity of clinical interest, and the pattern of the expected treatment effect. The final design should be based on assumptions that are as accurate as possible, and the potential impacts of deviations from these assumptions on the trial's statistical power should be carefully considered.

**Keywords:** clinical trials; misspecification; survival endpoints

## 1. Introduction

Regulatory approval of a cancer drug relies on the demonstration of its benefit compared to a control (whether a placebo or a current standard of care), typically in randomized clinical trials with a time-to-event endpoint, such as overall survival, progression-free survival, and disease-free survival [1].

Results from a well-designed trial—with the optimal survival benefit selected to reflect the mechanism of action of the experimental treatment, the design assumptions well-justified and reflective of the target patient population, as well as realistic expectations of the treatment effect—provide evidence to support approval of truly effective treatments or discontinuation of ineffective treatments. However, the information available at the time of trial design may be limited and change overtime, resulting in a trial whose design does not fully capture the effect of the new treatment or based on assumptions that deviate from the expected outcome which may lead to erroneous conclusions.

A deviation that has been noted in the past and has received more attention in recent years is the proportional hazards assumption. The log-rank test, which is often the basis for sample size estimation in phase III oncology trial, is the most powerful test when the hazard ratio between the new treatment and the control treatment is constant over time, known as proportional hazards [2]. However, Trinquart et al. [3] reported that 13 out of 54 (24%) published trials failed a formal test of proportional hazards assumptions. Even when a test of proportional hazard does not show statistically significant violation, the treatment effect can still vary over time and impact the trial outcome in a meaningful way [4,5]. With the recent surge of approvals of immune-oncology therapy, the proportional hazards assumption has become more questionable. Results of recent immuno-oncology trials indicate that the effects of immunotherapy are often delayed and the assumption of proportional hazards do not hold in immuno-oncology trials [6]. For example the KEYNOTE-045 trial [7] showed crossing survival curves (for both overall and progression-free), and the CheckMate 238 trial [8] showed late separation where there was no survival difference in the first 3 months.

In addition to the deviation in proportional hazard assumption, other deviations in trial design assumptions are possible. Yet design assumptions and the impact of their deviations from the observed data are rarely evaluated at trial completion or discussed in trial publications [9]. The deviation of baseline hazard in the control arm can occur when the survival rates of the control arms initially assumed during trial design do not accurately reflect the improvement in survival years later due to new scientific development or changes in standard of care. For example, the KEYNOTE-189 trial [10] was designed assuming the median overall survival for patients receiving chemotherapy alone as the first-line treatment for metastatic non-small-cell lung cancer was 13 months, however the observed median overall survival was 11.3 months; median progression-free survival assumed in the design was 6.5 months compared with the observed median of 4.8 months. This is an example where the observed survival experience in the control arm was worse than that was assumed in the design. Whereas the CheckMate 067 trial [11] is an example where the observed survival experience in the control arm was better than the design assumption. Specifically, the observed 24-month overall survival probability for patients receiving ipilimumab as the first-line treatment for advanced melanoma was 45% compared to the 24.4% assumed for the design.

Other deviations, such as deviations in enrollment rate and drop-out rate, have also been seen in clinical trials. For example, CALGB/SWOG 80702 (Alliance) planned to finish enrollment in 3.125 years but it took more than 4 years (June 2010 to November 2015) to reach full enrollment [12]. The PROSPECT trial started with a sample size of 1016 patients and subsequently increased the target enrollment to 1120 due to a higher than anticipated drop-out post-randomization [13]; it reached full enrollment with 1194 patients [14]. The prevalence of these type of deviations is difficult to gauge because the information is often omitted from the clinical trial manuscripts [15].

The aim of this work is not to compare the performance of various survival analysis methods, which have been well-published. Our aim is to evaluate how deviations in design assumptions affect statistical power (and Type I error when appropriate) for each method, while also accounting for the follow-up scheme associated with the method. Specifically, we consider the following deviations: (1) survival distribution of the control arm (referred to as baseline survival), (2) expected treatment effect (pattern and magnitude), (3) accrual rate, and (4) drop-out rate. In addition to evaluate the impact of deviations for the most common method, log-rank test, we also include other statistical tests, such as the difference in survival probabilities at a prespecified time point, the restricted mean survival time (RMST), and the MaxCombo tests, in our investigations.

The rest of the manuscript is organized as follows. In Section 2, we define the different test statistics used and describe their associated design, as well as detailing the simulation setup. The study power and Type I error from each test/deviation combination are described in Section 3. Sections 4 and 5 consist of the conclusion and discussions, respectively.

## 2. Methods

For simplicity, this exposition describes a two-arm randomized trial with a 1:1 randomization ratio. However, all concepts can be generalized to trials with multiple arms and to other randomization ratios.

### 2.1. Design Framework

Let $X$ be the time to the event of interest. Let $S(x) = \Pr(X > x)$ denote the survival function, the probability of an individual surviving beyond time $x$, and the hazard function be defined as $h(x) = \lim_{\Delta x \to 0} \frac{Pr(x \leq X < x+\Delta x | X \geq x)}{\Delta x}$. Let $S_C(x)$ and $h_C(x)$ be the survival function and hazard function for the control arm, respectively. Similarly, let $S_T(x)$ and $h_T(x)$ be the survival function and hazard function for the treatment arm, respectively. Below are the statistical hypotheses being evaluated in this paper, grouped by associated design.

#### 2.1.1. Event-Based Design

The log-rank test and the MaxCombo test are methods to evaluate the hazard rate, specifically testing the following hypotheses:

$$H_O : h_C(x) = h_T(x) \text{ for all } x \leq T \text{ versus } H_1 : h_C(x) \neq h_T(x) \text{ for some } x \leq T$$

where $T$ is the largest time at which both arms have at least one subject at risk. While the log-rank test statistic gives equal weight to differences in the observed and expected mortality over time, the MaxCombo test statistic is based on the maximum value of a combination of tests with varying weights (some give more weight to earlier differences and others give more weight to later differences). For the MaxCombo tests, it is necessary to specify the weight function and the components a priori.

In trials designed based on log-rank test and MaxCombo test, the size of a trial is stated in terms of the total number of events of interest. Under this type of design, all patients are followed until the time when the prespecified total number of events are observed, regardless of when they are enrolled on the trial. Therefore, follow-up duration of patients within the same trial can vary widely, with shorter duration for more recent enrollment and longer duration for earlier enrollment.

#### 2.1.2. Fixed Follow-Up Duration Design

In contrast to the log-rank test and the MaxCombo test, which are based on the hazard rate, the other two methods are based on the survival probability. The hypotheses for testing the difference in survival probability at a prespecified time $t$ are:

$$H_O : S_C(t) = S_T(t) \text{ versus } H_1 : S_C(t) \neq S_T(t)$$

where $t$ is the prespecified time of the survival probability of interest and the hypotheses for testing the difference in the RMST at time $\tau$ are

$$H_O : \mu_C(\tau) = \mu_T(\tau) \text{ versus } H_1 : \mu_C(\tau) \neq \mu_T(\tau)$$

where $\mu(\tau) = \int_0^{\tau} S(x)dx$ and $\tau$ is the prespecified restriction time. Although it is not within the scope of this work to discuss how to select $t$ and $\tau$, it is important to note that their selection should be based on the time point that is most clinically relevant for the trial being designed and that the statistical power of the survival probability test and the RMST test depend on time $t$ and $\tau$, respectively.

In trials designed based on survival probability and RMST, the trial size is stated in terms of the total number of patients enrolled. In both methods, survival experience beyond the prespecified time of interest (time $t$ for survival probability test and $\tau$ for RMST test) does not contribute to the hypothesis test. Under this type of design, patients are enrolled and followed until they experience the event of interest or reach the prespecified time, $t$ and $\tau$, whichever occurs first.

Table 1 summarizes the design framework, and Figure 1 illustrates the quantities being compared for the different endpoints.

**Table 1.** Design framework for randomized trials with survival outcomes.

| | **Hazard Rate $h(x)$** | | **Survival Probability $S(t)$** | **Restricted Mean Survival Time $\mu(\tau)$** |
|---|---|---|---|---|
| Statistical Test | Log-rank test | MaxCombo test | Test of difference | Test of difference |
| Treatment effect quantified by | Hazard ratio | No corresponding quantity | Difference in survival probability | Difference in mean survival time |
| Trial size stated in terms of | The total number of events | The total number of events | Total number of patients enrolled | Total number of patients enrolled |
| Follow-up | All patients are followed until the total number of events are reached | All patients are followed until the total number of events are reached | Each patient is followed until event or time $t$ whichever occurs first; follow-up beyond $t$ does not contribute to test statistic | Each patient is followed until event or time $\tau$ whichever occurs first; follow-up beyond $\tau$ does not contribute to test statistic |

**Table 1.** *Cont.*

| | Hazard Rate $h(x)$ | | Survival Probability $S(t)$ | Restricted Mean Survival Time $\mu(\tau)$ |
|---|---|---|---|---|
| Advantages | Uses all available data during follow-up; has the highest statistical power under proportional hazards assumption | Does not require proportional hazards assumption; uses all available data during follow-up | Does not require proportional hazards assumption; trial duration more predictable (depends only on the enrollment rate) | Does not require proportional hazards assumption; trial duration more predictable (depends only on the enrollment rate) |
| Disadvantages | Requires proportional hazards assumption (for optimal power and interpretability of hazard ratio); trial duration can be unpredictable (depends on time to reach number of events required) | Trial duration can be unpredictable (depends on time to reach number of events required) | Use only data up to time $t$ | Use only data up to time $\tau$ |

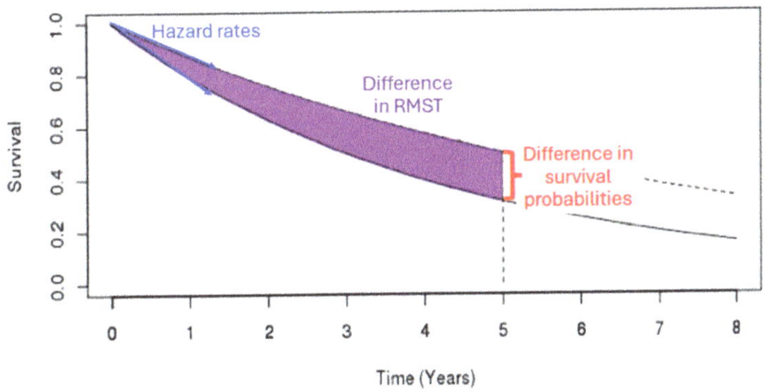


**Figure 1.** The survival quantity being compared for the different methods. The log-rank test and the MaxCombo test compare the hazard rate (a function of the slope of the survival curves, indicated by the blue arrows), the difference in survival probabilities at $t = 5$ years (distance denoted by the red bracket), and the difference in mean survival times restricted at $\tau = 5$ years (the difference between the areas under the survival curves, purple shaded area).

### 2.2. Simulation Setup

A simulation study was conducted to evaluate the impact of deviations on the statistical power and Type I error (when appropriate).

#### 2.2.1. Original Designs

The trial design that will be used as the reference for all comparisons in this paper is based on the following assumptions:

- Two arms randomized at a 1:1 ratio;
- Survival distribution of control arm:
  - follows exponential distribution;
  - median survival time = 3 years;
- Treatment effect:
  - proportional hazards;
  - hazard ratio (HR, experiment versus control) = 0.6;
- Type I error of one-sided 0.025 and 90% power;
- Accrual rate = 10 pts/month, uniformly distributed.

The resulting design based on the log-rank test requires a total of 162 events. With the assumed accrual rate, the trial needs to enroll a total of 350 patients (175 per arm) with an anticipated total trial duration of 5 years, defined as the time from first patient enrollment to statistical analysis of the primary endpoint. This design provides the same power for the MaxCombo tests. For this work, we focus on 2 MaxCombo tests: a 2-component with weights [(0,0) and (0,0.5)] and a 3-component with weights [(0,0), (0,0.5), and (0.5,0.5)] which are recommended for oncology trials from previously published work [16]. More details on MaxCombo tests are provided in the Appendix A.

Given that the goal of this work is to show how the deviations from the original design assumptions affect the statistical power within each of the different methods and not based on specific clinical setting, we selected $t$ and $\tau$ so that the original designs for the fixed follow-up duration designs achieve as close to 90% power as possible based on the same assumptions as the original log-rank based design. This leads to the selection of $t = 3.5$ years (empirical power 89.06%) for the survival probability test and $\tau = 4.5$ years (empirical power 90.36%) for the RMST test.

#### 2.2.2. Deviations Evaluated

The following deviations from the original design were considered:

1. Survival distribution of the control arm (Figure 2 insets): the observed median survival was set to be shorter than the expected time of 3 years (2 and 2.5 years, i.e., worse survival) and longer than expected (4 and 5 years, i.e., better survival).
2. Treatment effect:
   a. Magnitude (Figure 3 insets): the treatment effect was set to be larger than the expected hazard ratio of 0.6 (HR of 0.4 and 0.5) and smaller than expected (HR of 0.7 and 0.8).
   b. Non-proportional hazards (NPH):
      i. Early benefit (Figure 4 insets): Larger than expected early treatment effect (HR = 0.4) in the first $k$ years post enrollment and smaller than expected effect (HR = 0.8) after $k$ years where $k$ = 1, 2, 3, 4, and 5;
      ii. Late benefit (Figure 5 insets): Smaller than expected early treatment effect (HR = 0.8) in the first $k$ years post enrollment and larger than expected effect (HR = 0.4) after $k$ years where $k$ = 1, 2, 3, 4, and 5;
      iii. Crossing hazard (Figure 6 insets): Worse than expected survival in treatment arm (HR = 1.2) in the first $k$ years post enrollment and the same as expected treatment effect (HR = 0.6) after $k$ years where $k$ = 0.25, 0.5, 1, 1.5, and 2.

(a)

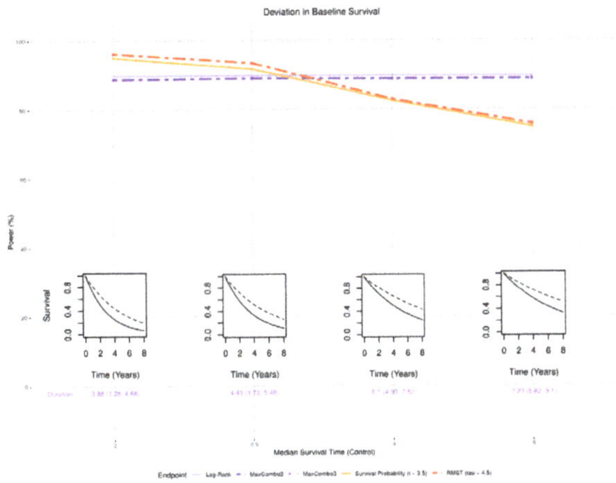


(b)

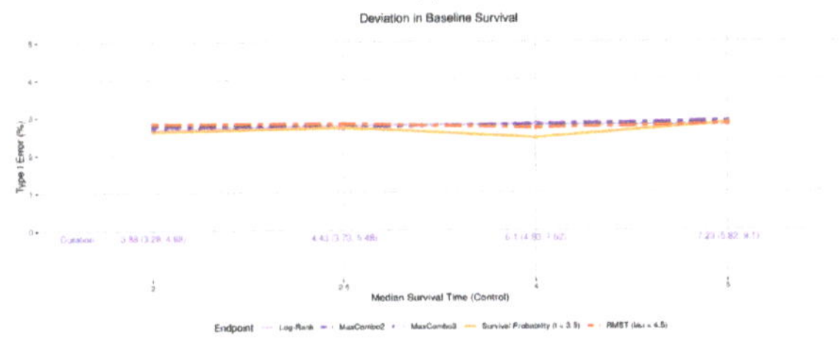


**Figure 2.** Changes in (**a**) statistical power and (**b**) Type I error associated with misspecified survival distribution of the control arm. The insets in (**a**) show four of the simulation scenarios where the control arm is drawn with solid black lines and the experimental arm is drawn with dashed black lines.

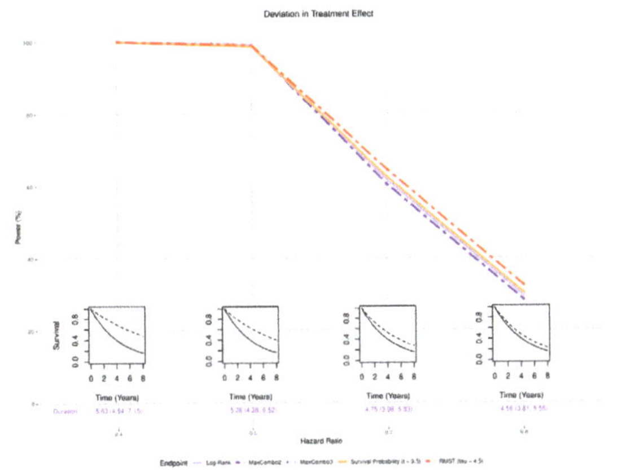


**Figure 3.** Changes in statistical power associated with misspecified magnitude of treatment effect. The insets show four of the simulation scenarios where the control arm is drawn with solid black lines and the experimental arm is drawn with dashed black lines.

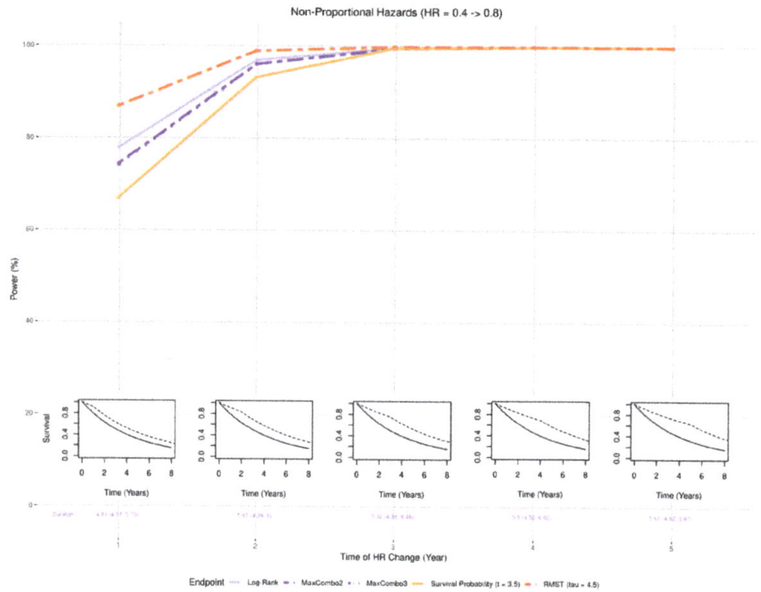


**Figure 4.** Changes in statistical power associated with misspecified treatment effect, non-proportional hazards with early benefit. The insets show five of the simulation scenarios where the control arm is drawn with solid black lines and the experimental arm is drawn with dashed black lines.

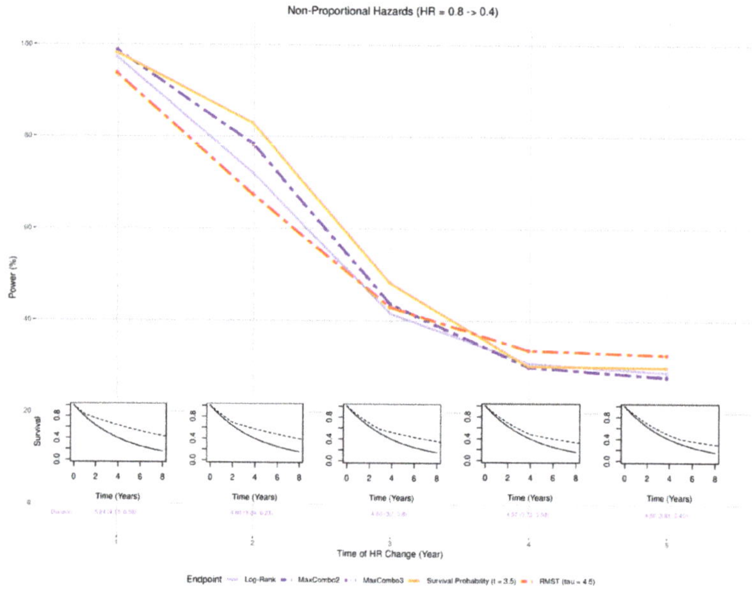


**Figure 5.** Changes in statistical power associated with misspecified treatment effect, non-proportional hazards with late benefit. The insets show five of the simulation scenarios where the control arm is drawn with solid black lines and the experimental arm is drawn with dashed black lines.

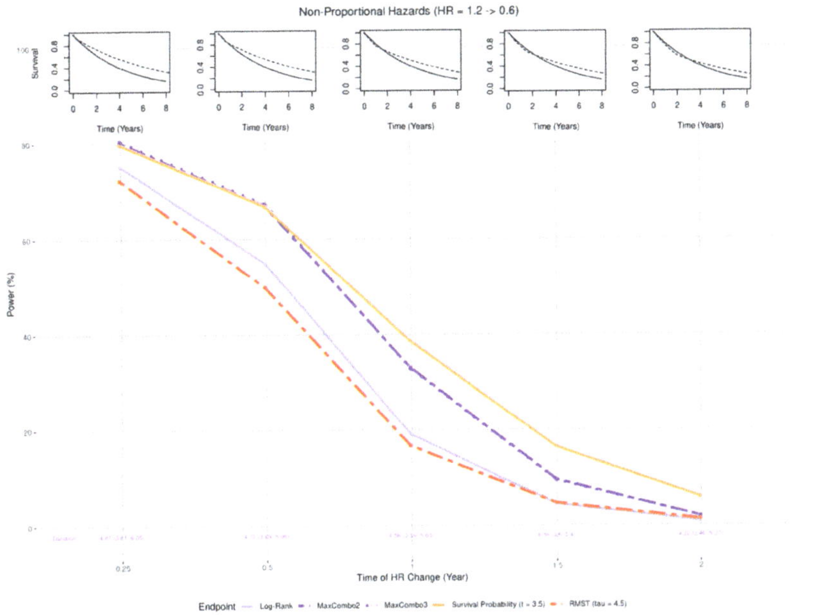


**Figure 6.** Changes in statistical power associated with misspecified treatment effect, non-proportional hazards with crossing hazards. The insets show five of the simulation scenarios where the control arm is drawn with solid black lines and the experimental arm is drawn with dashed black lines.

3. Accrual rate: Faster than expected accrual (i.e., full enrollment in 2 and 2.5 years) and slower than expected accrual (i.e., full enrollment in 3.5 and 4 years).
4. Drop-out rate: The original design assumes no drop-out. We incorporated various drop-out rates. The drop-out process is assumed to follow the exponential distribution with 15%, 30%, 45%, and 60% cumulative proportion by 5 years, independent of the survival process (i.e., non-informative censoring). Note that the observed drop-out rates vary based on the time of statistical analysis and are not the same as the cumulative 5-year rate. For example, for the 30% drop-out setting in simulation, the median observed drop-out rates by 3.5 and 4.5 years were 16.6% and 19.2%, respectively; for the 60% drop-out setting, the median observed drop-out rates by 3.5 and 4.5 years were 36.3% and 40.6%, respectively. Additionally, we did not incorporate informative censoring, where the censoring process and the survival process are dependent, as it would not only affect statistical power but also raise concerns about the validity of the trial. Addressing this issue is beyond the scope of the current manuscript.

All deviations were evaluated for their impact on the statistical power under each of the four statistical methods with corresponding follow-up schemes as described in Section 2.1. Type I error was also evaluated for deviations in survival distribution of the control arm, the accrual rate, and the drop-out rate.

Simulations were performed for each scenario with 10,000 iterations. The power was calculated as the percent of tests (out of 10,000) rejecting the null hypothesis (under alternative). The Type I error was calculated as the percent of tests (out of 10,000) rejecting the null hypothesis (under null). The simulation was performed using the R software version 4.4.1 [17]. The MaxCombo tests and RMST tests were performed using `nph` package version 2.1 [18] and `survRM2` package version 1.0-4 [19], respectively, in R.

## 3. Results

### 3.1. Deviation in Survival Distribution of the Control Arm

The log-rank, MaxCombo2, and MaxCombo3 tests maintained 90% power regardless of the median survival time of the control arm (Figure 2a). However, it is important to note that the trial duration is highly dependent on the baseline survival distribution (noted at the bottom of Figure 2). If the true median survival time for the control arm is 2 years (versus 3 years as assumed in the original design), the trial duration is much shorter (median trial duration: 3.88 years; range: 3.28–4.68 years) than the expected duration of 5 years in the original design; whereas if the true control arm median survival time is 5 years, the trial duration can take much longer (median trial duration: 7.23 years; range: 5.82–9.1 years).

On the other hand, the power of survival probability and RMST are affected by the deviation in the survival distribution in the control arm. When survival in the control arm is worse (median 2 or 2.5 years) than the original design assumption (median 3 years), the power for both survival probability and RMST are higher than the 90%. When the baseline survival is better than the original design assumption (median 4 or 5 years), the power for both tests decrease.

Type I error maintains stable for all tests regardless of the deviation (Figure 2b).

### 3.2. Deviation in the Treatment Effect

#### 3.2.1. Magnitude of Effect

Misspecified treatment effect size has similar impact on all five tests (Figure 3). A larger treatment effect (HR = 0.4 or 0.5) resulted in higher statistical power and a smaller treatment effect (HR = 0.7 or 0.8) resulted in lower power. The power loss is not substantially different across different tests. For log-rank, MaxCombo2, and MaxCombo3 tests which rely on event-driven follow-up, a larger treatment effect (HR = 0.4 and 0.5) resulted in a slightly extended trial duration (median trial duration of 5.63 and 5.26 years, respectively) a smaller treatment effect (HR = 0.7 and 0.8) resulted in a slightly shortened trial duration (median trial duration of 4.75 and 4.56 years, respectively).

#### 3.2.2. Non-Proportional Hazards, Larger Early Benefit

Overall pattern of change in statistical power is similar across all five tests when the proportional hazards assumption was violated. Figure 4 shows that when there is a larger early effect (HR = 0.4) and a smaller late effect (HR = 0.8), the power for all five tests increased as the time of the effect change ($k$) goes from 1 year to 5 years (corresponding to longer duration with larger treatment effect). When the HR changed from 0.4 to 0.8 at 1 or 2 years (i.e., $k = 1, 2$) the statistical power of the RMST test is the least affected while survival probably test is the most affected. When the HR change occurred at 4 years or later (i.e., $k = 4, 5$), all five tests reached the maximum statistical power of 100%. For log-rank, MaxCombo2, and MaxCombo3 test which rely on event-driven follow-up, the early change in HR (i.e., $k = 1$) slightly reduce the trial duration (median trial duration = 4.81 years) and a later change slightly prolong the trial duration (median trial duration = 5.61 years).

#### 3.2.3. Non-Proportional Hazards, Larger Late Benefit

Figure 5 shows that when there is a smaller early effect (HR = 0.8) and a larger late effect (HR = 0.4), the power for all tests decreased as the time of the HR change ($k$) goes from 1 year (corresponding to shorter duration with smaller treatment effect) to 5 years (corresponding to longer duration with smaller treatment effect) with the survival probability less affected than others when the larger benefit occurred before 3.5 years; whereas the RMST test is more affected than other tests when the HR change occurred before 3.5 years but becomes less affected when the change occurred after 3.5 years. For log-rank, MaxCombo2, and MaxCombo3 test which rely on event-driven follow-up, the early change in HR (i.e., $k = 1$) slightly prolongs the trial duration (median trial duration = 5.24 years) and a later change slightly reduces the trial duration (median trial duration = 4.56 years).

#### 3.2.4. Non-Proportional Hazards, Crossing Hazard

A more extreme case of non-proportional hazards is where the new treatment is associated with worse survival in the early period and better survival in the late period. Figure 6 shows the statistical power when the HR = 1.2 before time $k$ and HR = 0.6 after time $k$. The statistical power of all five tests decreased as the time of change ($k$) goes from 3 months to 2 years. Of note, in this scenario, the statistical power of the survival probability test is the least affected whereas the RMST test is the most affected. The statistical power of the MaxCombo tests is less affected than the that of the log-rank test in this scenario. Due to the faster rate of events early on, the trial duration is reduced for tests rely on event-driven follow-up (median trial duration between 4.22 and 4.87 years).

### 3.3. *Deviation in the Accrual Rate*

The deviation in accrual rate does not impact the statistical power nor the Type I error when sufficient follow-up is performed, i.e., patients are followed until pre-specified number of events for log-rank, MaxCombo2, and MaxCombo3 tests and followed until pre-specified duration of follow-up for survival probability and RMST. However, the accrual rate does impact the total trial duration for all tests. For tests under event-driven follow-up scheme, a faster accrual, 2 years instead of 3, resulted in a shorter total trial duration (median: 4.44 years, range: 3.58–5.22 years to reach 162 events) and slower accrual, 4 years instead of 3, resulted in a longer trial duration (median: 5.54 years, range: 4.66–6.83 years to reach 162 events). For survival probability and RMST, the total trial duration is approximately the accrual duration plus the fixed-duration follow-up; therefore, the total trial duration is directly impacted by the accrual rate.

### 3.4. *Deviation in the Drop-Out Rate*

Drop-out rate has minimal impact on the statistical power of the log-rank and the MaxCombo tests (Figure 7a). This pattern is expected given that the power of the log-rank and the MaxCombo tests depend on the number of events, and by design the analysis is conducted when the number of events is reached. However, when the drop-out rate is very high, e.g., in the 60% drop-out scenario, the total number of events required were never reached for 11% of the simulations, where the statistical analysis was conducted with less than 162 events, which slightly reduced the statistical power. It is important to note that, although the power was less impacted for event-driven tests, the trial duration can prolong dramatically, e.g., in the 60% drop-out scenario, the median study duration is around 9 years rather than the expected study duration of 5 years. In contrast, the impact of drop-out on statistical power is more pronounced for the survival probability and the RMST tests, due to more patients being censored at the pre-specified analysis time. However, the trial duration based on these methods is not affected since patients are followed for a fixed duration.

Drop-out rate has minimal impact on the Type I error (Figure 7b).

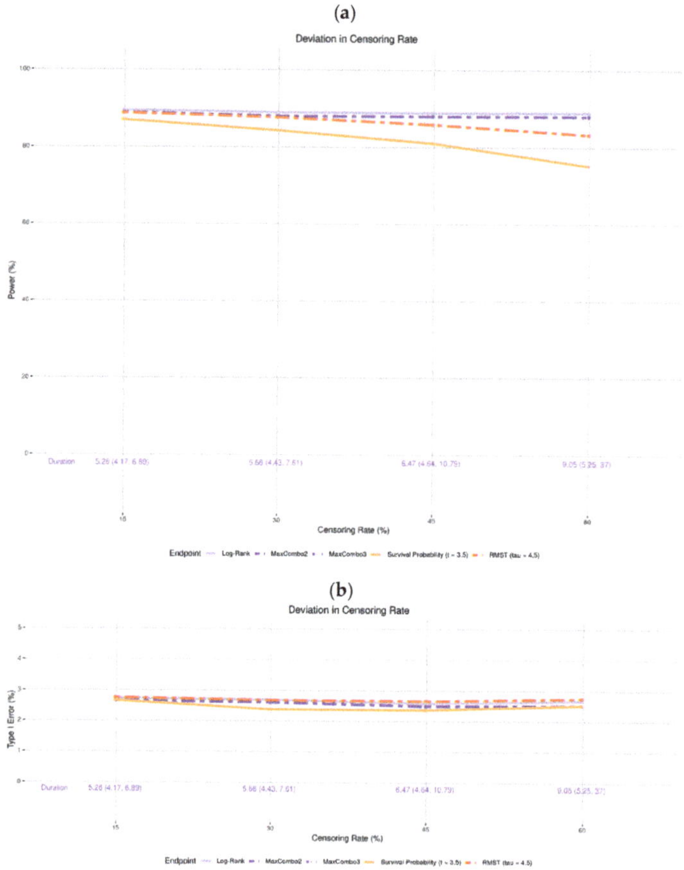


**Figure 7.** Changes in (**a**) statistical power and (**b**) Type I error associated with increased drop-out rate.

## 4. Discussion

This paper evaluated the impact of design misspecifications on the statistical power and Type I error on each of the 4 statistical methods that can be used to design clinical trials with survival outcomes. The methods include the log-rank test and MaxCombo tests for comparing the hazard rate, the test comparing the difference in the survival probability at a fixed time, and the test comparing the difference in the restricted mean survival time. In all parameters examined, misspecifications have similar impact in terms of direction and magnitude of the statistical power in all methods. The impact to Type I error is negligible.

Some notable observations include:

1. Deviation in the control arm's survival rate does not affect the power of the log-rank and MaxCombo but it affects the total duration of the trial. The power of the RMST test and survival probability decrease when the control arm's survival is better than the assumed distribution and increase when the control arm survival is worse than the assumed rate. These changes in power are due to an interplay between the change in the magnitude of the survival difference (in both survival probability and RMST, resulting from the deviation from baseline survival rate) coupled with the change in the estimation precision due to the censoring rate at time $t$ and $\tau$. This observation is consistent with the results found in Appendix 4 of Eaton et al. for RMST [20].

2. When the proportional hazards assumption is misspecified, the RMST test is least affected when there is a larger early treatment effect; the survival probability was least affected when there is larger late treatment effect, especially when the larger treatment effect occurs prior to the prespecified time of the survival probability; while the survival probability test and MaxCombo were the least affected with crossing hazards. Of note, in scenarios where the statistical power of the survival probability test is less affected than the other tests, it is due to the fact that the hazard-based tests and the RMST test evaluate the cumulative effect of treatment where small treatment effect in the early period dilutes the overall effect and, similarly, the harm of the treatment in the early period cancels out benefit of the late period. In contrast, the survival probability only evaluates the survival difference at 3.5 years regardless of the direction of early treatment effect. The power of the MaxCombo tests is less affected than the log-rank and the RMST in scenarios with crossing hazard since the method is designed to select the weight combination that maximizes the difference.
3. While deviations in the drop-out rate and accrual rate are seldom discussed in clinical trial manuscripts, they can significantly prolong the trial duration. An excessively prolonged trial can dramatically increase the monetary cost of the trial, and the standard of care may change during the trial period, rendering the trial conclusions less relevant. Additionally, a high drop-out rate can also reduce the study power.

It is well known that the magnitude of the treatment effect strongly impacts the trial statistical power. Advances in immuno-oncology in recent years have led to a heightened interest in understanding the impact of non-proportionality on the log-rank test and alternative statistical methods that are not constrained by the proportional hazards assumption. The survival probability at a fixed time and the restricted mean survival time were alternative endpoints that do not require the proportional hazards assumption, while the MaxCombo test is a method that allows flexible weighing schemes to focus on time period with the largest difference in survival between the two treatment arms. The survival probability at a fixed time and the restricted mean survival time also provide intuitive interpretation under nonproportionality. Of these alternatives, the survival probability at a fixed time is the appropriate endpoint if the goal of the trial is to show that the new treatment increases the likelihood of being alive at that time point, regardless of the shape of the hazard leading up to that time point. The restricted mean survival time, on the other hand, uses cumulative data up to the restriction time and the restriction time can be selected so that the power of the RMST test can approach that of the log-rank test. MaxCombo test, depending on the components and weights chosen, can be more robust against different type of deviations compared to the log-rank test.

Misspecification in other parameters such as the control arm survival distribution has received little attention in the clinical trial literature. Our simulation study shows that deviation in the control arm survival distribution can have a moderate impact on the statistical power for survival probability test and restricted mean survival time endpoints. Although in trials designed with the log-rank test and MaxCombo test where all patients are followed until a fixed number of events are reached, this deviation has no impact on the power of the log-rank test but the total trial duration can be highly contracted or extended, in some cases, trials may be extended for years to reach the few final events. An advantage of trials designed with survival probability or restricted mean survival time is that the trial duration is more predictable. Patients are followed to time $t$ for the survival probability and to time $\tau$ for the restricted mean survival time. Any follow-up beyond the prespecified time point does not contribute to the test statistics. A design with fixed follow-up duration is attractive for logistical reasons, for example, the time point of the final data analysis is known in advance so that resource allocation can be planned ahead of time. This design is also appropriate for trials with funding restricted to a fixed period. For designs using fixed follow-up duration, slower accrual rate directly affects the total trial duration which includes the accrual duration plus the fixed follow-up duration.

This manuscript uses simulations to evaluate the impact of deviations, which have inherent limitations. The simulations rely on specific parameter settings that may not fully capture the complexity of real-world data. We have chosen the parameter values to demonstrate the effect of deviations, but certainly, other parameter values are possible to represent the same deviation.

## 5. Conclusions

Selection of the appropriate quantity and associated statistical test to evaluate the survival benefit of a new treatment depends on multiple factors including the goal of trial, the mechanism of action of the experimental treatment, the survival quantity of clinical interest, and the pattern of the expected treatment effect. Although there are minor differences in how much misspecified assumptions affect the statistical power of the different statistical methods used, the overall pattern and impact of the mis-specified assumptions evaluated in this work seem to affect all methods considered in similar manner and the impact can be significant. Therefore, regardless of which method is used, the trial design should be based on as accurate assumptions as possible and potential impacts of deviations from these assumptions on the trial statistical power should be carefully considered.

**Author Contributions:** Conceptualization, J.G.L.-R.; methodology, J.G.L.-R. and F.-S.O.; formal analysis, F.-S.O. and T.Z.; writing—original draft preparation, J.G.L.-R. and T.Z.; writing—review and editing, J.G.L.-R., T.Z. and F.-S.O.; visualization, J.G.L.-R., T.Z. and F.-S.O. All authors have read and agreed to the published version of the manuscript.

**Funding:** This publication was made possible in part by the Daniel J. Sargent, Ph.D., Career Development Award in Cancer Research (FSO).

**Institutional Review Board Statement:** Not applicable.

**Informed Consent Statement:** Not applicable.

**Data Availability Statement:** R code is available upon request.

**Conflicts of Interest:** The authors declare no conflicts of interest. The funders had no role in the design of the study; in the collection, analyses, or interpretation of data; in the writing of the manuscript; or in the decision to publish the results.

## Abbreviations

The following abbreviations are used in this manuscript:

RMST Restricted mean survival time

## Appendix A

*MaxCombo Test*

MaxCombo test is a combination test based on the weighted log-rank test using the Fleming-Harrington weight family $G^{\rho,\gamma}$ [2].

Weighted log-rank test using the Fleming-Harrington weight family $G^{\rho,\gamma}$ has the test statistics:

$$\chi^2 = \frac{\left[\sum_{t=1}^{D} w_t(o_t - e_t)\right]^2}{\sum_{t=1}^{D} w_t^2(v_t)}$$

where

$o_t = d_{1t}$, observed number of events in group 1 at time $t$,
$e_t = n_{1t}\left(\frac{d_t}{n_t}\right)$, expected number of events in group 1 at time $t$,
$v_t = d_t\, n_{1t}\left(\frac{n_t - n_{1t}}{n_t^2}\right)\left(\frac{n_t - d_t}{n_t - 1}\right)$, variance of expected number of events in group 1 at time $t$,
$d_t$ is the total number of events at time $t$,
$n_t$ is the total number of events at time $t$, for each event time $t = 1, \cdots, D$,
$w_t = \{\hat{S}(t-)\}^{\rho}\{1 - \hat{S}(t-)\}^{\gamma}$, $\rho \geq 0$, $\gamma \geq 0$.

For example, considering $\rho = 0,\ 1$ and $\gamma = 0,\ 1$ as shown in the table below.

| $(\rho,\gamma)$ | $w_t$ | Type of Test |
|---|---|---|
| (0, 0) | 1 | Log-rank |
| (1, 0) | $\{\hat{S}(t-)\}$ | Test early difference |
| (0, 1) | $\{1 - \hat{S}(t-)\}$ | Test late difference |
| (1, 1) | $\{\hat{S}(t-)\}\{1 - \hat{S}(t-)\}$ | Test middle difference |

MaxCombo test was proposed by the working group with pharmaceutical companies initiated by the U.S. Food & Drug Administration [6]. The test statistics was proposed to maximum combination (MaxCombo) using the Fleming-Harrington $G^{\rho,\gamma}$ weight family $G^{\rho,\gamma}$, $\rho$, $\gamma \geq 0$ which has the form:

$Z_{max} = max_{\rho,\gamma}\{G^{0,0}, G^{0,1}, G^{1,0}, G^{1,1}\}$.

In this work, we considered the following MaxCombo tests.

- Two-component MaxCombo test with weights [(0,0) and (0,0.5)], defined as $Z_{2,\,0.5} = max_{\rho,\gamma}\{G^{0,0}, G^{0,0.5}\}$.
- Three-component MaxCombo test with weights [(0,0), (0,0.5), and (0.5, 0)], defined as $Z_{3,\,0.5} = max_{\rho,\gamma}\{G^{0,0}, G^{0,0.5}, G^{0.5,0}\}$.

We choose to use these combinations because these were recommended by the more recent research [16].

## References


1. U.S. Food and Drug Administration. Clinical Trial Endpoints for the Approval of Cancer Drugs and Biologics, Guidance for Industry. 2018. Available online: https://www.fda.gov/media/71195/download (accessed on 27 January 2021).
2. Fleming, T.R.; Harrington, D.P. *Counting Processes and Survival Analysis*; Wiley Series in Probability and Statistics; Wiley-Interscience: Hoboken, NJ, USA, 2005; pp. xiii, 429.
3. Trinquart, L.; Jacot, J.; Conner, S.C.; Porcher, R. Comparison of Treatment Effects Measured by the Hazard Ratio and by the Ratio of Restricted Mean Survival Times in Oncology Randomized Controlled Trials. *J. Clin. Oncol.* **2016**, *34*, 1813–1819. [CrossRef] [PubMed]
4. Holmes, E.M.; Bradbury, I.; Williams, L.; Korde, L.; de Azambuja, E.; Fumagalli, D.; Moreno-Aspitia, A.; Baselga, J.; Piccart-Gebhart, M.; Dueck, A.; et al. Are we assuming too much with our statistical assumptions? Lessons learned from the ALTTO trial. *Ann. Oncol.* **2019**, *30*, 1507–1513. [CrossRef] [PubMed]
5. Simes, R.J.; Martin, A.J. Assumptions, damn assumptions and statistics. *Ann. Oncol.* **2019**, *30*, 1415–1416. [CrossRef] [PubMed]
6. Lin, R.S.; Lin, J.; Roychoudhury, S.; Anderson, K.M.; Hu, T.L.; Huang, B.; Leon, L.F.; Liao, J.J.Z.; Liu, R.; Luo, X.D.; et al. Alternative Analysis Methods for Time to Event Endpoints Under Nonproportional Hazards: A Comparative Analysis. *Stat. Biopharm. Res.* **2020**, *12*, 187–198. [CrossRef]
7. Bellmunt, J.; Bajorin, D.F. Pembrolizumab for Advanced Urothelial Carcinoma. *N. Engl. J. Med.* **2017**, *376*, 2304. [CrossRef] [PubMed]
8. Weber, J.; Mandala, M.; Del Vecchio, M.; Gogas, H.J.; Arance, A.M.; Cowey, C.L.; Dalle, S.; Schenker, M.; Chiarion-Sileni, V.; Marquez-Rodas, I.; et al. Adjuvant Nivolumab versus Ipilimumab in Resected Stage III or IV Melanoma. *N. Engl. J. Med.* **2017**, *377*, 1824–1835. [CrossRef] [PubMed]

9. Nørskov, A.K.; Lange, T.; Nielsen, E.E.; Gluud, C.; Winkel, P.; Beyersmann, J.; de Uña-Álvarez, J.; Torri, V.; Billot, L.; Putter, H.; et al. Assessment of assumptions of statistical analysis methods in randomised clinical trials: The what and how. *BMJ Evid.-Based Med.* **2021**, *26*, 121–126. [CrossRef] [PubMed]
10. Gandhi, L.; Rodríguez-Abreu, D.; Gadgeel, S.; Esteban, E.; Felip, E.; De Angelis, F.; Domine, M.; Clingan, P.; Hochmair, M.J.; Powell, S.F.; et al. Pembrolizumab plus Chemotherapy in Metastatic Non–Small-Cell Lung Cancer. *N. Engl. J. Med.* **2018**, *378*, 2078–2092. [CrossRef] [PubMed]
11. Wolchok, J.D.; Chiarion-Sileni, V.; Gonzalez, R.; Rutkowski, P.; Grob, J.J.; Cowey, C.L.; Lao, C.D.; Wagstaff, J.; Schadendorf, D.; Ferrucci, P.F.; et al. Overall Survival with Combined Nivolumab and Ipilimumab in Advanced Melanoma. *N. Engl. J. Med.* **2017**, *377*, 1345–1356. [CrossRef] [PubMed]
12. Meyerhardt, J.A.; Shi, Q.; Fuchs, C.S.; Meyer, J.; Niedzwiecki, D.; Zemla, T.; Kumthekar, P.; Guthrie, K.A.; Couture, F.; Kuebler, P.; et al. Effect of Celecoxib vs Placebo Added to Standard Adjuvant Therapy on Disease-Free Survival Among Patients With Stage III Colon Cancer: The CALGB/SWOG 80702 (Alliance) Randomized Clinical Trial. *JAMA* **2021**, *325*, 1277–1286. [CrossRef] [PubMed]
13. Schrag, D.; Weiser, M.; Saltz, L.; Mamon, H.; Gollub, M.; Basch, E.; Venook, A.; Shi, Q. Challenges and solutions in the design and execution of the PROSPECT Phase II/III neoadjuvant rectal cancer trial (NCCTG N1048/Alliance). *Clin. Trials* **2019**, *16*, 165–175. [CrossRef] [PubMed]
14. Schrag, D.; Shi, Q.; Weiser, M.R.; Gollub, M.J.; Saltz, L.B.; Musher, B.L.; Goldberg, J.; Baghdadi, T.A.; Goodman, K.A.; McWilliams, R.R.; et al. Preoperative Treatment of Locally Advanced Rectal Cancer. *N. Engl. J. Med.* **2023**, *389*, 322–334. [CrossRef] [PubMed]
15. Argulian, A.; Karol, A.B.; Paredes, R.; Oguntuyo, K.; Weintraub, L.S.; Miller, J.; Fujiwara, Y.; Joshi, H.; Doroshow, D.B.; Galsky, M.D. Assessing patient withdrawal in cancer clinical trials: A systematic evaluation of reasons and transparency in reporting. *J. Clin. Oncol.* **2025**, *43*, e23003. [CrossRef]
16. Mukhopadhyay, P.; Ye, J.; Anderson, K.M.; Roychoudhury, S.; Rubin, E.H.; Halabi, S.; Chappell, R.J. Log-Rank Test vs MaxCombo and Difference in Restricted Mean Survival Time Tests for Comparing Survival Under Nonproportional Hazards in Immuno-oncology Trials: A Systematic Review and Meta-analysis. *JAMA Oncol.* **2022**, *8*, 1294–1300. [CrossRef] [PubMed]
17. R Core Team. *R: A Language and Environment for Statistical Computing*; R Foundation for Statistical Computing: Vienna, Austria, 2023.
18. Ristl, R.; Ballarini, N.M.; Götte, H.; Schüler, A.; Posch, M.; König, F. Delayed treatment effects, treatment switching and heterogeneous patient populations: How to design and analyzeRCTsin oncology. *Pharm. Stat.* **2021**, *20*, 129–145. [CrossRef] [PubMed]
19. Uno, H.; Tian, L.; Horiguchi, M.; Cronin, A.; Battioui, C.; Bell, J. survRM2: Comparing Restricted Mean Survival Time. 2022. Available online: https://cran.r-project.org/web/packages/survRM2/survRM2.pdf (accessed on 3 January 2025).
20. Eaton, A.; Therneau, T.; Le-Rademacher, J. Designing clinical trials with (restricted) mean survival time endpoint: Practical considerations. *Clin. Trials* **2020**, *17*, 285–294. [CrossRef] [PubMed]

*cancers*

MDPI

*Article*

# Robust Permutation Test of Intraclass Correlation Coefficient for Assessing Agreement

**Mengyu Fang, Alan David Hutson and Han Yu ***

Department of Biostatistics and Bioinformatics, Roswell Park Comprehensive Cancer Center, Buffalo, NY 14263, USA; mengyu.fang@roswellpark.org (M.F.); alan.hutson@roswellpark.org (A.D.H.)
* Correspondence: han.yu@roswellpark.org

**Simple Summary**

When different people assess the same medical image or patient test, it is important that their results agree to ensure accurate diagnoses and research findings. A common way to measure this agreement is with a statistic called the intraclass correlation coefficient. However, traditional methods for testing it rely on strong assumptions about the data, which often do not hold in real-world settings. This can lead to unreliable conclusions. We developed a new method that works even when the data is irregular or limited, using a technique called permutation testing. Through computer simulations and real medical examples, we show that our method provides more accurate and consistent results than standard approaches. This helps researchers and healthcare professionals better judge the quality of measurements, leading to more reliable science and clinical decisions.

**Abstract**

**Background:** Inter-rater reliability is critical in oncology to ensure consistent and reliable measurements across raters and methods, such as when evaluating biomarker levels in different laboratories or comparing tumor size assessments by radiation oncologists during therapy planning. This consistency is essential for informed decision-making in both clinical and research contexts, and the intraclass correlation coefficient (ICC) is a widely recommended statistic for assessing agreement. This work focuses on hypothesis testing of the ICC(2,1) with two raters. **Methods:** We evaluated the performance of a naive permutation test for testing the hypothesis $H_0$ : ICC $= 0$ and found that it fails to reliably control the type I error rate. To address this, we developed a robust permutation test based on a studentized statistic, which we prove to be asymptotically valid even when paired variables are uncorrelated but dependent. **Results:** Simulation studies demonstrate that the proposed test consistently maintains type I error control, even with small sample sizes, outperforming the naive approach across various data-generating scenarios. **Conclusions:** The proposed studentized permutation test for ICC(2,1) offers a statistically valid and robust method for assessing inter-rater reliability and demonstrates practical utility when applied to two real-world oncology datasets.

**Keywords:** ICC; agreement; permutation test

## 1. Introduction

The Intraclass Correlation Coefficient (ICC) is an important statistical measure for assessing the level of agreement or consistency between two or more continuous variables, frequently used in disciplines such as psychology, medicine, and social sciences [1–6]. It is commonly used for evaluating the reliability of measurements across different raters, instruments, or repeated assessments. By quantifying the proportion of variability in data attributable to the variables of interest rather than measurement error, ICC offers a means of evaluating the quality and consistency of data collection methods. Hypothesis testing on ICC is an important step for the conducting inference on this agreement statistic.

In cancer studies, the role of ICC is particularly critical due to the complex and often multi-center nature of clinical trials and diagnostic assessments [7–9]. Reliable and consistent measurement of tumor size, biomarker levels, or imaging interpretations across different observers or institutions is essential for ensuring valid comparisons and reproducibility of results [10,11]. High ICC values in such contexts confirm that observed variations are due to true biological differences rather than inconsistencies in measurement, thereby strengthening the integrity of research findings and supporting robust clinical decision-making. Compared to Lin's concordance correlation coefficient (CCC) [12], another commonly used measure of agreements which applies to two fixed raters, the ICC can be generalized to scenarios with randomly selected raters.

The commonly used test for ICC usually relies on normality assumptions, but often suffers from poorly controlled type I error when the assumption does not hold. A permutation test is often considered exact for testing zero Pearson and Spearman correlation coefficients, and this is a promising alternative for hypothesis testing of ICC as well. However, recent work has shown that such tests are not exact for testing zero correlation coefficients when the data does not follow the bivariate normal distributions, and a studentization of the test statistic can make the test asymptotically exact [13–16]. Further, Hutson and Yu showed that when the two variables do not follow bivariate normal distributions, a naive permutation test CCC generally does not control the type I error rate at the desired level [14]. Therefore, the question is whether a similar issue exits for ICC.

The inferences about ICC have been extensively studied [17–20]. However, the standard methods, such as the $F$ test, often assume that data follow a bivariate normal distribution, a condition that is frequently violated in real-world datasets. When data deviate from this assumption, such as in the presence of skewness, heavy tails, or outliers, traditional ICC methods can yield inaccurate or misleading results, undermining the reliability of conclusions drawn from the data. To address these challenges, this paper focuses on the ICC(2,1) with two raters, which is under two-way random model for assessing absolute agreements, and introduces a new testing procedure. Our proposed test can better account for the complexities of non-normal data distributions, allowing for more accurate and reliable agreement assessments. The goal of this paper is to present this novel test and illustrate its advantages through simulations and real-world examples. We believe that our method represents a significant advancement in the assessment of agreement between continuous variables, offering a more reliable approach for complex, non-normal data.

## 2. Intraclass Correlation Coefficient and Measurement of Agreement

ICC is a family of reliability indices used to assess the consistency or agreement of measurements made on units that are organized into groups. Unlike the Pearson correlation coefficient, which assesses the linear association between two variables, ICC is appropriate when the same quantity is measured multiple times, such as in repeated measurements, rater evaluations, or test–retest designs.

ICC models are derived from the analysis of variance (ANOVA) framework and can differ based on three main dimensions: the type of effects model (one-way vs. two-way; random vs. mixed), the unit of measurement (single vs. average), and the type of agreement being assessed (consistency vs. absolute agreement). Among different types of ICC, we focus on the two-way random effects model, ICC(2,1) with two raters, where all subjects are rated by the same set of raters randomly selected from a larger population.

Specifically, two-way random effects model with $n$ subjects and $k$ raters, where $x_{ij}$ is the rating for subject $i$ by rater $j$:

$$x_{ij} = \mu + s_i + r_j + e_{ij}$$

where $\mu$ is the overall mean, $s_i \sim (0, \sigma_s^2)$, $r_j \sim (0, \sigma_r^2)$, and $e_{ij} \sim (0, \sigma_e^2)$.

This model partitions the total variance into components due to subjects, raters, and residual error. Further, we define $MSB$ as the mean square between subjects, $MSR$ as the mean square for raters, $MSW$ as the residual mean square, $k = 2$ is the number of raters, and $n$ is the number of subjects. Thus, we have

$$E(MSB) = \sigma_e^2 + k\sigma_s^2,$$
$$E(MSW) = \sigma_e^2,$$
$$E(MSR) = \sigma_e^2 + n\sigma_r^2.$$

The single-measure, absolute agreement version, ICC(2,1), is given by [21]:

$$\text{ICC}(2,1) = \frac{MSB - MSW}{MSB + (k-1)MSW + \frac{k}{n}(MSR - MSW)}. \quad (1)$$

## 3. Permutation Test of Intraclass Correlation Coefficient of Agreement with Two Raters

The intraclass correlation coefficient ICC(2,1) is typically evaluated under normality assumptions, which often perform poorly when normality assumptions are violated. In such cases, permutation tests are considered a robust alternative. However, Romano and DiCiccio have demonstrated that a naive permutation test for Pearson's correlation coefficient fails to adequately control the type I error rate under non-normality due to violations of the exchangeability assumption. This issue can be addressed by using a permutation test based on a studentized statistic. Similar problems have been observed in other measures of agreement and correlation, including CCC [14], Spearman's correlation coefficient [22], and correlations for ordinal variables [15], where tests based on statistics studentized by the large sample variance can effectively control the type I error rate. Similarly, the large sample variance of ICC(2,1) was given as:

$$V(\hat{\rho}) = 2\hat{\rho}^4[(\frac{1}{\hat{\rho}} - 1)^2 + \frac{n}{k}\hat{u}^2], \quad (2)$$

where $\hat{u} = \frac{k(MSR-MSW)}{n(MSB-MSW)}$ [17]. However, this variance estimator tends to be unstable under $\rho = 0$. Studentization by this estimator does not provide a robust test (shown in Appendix B). To address this, we approximate the large sample variance of ICC(2,1) using the variance of Pearson's correlation coefficient. This approximation is motivated by the observation that when the between rater variation is low and the two raters have similar variance in their ratings. As demonstrated in Appendix A, under these conditions the between-subject and residual variances align with the covariance and variance components of Pearson's correlation coefficient, making its variance a reasonable surrogate for studentizing ICC. Therefore, we used the large sample variance of Pearson's correlation for studentization. The detailed procedure for the one-sided test is listed below.

- For $n$ pairs of i.i.d. observations $(x_{11}, x_{12})$, $(x_{21}, x_{22})$, …, $(x_{n1}, x_{n2})$, estimate the ICC(2,1) as $\hat{\rho}$.

- Estimate the approximated variance by

$$\hat{\tau}_n^2 = \frac{\hat{\mu}_{22}}{\hat{\mu}_{20}\hat{\mu}_{02}},$$

$$\hat{\mu}_{pq} = \frac{1}{n}\sum_{i=1}^{n}(x_{i1} - \bar{x}_1)^p (x_{i2} - \bar{x}_2)^q.$$

- Calculate the studentized statistic $R = \hat{\rho}/\tau_n$.
- Randomly shuffle $(x_{12}, x_{22}, \ldots x_{n2})$ for $B$ times. For each permutation, calculate the permuted studentized statistic $R^k, k \in (1, \ldots, B)$.
- Calculate the $p$-value by

$$p = \frac{1}{B}\Sigma_{k=1}^{B} I(R^k > R).$$

- Reject $H_0$ if $p \leq \alpha$.

## 4. Simulations

We examined Type I error control for the tests introduced above using distributions commonly found in the literature for these examinations in a wide range of settings in DiCiccio (2107) [13]. For our simulation study, we focused on testing $H_0 : \rho = 0$ versus $H_1 : \rho > 0$, with sample sizes $n = 10, 25, 50, 100, 200$. Each simulation used Monte Carlo replications $10,000$ and the number of permutations used is 1000. We compared the $F$ test, Fisher's $Z$-transformation (Fisher's $Z$ test), naive permutation test (Permute), and studentized permutation test (Stu Permute). The Type I error control for $\alpha = 0.05$ was examined. The specific scenarios are examined as shown below.

1. Multivariate normal (MVN) with mean zero and identity covariance.
2. Exponential given as $(X, Y) = rS^T u$ where $S = diag(\sqrt{2}, 1)$, $r \sim \exp(1)$, and $u$ are uniformly distributed on the two-dimensional unit circle.
3. Circular given as the uniform distribution on a two-dimensional unit circle.
4. $t_{4.1}$ where $X = W + Z$ and $Y = W - Z$, where $W$ and $Z$ are i.i.d. $t_{4.1}$ random variables.
5. Multivariate $t$-distribution (MVT) with 5 degrees of freedom.
6. Mixture of two bivariate normal distributions. Given as $(X, Y) = WZ_1 + (1 - W)Z_2$ where $W \sim Bernoulli(0.5)$, $Z_1 \sim N(\begin{pmatrix} 0 \\ 0 \end{pmatrix}, \begin{pmatrix} 1 & \rho \\ \rho & 1 \end{pmatrix})$, $Z_2 \sim N(\begin{pmatrix} 0 \\ 0 \end{pmatrix}, \begin{pmatrix} 1 & -\rho \\ -\rho & 1 \end{pmatrix})$. We use a range of $\rho$ values: 0.1, 0.3, 0.6 and 0.9 to simulate different degrees of dependency between $X$ and $Y$ (MVNX_1, MVNX_3, MVNX_6, MVNX_9).
7. Absolute normal distribution (ABNORM). $Y = ZX$, where $Z$ follows standard normal distribution and $X$ follows a folded standard normal distribution, thus $Y$ has a non-constant variance.
8. Binomial normal distribution (BINORM). $X = W + \epsilon$, where $W \sim Bernoulli(0.1)$, $\epsilon \sim N(0, 0.05^2)$, and $Y$ is defined to follow a normal distribution with mean 0 and a standard deviation dependent on $X + 1$.
9. Squared normal distribution (SQNORM). $X \sim N(0, 1)$, and $Y$ is a quadratic function of $X$ and a standard normal error.
10. Uniform distribution (UNIF). $X = W + Z$ and $Y = W - Z$, where $W$ and $Z$ are independent variables following $Uniform(-1, 1)$. This represents a scenario of dependency due to contrained support

The results in Table 1 show that all tests control type I errors well under bivariate normal distributions. However, the $F$ test, Fisher's $Z$ test, and naive permutation tests tend to be overly conservative for the circular distribution. Meanwhile, they tend to have inflated type I error rates for all other distributions. While for $t_{4.1}$, the type I error is consistently inflated. Note that for these tests, this deviation cannot be corrected as the sample size increases. Instead, they may converge to an arbitrary level, either lower or higher than $\alpha$.

Fisher's Z test for the ICC exhibits extremely conservative Type I error rates under non-normal distributions because its variance approximation and normality assumption rely on the data following a bivariate normal distribution in a random effects model. Non-normal data distort the sampling distribution of the ICC, altering the variance and shape of the Z-transformed statistic, which leads to underestimated or inflated standard errors, resulting in poor Type I error rates control. On the other hand, the proposed test consistently controls the type I error rate at desired level across the sample sizes and underlying distributions. Additionally, although the approximation in Appendix A relies on weak rater effects and similar variance between two raters, the test remains valid when these two conditions are not satisfied, such as in ABNORM, BINORM, and SQNORM scenarios.

In addition, we evaluated the power of all test methods under bivariate normal distributions to test $H_0 : \rho = 0$ versus $H_1 : \rho > 0$. The simulation of power was only conducted in bivariate normal distributions because the other tests failed to control type I error in other scenarios; thus, the comparison would not be meaningful. As shown in Table 2, the proposed test performs similarly to the F test and the unstudentized permutation test, with only small differences in power (less than 2%). A slightly larger difference occurs when the sample size is very small ($n = 10$) and the true correlation is strong ($\rho = 0.6$), but this difference quickly disappears as the sample size increases. The proposed studentized permutation test yielded a higher power across all scenarios than Fisher's Z test. These results suggest that the proposed test maintains good power while offering better control of type I error in other settings.

**Table 1.** Type I error rates across distributions and sample sizes.

| Distribution | $n$ | F-Test | Fisher's Z Test | Permute | Stu Permute |
|---|---|---|---|---|---|
| MVN | 10 | 0.048 | 0.036 | 0.050 | 0.052 |
| | 25 | 0.051 | 0.046 | 0.051 | 0.051 |
| | 50 | 0.053 | 0.050 | 0.052 | 0.051 |
| | 100 | 0.050 | 0.049 | 0.050 | 0.049 |
| | 200 | 0.052 | 0.052 | 0.053 | 0.054 |
| Exp | 10 | 0.107 | 0.090 | 0.114 | 0.054 |
| | 25 | 0.131 | 0.124 | 0.148 | 0.052 |
| | 50 | 0.145 | 0.141 | 0.163 | 0.054 |
| | 100 | 0.145 | 0.143 | 0.160 | 0.048 |
| | 200 | 0.148 | 0.147 | 0.164 | 0.048 |
| Circular | 10 | 0.012 | 0.007 | 0.018 | 0.054 |
| | 25 | 0.011 | 0.008 | 0.011 | 0.046 |
| | 50 | 0.012 | 0.010 | 0.011 | 0.047 |
| | 100 | 0.011 | 0.010 | 0.011 | 0.047 |
| | 200 | 0.012 | 0.012 | 0.012 | 0.050 |
| $t_{4.1}$ | 10 | 0.118 | 0.096 | 0.103 | 0.047 |
| | 25 | 0.146 | 0.137 | 0.139 | 0.041 |
| | 50 | 0.162 | 0.158 | 0.162 | 0.040 |
| | 100 | 0.184 | 0.183 | 0.184 | 0.044 |
| | 200 | 0.202 | 0.200 | 0.199 | 0.045 |
| MVT | 10 | 0.072 | 0.057 | 0.073 | 0.046 |
| | 25 | 0.096 | 0.089 | 0.096 | 0.046 |
| | 50 | 0.113 | 0.109 | 0.113 | 0.050 |
| | 100 | 0.113 | 0.111 | 0.114 | 0.047 |
| | 200 | 0.133 | 0.132 | 0.132 | 0.048 |

**Table 1.** *Cont.*

| Distribution | $n$ | F-Test | Fisher's Z Test | Permute | Stu Permute |
|---|---|---|---|---|---|
| MVNX_1 | 10 | 0.048 | 0.034 | 0.051 | 0.052 |
| | 25 | 0.050 | 0.045 | 0.052 | 0.049 |
| | 50 | 0.051 | 0.047 | 0.050 | 0.048 |
| | 100 | 0.052 | 0.050 | 0.052 | 0.052 |
| | 200 | 0.053 | 0.051 | 0.053 | 0.049 |
| MVNX_3 | 10 | 0.060 | 0.043 | 0.048 | 0.050 |
| | 25 | 0.064 | 0.057 | 0.063 | 0.052 |
| | 50 | 0.066 | 0.064 | 0.066 | 0.052 |
| | 100 | 0.065 | 0.063 | 0.052 | 0.049 |
| | 200 | 0.062 | 0.062 | 0.053 | 0.048 |
| MVNX_6 | 10 | 0.094 | 0.075 | 0.081 | 0.049 |
| | 25 | 0.104 | 0.097 | 0.101 | 0.049 |
| | 50 | 0.101 | 0.098 | 0.102 | 0.052 |
| | 100 | 0.105 | 0.103 | 0.103 | 0.051 |
| | 200 | 0.108 | 0.107 | 0.107 | 0.052 |
| MVNX_9 | 10 | 0.161 | 0.139 | 0.139 | 0.053 |
| | 25 | 0.159 | 0.145 | 0.138 | 0.050 |
| | 50 | 0.158 | 0.154 | 0.153 | 0.050 |
| | 100 | 0.155 | 0.154 | 0.152 | 0.048 |
| | 200 | 0.161 | 0.160 | 0.159 | 0.050 |
| MVN4_5 | 10 | 0.057 | 0.042 | 0.049 | 0.049 |
| | 25 | 0.050 | 0.046 | 0.049 | 0.048 |
| | 50 | 0.052 | 0.048 | 0.050 | 0.050 |
| | 100 | 0.050 | 0.048 | 0.048 | 0.049 |
| | 200 | 0.052 | 0.051 | 0.050 | 0.051 |
| SQNORM | 10 | 0.092 | 0.053 | 0.135 | 0.065 |
| | 25 | 0.124 | 0.098 | 0.175 | 0.060 |
| | 50 | 0.131 | 0.102 | 0.182 | 0.056 |
| | 100 | 0.134 | 0.107 | 0.186 | 0.054 |
| | 200 | 0.141 | 0.111 | 0.197 | 0.050 |
| ABSNORM | 10 | 0.081 | 0.058 | 0.107 | 0.077 |
| | 25 | 0.081 | 0.063 | 0.137 | 0.062 |
| | 50 | 0.085 | 0.069 | 0.158 | 0.066 |
| | 100 | 0.080 | 0.067 | 0.160 | 0.059 |
| | 200 | 0.080 | 0.069 | 0.169 | 0.063 |
| BINORM | 10 | 0.016 | 0.003 | 0.093 | 0.063 |
| | 25 | 0.014 | 0.010 | 0.151 | 0.074 |
| | 50 | 0.017 | 0.016 | 0.162 | 0.070 |
| | 100 | 0.020 | 0.019 | 0.167 | 0.068 |
| | 200 | 0.023 | 0.022 | 0.158 | 0.051 |
| UNIF | 10 | 0.009 | 0.004 | 0.090 | 0.050 |
| | 25 | 0.008 | 0.005 | 0.093 | 0.046 |
| | 50 | 0.007 | 0.007 | 0.096 | 0.045 |
| | 100 | 0.006 | 0.005 | 0.056 | 0.046 |
| | 200 | 0.005 | 0.005 | 0.066 | 0.044 |

**Table 2.** Power of testing $H_0 : \rho = 0$ versus $H_1 : \rho > 0$ under bivariate normal distribution.

| $\rho$ | N | F Test | Fisher's Z Test | Permute | Stu Permute |
|---|---|---|---|---|---|
| 0.2 | 10 | 0.131 | 0.103 | 0.127 | 0.121 |
| | 25 | 0.268 | 0.237 | 0.257 | 0.250 |
| | 50 | 0.375 | 0.399 | 0.373 | 0.360 |
| | 100 | 0.651 | 0.636 | 0.655 | 0.637 |
| | 200 | 0.884 | 0.880 | 0.883 | 0.877 |

**Table 2.** *Cont.*

| $\rho$ | N | F Test | Fisher's Z Test | Permute | Stu Permute |
|---|---|---|---|---|---|
| 0.4 | 10 | 0.342 | 0.271 | 0.327 | 0.256 |
| | 25 | 0.654 | 0.643 | 0.651 | 0.601 |
| | 50 | 0.915 | 0.894 | 0.911 | 0.897 |
| | 100 | 0.993 | 0.994 | 0.994 | 0.991 |
| | 200 | >0.999 | >0.999 | >0.999 | >0.999 |
| 0.6 | 10 | 0.655 | 0.561 | 0.626 | 0.454 |
| | 25 | 0.953 | 0.959 | 0.946 | 0.922 |
| | 50 | 0.997 | 0.999 | 0.999 | 0.997 |
| | 100 | >0.999 | >0.999 | >0.999 | >0.999 |
| | 200 | >0.999 | >0.999 | >0.999 | >0.999 |

## 5. Real World Examples

### *5.1. Inter-Rater Agreement in CT Radiomics*

To demonstrate the practical utility of the proposed studentized permutation test, we first applied it to a computed tomography (CT) radiomics dataset evaluating inter-rater agreement in 19 quantitative imaging features of renal tumors from 106 patients [23]. Two radiologists independently extracted variables including tumor size (volume, long/short axis), attenuation, and various texture features such as entropy, skewness, kurtosis, and uniformity.

We assessed whether the inter-rater ICC for each feature was significantly greater than zero using four methods: the *F* test, Fisher's *Z*-transformation test, a naive non-studentized permutation test, and our studentized permutation test. For features with high inter-rater agreement, such as tumor volume, attenuation, and entropy, all methods consistently yielded significant results ($p < 0.05$), indicating clear agreement between raters. However, differences among the methods became apparent for features with moderate or borderline ICCs. One illustrative example is the tumor UPP feature, where the *F* test, Fisher's *Z* test, and naive permutation test produced non-significant *p*-values of 0.175, 0.175, and 0.070, respectively (Table 3). In contrast, the studentized permutation test returned a significant *p*-value of 0.024, suggesting inter-rater agreement that the other methods failed to detect (Table 3). Another example is the kidney entropy feature, which yielded *p*-values of 0.458, 0.458, and 0.252 for the *F*, *Z*, and naive permutation tests, respectively, showing that none of them were statistically significant (Table 3). However, the studentized permutation test produced a strongly significant *p*-value (<0.001), identifying agreement that would otherwise be overlooked (Table 3).

To better understand these discrepancies, we evaluated the distributional assumptions underlying the traditional tests. Specifically, we applied the Shapiro–Wilk test for marginal normality and the Henze–Zirkler test for bivariate normality across all variables that have different test results. The results showed that most features significantly violated normality assumptions, with *p*-values < 0.05 in both tests. An exception was the kidney skewness variable, which did not show a violation in the Henze–Zirkler test ($p = 0.367$). Given these violations, our proposed studentized permutation test is recommended for more reliable inference in such setting because it offers better control of type I error under non-normal and small sample conditions, as supported by the simulation results.

**Table 3.** $p$-values from four inter-rater agreement tests for imaging features. The $p$-values that result in inconsistent conclusions are shown in bold.

| Variable | F Test | Fish's Z Test | Permute | Stu Permute |
|---|---|---|---|---|
| Tumor volume | <0.001 | <0.001 | <0.001 | 0.012 |
| Tumor longaxis | <0.001 | <0.001 | <0.001 | <0.001 |
| Tumor shortaxis | <0.001 | <0.001 | <0.001 | <0.001 |
| Tumor attenuation | <0.001 | <0.001 | <0.001 | <0.001 |
| Tumor attenuation SD | <0.001 | <0.001 | <0.001 | <0.001 |
| Tumor skewness | <0.001 | <0.001 | <0.001 | <0.001 |
| Tumor kurtosis | <0.001 | <0.001 | <0.001 | <0.001 |
| Tumor entropy | <0.001 | <0.001 | <0.001 | <0.001 |
| Tumor uniformity | <0.001 | <0.001 | <0.001 | 0.004 |
| Tumor MPP | <0.001 | <0.001 | <0.001 | <0.001 |
| Tumor UPP | **0.175** | **0.175** | **0.070** | **0.024** |
| Kidney attenuation | <0.001 | <0.001 | <0.001 | <0.001 |
| Kidney attenuation SD | <0.001 | <0.001 | <0.001 | <0.001 |
| Kidney skewness | **0.036** | **0.037** | **0.046** | **0.066** |
| Kidney kurtosis | 0.365 | 0.364 | 0.316 | 0.350 |
| Kidney entropy | **0.458** | **0.458** | **0.252** | **<0.001** |
| Kidney uniformity | **0.309** | **0.313** | **0.048** | **0.006** |
| Kidney MPP | <0.001 | <0.001 | <0.001 | <0.001 |
| Kidney UPP | **0.061** | **0.064** | **0.042** | **<0.001** |

### *5.2. Inter-Rater Reliability for iTUG Test*

The use of ICC extends beyond oncology to a wide range of other fields. We further applied our method to data from a clinical study evaluating inter-rater agreement for the instrumented Timed Up and Go (iTUG) test in patients with Parkinson's disease [24]. The iTUG test captures various movement parameters using wearable sensors, including total iTUG and TUG durations, sit-to-stand (SitSt) and stand-to-sit (StSit) transitions, and their respective flexion and extension phases. Each patient underwent multiple trials on two separate days, assessed independently by two raters. A total of 16 iTUG-derived features were analyzed for inter-rater ICC significance using the same four testing methods.

As shown in Table 4, the results again demonstrate consistent performance for features with high reliability. For example, total TUG duration and StSit durations on both days yielded $p$-values $< 0.001$ across all four methods, confirming strong inter-rater agreement. However, greater variation among the methods emerged for features with lower ICCs. On Day 1, the iTUG duration yielded non-significant $p$-values using the $F$ test ($p = 0.156$), Fisher's $Z$ test ($p = 0.160$), and the naive permutation test ($p = 0.080$) while it identified a statistically significant result using the studentized permutation test ($p = 0.002$), which suggesting that it is more sensitive to moderate agreement even in borderline cases. In addition, for the SitSt extension duration, the $F$ test ($p = 0.038$), Fisher $Z$ test ($p = 0.045$), and naive permutation test ($p = 0.026$) indicated significance, whereas the studentized permutation test ($p = 0.096$) did not.

A similar pattern was observed on Day 2 for the SitSt and extension durations. While the $F$ test, Fisher's $Z$ test, and naive permutation test all returned $p$-values below 0.05, the studentized permutation test yielded more conservative $p$-values of 0.056 and 0.096, respectively. These examples suggest that our method provides better control of type I error, avoiding potentially misleading significance when evidence for agreement is weak.

This interpretation is supported by the original study's [24] reported ICC values: the inter-rater ICC for iTUG duration on Day 1 was 0.95 (excellent reliability), while the ICCs for SitSt extension duration on Day 1 and Day 2 were 0.56 and 0.57, respectively (moderate reliability). Moreover, results from normality assessments (using Shapiro–Wilk and Henze–Zirkler tests) indicated that most variables deviated from both marginal and bivariate normality, reinforcing the need for methods that do not rely on these assumptions.

Taken together, the iTUG study further confirms the advantages of the studentized permutation test in applied settings. It consistently identifies meaningful inter-rater agreement while mitigating the risks of both inflated and deflated type I error that can arise from the limitations of traditional approaches.

These two real-world examples from CT radiomics and clinical mobility assessment collectively demonstrate the broad applicability and reliability of the studentized permutation test. Its robustness under non-normality, increased sensitivity in borderline cases, and interpretability in small-sample scenarios make it a valuable tool for modern biomedical data analysis, particularly where standard assumptions may not hold.

**Table 4.** Results of testing $H_0 : \rho = 0$ versus $H_1 : \rho > 0$ for iTUG durations. The $p$-values that result in inconsistent conclusions are shown in bold.

| Day | Durations | *F* Test | Fisher's *Z* Test | Permute | Stu Permute |
|---|---|---|---|---|---|
| 1 | iTUG | **0.156** | **0.160** | **0.080** | **0.002** |
| | TUG | <0.001 | <0.001 | <0.001 | <0.001 |
| | SitSt | 0.002 | 0.004 | 0.004 | 0.002 |
| | SitSt Flex | <0.001 | <0.001 | <0.001 | 0.034 |
| | SitSt Ext | **0.038** | **0.045** | **0.026** | **0.096** |
| | StSit | <0.001 | <0.001 | <0.001 | 0.002 |
| | StSit Flex | <0.001 | <0.001 | <0.001 | 0.002 |
| | StSit Ext | <0.001 | <0.001 | <0.001 | 0.002 |
| 2 | iTUG | <0.001 | <0.001 | <0.001 | <0.001 |
| | TUG | <0.001 | <0.001 | <0.001 | <0.001 |
| | SitSt | **0.004** | **0.003** | **0.004** | **0.056** |
| | SitSt Flex | 0.284 | 0.289 | 0.252 | 0.228 |
| | SitSt Ext | **0.001** | **0.001** | **0.004** | **0.096** |
| | StSit | <0.001 | <0.001 | <0.001 | <0.001 |
| | StSit Flex | <0.001 | <0.001 | <0.001 | <0.001 |
| | StSit Ext | <0.001 | <0.001 | <0.001 | 0.008 |

## 6. Discussion

In this study, we propose a robust concordance correlation permutation test for assessing the null hypothesis of zero ICC(2,1), $H_0 : \rho = 0$. Traditional methods for testing ICC(2,1) rely on normality assumptions, which, as demonstrated in our simulation studies, often result in poorly controlled Type I error rates when these assumptions are violated. While permutation tests offer a nonparametric alternative, previous studies [13–15,22] have shown that naive permutation approaches applied to correlation coefficients and the CCC fail to control the Type I error under non-normal conditions, particularly in cases where variables are dependent but uncorrelated.

We show that a similar issue arises when applying naive permutation tests to ICC(2,1). To address this, we develop a permutation test based on a properly studentized test statistic, which maintains accurate Type I error control even with small sample sizes (as few as 10) and under violations of normality. While this study focuses on ICC(2,1) for two raters under a two-way random effects model, the extension to multiple raters is a promising direction for future work. Conceptually, the same studentized permutation framework could be adapted by modifying the test statistic to accommodate the average of multiple ratings per subject. However, the derivation of a suitable variance approximation and the maintenance of exchangeability under permutation become more complex in higher-dimensional settings. Future research is needed to assess the theoretical properties and computational performance of such an extension.

## 7. Conclusions

In conclusion, we developed a robust studentized permutation test for ICC(2,1) that addresses the limitations of traditional parametric and naive permutation methods under non-normal conditions. Through simulations and applied studies, the test demonstrated consistent Type I error control, making it a reliable tool for agreement assessment, especially in biomedical research.

**Author Contributions:** Conceptualization, M.F., A.D.H. and H.Y.; methodology, M.F. and H.Y.; formal analysis, M.F.; writing—original draft preparation, M.F. and H.Y.; writing—review and editing, M.F., A.D.H. and H.Y. All authors have read and agreed to the published version of the manuscript.

**Funding:** This work was supported by Roswell Park Cancer Institute and National Cancer Institute (NCI) grant P30CA016056, NCI NRG Oncology Statistical and Data Management Center grant U10CA180822 and NCI IOTN Moonshot grant U24CA232979-01, NCI ARTNet Moonshot grant U24CA274159-01, and NCI CAP-IT grant U24CA274159-02.

**Institutional Review Board Statement:** Not applicable.

**Informed Consent Statement:** Not applicable.

**Data Availability Statement:** Code is available at https://github.com/hyu-ub/ICC_studentized_permutation_test (accessed on 3 August 2025). The original data presented in the study are openly available in [DANS Data Station Life Sciences] at https://doi.org/10.17026/dans-22j-5w67 (accessed on 19 June 2025) and https://doi.org/10.1371/journal.pone.0195270 (accessed on 19 June 2025).

**Conflicts of Interest:** The authors declare no conflicts of interest.

## Appendix A. Approximation of ICC(2,1) to Pearson Correlation for Two Raters

Here we show that the intraclass correlation coefficient, ICC(2,1), approximates the Pearson correlation coefficient $r$ for two raters ($k = 2$) in a two-way random effects model when rater effects are negligible ($\sigma_r^2 \approx 0$). Specifically, we show that $\text{MSB} - \text{MSW}$ is proportional to $\sum_{i=1}^{n}(x_{i1} - \bar{x}_1)(x_{i2} - \bar{x}_2)$, and $\text{MSB} + \text{MSW}$ approximates $\sqrt{\sum_{i=1}^{n}(x_{i1} - \bar{x}_1)^2 \sum_{i=1}^{n}(x_{i2} - \bar{x}_2)^2}$.

Consider a two-way random effects model with $n$ subjects and $k = 2$ raters, where $x_{ij}$ is the rating for subject $i$ by rater $j$:

$$x_{ij} = \mu + s_i + r_j + e_{ij}$$

where $\mu$ is the overall mean, $s_i \sim (0, \sigma_s^2)$, $r_j \sim (0, \sigma_r^2)$, and $e_{ij} \sim (0, \sigma_e^2)$. For ICC(2,1) with two raters:

$$\text{ICC}(2,1) = \frac{\text{MSB} - \text{MSW}}{\text{MSB} + \text{MSW} + 2(\text{MSR} - \text{MSW})/n}$$

where MSB, MSW, and MSR are the mean squares for subjects, error, and raters, respectively. When $\sigma_r^2 \approx 0$, $\text{MSR} \approx \text{MSW}$, so

$$\text{ICC}(2,1) \approx \frac{\text{MSB} - \text{MSW}}{\text{MSB} + \text{MSW}}$$

The Pearson correlation is:

$$r = \frac{\sum_{i=1}^{n}(x_{i1} - \bar{x}_1)(x_{i2} - \bar{x}_2)}{\sqrt{\sum_{i=1}^{n}(x_{i1} - \bar{x}_1)^2 \sum_{i=1}^{n}(x_{i2} - \bar{x}_2)^2}}$$

Firstly, we show the numerator MSB - MSW is proportional to $\sum_{i=1}^{n}(x_{i1}-\bar{x}_1)(x_{i2}-\bar{x}_2)$.
Define:

$$\bar{x}_i=\frac{x_{i1}+x_{i2}}{2},\quad \bar{x}=\frac{1}{2n}\sum_{i=1}^{n}(x_{i1}+x_{i2})\approx\frac{\bar{x}_1+\bar{x}_2}{2}$$

Assuming negligible rater effects ($\bar{x}_1\approx\bar{x}_2$):

$$\bar{x}_i-\bar{x}\approx\frac{(x_{i1}-\bar{x}_1)+(x_{i2}-\bar{x}_2)}{2}$$

$$(\bar{x}_i-\bar{x})^2\approx\frac{1}{4}\left[(x_{i1}-\bar{x}_1)^2+2(x_{i1}-\bar{x}_1)(x_{i2}-\bar{x}_2)+(x_{i2}-\bar{x}_2)^2\right]$$

$$\mathrm{MSB}=\frac{2}{n-1}\sum_{i=1}^{n}(\bar{x}_i-\bar{x})^2\approx\frac{1}{2(n-1)}\left[\sum_{i=1}^{n}(x_{i1}-\bar{x}_1)^2+2\sum_{i=1}^{n}(x_{i1}-\bar{x}_1)(x_{i2}-\bar{x}_2)+\sum_{i=1}^{n}(x_{i2}-\bar{x}_2)^2\right]$$

$$x_{i1}-\bar{x}_i=\frac{x_{i1}-x_{i2}}{2},\quad x_{i2}-\bar{x}_i=-\frac{x_{i1}-x_{i2}}{2}$$

$$\mathrm{SSW}=\sum_{i=1}^{n}\left[\left(\frac{x_{i1}-x_{i2}}{2}\right)^2+\left(-\frac{x_{i1}-x_{i2}}{2}\right)^2\right]=\sum_{i=1}^{n}\frac{(x_{i1}-x_{i2})^2}{2}$$

$$\mathrm{MSW}=\frac{\mathrm{SSW}}{n-1}=\frac{1}{2(n-1)}\sum_{i=1}^{n}(x_{i1}-x_{i2})^2$$

$$(x_{i1}-x_{i2})^2\approx(x_{i1}-\bar{x}_1-(x_{i2}-\bar{x}_2))^2=(x_{i1}-\bar{x}_1)^2-2(x_{i1}-\bar{x}_1)(x_{i2}-\bar{x}_2)+(x_{i2}-\bar{x}_2)^2$$

$$\mathrm{MSW}\approx\frac{1}{2(n-1)}\sum_{i=1}^{n}\left[(x_{i1}-\bar{x}_1)^2-2(x_{i1}-\bar{x}_1)(x_{i2}-\bar{x}_2)+(x_{i2}-\bar{x}_2)^2\right]$$

$$\mathrm{MSB}-\mathrm{MSW}\approx\frac{1}{2(n-1)}\left[\sum_{i=1}^{n}(x_{i1}-\bar{x}_1)^2+2\sum_{i=1}^{n}(x_{i1}-\bar{x}_1)(x_{i2}-\bar{x}_2)+\sum_{i=1}^{n}(x_{i2}-\bar{x}_2)^2\right]$$

$$-\frac{1}{2(n-1)}\left[\sum_{i=1}^{n}(x_{i1}-\bar{x}_1)^2-2\sum_{i=1}^{n}(x_{i1}-\bar{x}_1)(x_{i2}-\bar{x}_2)+\sum_{i=1}^{n}(x_{i2}-\bar{x}_2)^2\right]$$

$$=\frac{1}{2(n-1)}\cdot 2\sum_{i=1}^{n}(x_{i1}-\bar{x}_1)(x_{i2}-\bar{x}_2)+\frac{1}{2(n-1)}\cdot 2\sum_{i=1}^{n}(x_{i1}-\bar{x}_1)(x_{i2}-\bar{x}_2)$$

$$=\frac{2}{n-1}\sum_{i=1}^{n}(x_{i1}-\bar{x}_1)(x_{i2}-\bar{x}_2).$$

Next we derive the approximation of MSB + MSW

$$\mathrm{MSB}+\mathrm{MSW}\approx\frac{1}{2(n-1)}\left[S_1^2+2\sum_{i=1}^{n}(x_{i1}-\bar{x}_1)(x_{i2}-\bar{x}_2)+S_2^2\right]+$$

$$\frac{1}{2(n-1)}\left[S_1^2-2\sum_{i=1}^{n}(x_{i1}-\bar{x}_1)(x_{i2}-\bar{x}_2)+S_2^2\right]$$

where $S_1^2=\sum_{i=1}^{n}(x_{i1}-\bar{x}_1)^2$, $S_2^2=\sum_{i=1}^{n}(x_{i2}-\bar{x}_2)^2$.
Combine:

$$=\left(\frac{1}{2(n-1)}+\frac{1}{2(n-1)}\right)(S_1^2+S_2^2)+\left(\frac{1}{n-1}-\frac{1}{n-1}\right)\sum_{i=1}^{n}(x_{i1}-\bar{x}_1)(x_{i2}-\bar{x}_2)$$

$$= \frac{1}{n-1}(S_1^2 + S_2^2)$$

Therefore,

$$\text{MSB} + \text{MSW} \approx \frac{1}{n-1}(S_1^2 + S_2^2)$$

When $S_1^2 \approx S_2^2$, the arithmetic mean approximates the geometric mean:

$$S_1^2 + S_2^2 \approx 2\sqrt{S_1^2 S_2^2}$$

$$\text{MSB} + \text{MSW} \approx \frac{1}{n-1} \cdot 2\sqrt{S_1^2 S_2^2} = \frac{2}{n-1}\sqrt{\sum_{i=1}^{n}(x_{i1} - \bar{x}_1)^2 \sum_{i=1}^{n}(x_{i2} - \bar{x}_2)^2}$$

Therefore, we have:

$$\text{ICC}(2,1) \approx \frac{\text{MSB} - \text{MSW}}{\text{MSB} + \text{MSW}} \approx r$$

Thus, the variance can be approximated by:

$$\text{Var}(\text{ICC}(2,1)) \approx \frac{1}{n} \cdot \frac{\mu_{22}}{\mu_{20} \cdot \mu_{02}}$$

where $\mu_{22} = E[(X_1 - \mu_{x_1})^2(X_2 - \mu_{x_2})^2]$, $\mu_{20} = \sigma_{x_1}^2$, $\mu_{02} = \sigma_{x_2}^2$.

## Appendix B. Comparison of Large Sample Variance Estimator and Variance Estimator Based on Pearson Correlation When $\rho = 0$

To better demonstrate the instability of the classic large sample variance [17] when $\rho = 0$. We conducted a small numerical simulation to compare the sampling distribution of the classic ICC variance estimator ($var_{classic}$) and the estimator based on the Pearson correlation ($var_{pearson}$) (Appendix A). In this simulation, we focus on the data from multivariate normal distributions with mean zero and identity covariance where the sample size $n = 50$. And this simulation used Monte Carlo replication 10,000.

Figures A1 and A2 display the sampling distributions of two variance estimators for ICC(2,1) under the null hypothesis. The classic variance estimator (Figure A1) is highly skewed and concentrated near zero, indicating poor stability and potential underestimation of variance. In contrast, the Pearson correlation-based estimator (Figure A2) is more symmetric and centered away from zero, suggesting greater consistency and suitability for studentization. Figure A3 displays the sampling distributions of the studentized ICC under $\rho = 0$ using two different variance estimators. The distribution based on the Pearson variance estimator is symmetric and centered around zero, indicating valid standardization under the null. In contrast, the classic variance-based statistic shows a bimodal distribution shifted away from zero, suggesting poor calibration and potential distortion of type I error rates. These results support the use of the Pearson-based variance estimator in the proposed studentized permutation test.

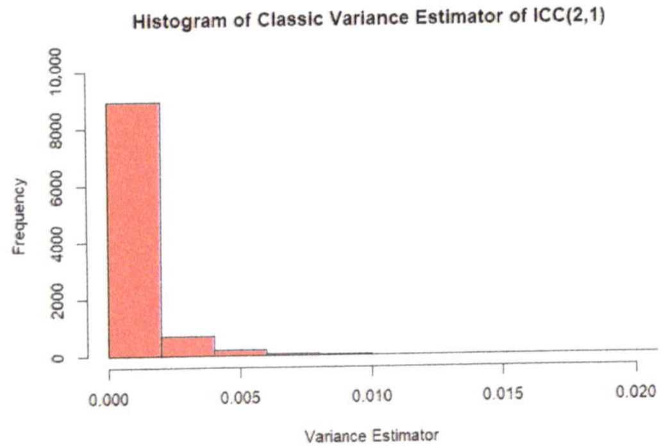


**Figure A1.** Histogram of Large Sample Variance Estimator of ICC(2,1).

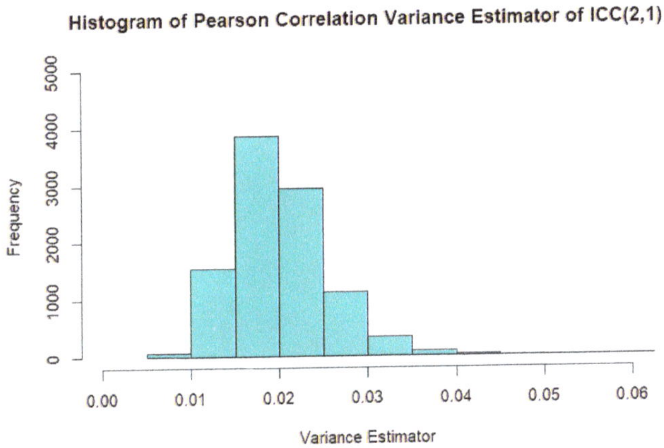


**Figure A2.** Histogram of Pearson Correlation based Variance Estimator of ICC(2,1).

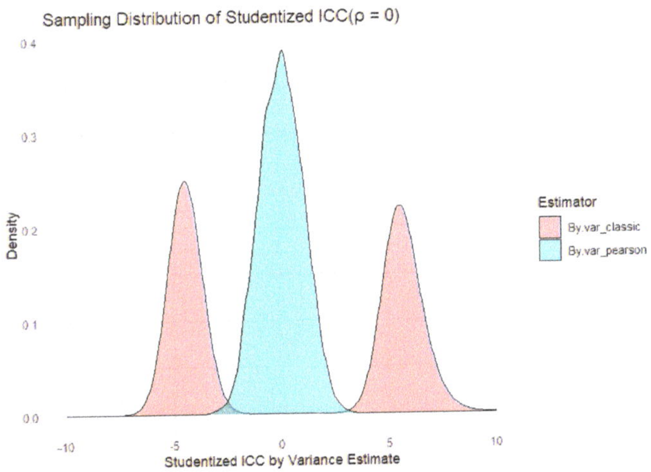


**Figure A3.** Sampling Distribution of Studentized ICC $\rho = 0$.

## References

1. Bartko, J.J. The intraclass correlation coefficient as a measure of reliability. *Psychol. Rep.* **1966**, *19*, 3–11. [CrossRef] [PubMed]
2. Bartko, J.J. On various intraclass correlation reliability coefficients. *Psychol. Bull.* **1976**, *83*, 762. [CrossRef]
3. Lahey, M.A.; Downey, R.G.; Saal, F.E. Intraclass correlations: There's more there than meets the eye. *Psychol. Bull.* **1983**, *93*, 586. [CrossRef]
4. Bland, J.M. and Altman, D. A note on the use of the intraclass correlation coefficient in the evaluation of agreement between two methods of measurement. *Comput. Biol. Med.* **1990**, *20*, 337–340. [CrossRef]
5. Leyland, A.H.; Groenewegen, P.P. Intraclass correlation coefficient (ICC). In *Encyclopedia of Quality of Life and Well-Being Research*; Springer International Publishing: Cham, Switzerlands, 2024; pp. 3643–3644.
6. de Raadt, A.; Warrens, M.J.; Bosker, R.J.; Kiers, H.A. A comparison of reliability coefficients for ordinal rating scales. *J. Classif.* **2021**, *38*, 519–543. [CrossRef]
7. Wu, S.; Crespi, C.M.; Wong, W.K. Comparison of methods for estimating the intraclass correlation coefficient for binary responses in cancer prevention cluster randomized trials. *Contemp. Clin. Trials* **2012**, *33*, 869–880. [CrossRef] [PubMed]
8. Xue, C.; Yuan, J.; Lo G.G.; Chang, A.T.; Poon, D.M.; Wong, O.L.; Zhou, Y.; Chu, W.C. Radiomics feature reliability assessed by intraclass correlation coefficient: A systematic review. *Quant. Imaging Med. Surg.* **2021**, *11*, 4431. [CrossRef]
9. Hade, E.M.; Murray, D.M.; Pennell, M.L.; Rhoda, D.; Paskett, E.D.; Champion, V.L.; Crabtree, B.F.; Dietrich, A.; Dignan, M.B.; Farmer, M.; et al. Intraclass correlation estimates for cancer screening outcomes: Estimates and applications in the design of group-randomized cancer screening studies. *J. Natl. Cancer Inst. Monogr.* **2010**, *2010*, 97–103. [CrossRef] [PubMed]
10. Dinkel, J.; Khalilzadeh, O.; Hintze, C.; Fabel, M.; Puderbach, M.; Eichinger, M.; Schlemmer, H.P.; Thorn, M.; Heussel, C.P.; Thomas, M.; et al. Inter-observer reproducibility of semi-automatic tumor diameter measurement and volumetric analysis in patients with lung cancer. *Lung Cancer* **2013**, *82*, 76–82. [CrossRef]
11. Pleil, J.D.; Wallace, M.A.G.; Stiegel, M.A.; Funk, W.E. Human biomarker interpretation: The importance of intra-class correlation coefficients (ICC) and their calculations based on mixed models, ANOVA, and variance estimates. *J. Toxicol. Environ. Health Part B* **2018**, *21*, 161–180. [CrossRef]
12. Lin, L.I-K. A concordance correlation coefficient to evaluate reproducibility. *Biometrics* **1989**, *45*, 255–268. [CrossRef] [PubMed]
13. DiCiccio, C.J.; Romano, J.P. Robust permutation tests for correlation and regression coefficients. *J. Am. Stat. Assoc.* **2017**, *519*, 1211–1220. [CrossRef]
14. Hutson, A.D.; Yu, H. A robust permutation test for the concordance correlation coefficient. *Pharm. Stat.* **2021**, *20* , 696–709. [CrossRef]
15. Hutson, A.D.; Yu, H. Exact inference around ordinal measures of association is often not exact. *Comput. Methods Programs Biomed.* **2023**, *240*, 107725. [CrossRef]
16. Yu, H.; Hutson, A.D. Inferential procedures based on the weighted Pearson correlation coefficient test statistic. *J. Appl. Stat.* **2024**, *51*, 481–496. [CrossRef]
17. Bourredjem, A.; Cardot, H.; Devilliers, H. Asymptotic Confidence Interval, Sample Size Formulas and Comparison Test for the Agreement Intra-Class Correlation Coefficient in Inter-Rater Reliability Studies. *Stat. Med.* **2024**, *43*, 5060–5076. [CrossRef] [PubMed]
18. Tian, L.; Cappelleri, J.C. A new approach for interval estimation and hypothesis testing of a certain intraclass correlation coefficient: The generalized variable method. *Stat. Med.* **2004** *23*, 2125–2135. [CrossRef]
19. McGraw, K.O.; Wong, S.P. Forming inferences about some intraclass correlation coefficients. *Psychol. Methods* **1996**, *1*, 30. [CrossRef]
20. Shrout, P.E.; Fleiss, J.L. Intraclass correlations: Uses in assessing rater reliability. *Psychol. Bull.* **1979**, *86*, 420. [CrossRef]
21. Liljequist, D.; Elfving, B.; Skavberg, Roaldsen, K. Intraclass correlation—A discussion and demonstration of basic features. *PLoS ONE* **2019**, *14*, e0219854. [CrossRef] [PubMed]
22. Yu, H.; Hutson, A.D. A robust Spearman correlation coefficient permutation test. *Commun. Stat.-Theory Methods* **2024**, *53*, 2141–2153. [CrossRef] [PubMed]
23. Bier, G.; Bier, S.; Bongers, M.N.; Othman, A.; Ernemann, U.; Hempel, J.-M. Value of computed tomography texture analysis for prediction of perioperative complications during laparoscopic partial nephrectomy in patients with renal cell carcinoma. *PLoS ONE* **2018**, *13*, e0195270. [CrossRef] [PubMed]
24. van Lummel, R.C.; Walgaard, S.; Hobert, M.A.; Maetzler, W.; van Dieën, J.H.; Galindo-Garre, F.; Terwee, C.B. Intra-Rater, Inter-Rater and Test-Retest Reliability of an Instrumented Timed Up and Go (iTUG) Test in Patients with Parkinson's Disease. *PLoS ONE* **2016**, *11*, e0151881. [CrossRef] [PubMed]

MDPI AG
Grosspeteranlage 5
4052 Basel
Switzerland
Tel.: +41 61 683 77 34

*Cancers* Editorial Office
E-mail: cancers@mdpi.com
www.mdpi.com/journal/cancers

www.ingramcontent.com/pod-product-compliance
Lightning Source LLC
Chambersburg PA
CBHW061617210926
51850CB00009B/2356